NEW YORK
HISTORICAL MANUSCRIPTS:
DUTCH

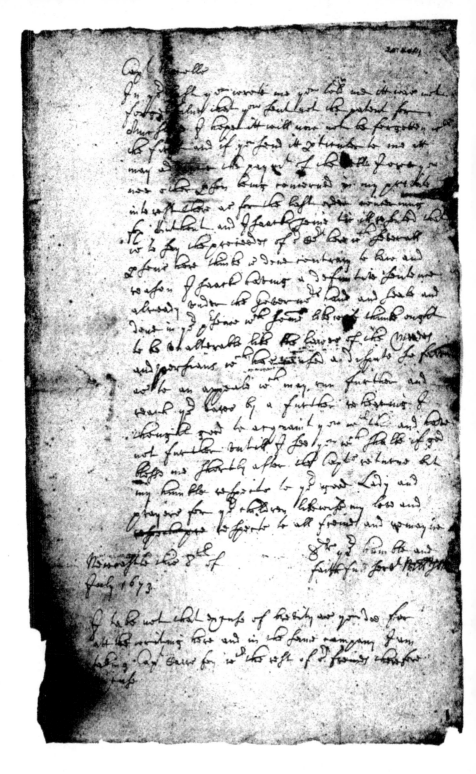

A letter from William Tom to Matthias Nicolls dated July 8, 1673

NEW YORK HISTORICAL MANUSCRIPTS: DUTCH

Volumes XX-XXI

DELAWARE PAPERS (English Period)

A Collection of Documents Pertaining to the Regulation of Affairs on the Delaware, 1664-1682

Edited by
CHARLES T. GEHRING

Published under the Direction of
The Holland Society of New York

CLEARFIELD

Genealogical Publishing Co., Inc.
Baltimore, 1977

Reprinted for
Clearfield Company, Inc. by
Genealogical Publishing Co., Inc.
Baltimore, Maryland
2000

Library of Congress Catalogue Card Number 76-41652
International Standard Book Number: 0-8063-0736-6

DEDICATED TO
THE HOLLAND SOCIETY
OF NEW YORK

whose prime object is "to collect and preserve information respecting the early history
and settlement of the City and State of New
York by the Dutch and to discover and preserve all still existing documents relating to
their genealogy and history." This purpose,
since 1885, has provided a stimulus for historical research and analysis of the New
Netherland era in America.

PREFACE

The historian's view of New York's colonial administration of the Delaware region has long been distorted because of Volume XII of *Documents Relating to the Colonial History of the State of New York*. This haphazard selection of records compiled by Berthold Fernow is marred by unsatisfactory translations from the Dutch and inaccurate transcriptions of English. With this present publication, however, we now have an accurate work containing complete texts of all documents in the New York Colonial Secretary's file of Delaware papers from the English period, 1664-1682. Two volumes for the Dutch period, 1646-1664, are in preparation. With these records the historian will have a wealth of material concerning the earliest history of Delaware, Pennsylvania, and New Jersey in a complete and accurate edition.

These volumes were prepared by a scholar who is well qualified for the task. Charles T. Gehring studied Germanic linguistics at the University of Freiburg, Germany, and at Indiana University. His doctoral dissertation, "The Dutch Language in Colonial New York," shows the relationship between social and linguistic change, and demonstrates his area of specialization. He further developed his knowledge of the Dutch language as a research assistant at the Royal Dialect Institute in Amsterdam, Holland. In addition to his academic training, he has added to his knowledge of the social and economic history of colonial New York by serving as museum administrator of the Fort Klock Historic Association and project director in the study of colonial agriculture. His writings concerning the colonial records have appeared in such journals as *New York History* and *Staten Island Historian*, and he is presently completing a new translation of the journal kept by Harmen Myndertsz van der Bogaert during an expedition up the Mohawk River in 1635.

Dr. Gehring has been working with the colonial manuscripts at the New York State Library for the past two years. He and the library staff have delved deeply into the history of the Delaware region, searching major works and obscure journals for information on such diverse topics as geography, law, medicine, farming, and religion. Dr. Gehring has also examined manuscript collections at other institutions throughout the middle Atlantic states as well as microfilm copies of records acquired by the State Library from agencies in The Netherlands and England. The library's collection of major multi-volume Dutch and English dictionaries was essential in determining the seventeenth-century meaning of terms, as were numerous texts in the library annotated by A. J. F. van Laer during his long career as translator of colonial records. The preparation of this edition involved months of careful scrutiny of the manuscripts. The transcribing, translating, typing, and indexing were continually reviewed and revised by comparison of the original records.

For the library staff, the hard work that went into this volume was often alleviated by the opportunity to read of the joys and tribulations of the irrepressible settlers on the Delaware. We hope that others will share our interest in the human insights that these records provide.

Peter R. Christoph
Associate Librarian
Manuscripts and History
New York State Library

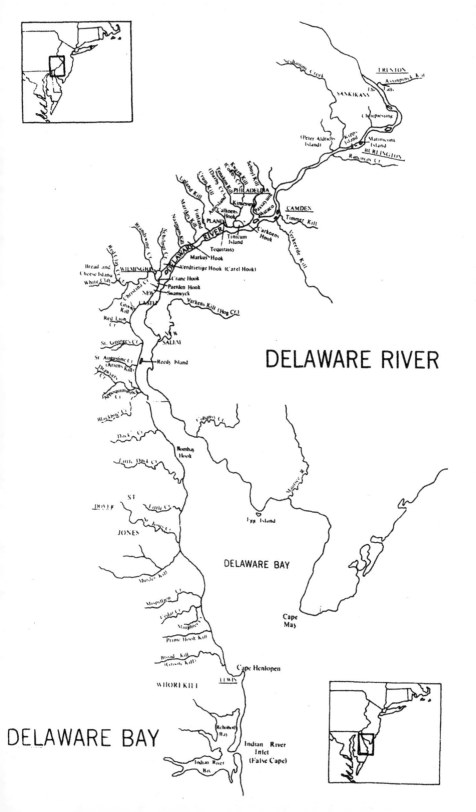

INTRODUCTION

The geographical shape of seventeenth-century New York bears little resemblance to the present boundaries of New York State. In 1664 Charles II granted an expanse of territory in North America to his brother James, Duke of York, which included Maine from the St. Croix River to the Kennebec River, all the land between the west bank of the Connecticut River and the east bank of the Delaware River and Bay, as well as Manhattan, Long Island, Martha's or Martin's Vineyard, and Nantucket. With the exception of the latter two islands and the territory in Maine, the boundaries of the grant coincided with the Dutch colony of New Netherland, which the English now intended to eliminate.

The principal settlement in the Delaware region at this time was located approximately halfway between Trenton Falls and Cape Henlopen. This upriver area, which was later named New Castle by the English, was first settled in 1651 when Petrus Stuyvesant, Director-General of New Netherland, ordered the erection of Fort Casimir at the Sand Hook in order to cut off the fur trade of the Swedes, who had scattered settlements from Christina Creek (Wilmington) to the Schuylkill (Philadelphia). Three years later Fort Casimir fell to the Swedes and was renamed Fort Trefaldighet (Trinity). In 1655 Stuyvesant led another expedition to the South River, as the Dutch called the Delaware region, during which he succeeded not only in retaking Fort Casimir but also in conquering all of New Sweden. Shortly thereafter the Dutch West India Company transferred control of most of the Delaware region to the City of Amsterdam. This was done not only to repay the city for its assistance during the late expedition against New Sweden, but also because the company realized that it no longer had the resources to settle the area. Amsterdam's colony, called New Amstel, came to an end less than a decade later with the seizure of the Delaware River and Bay for the Duke of York.

Several months before the English takeover of New Netherland in August, 1664, James granted a deed to Sir George Carteret and John Lord Berkeley for the territory that is now the state of New Jersey. This grant, in effect, ceded control of the Delaware trade to these two loyal supporters of the Stuarts and reduced the size of the Duke's future proprietary by one-third. Soon after the seizure of New Amsterdam by Richard Nicolls, first governor of New York, an expeditionary force commanded by Sir Robert Carr was sent to the Delaware region. Since the articles of surrender signed by Stuyvesant pertained only to the territory controlled by the Dutch West India Company, New Amstel in Delaware had to be dealt with separately. Carr's instructions were to reduce the place and summon the inhabitants "to yield Obedience to his majestie as the rightful Sovereign of that Tract of land."[1] These inhabitants, however, were living in settlements scattered along the west bank of the Delaware River and Bay on land actually claimed by Lord Baltimore of Maryland. Baltimore had made only feeble attempts to eject the Dutch because of his weak situation in Maryland, and because the tobacco merchants there found it profitable to circumvent English duties by dealing directly with the Dutch traders in New Amstel. After Carr seized control of the Delaware region by reducing New Amstel on the west bank, Nicolls anticipated that Baltimore would now assert his claim to the area. With this in mind he suggested to his superiors in England that Baltimore's rights to the region be considered "forfeited by act of Parliament for trading with the Dutch, or at least so much of his patent as hath been reduc'd at His Majesty's charge."[2] Nicolls's instructions to Carr also convey an awareness of the possibility of conflict with Baltimore's claim to the region, since Carr was instructed to inform Charles Calvert, Lord Baltimore's son and governor of Maryland, that he (Carr) had orders to keep possession of the region, but "if My Lord Baltimore doth pretend right thereunto by his Patent (which is a doubtful Case) you are to say that you only keep possession till his Majesty is informed and sattisfyed otherwise."[3] Thus the west bank of the Delaware River and Bay came under the control of New York at the expense of Lord Baltimore.

The English conquest of New Amstel did not proceed as smoothly, however, as that of New Amsterdam. The City of Amsterdam's director in New Amstel, Alexander d'Hinijossa, defended the fort with less than fifty men until the situation was hopeless, suffering thirteen casualties before the fort fell. After the surrender, Carr allowed his troops to plunder the houses and stores within the stockade. With the river firmly in English hands, Carr's attention then turned to Pieter Cornelisz Plockoy's Mennonite colony at the Whorekill near Cape Henlopen. Although there is no record of a defense, the English soldiers plundered and took possession of all effects belonging to Amsterdam and to Plockoy's colony "to a very naile."[4]

The severity of the initial English occupation was not followed by a harsh military rule, as the inhabitants of the Delaware region might have expected. The Dutch magistrates were to continue in office and were allowed to exercise their civil power as before: the *schout*, burgomasters, and other minor officials were to hold their offices for six months or until further notice. The magistrates were, however, to be subordinate to the English commander.[5] In 1668 Capt. John Carr, who replaced Sir Robert Carr as commander in Delaware, received instructions from New York to continue the civil government until further orders; also, "That the Lawes of the government Establisht by his Royall Highness be shewed and frequently Communicated to the said Councellors and all others to the end that being there acquainted the practise of them may also in Convenient tyme be established. . . ." [6] This order was issued in anticipation of extending the "Duke's Laws" to the Delaware region. These laws had been in force on Long Island, Staten Island, and in Westchester since 1665, but were not extended to Delaware until 1676. In the interim the magistrates at New Castle, Upland, and the Whorekill continued to administer justice according to forms more Dutch than English. Such accommodations to the predominately non-English population were probably made in realization that the continuance of familiar procedures might reduce the possibility of unrest.

A major step in the transition to English institutions was taken in 1672 when the government in New York ordered that New Castle be converted into a bailiwick and that English laws be established in all settlements on the Delaware. The office of *schout* was to be replaced with a *shrievalty*, and the town court was to have the power to try all cases of debt or damage below the value of £10 without appeal to New York.[7] Thus New Castle became the principal court in Delaware, holding monthly sessions, while the courts at Upland and the Whorekill met quarterly.

For nine years the west bank of the Delaware region remained under the control of the central government in New York. In 1673 the Dutch recaptured their former colony, including the Delaware, only to lose it again the following year as a result of the Treaty of Westminster. Charles II immediately reaffirmed his brother's proprietorship to New York, and the former Dutch claim to the west bank of the Delaware reverted to New York as well. In the meantime, John Lord Berkeley had sold his share of New Jersey to the Quakers Edward Byllynge and John Fenwick. Carteret had agreed to a partition that left him the region of East New Jersey, while the land west of a diagonal line, running from Little Egg Harbor to the Delaware River, was to be settled by the Quakers. Upon repossession of New York, James restored Carteret's claim to his share of New Jersey, east of the diagonal line, but refused to acknowledge Berkeley's sale to Byllynge and Fenwick. When the Duke's authority was re-established in New York, the east bank of the Delaware in West New Jersey was considered to be part of the Duke's territory. The east bank of the river and bay remained under New York's control until 1680, when the Duke of York finally recognized Byllynge's claim. Thus for six years all the land bordering Delaware River and Bay was administered by New York.

When the Duke of York regained control of his territory in 1674, he ordered governor-designate Edmund Andros to restore those laws and orders instituted by previous English governors of New York.[8] Andros was also ordered to extend the "Duke's Laws" to all settlements in New York, which included both sides of Delaware River and Bay.[9] The following spring he visited the Delaware region to dramatize the re-establishment of the Duke's authority. While there he attended a special court session in New Castle during which his commission was read and the local magistrates were sworn. Since the "Duke's Laws" were to be enforced in all settlements, he promised to send the court a copy of the laws as soon as possible. Instead of sending the laws, however, Andros waited a year before sending twelve "rules of government" that were to be followed by the local magistrates, including the order that "the books of laws Establisht by his Royall Highnesse, and practiced in New York . . . be likewise in force and practiced in this River and Precincts. . . ." [10] Still no copy of the "Duke's Laws" was available for use in Delaware. One was finally sent to New Castle in October, 1678. The reason for this delay of nearly four years is unknown.

In addition to the courts at New Castle, Upland, and the Whorekill, two new courts were established in 1677 on the east side of the river in order to accommodate the influx of Quakers at Burlington and Salem. These courts, however, were subordinate to the New Castle court, where appeals were heard for cases above £5 in value. In 1680 another court was established at St. Jones (now Dover, Delaware) after the inhabitants, mainly planters from Virginia and Maryland, complained of the hardships in reaching the Whorekill court.

During the Duke of York's possession of the Delaware region, three governors administered affairs from Fort James in New York City. Richard Nicolls, the first governor, was a member of the Duke's commission together with Sir Robert Carr, Samuel Maverick and George Cartwright. This commission was formed ostensibly to hear complaints in New England, but its primary mission was the overthrow of New Netherland. Nicolls was followed in 1668 by Francis Lovelace, who returned to England in debt and disgrace after the recapture of New Netherland by the Dutch in 1673. When the English re-established control over New York in 1674, Edmund Andros became the last New York governor to administer the Delaware region as part of New York. Anthony Brockholls served as deputy governor during Andros's visits to England in 1678 and 1681. Although the three administrations were as different in character as was the temperament of each governor, an administrative continuity was maintained throughout by the retention of Matthias Nicolls as provincial secretary.

Nicolls, one of the key figures in the early years of English rule in New York, was described by Samuel Maverick in 1663 as a person who "hath beene bred a scholar, and a student in Lincolnes Inne, and a good proficient as by many I have beene informed, and had he had now tyme, he could have brought Certificates from some sariants (savants) at law and other eminent persons, by what I have heard and seene, I most humbly Conceive he may be fitt for a secretary to the Commissioners. . . ." [11] After the takeover of New Netherland in 1664, Nicolls was appointed provincial secretary by Richard Nicolls (no relation) and remained in this office until 1680. During his tenure as secretary he was also a member of the provincial council, served as a presiding judge on the court of assizes, was twice appointed mayor of New York City, held a captaincy in a militia company, and was frequently appointed to special commissions. In addition to holding numerous offices, Nicolls is reputed to be the compiler and codifier of the "Duke's Laws" (1665) and the author of the "Charter of Libertyes" (1683). His knowledge of English law, his experience acquired as secretary and member of the provincial council, and his wide friendships with such colonial leaders as the Winthrops in Connecticut made Nicolls one of the most influential and indispensable men in the central government.

As provincial secretary, Nicolls maintained files of all outgoing and incoming correspondence and papers. Copies of letters, orders, warrants, commissions, and passes for the Delaware region were recorded in his "General Entries Book," while papers received from the various jurisdictions in Delaware were bundled together and marked as "Delaware Papers." It is uncertain whether Nicolls filed the papers of other regions and jurisdictions in New York separately in this manner. When E. B. O'Callaghan arranged the New York Colonial Manuscripts, then stored in the Secretary of State's Office, he may have retained this regional designation for papers related to Delaware since the area was no longer a part of New York. In any case, O'Callaghan's arrangement brings together the papers related to the Delaware region in a continuous series of manuscripts, from the beginning of the Dutch period through the period of English rule.

Volumes 20 and 21 of the New York Colonial Manuscripts, relating to the English period on the Delaware, do not, however, form a continuous historical record of judicial and administrative proceedings; rather, they consist of correspondence, reports, petitions, accounts, survey-returns, and copies of local court proceedings that were sent by official or private persons to the central government at Fort James. Among the papers are also copies of letters, orders, warrants, instructions, and patent records concerning the Delaware region that Nicolls retained for his files. The papers sent from the various jurisdictions in Delaware to Fort James comprise more than two-thirds of the manuscripts in volumes 20 and 21, representing court cases on appeal or suits outside the responsibility of the local courts. These volumes, therefore, do not contain the complete records of the Delaware region, but rather the central government's judicial and administrative contact with this remote area. In order to understand the local context of these "Delaware Papers," the records of the various courts in the Delaware region should be consulted.

The records of most of the courts in Delaware have survived starting from 1676, and many are available in print. Volume I of *Records of the Court of New Castle on Delaware, 1676-1681* was published in 1904 by The Colonial Society of Pennsylvania; and Volume II (1681-1699), consisting of extracts from the court records concerning land titles and probate proceedings, was published in 1935. The "Record of the Upland Court, 1676-1681" appears in the *Historical Society of Pennsylvania Memoirs*, Volume VII (1860). Records for the Whorekill appear in *Some Records of Sussex County, Delaware*, compiled by C. H. B. Turner (Philadelphia, 1909). These records begin in 1681, when the Whorekill had been renamed Deale County, and end in 1694. Records for the St. Jones court are published in the *American Legal Records* series as Volume VIII under the title *Court Records of Kent County, Delaware 1680-1705* (Washington, 1959). Records for the courts on the east side of the river are rather fragmentary. These courts either did not keep sytematic records, since they were subordinate to the New Castle court, or if they did the records have not survived. Records for Burlington begin in 1680, after Byllynge's proprietorship to West Jersey was recognized by the Duke of York. These records are published in the *American Legal Records* series as Volume V under the title *Burlington Court Book of West New Jersey 1680-1709* (Washington, 1944). For the Salem court there are only a few fragments of proceedings which are calendared in *Archives of the State of New Jersey*, Volume XXI, 1899.

Records preceding the Dutch repossession in 1673 have not survived at the local level. The only remnants from this period are those copies of proceedings and references to local affairs in the *Delaware Papers*.

After the re-establishment of the Duke's control over New York in 1674, William Tom was commissioned clerk or secretary at New Castle. He had come to the Delaware with Sir Robert Carr's invasion force in 1664 and was probably Capt. John Carr's secretary from 1666 to 1673. When Tom was replaced as secretary by Ephraim Herman in 1676, his records were found to be deficient. They were sent to New York for examination but were returned the following year with the admonition that Tom put his records in order, since the council in New York could make no sense of them. Tom died a few months later and the whereabouts of his "twoo small old paper bookes" is unknown. The loss of these records leaves a gap of almost two years in the court proceedings for New Castle and Upland. The *Delaware Papers* fill in part of this gap with copies of the more important of those proceedings that were sent to New York either on appeal or by order of the council. They include subjects ranging in importance from the 1675 New Castle riot, to a complaint over the discovery of a stone in a bag of feathers. Local records for the Whorekill begin with 1680, leaving even a larger gap than the one for New Castle and Upland. When Cornelis

Verhoofe, the secretary of the Whorekill court, was removed from office in 1681 for various offenses, he refused to turn his records over to the new secretary. The local sheriff was ordered to search for the records, and if they could not be located, Verhoofe was to appear before the Court of Assizes in New York. As with William Tom, Verhoofe died soon thereafter and his records have also been lost. Copies of those court proceedings at the Whorekill, which Verhoofe had sent to New York, have also been preserved in the *Delaware Papers*, whereas the minor or petty cases, which were disposed of locally, have been lost. The *Delaware Papers*, therefore, enable the historian to recover at least a class of the official records of this region for a period which would be otherwise undocumented.

In 1850 E. B. O'Callaghan began the enormous task of organizing the piles of manuscripts stored in the Secretary of State's Office, which now constitute the Colonial Manuscripts of New York. He had them bound in large folio volumes with title pages and identification numbers for each manuscript. In 1865-66 his *Calendar of Historical Manuscripts* was printed, and has for years served as the means of access to this indispensable source for the colonial history of New York. O'Callaghan's arrangement of the manuscripts in volumes 20 and 21 has here been maintained in order to preserve the usefulness of his calendar as a guide. The "Calendar of Manuscripts" printed in this volume is not intended to supersede O'Callaghan's but rather to facilitate access to those manuscripts cross-referenced by document number, and to correct errors found in O'Callaghan's calendar.

Many of the manuscripts transcribed and translated for this volume have suffered damage both as a result of the 1911 State Capitol fire and through neglect. Wherever possible, missing or damaged portions have been recovered from contemporary manuscript copies or from transcriptions made before the fire. All recovered portions are identified by brackets, and the source cited by footnote. Other printed transcriptions of the English manuscripts are also cited as well as the locations of final drafts of papers and letters sent by Matthias Nicolls to the Delaware. In some cases Berthold Fernow's well-known transcriptions in Volume XII of *NYCD* (see key to abbreviations at the end of the *Introduction*) were not used as a source because they were found to be unreliable, especially wherever it was clear that the manuscript was damaged before the fire. Fernow frequently supplied words in damaged portions by conjecture, without citation; in some instances his interpolations are quite different from contemporary copies of documents which have survived in sources unavailable to him. Fernow's transcriptions in general have proved to be unreliable and should be used with caution.[12] Any damaged portions that could not be recovered from other sources are marked by empty brackets with the space between them approximating the amount of lost material.

Although volumes 20 and 21 of the *Delaware Papers* are from the English period, Dutch continued to be used by officials for a short time after the takeover, and it appears in petitions written by non-English speakers. These Dutch manuscripts are noted in O'Callaghan's calendar with an asterisk, except for 20:81a and 20:82, which were left unmarked. All the Dutch manuscripts have been translated anew for this volume. Other printed translations of these Dutch manuscripts are cited by footnote; those manuscripts translated by V. H. Paltsits for *ECM* are accompanied by a transcription of the Dutch text.

The "expanded method" of transcription as outlined in the *Harvard Guide to American History* has been followed for the printing of the English manuscripts: all superior letters brought down to the line of text; abbreviations expanded if the final letter of the word is present; "-con" with a tilde printed "-cion"; the graph "y", when designating a spirant, replaced by "th-"; the use of "u" and "v" regularized according to modern spelling practices; "ff-" replaced by "F-"; "&" and "&c." printed as "and" and "etc."; "tailed-p" expanded to its appropriate form; all personal names capitalized, but otherwise transcribed exactly as they appear in the manuscript; and the Dutch abbreviation for the patronymic marker "-sen" transcribed as "-sz."

Descriptive titles have been added to all manuscripts that do not carry original titles, and appear in brackets. Original signatures are preceded by the marker [Signed:], and marks in lieu of signatures have been reproduced exactly as they appear in the manuscript. Marginal notations have been indented into the text with a citation of their source wherever possible. Addresses on covers follow the text, as well as all notations and endorsements. All dates have been left unchanged. It should be kept in mind that the English continued to use the Julian Calendar, or "old style," until 1752, whereas most of the Dutch provinces had adopted the Gregorian Calendar, or "new style," in the sixteenth century. According to "old style" dating, the new year began on March 25, and in the seventeenth century it was running ten days behind "new style" dating. Sometimes double dates were used for the period between January 1 and March 25, but if only a single date is given and the document is English, then it should be considered "old style." If the document has been translated from Dutch, then the date will either appear double or should be considered "new style." In a few cases only comparison with related documents will reveal a document's true date.

The file copies retained by Matthias Nicolls of correspondence and orders sent to Delaware are often rough drafts of the final document. In most cases the revisions are indicated in footnotes; a few documents, however, were so extensively revised that it was impossible to indicate all the alterations in this way. For these documents the revised version has been used in the body of the text, while the unrevised version appears in the *Appendix.*

The following abbreviations have been used to identify sources cited in the footnotes:

CLP   *Calendar of New York Colonial Manuscripts Indorsed Land Papers; in the Office of the Secretary of State of New York, 1643-1803*, Albany, 1864.

DYR   *The Duke of York Record, 1646-1679*, Wilmington, [1903].

ECM   *Minutes of the Executive Council of the Province of New York, 1668-1673*, two volumes, edited by Victor Hugo Paltsits, Albany, 1910.

MA   *Archives of Maryland*, ed. William H. Browne *et al.*, Baltimore, 1883-1956.

NCCR   *Records of the Court of New Castle on Delaware, 1676-1681*, Lancaster, Pa., 1904.

NYCD   *Documents Relative to the Colonial History of the State of New York*, Volumes I-XI, edited by E. B. O'Callaghan, Albany, 1865.
       Documents Relating to the Colonial History of the State of New York, Volumes XII-XV, edited by B. Fernow, Albany, 1877.

PA   *Pennsylvania Archives* (Second Series), Volume V, edited by John B. Linn and Wm. H. Egle, Harrisburg, 1877.

SCR   *Some Records of Sussex County Delaware*, compiled by C. H. B. Turner, Philadelphia, 1909.

UCR   "The Record of the Court at Upland 1676 to 1681" in *Historical Society of Pennsylvania Memoirs*, Volume VII, edited by Edward Armstrong, Philadelphia, 1860.

WWS   *Walter Wharton's Land Survey Register, 1675-1679*, edited by Albert Cook Meyers, Wilmington, 1955.

References to the other volumes of New York Colonial Manuscripts calendared by O'Callaghan are cited by volume and page number without an identifying prefix.

ACKNOWLEDGMENTS

I should like to thank the following people who were involved in the various stages of preparing this volume for publication: Peter R. Christoph, William A. Polf, Ralph L. DeGroff, Kenn Stryker-Rodda, Kenneth Scott, Michael H. Tepper, and Rosanne Conway; with special thanks to Mrs. Lewis Wilcoxen for preparing the *Index*, Thomas Schwartz, who drew the map of Delaware River and Bay, and Linda Rose, who typed the manuscript. The following agencies and institutions also deserve acknowledgment for providing the project with the necessary financial support: The New York State Library, The New York State American Revolution Bicentennial Commission, The Holland Society of New York, The H. W. Wilson Foundation, The Corning Glass Company, and The Eva Gebhard-Gourgaud Foundation.

Charles Gehring
Albany, 1976

NOTES

1. 20:1a (see end of *Introduction* for key to abbreviations).
2. *PA* 5:542.
3. 20: 1a.
4. NYCD 3:345
5. 20: 1b.
6. *PA* 5:573.
7. 20:29/30.
8. NYCD 3:218.
9. NYCD 3:226.
10. 20: 98.
11. *New York Historical Society Collections*, 2:57 (1869.)
12. See "New York's Dutch Records" in *New York History* (July 1975) for examples.

JAMES, DUKE OF YORK
(from the picture by Lely at St. James's Palace)

CALENDAR OF MANUSCRIPTS

Volume 20

Volume 21

NEW YORK
HISTORICAL MANUSCRIPTS:
DUTCH

Volume XX

Delaware Papers, 1664-1682

Instructions to Sir Robert Carr for the
          Reducing of Delaware Bay, and Settling
          the People there under his Majesties
          Obedience[1]

     When you are come near unto the Fort which is possessed by
the Dutch you Shall Send your Boat on Shoar to summon the
Governour and Inhabitants to yield Obedience to his Majestie
as the rightfull Sovereign of that Tract of Land And let him
and them Know that his Majestie is graciously pleased that all
the planters Shall enjoy their Farms Houses Lands Goods and
Chattels with the same privileges And upon the Same Terms,
which they do now possess them Only that they Change their
Masters, whether they be the West India Company or the City of
Amsterdam, To the Swedes you Shall remonstrate, their happy
return, under a Monarchicall Government and his Majesties good
Inclination to that Nation, and to all men who shall Comply
with his Majesties Rights and Title in Delaware without Force
of Arms.

     That all the Cannon Armes and Ammunition which belongs to
the Government shall remain to his Majestie.

     That the Acts of Parliament shall be the rules of future
Trading.

     That all people may enjoy Liberty of Conscience.

     That for Six months next ensuing the same Magistrates shall
Continue in their Offices, only that they and all others in
Authority must take the oath of Allegiance to his Majesty And
Publick Acts be made in his Majesties Name.

     If you find you Cannot reduce the place by force Nor upon
these Conditions You may add Such as you find Necessary upon
the place, but if those nor Force will prevail, Then you are to
Dispatch a Messenger to the Governour of Maryland with this
Letter to him And request his Assistance and of all other
English who live near the dutch plantations.

     Your first Care (after the reducing of the place) is to
protect the Inhabitants from Injuries, as well as Violence of
the Soldiers, which will be easily effected if you Settle a
Course for Weekly or Dayly provisions, by Agreement with the
Inhabitants which shall be Satisfyed to them, either out of the
profitts Customes or Rents belonging to their present Masters
or in Case of Necessity from hence.

     The Laws for the present Cannot be altered as to the
Administration of right and Justice between Partyes.

     To my Lord Baltimore's son You shall Declare, and to all
the English concerned in Maryland, that his Majesty hath at
his great Expence, Sent his Ships and Soldiers to reduce all
Foreigners in those parts, to his Majesties Obedience And to
that purpose only, you are employed, But the reduction of the
place, being at his Majesties Expence, You have Commands to
Keep possession thereof for his Majesties own Behoofe and Right
and that you are ready to Join with the Governour of Maryland
upon his Majesties Interest [in] all Occasions, And that if my

Lord Baltimore, doth prete[nd] Right thereunto by his patent
(which is a doubtfull Ca[se]) You are to Say that you only Keep
possession till his Maje[sty] is informed and sattisfyed
otherwise. In other things I mu[st] Leave you to your
Discretion And the best Advice you Can g[et] upon the place.

---

1. Other transcription in NYCD 12:457. Contemporary copy
   in General Entries 1:58; printed in State Library
   Bulletin: History, No. 2 (May, 1899) p. 125.

20:1b   Articles of Agreement between the Honourable
            Sir Robert Carr Knight on the Behalf of his
            Majesty of Great Britain, And the Burgomasters
            on the Behalf of themselves, and all the Dutch
            and Swedes Inhabiting in Delaware Bay and
            Delaware River[1]

1st   That all the Burgers and Planters will Submitt themselves
        to his Majesties Authority without making any Resistance.

2.   That whoever of what Nation soever doth Submit to his
        Majesties Authority shall be protected in their Estates
        reall and personall whatsoever, by his Majesties Laws and
        Justice.

3.   That the present Magistrates shall be Continued in their
        Offices, and Jurisdictions to Exercise their Civil power
        As formerly.

4.   That if any Dutchman, or other person Shall Desire to
        Depart from the river, That it shall be Lawfull for him
        so to doe, with his Goods, within Six months after the
        Date of these Articles.

5.   That the Magistrates and all the Inhabitants (who are
        included in these Articles) Shall take the oaths of
        Allegiance to his Majesty, and of Fidelity to the
        present Government.

6.   That all the people shall Enjoy the Liberty of their
        Conscience in Church Discipline as formerly.

7th   That whoever shall take the Oaths is from that time a
        free Dennizen and Shall enjoy all the privileges of
        trading into any of his Majesties Dominions, As freely as
        any Englishman and may require a Certificate for so
        doing.

8.   That the Scout the Burgomasters Sherriff and other
        Inferiour Magistrates Shall use and Exercise their
        Customary power in Administration of Justice, within
        their precincts for Six months or until his Majesties
        pleasure is further Known.

The Oath: I do swear by the Almighty God, that I will bear
           Faith and Allegiance to his Majesty of Great Britain
           And that I will Obey all Such Commands as I shall
           receive from the Governour Deputy Governour or
           other officers Appointed by his Majesties Authority.
           So long as I live within these or any other his
           Majesties Territories

                        Given under my hand and Seal this 1st day
                        of October in the Year of our Lord God
                        1664   Robert Carr

Given under our hands and seales in the
behalf of ourselves and the rest of the
Inhabitants the 1st day of October in
the Year of our Lord God 1664.

Fobb. Out Gout[2]
Henry Johnson
Gerrett Saunders Vantiell
Hans Block
Lucas Peterson
Henry Casturier

[Endorsed:] Instructions to Robt. Kerr for reducing Delaware
             bay.

---

1. Other transcription in Hazard's Register of Pennsylvania
   1:37. The transcription of a contemporary copy of 20:1b
   appears in NYCD 3:71.

2. Out Gout is a scribal error for Outhout; the correct
   spelling appears in the contemporary copy (NYCD 3:71).

20:2 [A CONFIRMATION GRANTED TO PETER ALRICHS FOR
       TWO ISLANDS IN THE DELAWARE RIVER][1]

Richard Nicolls Esq. etc. Whereas there are two certaine Islands
in Delaware River scituate lyeing and being on the West side of
the said River and about South West from the Island commonly
called Matiniconck The which is the biggest of the two Islands
haveing beene formerly Knowne by the name of Kipps Island and
by the Indian name of Koomenakimokonck conteining about a myle
in length and half a myle in breadth and the other Island lying
somewhat to the North of the former being of aabout half a
myle in length and the quarter of a myle in breadth and there
being also a small creek neare unto the lesser of the said
Islands fitt to build a mill thereupon Now to the end the best
improvement may be made of the said Islands and creek to which
there appeare no other lawfull Pretenders and for divers other
good reasons and considerations me thereunto especially moveing
Know that by Vertue of the Commission and authority unto me
given I have thought fitt to give and grant and by these

presents doe give ratify confirme and grant unto Peter Alricks
his heirs and assignes the afore recited two Islands with all
the Soyle, meadow ground wood land pastures marshes waters
creeks fishing hunting and fowling and all other profitts
comodityes and emoluments to the said Islands and premises belonging or in any wise appertaining as also the small creek
aformenciond neare unto the lesser Island running up a myle
within land to have Liberty to Erect and build a Mill thereupon
where shall be found most convenient as also a convenient pro-
portion of land on each syde of the said creek for Egresse and
Regresse to and from the mill and for other necessary
accomodacions thereunto belonging To have an to hould all and
singular the said two Islands Creek and proporcion of land on
Eeach syde thereof and premisses with their and every of their
appurtenances to the said Peter Alricks his heirs and assignes
unto the proper use and behoofe of the said Peter Alricks his
heirs and assigns for Ever, Yeilding and paying therefore
yearly and Every year unto his Majestys use Foure Otterskins as
a quit rent when itt shall be demanded by such person or
persons in authority as his Majesty shall please to establish
and empower in Delaware River or the parts and Plantations
adjacent. Given etc. The Pattent is Dated the 15th of
February 1667.

New York February 28th 1703
A True coppy of the originall taken out of the secrys. office
                              [Signed:] Geo: Clarke Secry.

[Endorsed:] A copy of a Patent Graunted in Coll. Nicolls time
             for the West side of Mattininconk Island[2]

---

1. Other transcription in NYCD 12:461. Other copy in DYR:
    125.

2. The endorsement is incorrect; the patent refers not to
    Matiniconck Island but to two islands south-west of it.
    cf., See The History of Bucks County Pennsylvania by
    W.W.H. Davis pp. 24-25 for a later reference to these
    two islands. Endorsement in Matthias Nicolls' hand.

20:3 [CONDITIONS UNDER WHICH PETER ALRICHS WILL
       LEASE MATINICONCK ISLAND]

Peter Aldricks will [   ] Mattinaconk Island for three y[   ]
certaine from the Time that Caleb Carman leaves it upon these
Conditions.

1st That hee may Enjoy the fruits of the Land free for three
     Yeares certaine.

2   That hee shall be accountable for halfe the increase of
     the Cattle which Caleb shall leave and of such Cattle
     Sheep Goates or the like as shall be delivered to him
     hereafter.

3   That hee shall make good the Number of all Cattle Oxen or
     horses that shall be delivered to him.[1]

4   That he shall keep the housing in repaire and leave both
     fences and housing in such necessary repaire as hee shall
     find good to keepe or renew them during the forsaid 3
     years.

5   That after the Expiration of 3 yeares the said P. Aldricks
     shall be obliged to hold the same condition aforesaid of
     half Increase of cattle and be accountable for halfe the
     Increase of the Corne yearly for 4 yeares more Except
     that the said P. Aldricks gives halfe a Yeares warning to
     the Governour [   ] the place or [   ] [ ]overnour
     shall soe Cause to [   ] P. Alricks warning to be gone of
     [before the expiration of the 3 yeares][2] in halfe a
     yeares Time. That the Governour and P. Aldricks are
     fully agreed upon the precedent formes with the addition
     that in case any Cattle oxen or horses sheep Goats or the
     like happen to dye or be killd by accident Each party
     shall beare halfe the losse.

     What is before mentioned to be agreed upon between the
Present Governour and P. Aldricks is to be understood with
reference to any Governour that shall succeed the present
Governour as likewise to the heires or Assignes of P Aldrickes
in case of Mortality.

     That Peter Aldrickes shall have a lease graunted with
these conditions annexed whereunto the Meadows lying over
against the said Island must be Inserted.[3]

     Jan Swarts Island lyeing South East from Matiniconck and
belonging to it for releife of the Cattle whereupon they allways
have run from [   ].[4]

---

1. Condition No. 3 is crossed out.

2. The phrase in brackets was marked to be inserted at this
    point.

3. This last condition was written by the same hand but at
    a different time. Color of ink is identical to that
    of the insertion.

4. This note concerning Jan Swarts Island was written in
    the lower corner in Matthias Nicolls' hand.

20:4 The forme of holding the Court at the Fort in
      Newcastle upon Delaware River, for the Tryall
      of the Long Finne etc. about the late Insur-
      rection, December the 6th 1669.[1]

Upon the meeting of the Court Let Proclamacion bee made by
saying O Yes, O Yes, O Yes, Silence is commanded in the Court
whilst his Majesties Commissioners are sitting, upon paine of
Imprisonment.

Lett the Commission bee read. And the Commissioners
called upon afterwards, [   ] any shall bee absent Let their
n[   ] bee Recorded.

Then Let Proclamacion bee made again by O Yes, as before,
after which say, All manner of Persons that have any thing to
doe at this speciall Court held by Commission from the Right
Honorable Francis Lovelace Esq. Governor Generall under his
Royall Highnesse the Duke of Yorke of all his Territories in
America, draw neare and give Your attendance, and if any one
have Plaint to enter or suite to prosecute, Let them come
forth and they shall bee heard.

After this Let a Jury of twelve good men bee empannelled.

Then Let the Long Finne (Prisoner in the Fort) bee called
for and brought to the Barr.

Upon which the Jury is to bee called over and numbered one,
two, etc. and if the Prisoner have no Exception against either
of them Let them bee sworne as directed in the Booke of Lawes
for Tryall of Criminalls, and bid to looke upon the Prisoner at
the Barre.

The forme of the Oath is as followeth

You doe sweare by the Everliving God that you will
conscientiously try and deliver your verdict betweene our
Soveraigne Lord the King, and the Prisoner at the Barre
according to Evidence and the Lawes of this Countrey, So helpe
you God and the Contents of this booke.

Then Let the Prisoner bee againe called upon and bid to
hold up his Right hand, viz. John Binckson alias Marcus Coningsmarke, alias Coningsmarcus, alias Matheus Hincks How [   ]

Then proceed with the Indictment as followeth

John Binckson, Thou standest here endicted by the name of
John Binckson, alias Coningsmarke, alias Coningsmarcus, alias
Matheus Hencks, alias xx[2], for that having not the feare of
God before thine Eyes, but being instigated by the devill, Upon
or about the 28th day of August in the 21st yeare of the Raigne
of our soveraigne Lord Charles the 2nd by the Grace of God of
England, Scotland France and Ireland King Defender of the Faith
etc. Annoque Domini 1669 at Christina.

And at severall other times and places before, Thou didst
most wickedly, traiterously, feloniously and maliciously,
conspire and attempt to invade by force of Armes this Government setled under the allegiance and protection of his Majestie,
and also didst most traiterously solicite and entice divers and
threaten others of his Majesties good Subject to betray their
allegiance to his Majestie the King of England, persuading
them to revolt and adhere to a forreigne Prince, that is to say,
to the King of Sweden, In prosecucion whereof, thou didst
appoint and cause to bee held many Riotous, Routous and Unlawfull Assemblyes [   ] the Peace of our [   ] Lord the

King, and the Lawes of this Government in such cases provided.

John Binckson, etc. what hast thou to say for thyselfe,
Art thou Guilty of the Felony and Treason layd to they Charge
or not Guilty?

If hee say not Guilty. Then aske him By whom wilt thou
bee try'de, If hee say by God and his Countrey, Say God send
thee a good Deliverance.

Then call the wittnesses and Let them bee sworne either to
their Testim[ ] already given in, or to what they will then
declare upon their Oathes.

Upon which the Jury is to have their Charge given them,
directing them to find the matter of Fact according to Evidence,
and then Let them bee called over as they goe out to consult
upon their Verdict in which they must all agree.

When the Jury returnes to deliver in their Verdict to the
Court, Let them bee called over againe, and then ask't. Gent.
Are you agreed upon your Verdict in this Case in difference
betweene our soveraign Lord the King and the prisoner at the
Barr. upon their saying Yes, Aske who shall speake for you,
Then they [ ] the Foreman [   ] in their Verdict and
the [   ] Then read the Verdict and say Gentle[men] this
is your Verdict, upon which you are [all] agreed, upon their
saying yes, Call that the Prisoner bee taken from the barre
and secured.

[Endorsed:] No. 15 Forme of Tryall. Long Finne. 1669 Dec.
6th.

---

1. Other transcriptions in ECM:314 and NYCD 12:467.

2. This may refer to another alias which was marked xx for
   insertion at this point.

20:5 A list of the inhabitants that was Confederets
with the long Fin and had the marke and their
fines[1]

gilders

	gilders			gilders
John Stolcup	1500		Mons Powson	300
Jens Ustas	0830		Henerick Anderson	200
Henerick: Coalman	0930		Lawsa Eskelson	050
[O]lla Francis	1500		Simon Johnson	100
John Powles	0150		Erick Urianson	200
Andries Johnson	0050		Mathias Bartleson	100
Hans Petterson	0100		Erike Matson	200
Neals Nealson	0300		Lawsa Wolson	100
Mathias Nealson	0100		Lawsa Corneleson	100

Charles Johnson............0300
Hans Wolason...............0100
Hans Hoofman...............0300
John Henerics..............0300
Paules Lawrson.............0100
Olla Torsa.................0100
Henerick Nealson...........0100
L[aur]ans Carolus minister.0600
M[arger]ett Matson widdow..0100
[John] Peterson............0100
[Bartle] Parker............0100
Samuell Peterson...........0050
                          ‾‾‾‾
                          7710

John Matson........150
Evertt the Fin.....300
Andries: Andrieson.050
Paules Lawrson....1[ ]
Mathias Matson.....100
Marcus Laurson.....050
                   ‾‾‾‾
                   2100

[Endorsed:] A List of Delinque[ ] with the Long Fin
             December 1669.

_____

1. Other transcriptions in NYCD 12:469 and ECM:317.

20:6   A liste of the fines about the Rebellion of the
       Long Finne.[1]

                                    Guilders   sewant

Evert Hendricksen..............   300
Mat Bertelsen..................   100
Simon Jansen...................   100
Las Oleson.....................   100
Erick Ericksen.................   100
Jan Matse......................   150
Samuell Pietersen..............   50
Las Eskell.....................   50
Erick Matsen...................   200
Bertle Hendricksen.............   100
Hendrick Anderson..............   200
                                ‾‾‾‾‾‾‾‾ 1450

Mons Paulsen...................   300
Las Cornelissen................   150
Andries Andriesen..............   50
Paul Larsen....................   100
Jan Stalcop.................... 1500
Olle Fransen................... 2000
Dirck Jansen...................   100
Hendrick Colman................   930
Matijs Matsen..................   100
Hans Pietersen.................   100
Paul Jansens Vrow..............   100
                                ‾‾‾‾‾‾‾‾ 5430

                                        Guilders   sewant

Neils Nielsen...............	300	
Hendrick Nielsen..............	100	
Mat Nielsen...................	100	
Olle Oelsen...................	100	
Paul Larsen...................	100	
Carel Jansen.................	300	
Mons Jansen..................	100	
Carel Monsen.................	100	
Hans Hopman..................	300	
Juns Junstersen..............	1500	
	3000	

Heer Lars....................	800	
Another Hans Pietersen........	100	
Jan Paulsen..................	100	
Andries Junsen...............	100	
Jan Hendrickse of Marcus Kill.	300	
Marcus.......................	50	

	1450
Besides this summe everyone or	3000
the greatest part paid to the	
Stebo[2]	5430
- 14G. and some 28G.	1450
	11330

Transcribed and Examined by mee at Newcastle
May 11th. 1675   [Signed:] Matthias Nicolls Secr.

[Endorsed:] List of the Fines about the Long Finne.
             Dec. 1669.

---

1. Other transcriptions in NYCD 12:470 and ECM:318.

2. Stebo is a variant form of Dutch steeboode or
    stadsboode meaning a "messenger of the court" or
    "summoner."

20:7 Charges about the long Fin[1]

To	John Henery...............	864
	Michaell Baroon............	2454
	Neals Matsa...............	0607
	John Harmons..............	0235
	Gisbert Dericks...........	1107
	Barnard the Smith.........	0110
	Albert Johnson............	0115
	Mathias Conradus..........	0200

```
Neals Lawsa............... 0100
Petter Alricks............ 0100
Mr. Tom................... 0650
                         ─────
                          6542
```

[Endorsed:] A list of Charges about the long Fin

---

1. Other transcriptions in NYCD 12:471 and ECM:320.

20:8   [MEMORANDUM RELATING TO THE DISPOSITION OF THE
        LONG FINN AFFAIR][1]

[ ]s Block[2]	27	135
Jur[ ]n Jansen[3]	25	5
Mattys Eschelsen	135	675
Hans Peitersen	54	
Andres Matsen	675	135
More 16		50
The Domini[4]		85
Harmen Reyners		
Neals Lawson and		
3 more		

                    Received 50 scheple of wheat of
                    C. Carre, there is due 85 scheple.
                    Dec. 13 1669

[Verso:]   The 2 schippers have recd. on board with each
           prisoner a bed, blanket, pair of bilboes and lock.

---

1. Other transcription in ECM:321. O'Callaghan's calendar
    entry stating that the names are those of prisoners, and
    the title in ECM: "Prisoners departed at Newcastle,"
    are questionable. The names are probably part of a
    list of persons who are paying their fines in wheat.

2. ECM:321 has H[an]s Block.

3. ECM:321 has Jur[ie]n Janse.

4. This is Laurentius Carolus Lokenius whose name appears
    as Laurans Carolus minister in 20:5.

20:9 [WILLIAM TOM AND PETER ALRICHS TO GOV. LOVELACE
ABOUT INDIAN AFFAIRS][1]

9th of March 1670

Right Honorable

Yours of the 28 of February wee have receav[ ] and to give
your honor a full answer is more th[ ] wee can doe being not
all one mens children and for us few English none of us able to
speake to the Indians but so farre as wee can advise your honor
is as followeth

1 first that wee are in a sad condicon is most certaine
being under the power of the Heathen and no power to defend by
reason a nomber of out plantacions are not able to secure them
selves and wee make a greate question if wee in the place can
well secure ourselves and to bring them into the Towne wilbe
there utter ruine and losse of the river for then they expose
there houses corne and cattell to the fury of the Indians and
wee not able to mainteyne them here for prevencion of which
our best proposall is if your honor could spare so much time as
to come over to treate with the Sachems without dispute the
reverence to your person would procure us 4 or 5 yeares respect
and by that time the numerous issue by the assistance of god
wilbe able to defend them selves

2 The Sachems of the Indians give for reason of there
warre that they threaten to make upon the Christians is they
say where the English come they drive them from there lands and
bring for instance the North Virginia and Maryland and feare if
not timely prevent[ ] shall doe so here.

3 Thirdly if possible to invite Capt. Carteret to beare
your honor company the most of the Indians living upon his side.

4 Fourthly with all reverence your honor having writt
that your honor if occasion was would expose yourselfe to the
trouble of comming over and desired to know what forces to bring
with you wee doe think that 25 men is enough for the guard of
your honors person and that number will not frighten the
Sachems and more may render your honors journe unprofitable by
there non appearance your honor now att the time of the yeare
not being to fight but to treate

5 fiftly if your honor comes as wee well hope be pleased
by the first to send an expresse and Peter Aldricks shall meete
your honor att the time prefixt to pilot your honor from the
Navecinck and informe the Indians of your coming that they may
not leave there houses att the sight of so many men to them
unexpected

6 sixtly our intencion here is to build a blocke house
40 foote square with 4 att every end for Flanckers in the
middle of the Towne the fort not being fitt to be repaired and
if repaired of noe defence lying att the extreame end of the
towne and noe garrison therefore wee begg that wee may have
liberty to pull itt downe and make use of the tiles bricks and
other materi[ ] for the use of our new intended fortificacion
which if wee have no occasion for as wee feare wee shall will
be convenient for a Court house notwithstanding

This being our duty in answer to your honors letter wee
present to more prudent consideracion and assure your honor wee
will not alone maintayne our owne interest so farr as god shall
inable us but to the furthest of our industry presse to save
the honor of your Royall Master and ours together the honor
of our countrey and then lett fate act with us as the greate
god is pleased in the meane time wee subscribe our selves

                    Right Honorable
                    your honors most humble
                    and faithfull servants
                 [Signed:] Will. Tom
                    Pieter Alrichs

[Endorsed:] A Letter from Mr. Tom and Mr. Alricks to the
             Governor, about the Indyan affayres there.
             Mar. 9 1670.

---

1. Other transcriptions in NYCD 12:493 and ECM:507.

20:10   [RELATION FROM THE WHOREKILL CONCERNING JAN
          DE CAPER'S SLOOP][1]

On the 20th of December 1670 a sachem of Nassawam, who
lives near Sachomok, came here to this place. I asked him
whether a vessel had been heard of at the South Sea. He informed me that a vessell had been found on the beach near
Cincketeck Inlet[2] belonging to Maryland. Whereupon I ordered
Hendrick Drochstraet[en], who was going to trade with the
Indians, to make careful inquiry about it. He returned the 3rd
of January having learned from the Indians that a vessel had
been beached when the corn was ripening and that they had
found one boat washed high up on the dunes with some goods in
it, and that they found a corpse on the beach along with various chests which had washed out of the yacht, and that the
vessel lay in pieces in the water against the shore, and that
they showed him one of the boats, which the Indians had worked
into the inner channel and brought to Sackamock, as well as the
arms of the yacht De Jonge Prins. The same Hendrick then proceeded from here to New Castle to report about the yacht. On
the 4th of January an Indian came from Sackamock who said:
"There are still some beavers and other goods there; come and
get them because the English intend to come and take them
away." Whereupon Pieter Groenendick along with Herman Cornelisz
went there and brought back the beavers and goods which appear
on the inventory.

On the 29th of January Hendrick Drochstraeten came back
again from New Castle together with Ule Swensen and Jan Boeyer
on their way to the Indians to find out about the people of the
sloop. At the same time I received a letter signed by Capt.
John Car, Will. Thom and Pieter Alrichs requesting of me to

accompany them there, which I did. When we arrived there we
questioned the Indians who said that they had gone to the place
two days after the storm to gather oysters. There they saw the
yacht lying broken on the beach and the boat in the dunes and a
dead body washed up on the beach, of tall stature, brown hair
and a very fat belly. We asked for an Indian with a canoe to
take us there which the sachem agreed to for 1 1/2 fathoms of
black sewant. We went about 2 Dutch miles further to a place
called Sinckoachkinck and because it was very cold and with a
strong North West wind, we dared not venture any further in the
canoe. We, therefore, had to waste 7 days among the Indians,
during which time the water froze, which is at least 3 Dutch
miles wide. Afterwards the Indian, whom we had hired, refused
to go with us. We could not wait any longer so we took a
canoe from the Indians to return to the mainland. We broke
through the ice and when we got out in the middle it was open
water due to the South wind which came up, and we were in great
danger with the ice flowing from one side with the ebb tide and
with the wind against the canoe on the other side. Through
much exertion, God be praised, we got across. When we returned
we went to the aforementioned Indians. We decided to go to the
English in Bocquetonorton[3] because the boat had been taken
there by an Englishman who had been among the Indians. We
arrived there two days later on the 14th of February. I
learned from several inhabitants that some of their neighbors,
after having heard from the Indians that a vessel was beached,
had gone there and brought back some goods. Therefore I met
with a Commissary of Pocomock, whose name is James Weedon now
residing in the Hoerkil, of whom I requested a warrant to inquire about the vessel and the goods which were taken from it
and to find out where the people might be. This was done, and
I went with the warrant to the constable who immediately went
with me from house to house. Those who had found something
were ordered to tell what they had: one showed us 2 iron bolts
from the yacht, another 3 iron bolts and an empty barrel and
yet another said that he had found 3 yards of Kersey buried in
the sand and seeing a small piece pulled it out of the water.
Everything that was shown was of little importance. We also
found the boat there with the rowing bench missing, which the
Indians said was gone when they found the boat. I have listed
in the inventory those pertinent items which each person in
Bocquetenorton has in his possession. When the weather improved we rowed the boat from there towards the wreck accompanied by an Indian boy, but the north-east wind came up so
that we barely made it to the James Mils Island,[4] where we
were held up by rain and wind. Afterwards we rowed, nevertheless, in the wind. When we came across we went along the
beach a good 3 Dutch miles and found the yacht partly covered
in the sand. All the hull planks were found strewn along the
beach; here and there a piece of the deck; pieces of the yacht,
and planks. The capstan lay about an hour's walk from the
wreck, which rests obliquely against the shore. We could not
find, however, either a body or bones. The people of
Bocquetenorton said that they had [   ] the body, but said
that the Indians had told them that the wolf had already eaten
it. The Indians also told us the same thing when we offered
them ten fathoms of sewant and a blanket, if they would show us
the body or bones. They said, "the wolf ate it and the bones
were covered by sand or water." Lastly we found the gighook
which we took along after burning off a short piece of wood
still attached to it. In the meantime news of the stranded
sloop spread in Maryland. As a result they arrested Jan
Deverus of Bocquetenorton because he had been among the

Indians without the knowledge of a Commissary, as well as an Indian boy about 16 or 17 years of age who confessed that the Indians had found a quantity of goods and had hidden them. But after having been sent to the Lord of Maryland and examined, they were released. When we arrived in Bocquetenorton they were already in prison and we could learn nothing from either the Indians or the English about the mast, sail, tackling or rigging, for we could not find a trace of mast or rigging when we came back to Bocquetenorton. I then ordered Hendrick Drochstraeten along with Ule Swensen and Jan Boeyer to go again to the Indians and bring back the people who might still be among them and the goods which they still had. I left for Manocken in order to find out about the disposition of the prisoners because there was a rumor that the Indians might have murdered the Christians. When I arrived there I found the prisoners, but since court would not be held for some time I proceeded homeward. I have learned, however, that they have been transferred to Petoxsen, but again set free. [   ] and I then came home. Jan Boeyer together with Uls Swensen and Hendrick remained with the Indians. On the 24th of February they left here for New Castle. On the same day 2 Indians arrived with goods from Sackamock which the aforementioned Hendrick had obtained through threats. On the 26th of February Hendrick himself arrived with more goods. Because there is a suspicion in Maryland and at this place that the people of Jan de Caper's sloop might have been murdered, we the magistrates of this place have convened an inquiry.[5]

[Endorsed:] A Relacion from the Whore Kill about Jan de Capres sloope 1670[6]

---

1. Other translation in ECM:532.

2. Possibly the southern passage into Chincoteague Bay which lies between the eastern shore of Maryland and Assateague Island.

3. This settlement was on the eastern shore of Maryland near Snow Hill Town.

4. Possibly Mills Island which lies between Brockatonorton Bay and the Accomack County line.

5. See 20:12 for the results of this inquiry. A copy of this report comprises the first page of 20:10 but has been omitted here in favor of 20:12.

6. i.e., 1671 new style; see 20:12, F.N. 3. Endorsement in Matthias Nicolls' hand.

20:11   [PROPOSITIONS OF CAPT. CARR CONCERNING DEFENCES
         IN DELAWARE][1]

On the proposition of the Hon. Capt. Caar to the Lords
High Councillors, that a suitable place be selected here in
New Castle in order to have some fortifications for defence in
times of emergency; and that a suitable place also be selected
above Christina Kill in order to make it defencible as a place
of refuge in times of emergency, on which proposition it was
answered and resolved:

1. That the market where the bell hangs is deemed the
most suitable location in New Castle to make a fortification of
block houses, which are to be situated in such a way that will
be judged most proper, provided that the Honorable Capt. Caar
shall cede forever the required land without retaining any claim
on it. Concerning the expenses and labor of the aforementioned
fortification and block houses, the citizens of New Castle
shall, for the present, each according to his means and
position, defray the expense of paying the workers, provided
that the inhabitants in this jurisdiction shall suitably ob-
ligate themselves in such labor and work each according to his
capacity.

2. Concerning the fortification above, this is left to
the discretion of the officials above, to arrange their defences
in the most suitable place or places.

3. All of this, however, with the provision, that, if
war does not break out with the natives, God forbid, the aforementioned block houses shall be used as public buildings, such
as Town hall, jails and other public needs, on the condition
that the expense shall then be charged to the general and public
account throughout the entire river.

4. This resolution is not to be put into effect without
having orders from the Honorable General, but necessary pre-
parations are to be made secretly without arousing suspicions
among the natives. Thus done and confirmed this 5th of
October 1670.

                    [Signed:]   John Carr
                                 Will. Tom
                                 H. Block
                                 Israel Helm
                                 The mark of *ℛℬ of Piter Rambo
                                 The mark ℛ of Piter Kock

[Endorsed:]   Proposicions made about the fortificacions at
              Delaware, under the hand of C. Carre and the rest
              of the high Court there. 1670. The order of the
              High Court.

_____

1. Other translations in NYCD 12:474 and ECM:497.

20:12 [REPORT OF THE JURY CONCERNING JAN DE CAPER'S SLOOP][1]

Be it known to whomever it may concern, that whereas there was a suspicion that the persons of the yacht De Jonge Prins out of New York may have been murdered while they were stranded near Inketeck Inlet, we, magistrates of the Hoerkill, not being able to learn the truth, deliberated and, for the execution of justice, assembled the first day of March 1671 twelve of the principle men of this place concerning a few goods which were salvaged by the Indians from Nassaawaam. Having come here to examine the evidence concerning the aforementioned, the verdict is as follows:

That the few goods in question were found to have been wet from salt water and that because of the evidence and in consideration of other circumstances it is their opinion that the yacht was lost at sea and the people were drowned and not murdered.

Helmanis W.
Sander Moelsteen
Ottho Wolgast
Willem Klasen[2]

Helmanis Wiltbanck, Coroner
James Weedon, Foreman
Jan Michiels
Pieter Gronendick
Antony Hansen
Pieter Hansen
Jacobus Klasen
Arian Hermens
Hermen Cornelissen
John Rots
Thomas Davies
Thomas Skidmor
Willem Klasen

[Endorsed:] The Report of the Jury about Jan de Capres sloope 1670[3]

---

1. Other translation in ECM:541. A copy of this report appears on the first page of 20:10 and is signed by Helmanis Fr. Wiltbanck.

2. This list of names does not appear in the 20:10 copy.

3. i.e., 1671 new style. c.f., the date of March 1, 1671 in the jury's report which was written according to the new calendar already adopted by most of the provinces of the Netherlands.

20:13 Account of expenses incurred by Hendrick de Backer and others who were sent from here to make inquiries about Jan de Kaper's yacht.[1]

Hendrick de Backer, for payments to the Indians while first looking for the yacht.

```
6 fathoms Sewant_____    f 12
5/4 duffels_____    f 15
3/4 gunpowder_____    f  4
Yet to be paid by agreement_____    f300
                                     ____
                                     f330
Still promised to Jan Boeyer_____    f128
                                     ____
                                     f458
```

Harmanus' account submitted for those concerned with Jan de Kaper's yacht: 13 ells of duffel for 4 loads of goods carried from the aforementioned yacht to the Hoere Kil by the Indians.

```
Figured at f12 the ell_____    f156
                                   f458
                          total   f614
```

The aforementioned Helmanus[2] submits another account for his personal expenses.

```
for provisions_____    f 24
for making the inventory
  of goods_____    f 20
for his lost time while              {which sum was not
  absent_____     f200 {taken into consid-
for provisions_____     f 16 {eration
Still owed Piter Groe[3]_____    f 45
                                 ____
                                 f305
```

[Endorsed:] A bill of Charges about Jan de Capres sloope. 1670.[4]

---

1. Other translation in ECM:530.

2. The aforementioned Helmanus actually appears above as Harmanus. This variation on Wiltbanck's given name occurs throughout the records.

3. i.e., Peter Groenendyk.

4. i.e., 1671 new style; see 20:12, F.N. 3.

20:14   [REPORT OF A MEETING WITH INDIANS ON THE DELAWARE ABOUT A MURDER][1]

The sachems present: Rinnawiggen Oebequeme Menninckta Oyagrakun	On Friday being the 23rd of September we, namely, Marten Roseman, Edman Kantwel, Pieter Cock, Pieter Rambo, Israel Helm and Matheus de Ringh, clerk, came, at the request of the Honorable Lords of Justice, to an Indian settlement or plantation called Annockeninck,

Quequirimen   where a group of Indians had been and still
Megeras   were meeting, in order to cantico[2] with some
Pemenacken   sachems whose names appear in the margin.
Colopapan   After having waited there 3 or 4 days for the
Magaecksie   arrival of the rest of the sachems and other
[ ]rensies   Indians, who did not all come, we placed our
Mannanengen   matter before them and asked them for what
                   reason they killed and murdered our people and
we named all of those whom they have murdered from the time when
the English came here into the country until the present,
being [t]en in number with many other details too long to
relate. [   ] replied that they did not know of
[   ] namely from Kohansy to [   ].
Whereupon they at once showed and presented us with a small
bundle of white sewant about 3 or 4 fathoms, on the condition
that we would be patient while they looked for the murderers
and brought them in, if they could find them. They then gave
us another bundle of white wampum adding these words: that
they did not seek war and that they desired to go out hunting
and trade up and down among the Christians just as before.
They then told the Minquaesen, that is the S[   ] Mincquaesen, whom we had among us, that they should kill no more
Christians. Whereupon they also give the Mincquasen a gift,
namely, a belt of sewant with a bundle of white sewant, after
the Mincquaesen had first given them a gift and delivered a
whole oration; saying, that we were brothers one to the other,
and that they wanted to remain brothers and friends, and that
they were sorry that they had done such things and that they
must know that they lived scattered among the Christians and
pointed out to them, "Christians are living here and Christians
are living there," and brought to their attention that since
they lived scattered among the Christians and if they made war,
where would they get their gunpowder and lead, along with many
more similar things which they recited to them. We answered
them, when we accepted this money or sewant, saying, that when
we accept this money or sewant we accept it not as atonement
for the murders which they committed but that we accept it only
provisionaly as a pledge that they would look for and bring in
the murderes; for our great sachem, we told them, was not
satisfied with money but wants you to bring in murderers. We
also said that we were surprised that not one of the sachems or
Indians knew who had committed the murders and themselves
named those whom we thought had committed the murders who were
by name Al[   ], Kecksioes, and the brother of Wissapoes.

    They then answered [   ] that they had [   ]
and that they [   ] the night when the murders
took place [   ] Allomgack in Assiskonck [   ]
Kecksioes was at home with the sachems and the brother of
Wissapoes was at the Maleboer's brother's house and further
that we should be content that they would look for those who
had done it. We also asked them why they had stolen and
plundered the goods belonging to Pieter Jiegoe and Pieter
Alrichs.

    They replied that they had not done that and had not
even known about it, but that the Indians from Assisconck had
done it and that they absolve themselves from it. These
being our dealings with the savage Indians.

Was signed   MATHEUS de RING
                                       CLERK

After collation this is found to agree with his original in

date and signature as above. At N. York the 6th of October
1670

Attestation [Signed:] D. V. SCHELLUYNE Not Publ. 1670

[Endorsed:]   [   ] the Examina[   ] [   ]
               Indyans concerning [   ] Murder. Oct. 6

---

1. Other translation in ECM:499.

2. In the Dutch it appears as Kintekayen; both are
   variants of Delaware Kantka, "to dance". The meaning
   intended here is a social gathering of a lively sort.
   c.f., Hodge's Handbook of American Indians, p. 202.

20:15   [LETTER TO CAPT. CARR ABOUT THREATS UTTERED BY
        SOME INDIANS]

[   ]

     These are to Informe you that heare ware one friday night
withine night a party of Ind[   ] aboute 4 or 5 and twenty and
would with vielence into our houses but wee kept them [   ]
only one, which said thay Cam from the [   ]awa[ ] and would do
us no hurt but for the English and all new Castll thay would
kill man woman and Child and burne the howll plase, so thay
say [   ] fare from our houses that night wee [   ] not a
Littell watch full I feare wee shall [   ] have order tell
tise two Latte pray bee Carful and Keepe good watch ·

                         Yours Thomas S[   ]

     one Satterday thay Cam to Andris Fines and thay did tell
them, thay would do them no hurt but for y[ ] and Mr. Tom,
thay would tappoose them and burne all man woman and Child,
that are Stout [ ]oug[ ] duble [   ]raggake the Chiefe, thay
are wel Loded[ ] [   ], and thay say thay will kill all
[   ] [   ] within 8 days time, thy Lay [ ]
[   ] and take way as wee thin[ ] [   ]
Rivere

                         Andris Andrisone
                         Mathis Mathisone
                         Walravne Jonsone
                         Juster Andrisone

Thay say wee must still s[   ] for thay will do us noe hurt

From Andris Andrisones
hous Sonday Instant

[Addressed:]   These
               From Capt. John C[   ]
               of New Castell
               Present

[Endorsed:] A paper se[   ] [   ] C. Carr concer[   ]
             the Indy[   ] [   ]

20:16   [ROBERT JONES TO CAPT. CARR ABOUT SETTLING IN
         DELAWARE]¹

                                       13th of March 1670

Sir

        Your letter of the 27th of Jan. I received the tenth of
March instant, whereby we are all confirmed of the report of
the great disaster that happened to the sloope,² and I should
have writt sooner to you by a sloope that went up the bay
wherein Mr. Wale did send, but I was from home and missed that
opportunity, however, new Mr. Wale and Mr. Wharton are goeing
themselves I have sent my draught of the survay of 400 acres
joyning to our Towne land, and that of 400 acres at Bumbyes
hooke³ which is between Mr. Wale and I, which I presume you
have already received by Mr. Wale, together with Mr. Merritts
who is gone for England, (but wilbe god willing here in October)
beseeching you to continue you[ ] great Kindness and to procure us our pattents. I doe purpose with gods leave to spend
all the next yeare with you at Delaware, but this yeare I cannot stir, in respect of my office. I can give you noe further
account of that Wm. Stone then I did in my last, but that it
is not that Dr. Stone mention'd in my letter, for his name is
John, this man must needs be very obscure for I have enquired
of the publiquest persons of that County concerning him and
can heare noe tideings of any such man: however pray send an
account (you may draw it as large as you think convenient) of
your due, by Mr. Wale, for if the man were found we cannot
proceed without it. I hope to receive good newes from you by
the bearers returne, of peace and plenty and noe obstruction
to our Noble Design. I pray present my dearest respects to all
your good Neighbours, but especially my humble service and
thanks to Madam Carr, for all her goodnes to us, strangers. I
have sent you a small roll of Tobacco to pipe it, but I am
confident you have better of your owne (though this be sweete
sented) for ours was all utterly spoiled with the gust in
August, however I beg your acceptance, assureing you that in
all respects wherein I am capable I will ever remaine

                    Sir your most faithfull and obliged servant
                        [Signed:] Robert Jones

[Addressed:] These for Capt. John Carr
              Governor of Delaware at
              New Castell

[Endorsed:] Mr. Robert Jones Virginia to C. Carre about
             comming to settle at Delaware. Mar. 13 1670.

1. Other transcription in ECM:509.

2. Probably a reference to Jan de Caper's sloop; see
    20:10/12.

3. i.e., Bombay Hook.

20:17   [WILLIAM TOM'S MEMORANDUM OF DEBTS IN MARYLAND]

    The bills [   ] by Alexander d'Hiniosa upon the
account of the Burgomasters of Amsterdam to severall persons in
Maryland and by the Right Honorable Collonell Richard Niccolls
delivered to me to be by vertue of his letter of Attorney
retouered there, are as followes

Nath Styles		62	5
Rich Bennett	5	61	16
Francis Stockett		52	9
Henry Stockett	1	86	16
Charles James	2	46	5
John Collett	1	11	7
	12	21	8

These are all delivered me by Generall Niccolls if any other
Clandestine bills by Sir Robert[1] I know not

    I have a receipt of the bills under Collonell Utyes[2] hand
where he ownes the receipt of another from Samuell Goldsmyth
but informed he hath delivered itt up I suppose his noate in
my hands if prosecuted in there Court will enforce him either
to pay the money or deliver the bill.

    George Goldsmyth not Knowne onely have heard that there
was a negro sold not payd for the other accounts not fully
ballanced Sir Robert did itt himself the last time he was there
and brought over peltrey but from whom or for what unknowne

    for the bills which are above menconed all but one the
Court of the County of Baltemore can take noe notice of itt for
that Court Holdes noe higher plea then three thousand pound of
tobaccoe and if his honor will further prosecute there must be
one sent to St Maryes

[In the margin opposite the next to last paragraph:]   widdow
Goldsmyth noe bill . his honor Knowes best

[Endorsed:]   Mr. Tom's note of debts at Maryland 1670.

1. i.e., Sir Robert Carr, commander of the English forces
   that captured the Delaware from the Dutch in 1664.

2. i.e., Col. Nathaniel Utie of Maryland.

20:18   [INVENTORY OF GOODS FROM JAN DE CAPER'S SLOOP][1]

Extract   Inventory of the peltries which were salvaged from
from the   Jan de Kaper's yacht, that was lost, and were sold
Protocol   to the highest bidder, namely, Mr. Hendrick
              Cousturier; as follows:

15 whole beavers at 20 guilders apiece-------------------f300
14 small beavers at 15 guilders apiece-------------------f210
6 otters and 12 lynx and 7 common otters
3 foxes, 1 wolf, one last of beaver and 4 half
beavers altogether for----------------------------------f200
For sewant ninty two guilders---------------------------f 92

                          amounts to the sum of   f802

Mr. Hendrick Cousturier shall pay this to Harmanes Freedricks,
13 ells of duffel at 12 guilders the ell, comes to-------f156
For one gesp[2] gunpowder and one knife, together----------f 6
To Harmen Cornelisz 2 and 3/4 ells duffel at 12 guilders
the ell, amounts to-------------------------------------f 32
which they gave to the Indians as a gift for the aforementioned
goods that they obtained.

Done at New Castel
The 30th of March Anno 1671
Agrees with the Protocol   [Signed:] Matt: De Ringh
                                                       Clerk

[Endorsed:] An Inventory of the Peltry etc. saved out of Jan
             de Capres sloope 1670[3]

1. Other translation in ECM:544.

2. A 17th century Dutch word for a measure formed by
   holding two cupped hands together.

3. i.e., 1671 new style. This endorsement is in English
   with the old style date while the above account and
   certification is in Dutch with the new style date.

20:19   [WILLIAM TOM TO GOV. LOVELACE ABOUT NEWCASTLE
          AFFAIRS][1]

To the Right Honorable

      1 here is a Towne erected which is the sthrength for the
river

      2 it has beene studyed by our neighbors of Mary land to
doe the same but could not attayne

      3 if our neighbors are so desirous then necessary

      4 if good then incourgament [sic]

      5 the way to incourage is that noe slopes passe above
this Towne to handle with the inhabitants

      1 for what before was used to be brought here is delivered
above and what debts is due to us cannot be receaved for that
they come not below

      2 then upon necessity the place must be forsaken and noe
man left to make resistance against the Indians having noe
profitt and must another way out of the land which will breake
the Towne and if so every man must stand upon his owne guard
single without any assistance which if the Towne had any incouragement was able to defend the whole river or at least
themselves but the sloopes going up and selling drinke by the
small measeaure and receiving there ready payment and with
furnishing with there petty wares by there doores getts themselves an advantage to our ruine which if permitted every man
may doe the like and then his Roy highness may with cost make
another Towne of defence as our neighbors have indeavered but
could not attayne to

[Endorsed:] Some Proposicions on the behalfe of the Towne of
             Newcastle in Delaware from Mr. Tom   1670.

_____

   1. Other transcriptions in ECM:505 and NYCD 12:480.

20:20   [A QUERY BY WILLIAM TOM ABOUT LAND TENURE][1]

      Wish to Know by what tenure wee hold our land not being
expressed in our patents

      In common Soccage as the Duke held his, as of the maanor
of East Greenewich[2]

[Endorsed:] A Quere of Mr. Tom's to bee resolved concerning
             the Tenure of land at Delaware

1. Other transcriptions in ECM:506 and NYCD 12:480.

2. Reply to William Tom's query written in the hand of
   Matthias Nicolls.

20:21   Instructions for Mr Walter Wharton about
         Delaware[1]

June 22nd 1671

1. To send mee[2] an Account (by the first oppertunity) of the
   names and number of the new Planters.

2. To affix a time by the which all the Patentees are to bee
   placed upon their Land and make their Improvements.

3. To draw a Cart of their Land and how the Plantacions are
   seated.

4. What publique Improvement may bee made thereabout either
   by Land or Sea.

5. What sort of Government will best suite with them when
   seated either as to Ecclesiastick, or Civil matters in
   point of Formalities. In the meane time that they have
   one of the Law Bookes, confirmed already by his R. Hs., and
   that they conforme themselves to that, as farre as is
   practicable.

6. How they will secure themselves against any attempt
   either of Indyans or others, by forming a Militia, and
   recommending Military officers to mee.

7. What tract of Land will remaine to invite new Planters
   besides those that are already Patented.

8. That some person bee appointed to undertake the collecting
   of the Quitt Rents for the which a Consideracion shall bee
   allowed for the whole River.

9. To view and enquire where the best and most convenient place
   or places will bee to fix one or more Townes.

10. Whether to associate with thos alrea[ ] seated at the
    Whore Kill bee not bes[ ] to strengthen their party.

    In a particular direction, Concerning a certaine Tract of
land which I have taken up in Delaware River, of which you
shall have the scituacion, and heads of the Patent out of the

Records, That you make a survey thereof and send mee a
draught of it.

[Endorsed:]   Mr. Whartons Instructions 1671

---

1. Other transcription in ECM:511.

2. i.e., Matthias Nicolls, in whose hand the document
    is written.

20:22   [PROPOSALS OF CAPT. JOHN CARR CONCERNING
         DELAWARE WITH ORDERS THEREON][1]

Some Matters to be tendred to the Consideracion of his
Honor the Governor and his Councell touching the Towne of New
Castle, and Plantacions in Delaware River now under his R. Hs.
Protection and Government.

That the Towne of New-Castle being the strength of the
[River,] and only capable to defend it selfe against the
suddain Violence and Incursion of the Indians, It's humbly left
to Consdieracion whether the Inhabitants should not have some
more then ordinary Encouragement.

1st.   As first That a Block-House may be erected in some
convenient Place of the Towne where a Constant Watch may be
kept (now the Fort is fallen to Ruine and Decay) for their
              Common Defence; the which will cost noe great Matter,
graunted. and may be risen at the Charge and Expence of the
              Inhabitants of the Towne and Plantacions upon the
River, who will not be backwards (if any Order shall be issued
forth for it) in contributing towards the same.

2ly.   That noe Sloope or Vessell from this or any other place
comeing to traffick or trade there be permitted to goe up the
River above the Towne (which hath of late been only tol[ ]ated,
              for that it will probably be the ruine of the
graunted. place (if continued) all Trade deserting them;
not to trafick. and those that goe up receiving ready payment
              in Peltry or Corne for their Liquors which
they sell by Retaile with the small Measure, or for their
petty Wares, the Inhabitants can neither be paid for what
formerly hath been due to them; nor shall be capable of getting a Livelyhood hereafter.

3ly.   That the distilling of Strong Liquors out of Corne,
being the Cause of a great Consumption of that Graine, as also
         of the Debauchery and Idleness of the Inhabitants, from
x   whence inevitably will follow their Poverty and Ruine,
         bee absolutely prohibited or restrayned.

[4ly.]   That the Number of Victuallers or Tappers of strong
Drinke bee ascertained; That is to say, three only for the
            Towne, and some few up the River, who the officers
graunted   shall thinke fitt to approve, and noe more then will
            be found convenient, who may have Lycense to doe the
            same; whereby Disorders will be prevented and
Travellers have better Accomodacions.

5ly.   That Constables may be appointed to keep the Kings
            peace, who shall have Staves with the Kings Armes
graunted.   upon them, as is practised in the rest of these his
            Royal High[   ] Dominions.

6ly.   That they may have the Kings Armes to be sett up in
            their Courts of Judicature, as well as on the
graunted.   Staves, the which they will bee at the charge of
            themselves.

7ly.   That what Land the Officers there have made Grants of
            for New Plantacions (being waste implanted Land)
x   and the which They had Encouragement to doe by your
            Honors Predecessor, and never had Order to the
contrary, may be Confirmed, There being generally Care had for
a Moderacion therein.

8ly.   That severall Orders past at and about the time of the
Tryall of the Long Finn, as well about Publique Charges, as the
            Whore-K[   ] haveing Officers subordinate to those
graunted.   of New-Castle, as also for clearing the High-wayes,
            maintaining Fences and other Matters relateing to
the Well-Government of that place be reinforced by your Honors
approbacion.

9ly.   That whereas their Neighbors of Maryland have made
Offer to cleare the one halfe of the way between Mr. Augustine
            Harmens Plantacion, and the Towne of New-Castle, an
graunted.   Order may be issued forth that those of Delaware
            should Cleare the other halfe next to them, the
which will be noe great Labour or Charge, and may prove of
great use and Benefit for Travelling and Commerce.

10ly.   That some Person may be appointed and Sworne at the
            Towne of New-Castle to be Corne-Meeter,
graunted and the who may not only see the Corne duely
laws in that case measured, but prevent the sending thereof
alterd.   abroad soe fowle, by ordering it to be well
            Cleaned; And also that the said Officer have
an Inspection, and doe View their Beefe and Porke that it be
well packt and merchantable.

11ly.   That there being a Mill, or most (if not all) the
            the Appertenances thereunto belonging,
graunted. The spare up Delaware River at the Carcoons
mill [sto]nes preserved Hooke, which did heretofore appertaine
[and] to bee let [out], to the Publique, and now is Endeavour'd
the profit [to] sarve to be engrossed by some particular
the public, untill persons for their private use; It may
further order. be recommended to be taken into his
            Royall Highness, or his Deputyes
hands; by which some Benefitt will accrew, and being kept in
good Repiare will be of a publique and Generall Good to the
Inhabitants.

12ly.   That noe Quantityes of Liquors be sold to the Indyans
           under a Quarter of an Ancker, halfe, or a whole
x   Ancker.

13ly.   That the Houses in the Forte being soe greatly decay'd,
          as they cannot stand long, their Tiles, Brick, Iron,
[grau]nted and other Materialls may be taken downe in time,
          and preserved for the building a new House in
their Roome, when opportunity permitts.

[Verso:] That they may bee acquainted by what tenure they
hold their land.[2]

[Endorsed:] Capt. Cars Proposalls. 1671.

---

1. Other transcriptions in ECM:558 and NYCD 12:480.
Material within brackets has been recovered from ECM.
The orders on each proposal appear in the margin in
Matthias Nicolls' hand. They appear here indented in
the text. The x may indicate refusal.

2. Written in the hand of Matthias Nicolls. Possibly a
reference to William Tom's query about land tenure
(see 20:20).

20:23   An Account of suc[h] [quit-rents] as are due
       and Payabl[e] [by] the severall Persons h[erein]
       named in Delaware[1]

Patents date		Bush:[ ] the [ ]
March:24th 1668/9.x	Jurian Janse..................	1
Mar: 25th 1669.x	Jacob vander Vere.............	2
Mar. 25th 1668.x	Hans Block...................	2
Mar. 25th 1669.x	Gerrit Sanderson.............	2
Mar. 26th 1669.x	Jan Sybrantse................	1
Mar. 26th 1669.x	Evert Gerritsen..............	1
Ditto Die......x	Paulus Jaques................	2
Aprill 8th 1669.x	Herman Reyners...............	1
Ditto..........x	Nealse Lawsa.................	1 1/2
May 28th 1669..x	Olla Towson..................	1
Ditto..........x	Bernard Eken.................	1
ditto die......x	Ditto........................	1
July 29th 1669.x	Will. Tom....................	2
ditto..........x	Will. Tom....................	1
Sept. 1st 1667.x	Charles Floyd and John Henry..	1
Janry 1st 1667.x	Capt. John Carre.............	[ ]
ditto..........x	Peter Andreas................	[ ]
ditto..........x	Thomas Woollaston............	1
ditto..........x	John Erskin, Tho. Browne and Mart. Gerrits.............	5
ditto..........x	George Whale and Geo. Moore...	2
ditto..........x	Andrew Carre.................	1

Janry. 1st 1669.x		Tho. Wollaston, Ja: Crawford,		
		Herman and Gerard Otto........		3
July 15th 1669..x		Capt. John Carre..............		2
Jan: 1st 1669...x		Robt Ashman. Jno. Ashman Tho:		
		Jacob etc....................		10

46

Wheat

[	] 18th 1668.x	Israel Helme...................		1.
[	] 1669.x	Ufro Popegay[2]................		1.
[	]......x	Israel Helme Hendrick Jacobs etc..		4.
[	] 1668.x	Renier Renierse................		1.
[	] 15th 1669.x	Samll. Edsall..................		5.
[	] 1669.x	Hanse Bones....................		2.
[	] 1668.x	Tho: Wollaston.Jno. Ogle. Jan		
		Hendrick etc..................		8.
[	]......x	Paulus Dux and wife............		1.
[	] 1668.x	Thomas Jackson, and Wolley		
		Poulston......................		3.
[	]......x	Juriaen Jansen.................		1.
[	]......x	Mattys Eschelsen...............		1.
[	]......x	Will Tom, at the Whore Kill....		2.
[	] 1668.x	Juriaen Keen...................		4.
[	] 1668.x	James Sandylands...............		2.
[	] 1669.x	Do. Laurenty Carolly...........		1.
[	] 1668.x	Andries Matesen................		1.
[	]......x	Hanse Pieters..................		1.
[	] 1668.x	Jan Erickse....................		1.
[	]......x	Olle Laerten[3]................		1.
[	]......x	Hendrick Claesen...............		1.
[	]......x	Pieter Ollesen.................		1.
[	]......x	Paul Ponsen[4].................		1.
[	]......x	Mattys Jansen..................		1.
[	]......x	Paul Laersen...................		1.
[	]......x	Juriaen Jansen.................		1.
[	] 1669.x	Another Paten to these 8 persons..		2.
[	] 1669.x	Jan Sybrantse..................		1.
[	]......x	Evert Gertse...................		1.
[	] 1669.x	Andries Andriese, Synick Broers		
		etc..........................		8.
[	] 1669.x	Pieter Rambo...................		1.
[	]......x	Andries Andriesen and Company.....		1.
ditto..........x		John Askue.....................		1.
ditto..........x		Hanse Bones....................		1.
ditto..........x		Andrew Carre...................		2.
ditto..........x		Tho: Woolaston.................		1.

- 66 -

B. Whe[ ]

October 1st 1669.x	John Askue.....................	2
Ditto...........x	Robert Scott, John Marshall etc.	4
Ditto...........x	Tho: Jackson, Wooley Poulson etc	1
Ditto...........x	Pieter Cowenhoven..............	1.
Ditto...........x	Robert Jones...................	1.
Ditto...........x	Pieter Rambo...................	3
Ditto...........x	Pieter Cock....................	1
November 5th. 69.x	Pieter Claesen.................	[ ]
Ditto...........x	Juriaen Juriansen and Olle	
	Clementse.....................	2
May 14th. 69.x	Hanse Monsen...................	[ ]
May 16. 69.x	John Eustace...................	1
June 6. 1670.x	Robert Jones...................	[ ]

June 13. 70.x	James Sandylands................	[ ]
Ditto.......x	Neals Matson....................	3
May 25th 1670.x	Dirck Pieters...................	[ ]
August 11th 1670.x	Dirck Alberts...................	[ ]
Apr. 2d 1670.x	James Bollen and Pieter Jego.....	4
August 16th 1670.x	Pieter Alricks..................	[ ]
Ditto.......x	Pieter Alricks..................	[ ]
August 14th 1671.x	Barent Hendrickse...............	[ ]
August 4th 1671.x	John Sherricks..................	3
July 1st 71.x	Hermanus Fredricks..............	8
June 1st 71.x	Leendert Teunisse...............	2
Ditto.......x	Cornelis Wynhart................	3
June 17th 71.x	George Whale....................	4
Ditto.......x	Geo: Weale Senior and Robert Jones........................	[ ]
Ditto.......x	John Bradborne..................	[ ]
Ditto.......x	Thomas Young....................	[ ]
Ditto.......x	Robert Jones....................	[ ]
Ditto.......x	Thomas Merritt..................	4
Ditto.......x	John Bell, and Peter Pernon.....	[ ]
Ditto.......x	Lucas Abel, Cornelis Buys etc....	9
Ditto.......x	Patrick Carre...................	4
Ditto.......x	William Eves....................	4
June 19th 71.x	Charles Hutchins................	5
		105

		B: Wheat
[ ] 19th 1671.x	James Crawford..................	4 1/2
[ ]..........x	John Johnson....................	5.
Ditto.............x	Christopher Sentill.............	4.
Ditto.............x	William Sincleer................	4.
Ditto.............x	Charles Hutchins.a mistake......	5.
[ ] 18th 67...x	Hendrick Jansen.................	1.
[ ]........x̄	Johannes Hendricks Niel Niels etc.....................	5.
[ ].........x	Capt. John Carre................	2.
[ ] 67......x̄	Capt. John Berry and Mr. Edsall.	2 Otters
[ ] 67......x	Pieter Alricks 4 Otter Skins....	
[ ] 67......x̄	James Crawford..................	2.
[ ] 1665....x̄	Will. Tom. for an Island........	8.
[ ] 1665....x̄	C. John Carr[5].................	8
		48-
		105-
	Foure Otters skins	66-
		46 1/2
		257 1/2
	Albany - Mr. Renzlaer	225-
	Esopus - ~	50-
	Staten Isl: after 3:-⎱ yeares - 100 - Lotts ⎰	400

---

1. The title for this document is badly damaged. The
   missing portions have been recovered from O'Callaghan's
   calendar entry and appear in brackets. Other transcription in NYCD 12:490.

2. Armegart Printz, the widow of Johan Papegoja. <u>Ufro</u> is
   an English attempt at 17th century Dutch <u>Juffrouw</u>
   meaning "madame" or "gentlewoman."

3. Possibly a scribal error for <u>Laersen</u>.

4. Possibly a scribal error for <u>Pousen</u>, i.e. "Paulsen" or
   an abbreviated variant of "Paulensen."

5. From this entry on, the handwriting changes to that of
   Matthias Nicolls who also noted a <u>mistake</u> after Charles
   Hutchins' name above. The check marks before each name
   were probably done by Nicolls also.

20:24   [WILLIAM TOM TO GOV. LOVELACE ABOUT WAR WITH THE
        INDIANS][1]

                                        25th of October 1671

Right Honorable

     by this conveyance I shall informe your honor that Mr.
Aldricks and my selfe going up the river with a perfect intention with your honors order this winter to make a warr and
there advising with the Sweedes about itt there miserable moane
for the losse of their beasts for want of Hay and the consideracion that the winter being so neare att hand that itt was
impossible for ice to build a strenght att Mattinacunck and to
lay in provisions there which must bee for when men march they
must not come hither every six or seaven dayes for victualls
therefore before wee begin a warr provision must be layd in all
convenient places itt may be your honor att first sight may
looke upon the warr as frivolous but way itt further and your
honor will find that all the Kings interest in this part of the
world depends upon itt (for this river lying in the middle and
the worst to be wonne from the Indians by reason of the broken
lands and Crewples[2] which are a shelter for them against any
Christian force without helpe of other Indians) if deserted
Mary land has noe strenght to follow them here for want of provisions and distance of place and so cutt of by degrees and
Virginia much lesse for the same reason the Indians as is dayly
found not caring bee itt middle winter to march 4 or 5 hundred
mile for 2 or 3 heads of Haire much more when they can have
that with plunder how New Jarsey stands your honor best knowes
then if your honor concludes with us this river must upon
necessity be maintayned were itt for noe other reason as a
magazine for the rest of his Majesties territoryes hereabouts
and refreshing which cannot otherwise be done as with men
money and ammunition for at present a little money in regard to
the Kings purse which ought always to be open upon such affaires
may be may stop this issue of bloud which is likely to ensue
when afterwards thousands will not doe itt here is rumor come
by the Indians that the Assateack[3] Indians they who were the
murtherers of John the Capers sonnes with the rest have since
killed an Englishman and that Sir William is in persuite of the

murtherer tis but Indyan newes therefore beleive as you please
I have hereby this opertunity sent your honor Collonell
Scarboroughs his letter which was mislayd another report wee
have from Maryland by Patrick Carr one of our soldiers an
honest fellow and noe statesman and not likely to rayse such
reports if not true that Mr. Charles Calvert Leiuetenat of
Mary land has sent up order to Mr. Augusteene[4] and the rest in
the head of the bay that they stand upon there guard and likewise that so soone as the new Governor comes he shall send him
notice and he will give him a meeting therefore wee conclude
that if your honor have noe advice for the exchange he has itt
there being two ships arrived att Pattuxunt if thought convenient that with the next sloope 25 soldiers were sent itt
would much depresse the Indyan courage and assist us but
betimes in the spring a greater supply of men and if possible
Northerne Indyans when ours are coming from there hunting
quarters

I thinke I need not write further Mr Aldricks and Mr
Helme comming with this onely presse your honor to weigh this
seryously and send us full supplyes your honor must pick out my
meaning for my finger is so soare I can hardly lay itt to the
paper further I have sent to Capt. Howell to know the certainty
of there reports which you may expect to heare by Thomas Lewes
but desire that noe provision may be exported out of this river
untill your honor has fully discussed this business noe more
att present but I am

> Right Honorable your honors
> most Humble servant
>
> [Signed:] Will. Tom

[Addressed:] for the Right Honorable
Collonell Francis Lovelace
Esq. Comander in Cheife of
all the forces belonging
unto his Royall Highnesse
the Duke of yorke and
Governor of New yorke
these present in

[Endorsed:] Mr. Toms Letter to the Governor
Delaware - Oct. 25 1671 about the Murder.

---

1. Other transcription in ECM:599.

2. From Dutch Kreupelbosch : "thicket".

3. cf., See 20:10 for relation of John De Caper's sloop which
   was stranded on what is now called Assateague Island.
   ECM:600 has incorrectly transcribed Assawack.

4. Augustine Herrman.

20:25   [CAPT. JOHN CARR TO GOV. LOVELACE ABOUT INDIAN
        MURDERS][1]

Sir

        I receaved your Honors letter by Petter Aldricks wherin
your Honor seemes to lay all the blame upon me, for my remisnese
in not getting the murtheres, both for the woman at Pertt hooke
and allsoe for the murther now last Comitted, Sir as for the
first when it was done I was comeing for new yorke, but hearing
of that sad accident returned back, makeing your Honor ac-
quainded of the murther, after which I receaved your Honors
order for to gett the murtherers to be brought to Condigne
punishment, your order I did follow, for I went up the River to
the Magastrats, who sent for the Sachams, who execusd them-
sealfs that his men had not done it another saied the like, I
knew not the villans nor theyr names that Comitted the fact, soe
that from the time I receaved your Honors order I was Continualy
above the River demaunding the murtherers with as much vigor as
I could; I was not alone but the rest of the magastrats was
there, soe that my Conscience shall wittnes that there was noe
remisnes of my part, and I beseech god that all my sins be
remitted soe Cleare as that, as for the last murthers Comitted
I was at the same time desperat sicke, and hath Continued to
this day that I have not been without my doores; but I hope now
Doctor Jardin is with me he will usse his best skill to take
away my violent fever, soe that I hope your Honor will excuse,
what god doth inflict upon me by sicknes, soe there could be
noe remisnes of my part, in getting the last murtherers, being
I was not able to sture abrood If any one can prove that I
have been backeward in not followeing your Honors orders from
time to time ore hath not done to the utmost of my endeavouer
to gett the murtherers, then lay a penalty upon me, but not
without Cause, allsoe lett me Answer for my sealf as for the
backwardnes of the Inhabitants of this River in raiseing forces
as well as new Jarsy your Honor must excuse me though the Cheife
Comaunder, for I was not able to goe abrood, and trully new
Jarsy had a great deale of reson being the murtherers lived
within theyr Juradiction, when your Honor gave me my first
Instructions I was allowed twenty souldiers out of that number
was discharged by Coll. Nicolls and some by your Honor, fower
died soe that we was reduced to ten, I had a strict orders from
Coll. Nicolls not to raise a man without your Honors Consent
which I observed, untill your Honor gave me order for raiseing
of men when the woman and Children was murthered, and when I
came last from thence, your Honor gave me order to dismise
them, which I did soe that your Honor will find by my account
with Mr. Bedloo that there is but ten old souldiers, and how it
is posible for me with ten men to repaier such a decayed fortt
whilst I was there it Cost me mony for the repaier of the
houses, though your Honor knowed you could not ly dry in your
bed when you lay there, had I a gaurd house, and souldiers
sufficient to mount gaurds I should be as ready as any officer
belongs to your Honor, soe that if I receave pay soe long as I
have Comision and being not reduced, we was sent over by his
Royall Highnes for souldiers, and if I be able, and in health,
I shall goe as farr to doe my Prince service, to any place
where your Honors order shall Comaund me, Sir Peter Alricks
Mr. Tom and the rest of the Swead magastrats spook with the
Sachams, who promised by friday last to bring theyr heads but
since heere is noe newes from above, but assoone as it come we
will send your Honor the newes, I have noe more but that I
ame Your Honors obedient servant

[Signed:]   John Carr

New Castle 27th
November 1671

[Addressed:]   Thesse For Generall Francis Lovelace
               New Yorke

[Endorsed:]   Capt. Carre to the Governor.   Newcastle
              November 27. 1671.

---

1. Other transcription in ECM:606.

20:26   [PETITION OF ARMEGART PRINTZ FOR PAYMENT OF
         DEBT BY ANDREW CARR; CERTIFICATE BY WM. TOM
         CONCERNING SAME][1]

The Honorable, Prudent and Most Discreet Lords,
Capt. John Caar the Schout, and the Honorable
Justices of New Castle.

My Dear Lords---

        In view of the fact that not only equity and reasonable-
ness, but also all statute laws permit and allow every person,
whoever it may be, irrespectively, to seek and claim that to
which he is entitled, whether by demanding or complaining and
also, if need be, by arrest and detention in order to obtain
justice / it is now well known to Your Honors that Mr. Andris
Caar in the full possession of the chattles of Tinneckunck,
which his forefather de la Grange bought from me, has under-
taken to pay the same just as he has done with his own goods
and has been obliged to do. However, he is now planning to
move his residence to Holland without giving me any satisfaction. Therefore I respectfully petition Your Honors, if it
pleases, and for the sake of justice, to cause him, Mr. Caar,
before he departs, to settle with me for the three thousand
guilders by payment or by security, or if it cannot be otherwise, to turn over to me once again Tinnekonck with the
chattles belonging thereto; but in case of refusal of these
reasonable condition, I respectfully petition Your Honors
that he be arrested and detained until the arrival of the
Honorable General Lovelace; and await his justice and judgement
with which we both shall have to be content.

        Doing this I remain Your Honors'

                              humble servant
New Castle this 8th of March   [Signed:] Armmegartt Printz
      1671

I doe attest that Capt John Carr is full procurater for Mr
Andrew Carr to answer all that shal be demanded of him in his
absense witness my hand[2]

                         [Signed:] Will: Tom

[Endorsed:] Certificate from Wm. Tom that C. Carre was to
             answer for Andr[ ] Carre.

---

  1. Armegart Printz' petition is written in Dutch, while the
     certificate from Wm. Tom, which appears directly below
     the signature, is in English. Although Armegart Printz
     signed the petition it was written by someone else.

  2. This declaration also appears in 20:42a.

20:27   March 24. Order extending the time for settling
         Chiepiessing on the Delaware river, granted to
         John Berry and company, three years.[1]

---

  1. There is a notation in the MS. folder that this
     document is missing. The heading has been taken
     from O'Callaghan's Calendar.

20:28a   Directions for the holding of the Speciall
          Court of Oyer and Terminer for the Tryall
          of Wm. Syncleer at New Castle in Delaware
          the 5th of Apr. 1671.

     At the meeting of the Court lett the Cryer with a loud
Voyce make Proclamacion and say, O yes, O yes, O yes;

     Then lett him say after the Clarke.
     Sylence is commanded in the Court, whilest his Majesties
Commissioners of Oyer and Terminer, are sitting, upon paine of
Imprisonment.

     After Sylence in commanded, the Clarke is to read the
Commission of Oyer and Terminer and then call over the Commissioners names, who as they are called, are to stand up and

make Answer to their Names.

Lett then the Prisoner bee call'd for, and brought to the
Ba[   ]

Which being done, the Cryer is againe to make Proclamacion
and say, O yes thrice.

Then lett him say aloud after the Clarke.
All manner of Persons who have been summoned, or have
anything to doe, at this Speciall Court of Oyer and Terminer,
and can give in Evidence, for our Soveraigne Lord the King,
against the Prisoner at the Barr, Draw neare and give your
attendance;

The Clarke is then to make Enquiry of the Returne of a
Jury for the Tryall of the Prisoner at the Barr.

Upon the Returne of the Jurors names to proceed to
impannell a Jury by calling over their Names, the which is to
be done of the whole Lyst returned; and the Clarke is to
marke the Names of the Defaults of Appearance.

After that the number of twelve shall bee pitcht upon,
out of the whole Returne before they bee sworne, The Prisoner
at the Barr is to bee called upon to Know as they are named if
hee hath any Exception against any of their Persons; The which
hee is to have notice, that hee doe it before they are sworne,
for that afterwards it will bee too late.

Upon the Prisoners lawfull Exception against any Person,
another of those returned is to bee putt in his Place, and
none of the Persons returned are to bee dismist or depart the
Court, untill the Jury bee compleated.

Then they are to bee sworne, the Jurors being [   ] as
the Oath is read to them, to looke upon the Pr[   ] at the
Barre. [read the Oath to the Jurors.][1]

Soe, proceed, and lett Mattheus Eschelssen the Prosecutor
bee called upon to come into the Court.

Upon his appearance, Read the Presentment, Then the Indictment; only before the reading of the Indictment the Prisoner is to bee calld upon to hold up his hand at the Barr; in
these words. vizt. Wm. Syncleer hold up thy hand.

The Indictment being read, if the Prisoner plead not
guilty, Then ask him, by whom wilt thou bee tryed.

If hee stand upon his Tryall, Hee must say, by God and
Countrey, upon saying whereof, say, GOD SEND THEE A GOOD
DELIVERANCE.

Then goe on to Tryall.

First, call for the Corners Inquest, which is to bee
brought into the Court, and read to the Jury.

Then the Evidences for our Soveraigne Lord the King
against the Prisoner at the Barr are to bee calld upon and
sworne. [read the Oath to the witnesses.][2]

After which, the Prisoner hath Liberty to plead for himselfe.

After all, the President is to give a Charge to the Jury, who then are to retire by themselves, and the Prisoner is to bee withdrawn. [ad hoc: in antemeridiano.][3]

The Jury are to bee called over as they goe out.

When the Jury returne, to bring in their Verdict, they are to bee call'd over againe, and the Prisoner is to bee sett to the Barr.

Then the Clarke is to say,
Gentlemen of the Jury, look upon the Prisoner at the Barr.

After which hee is to ask them, if they are agreed upon their Verdict as to the matter in issue between our [   ] Lord the King and the Prisoner at the Barr.

If they say, Yes; Ask, who shall speak for you;

They are to say, Their Foreman; Then ask them, how they doe finde; If they say guilty; then ask whether of Murder or Man-slaughter? Enquire what Goods and Chattells the Prisoner had at the time of his Impeachment, the which is to bee secured for the use of his Majestie.

[Terminus][4] If the Prisoner bee found guilty of Murder hee is, (if the Bench for extraordinary Reasons, differ not from the Verdict of the Jury) to receive the Sentence of Death; and to bee tyed up, and secured in Irons untill the Generalls pleasure bee Knowne for the time and place of his Execucion.

If hee bee brought in guilty of Man-slaughter only, hee is to have the Benefitt of his Clergy, and if hee can read, then hee is to bee burned in the hand, before the riseing of the Court, and to bee returned to Prison, there to remaine for a yeare and a day, unless the Generall shall please to remitt the time, or order his Disposall otherwise.

When it is askt of the Prisoner upon the returne of his being guilty of Manslaughter, what hee hath to say for him- selfe that Sentence of Death should not pass upon him; Hee is to desire the Benefitt of his Cler[   ] and the Favour of the Bench.

And after being burn't in the hand, hee is to fall down on his Knees, and say,

GOD SAVE THE KING

All manner of persons, who have given your attendance, or have had any thing to doe, at this speciall Court, of Oyer and Terminer, You are for the present dismist, and You are to give your attendance here againe by two[5] of the clock.

God save the King.[6]

To gett the Forme of Dissolving the Court.[7]
    the Jurors Names.
    the Commissioners Names.[8]
    the Oath for Jurors.
    the Oath for Wittnesses or Evidences.

The Court adjourns till Tomorrow 8 a[   ]

[Endorsed:]   No. 14 [   ] Speciall Court of Oyer
               and Terminer about Wm. Syncleer etc. Aprill
               5th, 1671.

----

1. This instruction within brackets appears in the margin.

2. This instruction within brackets appears in the margin.

3. This instruction within brackets appears in the margin.

4. This notation within brackets appears in the margin.

5. The number two was written by another hand in the space
    provided here.

6. This phrase and the passage immediately preceding was
    written later in the hand of Matthias Nicolls.

7. This memorandum appears at the bottom of the last page.

8. See 20:32 for commission with the names of those
    appointed as commissioners.

20:28b   The Presentment

     Mattheus Eschelsen doth present for our Soveraigne Lord
the King, That William Sincleere late a souldyer, since an
Inhabitant of this Towne, upon the 9th day of March last past,
being in company with Lausa Eschelsen his brother at the
dwelling house of the said Mattheus Eschelsen, within the
Jurisdiction of the Towne, did then and there assault, and with
divers blowes with a Can[1] or some other unlawfull weapon strike
upon the head, the said Lausa Eschelsen, with the which blowes,
hee received such wounds and bruises, that thereof hee suddenly
dyed, which said assault and murder of one of his Majesties
good subjects, is against the Peace of our Soveraigne Lord the
King and the Lawes of the Realme establisht and in such cases
provided, whereupon hee the aforemencioned Mattheus Eschelsen
desires justice against the Delinquent on the behalfe of our
soveraigne Lord the King for the death of the said Lausa
Eschelsen his Brother, and humbly referrs his case to the Court.

----

1. i.e., cane.

20:28c   The Indictment

William Sincleere, Thous standst here indicted by the
name of William Sincleere of the Towne of Newcastle in Delaware
River, for that having not the feare of God before thine Eyes,
but being instigated by the Devill, thou didst upon the 9th day
of March last past, at the dwelling house of Mattheus Exchelsen,
assault the person of Lausa Eschelsen, and with a wooden Can[1]
or some other unlawfull weapon, malitiously, violently, wickedly
and feloniously, strike him the said Lausa Eschelsen upon the
head, with which assault and blowes he was immediately done
unto death, [   ] against the Peace of our Soveraigne Lord
the King, and as a guilty person didst fly for the same.

William Sincleere, what sayst thou, art thou guilty of
the Murder and felony layd to thy Charge or not Guilty.

---

1. i.e., cane.

20:29/30   [COUNCIL MINUTES CONCERNING DELAWARE;
             PROPOSALS TO THE COUNCIL FROM CAPT. CANTWELL
             WITH ITS REPLY THERETO][1]

At a Councell held at Forte
James in New Yorke. May
the 17th 1672.

Severall Matters being taken into Consideracion relating
to the Government, and other Affayres at Delaware, It was
Ordered as followes. Vizt.

That for the better Government of the Towne of New Castle
for the future, the said Towne shall bee Erected into a Corporacion, by the Name of a Baylywick, That is to say, It shall
bee Governed by a Baily and six Assistants, to bee at first
nominated by the Governour, and at the Expiracion of a yeare
foure of the six to goe out, and foure others to bee chosen in
their Places, The Baily to continue for a yeare, and then two
to bee named to succeed, out of whom the Governour will elect
one; Hee is to preside in all the Courts of the Towne, and to
have a double Vote; A Constable is likewise annually to bee
chosen by the Bench.

The Towne Court shall have Power to try all Causes of
Debt or Damage to the Value of ten pounds without Appeale.

That the English Lawes according to the Desire of the
Inhabitants, bee Establisht both in the Towne, and all
Plantations upon Delaware River.

That the Office of Schout bee converted into a Sheriffalty,
and the High Sherriffs power extend both in the Corporacion and
River, and that hee bee annually chosen by two being presented

to the Governour, of whom hee will nominate and confirme one.

As to the Clause given in by the Officers and Magistrates there, about having a free Trade without being obliged to make Entry here, but that it may bee done there, paying his Majesties Customes and Dutyes; It is thought fitt that the Determinacion thereof bee for the present suspended, untill Directions bee sent about it out of England or some farther Consideracion had thereupon here.

And for the Matter of the Whore-Kill brought to Capt. Carr certifying that some person[ ] from Mary-land pretend Interest there, and seat themselves without Leave, The Officers are to take care that his Majesties and his Royall Highness Interest there bee not infringed, and that they submitt themselves to nor acknowledge any other Government, unless they have Order to doe the same from the Governour here.

By Order of the Governours
Councell.

Proposalls from Capt. Edmond
Cantwell to his Honour the
Governour on the behalfe of
himselfe, and the rest of his
Neighbours the Inhabitants at
Delaware.

1. That his honour would please to give his Instructions about the finishing the Blockhouse in Delaware, which standeth still in that posture his Honour left it; It is high time that some speedy Order bee taken therein, in regard not only of the Troubles now likely to ensue from the Warrs in Europe, but that what is already expended thereupon will bee as good as thrown away by reason as it is now, it only stands and rotts; It is humbly conceived that the most effectuall means to bee used for the Accomplishment will bee by a Generall Tax to bee imposed both upon Towne and River.

2. That his Honour would please to make some Order for the restrayning of Persons to goe amongst the Indyans with Liquours and Drink to sell, whereby great Mischiefe doth frequently arise; there being diverse of late that leaving their owne Homes have taken what quantityes of Drink (and other Trade) they pleas'd, and gone a hundred or two of Miles to the Indyans Plantations, and there (for a little proffitt) selling what they had to the Indyans, great Uproars and Disturbances have arisen, insoemuch as the Christians living near them have been putt into great Frights, and unless great Wisdome had prevented, tis believed that Murder had many times been committed by the Salvages meerly through that Occasion; It were very necessary that this Abuse were regulated.

3. That his Honour would please to Nominate some Person or other to receive the Quit Rents there, there being diverse persons who pretend they are ready to pay them if they Knew to whom.

4. And that in regard there hath been great Complaints from Maryland (about Servants runn[ ] away from thence, who pass

thorough New Cast[ ] that the Inhabitants of New Castle doe
rather help to convey them away then stop them, and soe are
accused as being instrumentall to their [ ]ape, It were
necessary some Order were made as to that particular; Em-
powering some Person at New Castle to grant Passes or Ticketts
to People that pass to and againe in those Parts (which person
is to question and examine them) and also laying a Fine upon
those who shall bee found to convey away such Persons as are
Runn-awayes.

                    Whereas the Proposalls hereunto
                    annexed were presented unto mee
                    by Capt. Edmond Cantwell I have
                    thought good to give this Result
                    thereupon, together with the
                    following Orders concerning the
                    Regulation of Affayres in Delaware.

     In Answer to the first Proposall about the New Blockhouse
at New Castle in Delaware; Since my former Orders concerning
the finishing thereof have been noe better observed, I doe
once more enjoyne them the compleating of it, before the first
day of November next, and that under the penalty of one thousand guilders Seawant in case of Default; As to the way of
raising a Tax or Contribucion for the Effecting thereof, It
shall bee left to the Discretion of the Officers there either
to raise it by the way proposed, or any other they shall judge
most convenient.

     To the second concerning the great Abuse in selling strong
Liquours to the Indyans, I doe hereby Order, and strictly
enjoyne the Magistrates and Officers at New Castle and other
parts in Delaware River to cause the Lawes and Orders heretofore
made on that behalfe to bee more carefully and severely putt
in Execucion for the future to prevent such Danger and ill
Consequences as otherwise might thereby ensue.

3. As to the third, That a Person be nominated to receive the
Quit-Rents in Delaware River, I have thought fitt to Order and
Appoint Capt. Edmond Cantwell, who is to bee the present High
Sheriff, to bee Receiver and Collector of the said Quitt-Rents,
for the which hee shall have my Authentick Commission, and for
his Trouble and paines therein, hee shall have a reasonable
Allowance.

4. And as to the fourth about the Runn-away Servants that
frequently pass through Delaware either in coming from or goeing into Maryland and Virginia, It is ordered that noe Person
or Persons, but such as have Passes and Certificates, or can
give a good Account of their Travailes towards these parts, or
goeing from hence, shall bee permitted to travaile, but shall
bee apprehended, and kept in safe Custody, untill it bee made
known what they are, and to whom they doe belong; The Care
hereof is to bee committed to the Bayliff of New Castle, and
the High Sheriffe, who are to Act joyntly herein, both as to
the Examining of their Ticketts or passes, and likewise to give
Ticketts to such as shall have Occasion thereof; And noe person
is to presume privily to conceale or convey away any such
Servant, but if hee bee acquainted therewith, that hee give
Notice of any such Run-away unto the Magistrates or Officers

under the penalty of [space left blank   ].

It is likewise Ordered, That Capt. John Carr the present
Bayliff, and High-Sherriffe, Mr. Wm. Tom, and Mr. Hans Block,
or any three of them have Inspection into the Arreares of the
Quitt-Rents, the Fines about the Long Finn,[2] as also the Taxes
and Rates for the keeping the High and Low Courts in New Castle
and Delaware River, and all other publick Rates and Taxes, to
make Enquiry how and where they have been disposed of, or in
whose hands they are, and where any persons are in Arreare to
levy the same by Distress; Of all which they are to render mee
an Exact and speedy Account that all Abuses, therein may bee
regulated.

WHEREAS his Majestie hath been pleased to give Order that
his Declaracion of Warr against the States Generall of the
United Belgick Provinces, should bee proclaimed in all his
Colonyes and Territoryes, It is ordered That forthwith after
the Arrivall of Capt. Edmond Cantwell at New-Castle the said
Declaracion is publickly to bee read there, and also at the
Whore-Kill as soon as Opportunity shall present to send from
thence thither.

That the great Gunns bee with all convenient speed sent
up to the Block-houses in Delaware River according to my former
Order, And that the greatest bee disposed of according to the
distance of the Places.

As to the Determinacion of the Busyness between Foppe
Outhout and Isaack Tyne which soe long hath been in Dispute,
That the Orders made by the Court at New Castle concerning the
same bee inspected and examined into by the present Bayliff
and Assistants in the presence of Capt. Carr and Mr. Tom, or
one of them, who together are to make a finall result thereupon, there having been some Misinformacion heretofore given
unto mee, as to that particular Affayre, which is the Occasion
of it's being now calld in question.

And Lastly, It is to bee taken notice of, That although
there is an Alteration as to the Officers and holding of
Courts at New-Castle, yet this doth noe way intrench upon the
Priveledges of the High Court for the Towne and River which is
to continue in the same manner it did formerly without any
Molestation or Interruption upon this or the like Accompt.

Given under my hand at Forte James in New Yorke this
[blank] day of August in the 24th yeare of his Majesties
Reigne, Annoque Domini 1672.

[Endorsed:]

Delaware Papers of   Delaware affaires
severall Concernes from   May 17 1672.
1668 to some time in
1673.   Viewed March the 23rd
Some papers of Maryland   1676.
Concernes before and in
that time.   Maryland etc.

---

1. Although these documents are recorded in O'Callaghan's
    Calendar under two separate entries, they represent a

copy made of three documents concerning affairs in
Delaware. The documents were copied in the same hand
and filed together with a single endorsement. Other
transcriptions in ECM:670-74 and NYCD 12:496, 501 and
502.

2. See 20:6 for a list of these fines.

20:31/32/33   [ORDER AND COMMISSIONS CONCERNING
                DELAWARE][1]

                    An Order for Mr. Tom to render an
                    Account of the Quitt Rents.[2]

WHEREAS you have been by mee employed to Collect and
receive the Quitt-Rents in this Towne and the Plantacions in
the River for the use of his Royall Highness; These are to
require you, That you render mee an Account of what you have
received, and what is in Arreare, forthwith before my departure, if possible, otherwise in some short time at New Yorke,
that I may returne the same to the Auditor Generall who is to
have an Account from mee by his R. Hs. Order of the Quitt-
Rents, as well as of other his Revennues committed to my
Charge. Hereof you are not to fayle. Given under my Hand at
New Castle in Delaware River Aprill the 6th 1671.[3]

To Mr. Wm. Tom Schout.

                    Commission for Capt. Walter Wharton to
                    bee a Justice of the Peace in Delaware
                    River, and parts adjacent.[4]

WHEREAS I have conceived a good Opinion of the fittness
and Ability of Capt. Walter Wharton to bee a Justice of the
peace at Apoquemini, and the parts and Plantacions adjacent in
Delaware Bay or River for to putt his Majesteis Subjects there
into a regular Forme of Government according to his Majesties
and his R. Hs. his Lawes, I have therefore Constituted and
Appointed, and by this my Speciall Commission doe hereby
Constitute and Appoint the aforenamed Capt. Walter Wharton to
bee Justice of the peace in the parts and Plantacions aforemencioned, giveing and granting unto him the said Justice power
to Nominate or cause to bee Elected a Constable for the preservation of his Majesties peace, and two other Persons as
Overseers, with whom at his pleasure hee may sitt to heare and
determine small Causes of Debt or Trespass to the vallue of
five pounds; And all Persons are to give unto the said Capt.
Walter Wharton the respect and Obedience due unto a Justice of
the peace; and hee is in all things of Government to follow
and observe the Lawes Establish[ ] in his Royal Highness his
territoryes, and [   ] follow such Orders and Directions as

from ti[ ] to time hee shall receive from mee. Given under
my Hand and Seale at New Castle in Delaware River this 9th day
of Aprill in the 24th yeare of his Majesties Reigne, Annoque
Domini 1672.

                              Fran: Lovelace

                    Commission of Oyer and Terminer for
                    the Tryall of Wm. Syncleer.

           Francis Lovelace Esq. etc.

                    To the Commissioners of Oyer and
                    Terminer herein mencioned.

     WHEREAS not long since his Majesties Peace hath in a High-
Nature been violated and broken within the Jurisdiction of this
Towne whereby one of his Majesties good Subjects hath been
assaulted, a nd by some violent way or meanes done unto Death,
of the which one William Syncleer now lyeing a Prisoner, and in
Custody for the same, is suspected and accused to bee guilty;
To the End the due Course of Justice may in these his Majesties
Dominions and Territoryes bee prosecuted according to Law and
good Conscience, I have thought fitt to nominate, constitute,
and appoint, and by these Presents doe hereby nominate, Con-
stitute, and appoint you Capt. Matthias Nicolls, Capt. John
Carr, Mr. Wm. Tom, Mr. Peter Alricks, Mr. Hendrick Cousturier,
Mr. Walter Wharton, Mr. Peter Rambo, Mr. Peter Cock, Capt.
Israel Helme, Mr. Hans Block, Capt. Edmond Cantwell, and Mr.
Ernestus Otto (of whome Capt. Matthias Nicolls to bee President, and to have the Casting or decisive voice) to bee
Commissioners of a Speciall Court of Oyer and Terminer to
Examine, Enquire into, heare, and determine the Matters of Fact
concerning the Murder of Death of Lausa Eschelsen; And that you
put the said William Sincleer upon his Tryall by a Jury of
twelve good Men; And for the better Knowledge and Clearing of
the Truth, you are hereby Authorized to call before you by
Sub-poena or Summons, all such Persons who can give in Evidence,
concerning the same, and them to examine upon Oath, which Oath
you are hereby empowered to give. And upon Conviction of the
Delinquent if hee shall bee returned guilty that you proceed to
Sentence and Condemnacion, according to the nature of the Fact,
and the Lawes in such Cases provided; And for what you shall
lawfully Act or Doe in prosecucion hereof, This my Speciall
Commission of Oyer and Terminer shall bee your sufficient
Warrant and Discharge. Given under my Hand and Seale with the
Seale of the Province at New Castle in Delaware River this 4th
day of April in the 24th yeare of his Majesties Reigne,
Annoque Domini 1672.

                    Forme of the Commission granted to the
                    Militia Officers at Delaware and parts
                    adjacent, whose Names are as followeth.

           To Edmond Cantwell Capt.

     By vertue of the Commission and Authority unto mee given
by his Royall Highness James Duke of Yorke and Albany etc. I
have Constituted and appointed, and by these Presents doe

hereby Constitute and appoint you Edmond Cantwell to bee
Captaine of the Foot-Company risen or to bee risen within the
Towne of New Castle in Delaware River and parts adjacent. You
are to take the said Company into your Charge and Care as
Capt. thereof; and them duely to Exercize in Armes, and all
Officers and Souldyers belonging to the said Company are to
obey you as their Captaine; And you are to follow such Orders
and Instructions as you shall from time to time receive from
mee or other your Superiour Officers according to the Discipline of Warr, For the doeing whereof this shall bee your
Commission. Given under my Hand and Seale at New-Castle in
Delaware River this first day of Aprill in the 24th year of
his Majesties Reigne Annoque Domini 1672

Fran: Lovelace

---

1. The following series of documents represents the remains
   of a copy book for orders, warrants and commissions in
   Delaware. The leaves are numbered 17-21 consecutively;
   the verso of leaf 21 is blank.

2. Other transcription of this order in NYCD 12:495.

3. Possibly an error for 1672.

4. Other transcription of this commission in NYCD 12:495.

20:34   [REPORT ABOUT THE DEPREDATIONS OF JOHN SMIT
         IN THE GROOTE KILL][1]

     [   ] January a sloop came here into the Kill with
[   ] John Smit with a crew of six men and [   ] made
some caulking and tarring repairs on their sloop [   ]
they made it ready to sail [   ] with two runaways
from Maryland. They set sail the first of March. After they
were gone we discovered [   ] the mill stones were missing.
The skipper proceeding by canoe with 2 [   ] the marsh, went
to the house of Daniel Bruy[ ].[2] Ottho Wolgast seeing the
canoe there [   ] here to this place. After which the skipper
John [   ] and was at his wit's end over the seizure
of the canoe. [   ] interrogation he admitted having the
millstones on board [   ] was held in arrest. [   ] the
schout with the Commissary's permission [   ] Herman
Cornelissen's boat in order to go on board [   ] Smit and
recover the millstones. Whereupon the men on board readied
their weapons threatening to shoot and would not let [   ]
come aboard. They, therefore, had to return and could not
enter [   ] but had to [   ] to the Groote Kill and
leave their boat there. [   ] the crew of the sloop came back
to [   ] Kill and by order to John Smit [   ] brought the
millstones ashore.

     [   ] the schout with the approval of the Commissary
sent [   ] to the boat, which began to roll and pitch in sand

[   ] to push off and bring it back here. When the men
had gone there, the crew came in the canoe to the [   ] of the
schout armed with muskets and pistols and took the schout by
force out of his house. They brought him along in their canoe
to Sander Moelsteen's house where John Smit was being confined.
They demanded the release of their captain or they would not
[   ] the schout. Whereupon the two guards set John Smit
free. [   ] released the schout and they went then [   ].
When the boat came out of Groote Kil [   ] the crew with
sharp shooters said they have [   ]. The men in the boat
[   ] back again to the Groote Kil [   ] beached the boat
there and brought the oars to the crew of the sloop. John
Smit then said, "If [   ] Cornelis brings us nothing to drink,
we will [   ] his boat." Herman Cornelis and Jan Michiels
went to [   ] and found the boat lying on one side, the
rudder [   ] and fetched [   ]. On the 11th of March
Herman Cornelis went aboard [   ] demanding payment for the
liquor which John Smit had consumed. Whereupon the same John
Smit detained the same Herman [   ] of which none of us
knew, but [   ] here. The schout then [   ] a man there who
asked John Smit why he [   ] held. He replied that they
[   ] here so long and that they needed provisions in order
to go to sea. [   ] not let Herman go if they need
provisions [   ].

     On the 12th of March the schout sent officers to the
[   ] the warrant reading as follows:

                    This [   ] in the Name of [   ]
                    Duke of Yorcke To Comma[   ]
                    ye man that you [   ]
                    yr sloope by neame Herman [   ]
                    in so set give under [   ]
                    1672   [   ]

     When this warrant was read [   ] threw [   ]
board and these men came back again [   ] shooting after them.
[   ] which they did. They sent an order [   ] signed
by Herman Cornelis to [   ] 2 pigs and 6 lb gunpowder
aboard the sloop. On the 13th of March we went to the sloop
[   ] 2 pigs with 6 lb gun powser which the crew [   ] took
aboard. They then released Herman Cornelis after [   ] he had
been prisoner [   ] and 2 nights. On the 14th of March John
Smit sailed his sloop out of this Kill and anchored near the
Groote Kill. [   ] the night of the 16th a strong N West
wind [   ]. [   ] morning seen no more.

[Endorsed:] John Smit, Privateer
             His depredations

---

1. Translated from the Dutch with the exception of the
    text of the warrant which is in English. The Groote
    Kill was called Great Creek and Broad Creek by English.
    It is now known as Broadkill Creek. This creek should
    not be confused with the Groote Kill which was also the
    Dutch name for a creek about three miles south of New
    Castle.

2. Probably Daniel Bruyn.

20:35   [REPORT FROM THE WHORE KILL CONCERNING A
        SURVEYOR FROM MARYLAND][1]

                    27th of Aprill 1672

     This morning appeared before us Harman Cornelius and
John Kipshaven who informed that a certaine person by name
Mr. Jenkins who came into the Hoer Kill and there surveyed
severall lands in the bay by pretended Commission from the Lord
Baltemore threatning the Inhabitants that denyeth his power
that they shall be sent for into Maryland there to be punished
whether he has Comission or noe is uncertayne these wee thought
fitt to acquiant your honor with to wayte your honors further
order.

                    [Signed:] Will. Tom
                               Pieter Alrichs
                               Walter Wharton
                               Ed. Cantwell

[Endorsed:]   A Certificate from the Whore Kill, about a
              Surveyor sent there from Maryland.   1672

---

1. Other transcriptions in ECM:669 and NYCD 12:496.

20:36 [RICHARD PERROT TO GOV. LOVELACE ABOUT
        ACQUIRING LAND IN THE WHORE KILL][1]

May it plese youre Honer

     In May Last my selfe with sume other Gentelmen of ver-
geney Came over to deliware to see the plase and Liking the
plase wee made Choise of severall tractes of Land for our
selfes and nabores and had made bolde to Have given youre Honer
A visitt had not one of our Companey falen ill so that wee
implied Mr. Walter Whar[ten] For to paten our Land: now may it
plese youre H[oner] About tenn dayes before I Came to seet the
Mare[lande]men Have sarvaed it agane in the Lordes name I much
fere it will disherten the Rest of the gentelmen from Cuming
up at the falle and severall more of our nabores that would
Cume up at the fale of the lefe very Honest men and good House
Keepers they desired me to take them up sum land which I am
doutfull to doue unlesse youre Honer will bee plesed to give
me permishon for it: I dout not but to se the plase well
seted in tow or three yeares at the [   ] and A trade from
London the plase is good and Helthf[   ] and wanteth nothing
but peple I was in good Hopes I should have had the Hapines to
have got up before you[ ] Honer left deliware but my hopes was
in vaine I Hope youre honer will bee plesed to honer mee with
A line or two whoe is youre faithfull and Obedient servant
unkno[ne]

                    [Signed:]   Richard: Per[rot]

From the Horkill
     June the 21th 1672

     If youre Honer plese to grant us all the Land [to us]
vergenianes that lieth betwene the Horekill and the moth[ ]
kill[2] wee shall take spedey Care for the seating of it as may
bee Expeted at so great A distance when Layed out acording to
menes familise what good Land ther maye bee found in the distance I know not at present wee Ha[ve] A desire to be neare
together as the plase will aforde In Ag[ust] I intend to ver-
geney for sum Occasione of bisnes and send up my sonn

                              [Initialed:]   R: P:

[Addressed:]   These
           For the Honered
           Fransis Lovlis Esqr.
           Governer and Captane
           Generall of nue yorke
           per with
             Care

[Endorsed:]   [Mr.] Perrot
           Whorekill - June. 21, 1672

---

1. Other transcriptions in NYCD 12:498, ECM:671

2. Mother Kill, which is a later English form of the
   Swedish Mordare Kijhlen, i.e. "the Murderer Creek."

20:37   [CAPT. CARR TO GOV. LOVELACE CONCERNING
         THE WHOREKILL AND MARYLAND][1]

Sir

     According to your Honors order we sent t[hose] papers to
the Horekill by Mr. Whart[on] where they found noe reception,
I need not give your Honor the resons, for your Honor will find
them in the papers inclosed taken by Mr. Wharton, the number of
men and horse that came to the Horekill was but thirty, but
they were sixty halfe way, where meeting Mr. Parrott going to
Acamake and soe to Virginia and understanding by him there was
noe other forces from your Honor but the Inhabitants of the
Horekill thirty Horse was sent ba[ck] to Maryland this Mr.
Parrott is a gentleman seated near the Horekill by your Honors
Patant, the Horekill boat is come hee[re] with fower of the
Inhabitants and desier[s t]o take a tract of land up the River
neare your Honors Land, they say before they came from thence
Harmanus and Sanders[2] [was] returned from St. Maries, who
brings ne[wes] that in Maryland they are Leviing a Considerable
force to bring this place and soe fare up the River to the
degree Forty northerly under theyr obedience, we shall know

more when Cantwell returns with Answer of your Honors Letter,
which I shall dispatch t[o] your Honor with all expedition, I
have not els[e] but waite your Honors Comaunds, and Subscribe
my sealf as in duty bound Sir

  Your Honors most Faithfull and obedient servant

[ ]w Castle 27th   [Signed:] John C[a]rr
[ ]pt. 1672.

[Addressed:] Thesse
    For Generall Francis
     Lovelace
Hast post Hast   New yorke.
 John Carr

[Endorsed:] C. Carr to the Gov[ ] Newcastle Sept. 1672

---

 1. Other transcriptions in ECM:679 and NYCD 12:503.
   For a transcription of Gov. Lovelace's reply to
   Capt. Carr see ECM:680.

 2. i.e., Helmanus Wiltbanck and Alexander Molestine.

20:38 [CAPT. CANTWELL TO GOV. LOVELACE ABOUT
    AFFAIRS AT THE WHOREKILL][1]

Right honorable Sir

   your honor writts Mr. Alrichs of my not wri[ ] to your
honor I had writt to Capt. Nicolls [att] Large of what I heard
and saw att m[ ] Land I thought Capt. Nicolls would ha[ve]
informed your honor of all I heard so [much] that my lorde
thus intend for to keepe the whore kill I saw Jones power to
seas[2] all Indyan goods or skins att the whore kill and one
Smith the Juge of the Court att the whore kill tould me that
my Lorde Baltemore gave him order for to drive a 20d naill in
the touch hole of the great gon and seas the gone and mill
stones att the whore kill his Comission was soe Large as your
honor Can Imagen when I Came to St. Marys Jones went to the
gou[ernor] and he writt upon the back side of his Comiss[ion]
that he would mantane his Comission I tould them that itt was
a folly for them for to strive aganst your honors power and
tould them If your honor gave but order for to beat a drom all
the servans would Com away from them the most part o[ ] the
people thus fear that theire servan[ ] will run away from them
all the people w[ ] be glade submitt them selves onder your
honor Goverment and they plaenly say that they will not Resist
your honors power nor will have noting to doe with what my
lorde has done

   Capt. Nicolls writts to me about Derick Smith goin up the
River I gott him for to goe for the quit Rent the which he
has aboarde for to be sent to your honor what he has not in I

shall thake Care for to send in the spring nor Derick Smith
should not goe [up] the River If itt had not bene for the quit
Rent without your honors order the vessell is just going away
and I shall end and Remane

                    Your honors
                      most faithfull servant
                               To Comand
                    [Signed:] Ed: Cantwell

[Addressed:] For the Right honorable
              Coll. Francis Lovelace Esqr.
              Governor off all his
              Royall highnesse Terotories
              In Amerikae att
              new yorke
              present

[Endorsed:] Delaware fr[om Cap] Cantwell of the 10th of
             December 1672

---

1. Other transcriptions in ECM:682 and NYCD 12:505.

2. i.e., "I saw Jones' power to seize..."; Capt. Thomas
   Jones was sheriff of Somerset County, Maryland. See
   MA 65:37 for a reference to this seizure of goods.

20:39   [MAGISTRATES OF DELAWARE TO GOV. LOVELACE
        CONCERNING WAR WITH THE INDIANS][1]

Right Honorable

     the Indyans not bringing in the murtherers according to
their promise I[2] went up with Mr. Aldricks[3] to Peter Cocks and
there called the Raedt[4] together to informe your honor what wee
thinke most for our preservacion and defense of the river

     first wee think that att this time of the yeare itt is to
late to begin a warr against the Indyans the hay for our beasts
not being to be brought to any place of safety and so for want
of Hay wee must see them starve before our faces the next
yeare wee can cutt itt more conveneint

     2dly our corne not being thrashed or ground wee must
starve for want of provision which this winter wee can grind
and lay up in places of safety

     3dly that there must upon necessity a warr in the Spring
and by that time wee shall make so much as wee can preparacion
but wayte from your honor assistance of men ammunition and
salt

     4thly wee intend to make Townes att Passayuncke Tinna-
combe Upland and Verdrieties Hoocke whereto the out

plantacions must retire

5thly wee thinke that your honors advice for a frontire about Mattinacunck Island is very good and likewise another att Wicaquake[5] for the defence whereof your honor must send men

Is there any thing else unwritten wee have sent Mr. Aldricks and Mr. Helme to advice your honor what is best to be done but intend to stop Thomas Lewes untill your honors order for wee thinke itt not convenient any corne or provision be sent out of the river untill this bruit[6] be over for wee Know not the next yeare whether wee shall have any corne or noe wee have not more att present but to informe your honor that Capt. Carr is not recovered but remayne

	Right Honorable
	your honors most humble servants
[P.S.] that if possible	[Signed:] Will. Tom
there be Hired fifty or	the mark of ⨂ Peter Rambo
sixty North Indyans who	the mark of ⅆ Peter Cock
will doe more then 200	H: Block
men in such a warr	Henrich Janssen
	Ed. Cantwell
	M. Roseman
	the mark of ⧢ Ole Torsen

[Endorsed:]   The Result and Reasons of the Commissories and Magistrates at Delaware about prosecucion of the warr against the Murderers. 1673[7]

---

1. Other transcriptions in ECM:602 and NYCD 12:505.

2. i.e., William Tom.

3. i.e., Peter Alrichs.

4. Dutch word for "council".

5. i.e., Wicaco.

6. i.e., "uproar."

7. Either the date is incorrect or it represents a file date. The contents of this letter when compared with 20:24 indicate that it was written in the fall of 1671. In ECM:604 it is conjectured that this letter was an enclosure with 20:24 dated October 25, 1671.

20:40   [WILLIAM TOM TO MATTHIAS NICOLLS ABOUT A
         PATENT AND OTHER AFFAIRS IN DELAWARE]

Capt. Niccolls

        In your last you wrote me you told me itt was not for-
getfulnes that you sent not the patent for [Amesland][1] I hope
itt will now not be forgotten with the first and if you send
itt perticuler to me itt may advance the payment of the debt
I owe you noe other person being concerned in my private interest there as for the last order concerning Fop Outhout and
Isaack Teine tis ill resented that is to say the proceedes of
our Court here with severall persons here thinke is done contrary to law and reason Isaack having a definitive sentence
already under the Governors hand and seale and done in your
presence which somme likewise thinke ought to be unalterable
like the lawes of the Meedes and Persians which has caused a
dispute so farr as to an appeale which may run further and
reach your eares by a further rehearing I thought good to
acquaint you with this and have not further untill I see you
which shalbe if god blesse me shortly after the Capts. returne
but my humble respects to your good Lady and prayers for your
children likewise my love and respects to all freinds and
remayne

Newcastle this 8th of   Sir your humble and faithful
July 1673   servant [Signed:] Will. Tom

[P.S.]   I take not that excuse of brevity as you doe for att
         the writing here and in the same campany I am taking
         Capt. Carrs fey with the rest of our freinds
         therefore excuse

[Addressed:]   for his Honord freind Capt. Mathias Niccols
               Secretary att New York these present in

[Endorsed:]   Mr. Tom
              Newcastle July 8 1673

_____

1. Wm. Tom's handwriting is unclear at this point. The
    name in question appears to be Amcsland which could be
    a mistake for Amesland.

20:41   An Inventory of the Goods, Lands and Houses
         (belonging to Tinaconk in Delaware River left
         there by Mr. Andrew Carr) taken and apprized
         by us whose names are subscribed by order of
         the Right Honorable the Governor and his
         Court, as followeth, (vizt.)

	Gl. St.[1]
1 Dutch plough with 2 Coulters, and one plough chaine	060
2 Sweedes plough Irons...............................	025
1 Harrow with 24 teeth, and 27 teeth more all Iron	070

	Gl.	St.
2 Dung Forks		016
3 Hay forks		020
2 Augers		030
2 small Wimbles at		006
1 Old broad Axe at		004
2 Old Sweeds axes at		006
2 Iron Wedges at		020
1 Spade at		012
1 Spade without a handle		008
1 wooden corn shovell at		005
1 great Padlock att		012
1 Dutch syth att		016
2 Syth hammers at		025
1 hanging Iron att		010
1 frying pan at		010
1 great Iron Pott at		060
1 little Iron Pott att		010
2 pott hangers att		020
1 great Pewter dish at		016
2 Old little pewter dishes at		006
1 brass Candlestick with snuffers		012
1 pewter saltseller att		002
1 Sweeds Jack with 1 spitt att		080
1 Dripping pan att		030
1 Andiron at		010
2 pair of tongs att		012
1 fire shovell at		002
5 reap hooks att		015
1 great presse stand in the Chamber		050
1 little hanging Cupboard in the Chamber		008
Summa		688

	Gl.	St.
2 Old powdering tubbs att		006
2 Meale Chests att		025
2 brasse skimmers att		016
1 pewter Cann without a Cover att		010
1 wooden Cann conteyning 2 Fans att		003
1 great table with 2 benches in the fore roome		050
1 great Table in an out house att		015
1 middling table in the yard att		004
1 bench in the Chamber att		010
1 pair of wooden scales with 14lb. weight att		030
1 drawing Knife att		006
1 hand saw att		010
1 file att		003
1 hammer att		006
1 Old Cart and wheeles att		030
1 old brewing Tubb qt. 6 scheple att		004
2 water pailes att		010
1 Kneading Trough att		010
1 old wooden Scheple att		003
1 Iron Croe att		030
2 yoaks with Iron hooks att		030
1 old pewter chamber pott att		008
1 Sow, 1 Boar, and 1/2 Barrow att		070
4 drawing Oxen att		600
3 Cows att		450
1 bull 3 years old att		100
1 year old bull att		040
the halfe of a Cow Calfe att		013

```
                                            Gl.   St.
1 young Oxe in the hands of Albert att       100
1 ditto with a bull in the hand of Capt. Carr att 200
                                 Summa      1892
             Summe from the other side       688
                                            2580
    The Island with it appurtenances    ⎫
    together with all housing and houses │
    thereon (the Church only excepted,  ⎬   6000
    which is left as it was before)     │
    Amounts to the sume of............. ⎭
                                            8580 Gl.s[   ]
                           Holl: money      2145 Gl.[   ]
                                             lb. St.[   ]
                 Or in Money Sterling      214=10 [   ]
```

Memorandum that Albert (who is the husbandman) is to performe
his Condicion formerly made with Mr. Andrew Carr to Jufroe
Popegay.[2]

Witness Our hands   Pieter Alrighs
the 23rd day of Aprill 1673.   Will: Tom
                                      Walter Wharton
                                      Ed: Cantwell
A true Copie
[Signed:] Matthias Nicolls Secr.

[Endorsed:] No. 13 A Copie of the Inventory of Goods at
             Tinnicum Isl. apprized by Order 1673.

---

1. i.e., appraised in guilders, sewant value.

2. This is Armegart Printz, the wife of Johan Papegoja.
    Jufroe is Dutch Juffrouw meaning "madam."

20:42a   [COPIES OF RECEIPTS CONCERNING ANDREW CARR][1]

Albert[2]

     Deliver unto James Sanderlins one bull of Mr. Andrew Carrs
and this shall be your discharge witnesse my hand.
Opland 22nd
October 1672   John Carr

     Received of Albert of Tinicum one Oxe belonging to Mr.
Andrew Carr I say by me receaved this 19th of October 1672.
                                John Carr

     Capt. Carr hath received from mee on the Account of Mr.
Andrew Carr the somme of three thousand six hundred pound of
Tobacco I say received of mee
Sassafrax River in   John Gilbert
Baltimore County Marty
10th 1672/3

On the backside of a Peticion from Jufrow Armigaert
Prince was written thus vizt.

I do attest that Capt. John Carr is full procurator for
Mr. Andrew Carr to answer all that shall bee demanded of him in
his absence wittnesse my hand
                                        Will Tom

Ick ondergescreven bekenne schuldigh te wesen aen Mr.
Andris Carr volgens myn bill gedaen Vierteen hondert lb. goede
leverbare toback. waer van twee Oxhovden van Capt. John Car
[blank] syn ditt gedaen synde voor ondergeschreven
getuygen inde[3]

A bill in dutch signed by Mons Andries of fourteen hundred
lb. Tobacco that he is indebted to Mr. Andrew Carr
Wittnesses   Andies Pietersen
                 Jan Boyer

John Martiall received of mee Axell Stelle by the Order of
Mr. John Carr eight hundred and fifty pounds of Tobacco and
Cask which was due to Andrew Carr testifyed per me.
March the 11 1672   Axell Stelle

[Endorsed:] Copies of the bills about C. Capt. Carrs receiving
             Andrew Carrs Tobacco.

----

1. These receipts were copied from the originals which
   appear as 20:42b, 43b and 43c.

2. Albert was Andrew Carr's "husbandman" on Tinicum
   Island. See the memorandum at the end of 20:41.

3. This bill is not completely transcribed because the
   clerk apparently had difficulty with the Dutch handwriting. See 20:43c for a translation of this document
   from the original.

20:42b   [RECEIPT CONCERNING ANDREW CARR]

Albert[1]

Deliver unto James Sanderlins one bull of Mr. Andrew Carrs
and this shall be your discharche wittnes my hand
Opland 22nd   [Signed:] John Carr
October 1672

[Endorsed:] Capt. Carr

----

1. Albert was Andrew Carr's "husbandman" on Tinicum
   Island. See the memorandum at the end of 20:41.

20:43a [ORDER TO PAY CAPT. CANTWELL]

17th of October 1672

being present Capt. John Carr Mr. Peter Aldricks Bayleffe
William Tom Mr. Hans Block The Sherriffe being present itt was
ordered that Capt. Cantwell bee payed the somme of nyne hundred
seaventy and three guilders eleeven stivers which he has dis-
bursed for the publick out of the publicke [   ]1 for Car-
riages and publick worke.

vera copia   283-10 paid Mrs. Cousturier
[Signed:] Will. Tom   for the duffells given by
                                Coll. Lovelace by C. Cantwell.

[Verso:] 6417 paid by Capt. Cantwell hee to bee paid by
          the Gov. at Delaware.

[Endorsed:] An Order for Payment of 973 Guilders 11 Stivers to
             Capt. Cantwell, for what hee disburst. 17th
             October 1672.

---

1. Word crossed out.

20:43b   [RECEIPT CONCERNING ANDREW CARR]

Capt. Carr hath received from mee one the account of Mr.
Andrew Carr the somme of three thousand six hundred pound of
Tobac[ ] I say received of mee:
                              [Signed:] John Gilbert
Sassafrax River in Baltimore
County Marty 10th 1672/3

[Verso:] 3600
          1400
           850
          ────
          5850
           800
          ────
          6650

20:43c   [RECEIPTS CONCERNING ANDREW CARR]1

I the undersigned acknowledge to be indebted to Mr. Andris
Carr, done according to my bill, for fourteen hundred lbs. of
good marketable tobacco of which two hozsheads were from

Captain Jan Car. This having been done before the undersigned
witnesses in the province of Maryland. The 10th day of March
1672/3.

The **AP** mark of Andris Pitersen
The mark ✳ of Mons Andrisen
[Signed:] Jan Boeyer

        John Martiall received of me Axell Stelle by the order of
Mr. John Carr eight hundred and fifty pounds of tobacco and
Cask which was dew to Andrew Carr testified per me March the
11 1672
                            [Signed:] Axell Stille

---

1. The first receipt is written in Dutch. See 20:42a for
    an incomplete transcription which was made for a copy
    of all receipts concerning Andrew Carr.

20:44   [PERMISSION TO CASPARUS HERMAN TO CULTIVATE A
         PIECE OF LAND ON APPOCQUENEMIN KILL][1]

    ...north [   ] a certain Kill named [   ] Kill,
which flows from the west, and on the west side by the common
woods; so that its width is from Ariens Kill to the aforesaid
Appocquenemin Kill, and its length from the riverbank to the
source of the Ariens Kill; westward into the woods and then to
the south until Appocqueneemins Kill, measuring about 250
morgens.

    Which aforesaid piece of land, being in compliance with
the aforesaid grant, and moreover, which is in the possession
of the aforementioned Casparus Herman, who has built a
dewlling house on it and fenced part of it in, I have, therefore, at the request of the aforementioned Herman, given my
consent and permission to the same to continue cultivating the
aforementioned parcel of land, bounded and situated as described, and to use as his own property provided that he
obtain letters-patent and a confirmation for the same from the
Honorable Governor. Done at N. Amstel on the South River of
N. Netherland.

The 5th of Feb. 1674[2]   [Signed:] Pieter Alrichs

---

1. The surviving lower half of this document has been
    translated from Dutch. Other translation in NYCD
    12:517.

2. This date is new style.

20:45   [A LIST OF PAPERS DELIVERED TO CAPT. CANTWELL]

Deliver'd to Capt. Cantwell, these particular papers
following

A Commission to be Sherriffe or Schout of New Castle, and
   places adjacent on the west side thereof.
Copy of Governor Colves Resignacion.
The Rates for the Customes.
Mr. Toms Commission, to be Clarke or Secr. his owne Commission
   to be Capt.
Johannes De Haas his Commission for Lieut.
John Williams Commission to be Ensigne.
A Commission to receive the Quit Rents.
A Commission to Mr. Capt. Cantwell and Mr. Tom to take
   Possession of Delaware.
A Lettre and Commission to the Commissaryes at Whorekill.
The like to the Commissaryes at New Castle.
The like to the Commissaryes up the River.
A Lettre to Sir William Barkley.
A Lettre to the Governor of Maryland.
A Commission to Administer an Oath.
An Order to receive the C[   ]rs.

20:46   [DECLARATION CONCERNING THE THEFT OF A CANOE]

Samuell Edsall plaintife
William Oryon defendant

    The plaintife declareth Against this defendant that hee
Comeinge to the plantatyon of this plaintife About the Later
end of Feryary Last And theare remaininge till the begininge of
marche did borowe of the plaintifes overseare A Canow with two
men to Cary him to Governour Cartterets piont [sic] with promise to returne the Canow with men bake with All expedityon:
but Contrary to his promis hee did Cary both men And Canowe
downe to wood bridge And theare sould the Canowe And Caryed the
men with him the one of them beeinge A servant to the plaintife
for the space of one yeare and had receaved great part of his
wages And stole At theire goeinge Away to the valew of five
pounds thearfore the plaintife humbly desireth this honorable
Court to order the defendant to returne the produce of what
hee reteined for the Canow And to make satisfactyon for the
damadge sustained by the plaintife by Caryinge his men Away:
the which may Apeare was by his Instigatyon by Reson hee
neaver did aquaint Any of the oficers of this towne At theire
passinge by to Mary Land And your petityoner shall Ever pray

[Endorsed:]   Sam: Edsall plt.
              Will: Oryon deft.

20:47   [DECLARATION CONCERNING PAYMENT OF A DEBT]

Samuell Edsall Atorney to John Sharpe plaintife
William Oryon deffendant

    The plaintife declareth that the defendant standeth
indepted to him by bill bearinge datt the 20th of May 1670:
the sume of fivety fowre gillders eight stivers the which
beeinge demanded of him hee refuseth to mack payment therfore
the plaintife humly prayeth this honorabe Court to order the
payment of the Above specified sume with Cost And hee Shall
Ever praye

[Endorsed:]   No. 20   Sam: Edsall plt.
                          Wm. Oryon deft.
                          Declaracon.

20:48a   [DECLARATION OF WM. TOM CONCERNING A PIECE
          OF LAND][1]

William Tom plt.   5th of January 1674
Dirick Albertsen deft.

    The plt. complaynes against the deft. that he the plt.
having obteyned a patent under the hand and seale of Collonell
Francis Lovelace bearing date 25th day of July 1669 for one
halfe of the lott where the mill stood and the deft. denying
the said halfe of the lott by vertue of a transport from William
Beakeman he having by that transport sold him 38 foote of the
abovemencioned [   ] then halfe of the said lott
itt is by the Court ordered that itt be referred to New Yorke
for the determinacion
                    by the Court [Signed:]   Will. Tom

[Endorsed:]   Mr. William Tom
              Mr. Wm. Beeckman
              Recommended at the goeing of th Go: to
              Delaware.
              Referred to the Magistrates.

---

1. Other transcription in NYCD 12:517.

20:48b [MEMORANDUM BY MATTHIAS NICOLLS CONCERNING
WM. TOM'S LAND DISPUTE]

Mr. Tom claymes of the Guift[1] of Webbers Lott to come to
Mr. Beekmans house, and takes no notice of the passages
betweene, which is against prejudice; hee desires releife
etc.

_____

1. i.e., gift.

20:49 [JOHN MOLL TO MATTHIAS NICOLLS ABOUT PAYMENT
ON A HOUSE; RECOMMENDATION CONCERNING SAME BY
WM. TOM]

Capt. Matthuw Nicols.

New Castle Aprill the 15th 1675

Sir After my Humble Servises unto You Presentet, Whar as I
have taken Possion[1] off the House whare Mrs. Coutrie Leved in
Laest heer, which is as I am Informed by Capt. Cantwell seased
for your house, I crave that [   ] from you as to have
the refusall off the Teale[2] thar[ ] off, I hope to make you as
prompt and Honest payment as your own Selve Shall desier, I
Question not butt shall bee so happi as to Embrace your Good
Sosiety att the Arivall off the Hon. Gouvernor Andross heer,
In the meane tyme I make bold to acquand You my desier, and to
tender unto you this My Request, In the Admittance off which
you will Infinely Oblidge him hoo Kisses your hand and desiers
to Remaine
                              Sir Yours att Commande
                              [Signed:] John Moll

[Notation below signature:] if you can obleige my freind Mr.
Moll in his request you may for nothing has beene wanting to
your assistence in recovery of your pay from Capt. Carr for
that you have Judgement for so many beavers although uncertayne as Cantwell alleadged I am so short not Knowing of
this speedy dispatch but will see all your ends effected att
your coming not else but desiring you to pleasure my freind as
alone I rem.   your assured servant
dated as above   [Signed:] Will. Tom

[Addressed:] To Capt. Matthew Nicolls
             Secretary Att New Yorke
             in Ami.[3]

[Endorsed:] [   ] 30 John Moll and [   ] Wm. Tom
            New Castle Apr. 15th 1675.

_____

1. i.e., possession.

2. i.e., tail : "entail."

3. Abbreviation for: America.

20:50a/50b   [CAPT. CANTWELL'S COMMISSION TO BE
               SURVEYOR; INSTRUCTIONS FOR THE SAME][1]

Edm: Andros Esq. etc.

By vertue of the Authority unto mee derived, I do hereby
constitute and appoint you Capt. Edmund Cantwell to bee surveyor of this place River and precincts In which Employment
you are to act according to the best of your skill and Knowledge in surveying of such lands, for which you shall from
time to time receive warrants or Orders from mee and to make
due and exact Returnes thereof, with the particular distinctions
of their buttings and boundings as well as Quantity, in order
to a Confirmacion by Patent you taking and receiving for the
same such reasonable Fees as belongs to your said place, and
have beene, or shall bee allowed of by myselfe, or the Generall
Court : Given under my hand and seale at Newcastle in Delaware
River this 12th day of May Annoque Domini 1675.

To Capt. Edm: Cantwell
Surveyor of Delaware.

                    By the Governor[2]

     Whereas you are appointed Surveyor for this River and pre-
cincts, the which being at so great a distance from N. Y.
Therefore the better and more speedy accommodacion of such
fitting persons as daily resort hither to settle under his
R. Hs. Government, you are hereby further authorized as
followeth:

     That you admitt of any such new Commers and assigne them
such Tracts of land proper for them, as hath not beene yet
taken up or settled according to the Law and Custome of the
Government within three yeares, allowing to each head 60 acres
of land, they not parting with such land assigned them untill
it bee setled. And for their better Encouragem[ ] such as
take up new Land, shall bee free of paying any Quitt Rent for
the first three yeares.

     That upon all occasions of New Commers you do advise with
the Magistrates concerning the quantitye of land to bee given
them, and the most proper Places.

     That from time to time you give me an acompt and send me
due surveys of all new lands taken up, as also of all lands
setled that have nott been surveyed, and Patented, that there
may be Grants and patents sent for the same and duly recorded
in the Courts of the severall juresidctions or Precints [sic]
to prevent all future litigious sutes.
Given under my hand in N. Castle the 15th of may 1675.

To Capt. Edm: Cantwell
Surveyor of Delaware

By the Governor

Whereas there was an obmision att the last Generall Court
in this place by the nott presenting the want of corn milles
or nott Keeping of them in due repaire in this River, the de-
fect of which is a great prejudice to the inhabitants and
Traders. I doe therefore recomend to the justices of the 3
severall Courts[3] that without delay they Examine the same and
cause all such mils already made and the bancks, to be well
fited and kept in due repair and if there bee Cause others to
be built in such Convenient and fitting places where none are
for the most convenience and service of the inhabitants in
order to which that they regulate the tols or prises for
grinding and give such other fitting incouragement as they shall
judge proper, for the said millers, and owners wheather of Publick or private mils are to regulate and Conforme themselves
thereunto, the said regulations to be in force till the next
generall Court,

And whereas there hath been heitherto a neclect in duly
recording of lands which often ocasions litigious sutes, and
the losse of some mens reall Estates I have therefore ordered
that all new lands be duly survey'd and patented and the same
to be recorded in the Court books of the severall juresdictions
or precints [sic], and doe also require that all lands already
or formerly taken up and setled but nott surveyed and the
owners have noe patents for the same, that such owners doe
fortwith before the next Generall Court give notice to the
surveyor Generall that it be done and they take out patent for
Confirming, and asuring unto them so to prevent all future
sutes or doubts for the samme and that itt be recorded in
order to which that you give publick notice att your next
monthley or quarterly Courts, or by Such other means as you
shall judge most proper in the severall precints [sic] that
all persons concerned may be advertised and conforme themselves thereunto acordingly, itt being a generall concerne and
good of the inhabitants.[4]

To the three severall
Courts of Delaware River
[   ] Day [   ]

[Endorsed:]   From the Go: orders 1675 in Delaware. Quere
              if entr'd.

---

1. The following are copies of orders issued by Matthias
    Nicolls while visiting Delaware with Gov. Andros in
    1675.

2. This phrase replaces: Instructions for Capt. Edmund
    Cantwell Surveyor etc., which has been crossed out.

3. The three courts were at Upland, New Castle and
    Whorekill.

4. See NCCR:47 for the court's copy of these final two
    paragraphs.

20:51   [CAPT. CANTWELL'S RECEIPT FOR BILLS AND
         PAPERS FROM MATTHIAS NICOLLS][1]

Received at Peter Rambo's the under written Bills and Papers.
May 17 1675.

Capt. John Carrs Account and Copie of Court Charges betweene Jeuffrou Prince and Capt. Carre Amounting in all to.................	Guilders 1815 Sewant
Mr. Walter Whartons bill of 45 beavers dated June 21 1671 and Account, being in all due..	G: st. 1212.18
Mr. William Tom's bill of his hand for 17 lb. money value and a beaver and Account, where rests due...............................	613.5
In all	3641.3

                              [Signed:] Ed. Cantwell

[Endorsed:] Capt. Cantwells Receipt of my[2] bills and papers
             at Delaware.

---

1. The receipt is written in the hand of Matthias Nicolls
    and signed by Capt. Cantwell.

2. i.e., Matthias Nicolls.

20:52   [DEPOSITIONS CONCERNING JOHN LAURENSON'S CHEST
         OF GOODS]

Johannes de Haiz[1] in full Court sworne declares that one
morning John Laurenson came to his house desiring him house
roome for one Chest which should not stay Long there for that
John Tarkinton would comme with more goods and ship them for
New Yorke and that he was alwayes ready and would upon all
demands have delivered the said goods to Tarkinton by the said
order and further that he has heard Tarkinton affirme with
many oathes that the goods were his

Henry Williams Sworne declares that there was a Chest of
goods brought into his house and afterwards carryed to the
House of Johannes de Haiz and afterwards he heard Laurenson
say that he had bought that chest with goods

Gisbert Dirickson declares That Tarkinton being his debtor
and Lawrenson likewise Tarkinton came by this deponent and said
he would pay him out of the chest both for himselfe and
Laurenson [   ] chest was attatched came againe by this
deponent and said that the chest was attatched and my goods
away and now neither pay for himselfe nor the other therefore
he must have patience

George Moore under sherriffe sworne declares that going to attatch the chest as the goods of Laurenson for the somme of 5000 lb. tobaccoe for James Crawford Tarkinton came by him and with many oathes affirmed th[ ] the chest and goods were his and not Laurensons upon which he forbore to proceed with the attatchment any further

Judith Crawford the wife of James Crawford Sworne declareth that when her husband had attatched the chest as the chest and goods belonging to John Laurenson th[ ] Tarkinton came and affirmed the goods to bee his whereupon Crawford answered if you will give me your bill I will discharge the attatchment which he promised to doe but afterward when itt was attatched as his owne he then denyed itt affirming the goods were neither his nor Laurenson[ ]

John Vidett Sworne declares that when the Chest was sent for from Johannes de Haiz Tarkinton was mightily troubled att itt affirming the goods to be his

[Endorsed:] No. 31 Severall deposicions about a Chest left in Delaware. April 1675

---

1. i.e., Johannes de Haes.

20:53   [COMMISSION FOR MILITIA OFFICERS ON THE DELAWARE][1]

Edmond Andros Esq. Seigneur of Sansmarez Lieut. and Governor Generall under his Royall Highnesse James Duke of Yorke and Albany etc. of all his Territories in America.

By vertue of the Authority unto mee given, I doe hereby constitute and appoint you [blank] to bee Capt. of a foot Company of the Militia composed of the Inhabitants of Newcastle in Delaware River[2] and Dependences : you are therefore to take the said Company into your Charge and duely to exercise both Officers and souldyers in armes, and Keepe them in good order and discipline, And the said Officers and souldyers are required to obey you as their Capt. and you to observe such Rules and Orders as from time to time you shall receive from mee or other[ ] your superior Officers according to Law, and the Rules and discipline of warre : This Commission to bee of force for the space of one whole yeare after the date hereof or further order : Given under my hand and seale at Newcastle in Delaware River this [blank] day of May 1675

Newcastle - Capt. Lieut. and Ens.[3]
Cranehooke
Verdreede Hooke
Upland

Passyunck
Apoquemini   The like
Whorekill

[Endorsed:] No. 29 President of Military Commissions at
             Delaware May 1675.

---

1. Other transcription in NYCD 12:520.

2. This phrase was inserted to replace: Inhabitants of the
   Towne of Newcastle, which was crossed out.

3. i.e., Ensign.

20:54   [COURT ORDER CONCERNING SOME MEADOWLAND
        CLAIMED BY WM. TOM][1]

                     At a speciall Court etc.

        In the Case of the Inhabitants of Verdreetyes Hooke[2] in
this River, complayning that Mr. William Tom doth molest them
in the Enjoyment of the Meadow Ground next to their Plantacions,
and Mr. Tom making clayme thereunto by Vertue of a Patent obtayned by him from Coll. Richard Nicolls, The necessity of the
Petitioners for the said Meadow, or a sufficient proporcion of
it and Mr. Toms Allegacions being discourst and taken into Consideracion As also Mr. Toms Proposall[3] That is to say That
those of Verdreetyes Hooke should by Consent[4] Enjoy the said
Meadow in Question Provided That hee the said Mr. Tom, might
have liberty to admitt the Inhabitants of some other Neighbors
Plantacion who stood in Need thereof, to have equall[5] benefit
likewise of some of the Meadow next unto them (there being
sufficient for them all,) and that the said Mr. Tom should
likewise reserve freedom of Commonage there for himselfe; The
same said Proposall was allowed and ordred accordingly

                     By order etc.

[Endorsed:] No. 23 Mr. William Tom, and the Inhabitants of
             Verdreeties Hooke, about some Meadow. May 1675

---

1. Written in the hand of Matthias Nicolls.

2. i.e., Verdrietige Hook.

3. Proposall was inserted here to replace: making of
   Moderacion betweene them and his clayme, which was
   crossed out.

4. should by Concent was inserted here to replace: might
   have liberty, which was crossed out.

5. equall was inserted here to replace: the, which was
    crossed out.

20:55   [DECLARATION IN A SUIT AGAINST CAPT. CARR]

                        To the Right Honnorable
                        Mayor Edmund Andros
                        Governor Gennerall under his
                        Royall Highnesse and his
                        Honnorable Councel and
                        Court now Sitting at New
                        Castel in delowar.

Gabriell Minvielle Plt.
         Contra
Capt. John Carr Deft.

        The plt. declares that this deft. became indebted unto
him in the Yeare 1671 for Linning[1] Sould unto him at New
Yorke the Summe of f521: wampum vallue to be paid in
Small furres uppon demand wich summe this plt. hath not
Received to this day, wich Caused him to Commence this
his Sute humbly praying that Your honnor will be pleased
to Grant the plt. Judgement against the said deft. or
his Estate here in these parts for the payment of the
said summe together with Cost, and this plt. shall ever
pray etc:

[Endorsed:]   No. 24   Mr. Minvielle Plt.
              The Estate of ⎫ Deft.
              Capt. Carre   ⎭

        allowed as an Attachment 1675[2]

_____

1. i.e., linen.

2. This notation and the endorsement are written in the
    hand of Matthias Nicolls.

20:56   [DIRECTIONS FOR A SPECIAL COURT TO BE HELD
         AT NEW CASTLE][1]

At the Meeting of this speciall
Court to bee held by the Governor
this 13th day of May 1675, in
Newcastle, Let these directions
bee observed.

At the first meeting of the Court, The Cryer is to make
Proclamacion and say O yes, O yes, O yes: Silence is commanded
in the Court, whilst his Royall Highnesse Governor, Councell
and Justices, are sitting, upon paine of Imprisonment. This
is to bee said by the Cryer, after the Clarke.

Then the names of those appointed by the Governor to sitt
in Court, if it bee the Governors pleasure, of which you will
have a list. The which are to bee distinctly read one after
the other; Those present to answer to their names, the absent
to bee markt. After that, Let the Cryer againe make Proclamacion of O yes, And say, All manner of persons that have
any thing to doe, at this speciall Court now held by his Royall
Highnesse Governor, draw neare, and give your attendance; And
if any one shall have any Plaint to enter or suite to prosecute, Let them come forth and they shall bee heard.

Upon calling of the Docket The Cryer shall after the
Clarke, call for the Plaintiffe: A . B . Come forth and prosecute thy Action against C . D . or else thou wilt bee non-
suited. Then the Cryer upon his Appearance, shall call for the
Defendant. C.D. come forth and save thee and thy bayle, or
else thou wilt forfeit thy Recognizance.

When the Court Adjournes. The Clarke shall say, and the
Cryer after him, All manner of Persons, who have had any thing
to doe, at this speciall Court, they are for the present
dismist, and are to give their Attendance here againe at
[blank] of the clock, in the afternoone, or tomorrow morning by
[blank] of the clock.

When the Court is ended, The Cryer after Proclamacion
shall say after the Clarke, All manner of persons, who have
given their Attendance, or had any thing to doe at this speciall
Court, They are dismist from giving any farther Attendance
thereon: The said speciall Court being dissolved.

Present

The Governor   Go. Carteret
The Sec.   C. Salisbury
                 Mr. Minvielle
                 Mr. Cornell

The names of the Justices
for Newcastle, and first
Capt. Edmond Cantwell High Sheriffe   For the River
Mr. Hans Block   ⎫   Mr Peter Cock
Mr. John Moll   ⎪   Mr. Peter Rambo
Mr. Foppe Outhout   ⎬ Justices   Mr Israel Helme
Mr. Joseph Chew   ⎪   ab.xMr Laes Andriesen[2]
Mr. Dirck Alberts   ⎭   Mr Woole Swain
The Clarke   Justices

For the Whorekill
ab. Mr Hermanus Wiltbanck ⎫
ab. Mr. John Avery   ⎬ Justices
ab. Mr Sander Meulesteyn ⎪
    Mr Jan Kipshaven   ⎭

[Endorsed:] Directions for the Court
             Newcastle May 13 1675
             When the Governor was there.

────────────────────────

1. Written in the hand of Matthias Nicolls.

2. The ab. before this name and those justices from the
   Whorekill indicate absentees. The significance of the
   x is unknown.

20:57   [PRESENTMENT OF JAMES SANDYLANDS FOR MANSLAUGHTER;
         JUDGMENT OF THE COURT THEREON][1]

                    A Presentment

     Edmond Cantwell High Sheriffe of Delaware doth present to
this Court, for our Soveraigne Lord the King; That by Informacion brought unto him, hee hath heard, That James Sandylands of Uplands in this River, at a certain time in the last
Fall; about the month of Sept. or October did with force and
violence, thrust out of his dewlling house, in the place
aforesaid, a certaine Indyan commonly called or known by the
name of Peeques. Whereby the said Indyan fell to the Ground,
without the doores and (as is supposed) by the said Fall was
sorely bruised in his body, whereby in some short time after,
That is to say within the space of two Months hee dyed: The
which being against the Peace of our Soveraigne Lord the King,
and the Lawes of this Government in such Cases provided: Hee
the said High Sheriffe brings this Presentment against the
said James Sandylands, now Prisoner upon suspicon of the said
Fact.

                              [Signed:] Ed. Cantwell

[Verso:] All manner of Persons may hereby take Notice that
James Sandylands who stood presented to this Court upon
suspicion of being guilty of the death of one Peeques an Indyan
of which being acquitted by a lawfull Jury is by Judgement of
Court cleared and is hereby proclaymed accordingly.

[Endorsed:] No. 19 The Presentment of James Sandylands
             Newcastle May . 13 . 1675. The Jury acquitting
             him Hee was ordered to bee cleared by Proclamacion.

────────────────────────

1. Written in the hand of Matthias Nicolls.

20:58   [SHIPPING PERMIT FOR JOHN MOLL AND PARTNERS][1]

By the Governor

Upon the Request of Mr John Moll Merchant, an Inhabitant
of this place, I doe consent that the said Mr.
Moll and par-
tners have permission for a ship or vessell with her loading
to come from New England or any other his Magesties Dominions
allowed of by Act of Parliament, directly to this Place, and
to loade or fraight her out againe, hee making due Entryes and
paying the Customes, to such officers as are or shall bee
appointed in this Towne; This liberty to continue for the
space of one yeare after the date hereof: Given under my hand
at Newcastle in Delaware River this 13th day of May 1675.

[Endorsed:]   No. 28 Liberty graunted to Mr John Moll and
Partners, to have a Ship or other Vessell with
English Goods to come and unload here. 13th May
1675.

_____

1. Written in the hand of Matthias Nicolls.

20:59   [PETITION OF JACOBUS FABRICIUS CONCERNING A CHARGE
OF RIOTOUS CONDUCT][1]

To the honorable Mayer Edmond Andros
Governor Generall under his Royal Highnesse of all his Territoryes in America.

The humble Peticion of Jacobus Fabricius.

Sheweth your honors humble Peticioner as that your honor
having beene pleased to send a warrant to New Castle, ordering
your Peticioner forthwith to make his personall appearance
before your honor in this place, to make answer, to what shall
bee objected against your honors Peticioner concerning a disturbance hapned at Delaware in New Castle the 4th day of June
Last, in contemning and Disobeing the orders Sett forth by the
Magistrates in a riotous manner. In obedience to your honors
order and comand, your honors Peticioner doth appeare before
your honor and as for what is Laid u[ ]on him your honors
Peticioner finds himselfe not guilty as may appeare by Severall
wittnesses.

Therefore its your honors Peticioner humble Request, that
an order may be given with a comission to examine the Burgers
and Inhabitants of New Castle whether your honors Peticioner
ha[ ] beene tumultuous against the Mag[   ]ates [   ]
whether hee has given base Language to the powers, or came
armed or had any weapons, or made any resistance. To the contrary thereof your honors peticioner being desired by the
people to speake for them, was affrontuously dealt by the
Commander there: upon the Returne of the examinacion;

your honors peticioner hopes your honor to be better informed,
and shall Know the very truth; and to judge that your honors
Peticioner is much wrongd, and damaged in coming hether, in
loosing his time and leaving his employment with dayly expences: which your honor bee pleased to consider, and to give
Such order, that after your honors Peticioner is cleared of
the accusation Laid on him, his costs, expenses, damages and
Loss of tyme may bee allowed to him; not being reasonable to
bee So much troubled in a vexatious cause

And your honors peticioner Shall ever pray

[Endorsed:]   The humble Peticon of Magister Jacobus Fabricius
1675

---

1. Other transcription in NYCD 12:521. See 20:68 for the
   report on the "riot."

20:60   [PETITION FOR A GRANT OF LAND ON THE DELAWARE][1]

Right honireabill Ed: Andros governor

For we thought good to propound Fewe things unto your
honners Considireation for the seatilment of our selves and
famelies at the Falles of delaway Riv[ ]

First: we Request of your honner Such a trackt of Land
in the please aforesaid Contayneing Fowar thousand eakers of
Land lying by the River that is to saye Fowar mile above the
fales and fowar miles belowe with the ylands thereby and that
the yland callid by the name of Mr. Olderidges yland[2] may be
procuarid For us and that your honner wolde be pleased to give
us such a Pattin For the same where by it maye be Confermid
unto our selves and ayares or Sucksesars For ever and besids
this Fowar thousand eakeres of Land we Request a nother parte
of Land to ley as Comman and Free From any payments but For
the Fowar thousand Akers afar the expireation of 7 yeres
paying For evry hondred eakeres one scipill of wheate yerely
shall then be Freid From any other payments as to the publick.

2ly that we maye have our Liberty in point of worship and
the Choise of our owne ministar and that nothing may be imposed upon him which may be ofensive unto his Consho[ ][3]

3ly that we may have the Liberty For the judeing [sic] of
such difarans[ ][4] as may any way hapin amongt as to give a
Finall determinat[ ] thereof exsept of mattars which moste
properly belong to the Courte of Asisis.

That we maye have the Liberty of treade and make the
b[ ] of what we shall Rayes or any waye produce and tran-
cep[   ][5] into any parts of his maiestyes dominyones either
yorke, Boston or berbatos or where we maye make the best of
wh[ ] we shall any waye produce Previdid we paye the King[ ]

Custom as in new yorke we then be Free to trancepor[   ] it
where we please without any Furdar payments

[Endorsed:]   [   ] [ ]675
              [   ] of Land att Delowerr fals.

---

1. The petitioners' names do not appear on the document.
   Other transcription in NYCD 12:521.

2. i.e., Peter Alrichs' Island.

3. i.e., conscience.

4. i.e., differences.

5. i.e., transport.

20:61   [FRAGMENT OF A MEMORANDUM BOOK KEPT BY MATTHIAS
         NICOLLS WHILE GOV. ANDROS WAS VISITING DELAWARE][1]

         [top portion destroyed   ]

         An order abou[   ]etching [   ] guns above in the River,
         [   ] two smaller up the River.
11.   An warrant of Survey of 1000 Acres to Mr. Cantwell for
         Mr. Pitts a Quacker, to put in to Account
13.   The 3 Commissions for the Jurisdictions, delivered in
         Court after they were sworne. C. Cantwells Commission
         of High Sheriffe and hee sworne.
14.   Yesterday the Military Officers of this Towne had their
         Commissions,[2] this day those of the Whorekill and
         Apoquemini, to Capt. Jos: Chew of Appoqu[   ]. Delivered
         Mr. Moll A Graunt to bring a Vessell direct hither and
         goe back, for a yeare[3]; another A warrant for him and
         Mr. Ward to C. Cantwell to lay out a Considerable
         Quantity of land.
15.   Delivered severall Orders of Court
         1.   to the wid: Young.
         1.   to Ralph Hutchinson.
         1.   To Sam: Edsall for Mrs. Young
         3.   more to him - betweene him and Oryon.

         [top portion destroyed   ]

         his fine [   ] my hand. I have of him a good offer.
         The hue and Cry to one Pitcher [   ] 3 Run-awayes.
         and a Copie taken of his warrant from the Chance Rd of
         Maryland. hee saith C. W. Dyre will pay.

         Mem. I left with Capt Cantwell C. Carrs, Mr. Whartons and
         Mr Toms Accounts with the old Accounts of mine to Mr
         Wharton - A Copie I have.

To remeber for him An account of the Fees as Surveyd, and Sheriffe, To Mr Tom, as Clarke, his Fee,

I gave Will: Oryons Engagemt to pay 3 - actions - with C. Cantwell.

A Graunt to C. Cantwell to servey 400 acres for James Crawford.

Given C. Cantwell the Rem.[4] of the orders, most double,

[top portion destroyed   ]

A warrant to C. Ca[ ]well to survey. 300 - acres of Land at the Who[ ]ekill for Tho: Evans, 400 - for Rich: Fli[ ], and 200 - for James Chisham. To pay when the Patent comes:

[Endorsed:]   [   ] when [   ]s in [   ]ware.
            May 1675

---

1. Only the final two pages of this memorandum book survive.

2. See 20:53 for the form of these commissions.

3. See 20:58 for a copy of this grant.

4. Perhaps an abbreviation of "remainder."

20:62   [CONFERENCE BETWEEN GOV. ANDROS AND FOUR INDIAN CHIEFS][1]

At Newcastle May 13th 1675

Upon an Appearance of the Indyans before the Go: and the New Magistrates in the afternoone, They were those who came in the morne, with Mr. S. Edsall, Mr. Izr: Helme and Lausa Cock. The names of the Cheifs were Renowewan of Sawkin on the Easterne side, Ihakickan of Rancokes kill Ketmarcas of Soupnapka, Manichty of Rancokes kill heretofore all of N. Jersy side The Governor delcares his desire to continue in friendship with them, and his readines to protect them and thanks them for their coming downe.

They by Izrael Helme the Interpreter expresse their readinesse to continue in good friendship, and returne their thanks to the Go.

They are told that it is not that the Governor wants their helpe, if the other Indyans will bee bad, hee can deale well enough with them but is willing to bee kind to those that will live quietly and well.

They believe so they say.

They are told they must not Kill the beasts or swine belonging to the Christians, and the Christians shall not doe them any Injury, but Justice shall bee done, as they might see today in the Case of James Sandylands.

The first Sachem rises up and walkes up and downe taking notice of his old Acquaintance P Rambo and Peter Cock, Lausa Cock with C Cantwell then taking a band of Sewant, he measured it from his neck to the length downeward and [   ] his heart should bee so long and so good to the Go. and the Christians, and should neer forget the Go. So presents the belt of Wampam, throwing it at the Go. feet.

The next rises up and professing much friendship and thanks to the Go. for his kind Expressions presents another belt of wampam.

The Go. tells them the two belts shall bee Kept as bands of friendship betweene them.

The belts of Sewant were written upon, to bee kept in token of a continuance of Peace.

The first belt was 15, t'other 12-wamp: high

The Go: presents them with 4 Coates and 4 lapp Cloathes.

They returne thankes and fall a Kintecoying[2] with expressions of thankes: singing Kenow, Kenow.

[Endorsed:]   No. 32 The Indyans Appearance before the Go: at Newcastle. May 13 1675.

---

1. Written in the hand of Matthias Nicolls. Other transcription in NYCD 12:523.

2. A lively social gathering which includes dancing. c.f., 20:14, F.N. 2.

20:63a   Actions entered for Tryall and some other Matters to bee called upon at the speciall Court to bee held by the Governor at Newcastle in Delaware May the 13th 1675.[1]

Samuell Edsall.............Plt.
x William Oryon..............Deft.
In an action of the Case.

Samuell Edsall as Attorney⎫
x   to John Sharpe.........⎭ Plt.
William Oryon..............Deft.
In an action of Debt.

```
  William Oryon...............Plt.
x Samuell Edsall..............Deft.
  In an action of debt to the
  value of, or for the summe
  of 175 Guilders sewant.
```

```
  A Presentment by the Sheriffe against James Sandylands
x about the death of an Indyan.2
```

All Claymes that shall bee brought in for Titles etc.

Several Petitions etc.

```
  A Memorandum About Bridges and Highwayes, and that a Ditch
x bee made through a Swampe at one End of the Towne, and a
  Ditch or banck through that at the other.
```

```
  Matthias Nicolls.......Plt.
  Capt. John Carr........Deft.
```

```
  Gabriel Minvielle......Plt.
x Capt. John Carr........Deft.
```

[Endorsed:] No. 18 The Docket Newcastle May 13 1675.

---

1. This document is written in the hand of Matthias Nicolls.
   See 20:63b and 64 for the proceedings of this special
   court.

2. See 20:57 for this presentment.

20:63b   At a speciall Court held at Newcastle in
          Delaware. May 13th 1675.1

Present
The Go: etc.

The Dukes Commission to the Go: read.

The Sheriffes Commission read and hee sworne.

The 3 Commissions for Newcastle, Upland and
Whorekill read, and those present sworne.2

The orders of Regulacion read.

The bench called over and placed on the Go; left
hand, Go: Carteret on the right with C. Salis-
bury3 Mr. Minvielle and Mr. [   ] next Mr.
Tom.

A Jury empanneld-vizt. Mr. Sam: Edsall, Mr.
Tho: Wandall, Mr. Jos: Smith, Mr. John Jackson,
Mr. Wm. Osburne.

The Jury.

{ Mr. John Desjardins, Marti Rosamond, Otto Ernest,
Hendr: Jansen, Gysbert Dircksz, Henry Jones,
Ralph Hutchinson.

James Sandylands brought to make answer to a
Presentment[4] brought in against him by the
Sheriffe for a suspicion of being the cause of
the death of an Indyan.   The Presentment read.
Hee pleads to it not guilty; and relates the
whole manner of the Indyans being at his house
and his putting him out of doors etc.

Severall Indyans being brought downe from Peter
Rambo's this morning, by Sam: Edsall, Izr:
Helme and Laus Cock, who went up for them, they
were sent for to the Court, to heare the Tryall.

Mr. Izrael Helme Interpreter.

One of the cheife Indyans relates the matter as
hee heard it, but disagrees about the time the
Indyan lived after his fall. Saying it was but
about 5 dayes, and others 6 or 8 weekes.

The difference betweene wilfull murder and
accidentall delcared to them.

James Sandylands hath leave of the Court to
speake [   ] Indyans.

Another Indyan saith hee lived two months.

The Go: having given the Charge to the Jury,
They goe out upon the matter.

The Peticion of Michael Judd, wherein Jacob
Young is concerned, Hee being absent, It put
off till tomorrow.

The like of Sarah Young and Children; Hee being
therein concerned also.

The Peticion of James Boyde about Goods sold at
an Outcry here, to pay a debt to Mr. Tom. Mr.
Cornell, Mr. Osburne and Ralph Hutchinson Att.
for Boyde.

x { The Proceedings being found irregular, The
Sherriffe is to make good the value the Goods
were sold for, and the persons who bought them
to bee accomptable to him:
The Determinacion to bee left to the Law
To bee heard to morrow morne. 8 a clock.

x { A peticion of Henry Jacobsz against monsr. Peter
Jegoe about a bargaine for a still, which hee
complaines of and would bee releast.
To bee referred to a Rehearing at the next
Court at Upland

The Jury bring in their Verdict, That they find
the prisoner not to bee Guilty. He is ordered
to bee cleared by Proclamacion.[5]

Fryday May 14 1675.

Sam: Edsall - as Att. to John Sharpe...Plt.
Wm. Oryon.............................Deft.

A bill is produced for 54 G. 8 st. The Deft.
denyes the bill. Its only his marke. The Plt.
shews a deposicion from Mr. Richbell sworne
before Mr. Delavall acknowledging a debt but
no certain summe.

x
{ The Deft. to give security to answer the Action
at N. Y., or the Plts. Att. upon his paying the
debt, to give security to make good the bill
or answer the determinacion of the Law, with
all Costs and damej[   ]

Samuell Edsall - plt.
William Oryon - deft.

A delaracion put in by the Plt. against the
Deft. about taking away a Canooe from his
Plantacion etc. and enticing away 2 servants.
The Deft. denyes taking the Canooe
Its prooved by his owne Confession before Mr.
Des Jardin Champagne and James Sandylands.
Hee denyes taking the servants with him, but
its proved one only was a servant.

x
{ The Deft. to pay the Action, or give security
[   ] it upon the place in N Jersey.

William Oryon - plt.
Samuell Edsall - deft.

Hee demands 175 g. due for curing of 4 horses
and looking after his horses.

x
{ The Plt. making nothing appeare is non suited.

The Peticion of Sarah Young in behalfe of her-
selfe and Children being read.
An order of Cort. in the Dutch time.
Her son in Lawe's deed of Guift[6] produced.
T'was alleadged he was under age when hee did it.
That the former order of Cort. stand Good, and
the deed of the son Confirmed.

The peticion of Michael Judd.
In the absence of Jacob Young, his wife appears
to answer the Complaint.

x
{ The first bond to bee paid as performer order
of Court.
hee to have his remedy for the 1st. etc.

The businesse of Boyde about the Chest of Goods
etc.

x
{ referred to this morning.
The Goods or Value to remaine in the Sherriffes
hands till the law determines who they belong to.

Ralph Hutchinsons peticion about Mr. Richbells
debt Respited till Mr. Laurence's letter bee
seene, which C. Cantwell hath Afterwards
ordered That the former Judgements should bee
allowed, and the pretended Attachment of Goods
in the hands of Capt. Cantwell bee taken off.

Mr. Will. Tom and those of Verdrietys Hooke
about Meadows.   The same as in Coll. Lovelaces
time.
Mr. Toms proposall accepted by the Court That
the Inhabitants shall have proporcionable Meadow there So hee may have liberty to dispose of
the remainder to oth[ ] and have the use of
Commonage himselfe.[7]

That the Magistrates up the River have liberty
to build a Church at Wiccakoe, to bee for the
Inhabitants above Passayunck, with power to
raise a taxe for its building and to agree upon
Maintenance for the Minist[ ] and give account
of it to the Generall Court, and from thence
to [ ] Governor.

For Upland etc. The Church at Tinnicum Island.
For Crane Hooke another.

The buisnesse for the highwayes taken into
Consideracion.
That some way bee made passable betweene Towne
and Towne.
That C. Carrs meadow at the Townes North End
being represented to the Court to bee a great
Nusance to the Towne as it lyes, there being
neither bridge nor fitting way to passe, and the
Towne being in great ruan thereof: It is
ordered That the said Meadow Ground shall be
apprized by different persons, and the Towne to
have the refusell, Condicionaly[ ] if they have
it that the maintaine sufficient bridges and
ways through their limitts, To bee a Cartway.
The Apprizers to bee 2 appointed by the Magistrates of the Towne, and 2 by the Court of Uplands and that the Apprizement bee returned to
the next Court in the Towne.

As to the small piece of Swampe on the Souths[ ]
of the Towne, to bee ditched within one month
by [ ] Owners if any, otherwise to bee done by
the Towne, within a month after, and to enjoy it.

A prohibicion for selling strong Liquors to the
Indyans by retayle, or lesse than two Gallons.
penalty 5 lb. Go: Carteret will give the like
order.

No Corne or Graine to bee distill'd in the River,
pen[ ] 5 lb.

That these Orders about highways bridges etc.
bee put in Execucion by the Magistrates within
[ ] space of three months after the date
hereof, or the sheriffe shall have power to
have it done and the Countrey to pay double the
Charge.

A Ferry boate to bee maintayned at the Falls on
the Westside, A Horse and Man to pay 2 g.   A
Man 10 st.

The buisnesse of Mr. Tom and Dirck Alberts,
referred by the Court to N. Y., Is by the Court
referred to the Magistrates to view or cause
x   the Ground [   ] to bee viewed, and if they
doe not thinke it proper to determine it, Then
to returne their Report and Judgments thereof
to the Go: for a finall Determinacion.

George Moores peticion for Administracion,
which was refused by the Court.
It is to bee graunted by the Magistrates
x   according to Law. Hee making proofe of the
Nuncupative Will of the deceased.

Gabr. Minvielle........Plt.
The Estate of C. Carr...Deft.

His debt 521 g.
The same to bee entred, and to have his Remedy
x   at Law against the Estate, and this to bee as
an Attachment.

x   James Sandylands cleared by Proclamacion.

The next Generall Court to begin the 2nd Tuesday in May next, unlesse called upon extraordinary Occasion.

[Endorsed:]   Proceedings in the speciall court at Newcastle.
May 13.14-75

---

1. See 20:64 for a later draft of most of these same proceedings written in a more expanded prose style. Other
transcription in NYCD 12:524.

2. See 20:53 for the form of these commissions.

3. i.e., Capt. Silvester Salisbury.

4. See 20:57 for this presentment.

5. This is the verdict in the James Sandylands case.

6. i.e., deed of gift.

7. See 20:54 for the court's decision in this matter.

20:64   At a speciall Court held by the Go: at Newcastle
in Delaware River, the 13th and 14th dayes of
May 1675.[1]

It was ordered As followeth

1. That the Church, or place of Meeting for divine worship,
   in this Towne and the affayres thereunto belonging bee
   regulated by the Court here in as orderly and decent
   manner as may bee.

2. That the place for meeting at Crane hooke, Doe continue as
   heretofore.

3. That the Church at Tinnicom Island Do serve for Upland and
   parts adjacent,

4. And whereas there is no Church or place of meeting higher
   up the River then the said Island for the greater Ease and
   Convenience of the Inhabitants there Its ordered that the
   Magistrates Doe cause a Church or p[lace of] Meeting for
   that purpose to bee built at Wickakoe, the which to bee
   for the Inhabitants of Passayunck and so upwards, The
   said Court being empowered to raise a Tax for its building,
   and to agree upon a competent Maintenance for their Minister, of all which they are to give an account to the next
   Generall Court, and they to the Governor for his Approbacion.

   The buisnesse for Highwayes being taken into Consideracion,
It was ordered, That some convenient way bee made passable betweene Towne and Towne in this River, The manner of doeing it,
to bee ordered by the respective Courts, and likewise the
Charge.

   And That Capt. Carres Meadow at the North End of the Towne,
being represented to the Court to be a generall[2] Nusance to
this place and Country[3] as it now lyes, there being neither
bridge nor fitting way to passe by, or through it and that
the Towne is in great straight for want of it as they might
improve it: It is ordered, That the said Meadow Ground shall
bee apprized by indifferent Persons and the Towne to have the
refusall, but whosoever shall enjoy it shall bee obliged to
maintaine sufficient bridges and wayes through the limitts
thereof, with a Cartway; The Apprizers to bee two persons
appointed by the Magistrates of this place, and two more, by
the Court of Upland and the Apprizement to bee returned in
to the next Court held in this Towne.

   As to the small piece of Low Ground or Swampe on [sou]th
side of the Towne It being in like manner represented as a
Nusance It is ordered to bee dit[ched] within one month in order
to its draining, by the Owners if any, Otherwise to bee done
by the Towne within one month after the Expiracion of the
former, and they to enjoy it for the time to come.[4]

   That the orders about highwayes, bridges etc. bee put in
Execucion by the Magistrates within whose precincts they shall
bee in the time of 3 months after the date hereof, or the
Sherriffe shall have power to get it done and the Country to
pay double the Charge for their Defaults.

   That a Ferry boate bee maintained and kept at the Falls
on the West side of this River, A horse and man to pay for
Transportacion 2g. A man without horse - 10 st.

   That care bee taken for the erecting of Mills in
convenient places.[5]

That there bee a Prohibicon against selling strong drinke
or Liquors to the Indyans by Retayle or a lesse Quantity then
two Gallons at a time, under the penalty of five pounds for
any such offence.

And that no Corne or Graine bee distilled by any of the
Inhabitants in this Place, River, or Bay under the like penalty
of five pounds.

That the Generall Court to bee held in this place for the
Towne, River and Bay doe begin the 2d Tuesday in the Month of
May next, which shall bee in the yeare 1676 Unlesse upon
extraordinary occasion, It shall bee called before.

> At a speciall Court held by the
> Governor at Newcastle in Delaware
> River the 13th and 14th dayes of
> May 1675.

The Petition of James Boyde being presented to this
Court by Mr. William Osburne, as his Attorney, wherein hee
Complaines that a certaine Chest of the petitioners with Goods
herein had beene condemned in Court not long since by the
Magistrates of this place and exposed to [   ] by the
Sheriffe as belonging unto one Tarkenton The matter having
beene debated, and the former Proceedings judged Irregular.
It is ordered, That the Sheriffe shall make good the value of
the Goods at the Rate they were sold for, and the persons who
bought the said Goods are to bee accomptable for them to him,
The same to remaine in his hands undisposed of, Till the Law
shall determine more clearely to whom the said Goods did
belong.

> By order of the Governor and
> speciall Court

At a speciall Court etc.

The Peticion of Henry Jacobs, being taken into Consideracion wherein hee complaines against Mr. Peter Jegoe, for
sueing him at the Court of Uplands upon pretence of a bargaine
for a certaine Still, for the which hee obtayned Judgment
against the Petitioner in his absence It is ordered to bee
referred to a Rehearing at the next Court of Justices, to bee
held in the said Towne of Upland, who are to give their
Judgment therein and determine the same accordingly.

> By order etc.

At a speciall Court etc.

Samuell Edsall as Att.
    to John Sharpe........plt.
Wm. Oryon...............deft.

The plt. producing a bill of 54g. 8 st. signed in the name
of the Deft., with a Marke, the which hee denyes to bee his
act, disowning the debt likewise, the which the plt. could not
make punctuall proofe of in this Court, It is ordered that the
Deft. give security to answer the action at a Court in New
Yorke, within 3 months after the date hereof; Otherwise upon
his paying the debt, the plts. Att. shall bee obliged to give

security to make good the bill, or abide the determinacion of
the Law, and pay all Cost and damages
By order etc.

At a Court etc.

Samuel Edsall plt.
William Oryen deft.

The plt. complaining that the deft. had borrowed a Canooe
of his Overseer at his Plantacion in New Jersey, the which hee
hath not returned, but converted to his owne use, and that the
Deft. did likewise entice away a servant of the plts.; It is
ordered that the Deft. do forthwith make satisfaction to the
Plt. for his action, or that hee give security to answer the
suite in New Jersey, where the Cause of Action did ari[ ]e
within the time of 3 months after the date hereof
By order etc.

At a Court etc.

William Oryon Plt.
Samuell Edsall Deft.

The Plt. demanding the sume of 175 Guilders as due to him
from the deft. for worke done by him as a Smith or Farrier,
between 9 and 10 yeares agoe, The same not appearing, or that
hee ever demanded such a Debt from the Deft. ever since, The
Court doe order a Nonsuite and that hee pay the Costs of
Court
By order etc.

At a Court etc.

Another   The peticion of Michael Judde being taken into Con-
copie[6]   sideracion, wherein hee desires to be freed from an
           Obligacion of 8000 wt. of Tobacco wherein hee is
jointly and sevarally bound with one Evan Salisbury to Mr.
Jacob Young, and that hee may have the benefit of a bond of
10 lb. given him by the said Evan Salisbury condicionally to
save him harme lesse from all bargains, Contracts etc. betweene
them: It is ordered that the first bond doe stand good against
the petitioner as per former order of Court, and for the last
hee may have his Remedy at Law.
By order etc.

At a Court etc.

The Peticion of Sarah Young being taken into Consideracion,
wherein shee desires to bee possest of the Estate which was
left by her husband, towards the maintenance of her selfe and
three small Children for the which shee obtayned an order of
Court in the time of the late Dutch Government; And also that
the Petr. may enjoy a parcell of Land of her husbands conveyed unto her and her children by her son in Law, the eldest
son of her husband; It is ordered, that the order of Court
heretofore made shall stand good, That is, that what shall
remaine of her husbands Estate after debts paid, shall bee to
the use of the petitioner and her Children, and that the land
remaine likewise to the uses in the deed Exprest.
By order etc.

At a Court etc.

The matter in difference betweene Mr. Will Tom, and Dirck
Alberts about the limitts of two Lotts here in the Towne,
referred heretofore by their Court to bee determined at New
Yorke, The same being taken into Consideracion, It is ordered
that the Case bee remitted back to the Magistrates of this
place, to view or cause the Ground in dispute to bee view'd,
and if they cannot or shall not thinke it proper for them to
decide Then to make Report of the whole matter and their
opinions thereupon to the Go. for his finall order and
determinacion.

By order etc.

At a Court etc.

Upon a declaracion of debt put in to the Court by Mr.
Gabriel Minvielle against Capt. John Carre or his Estate in
these parts, It being for the sume of 571 g. sewant or value,
The Court doe allow of the said clayme of Mr. Minvielle as
an Attachment upon the Estate of the said C. Carre, the which
hee hath liberty to prosecute according to due course of Law.

By order etc.

At a Court etc.

The Petition of George Moore being taken into consideracion, wherein hee desires Letters of Administracion upon a Verball
or Nuncupative will made by Thom[ ] Lane deceased wherein hee
named him his Executo[ ] hee having upon presumption thereof
paid already to me of his Debts, Its' ordered that the Court
of Justices of this Towne, doe graunt Letters of Administracion of the Estate of the said Tho: Lane within this
Government unto the Petitioner, according to custome, and the
directives in the Law sett forth.

By order etc.

At a Court etc.[7]

The case of the Inhabitants of Verdreetge Hooke and Mr.
William Toms being taken into Consideracion. the former urging
                        their Necessity as the Latter Coll. Nicolls patent
To bee   } for the Meadow Ground there, It was agreed that
rectifyde } each Lott of the Inhabitants there should have a
                        sufficient proporcion or Quantity of Meadow for
their Convenience, and that Mr. Tom may have liberty to dispose of the Remainder to such as shall have occasion, Retening
also freedome of Commonage to himselfe.

By order etc.

At a Court etc.

The Case of James Sandylands being taken into Consideracion, who having beene a Prisoner and presented to this
Court by the Sheriffe, upon suspicion of being Guilty of the
death of one Peeques an Indyan and acquitted of the same by a
Lawfull Jury, Hee was by the Judgment of Court cleared, and so
proclaymed accordingly.

By order etc.

---

1. The following court minutes represent an expanded

prose version of those proceedings which appear in
20:63b. They do not cover all of those proceedings
because the final pages of this document are missing.
This copy of the court minutes has undergone considerable revision, especially in the first entry concerning
the churches. The other transcription in NYCD 12:526
neither reflects any of these changes nor represents
the complete document. See NCCR:46 for copy of the orders.

2. generall replaces: great, which is crossed out.

3. to this place and Country replaces: to the Towne,
    which is crossed out.

4. for the time to come replaces: afterwards, which is
    crossed out.

5. This entry is completely crossed out.

6. This notation appears in the margin.

7. This entire case is crossed out. The indented
    notation appears in the margin.

20:65a   [PROVISIONAL GRANT OF LAND TO DR. JOHN DES JARDINS][1]

By the Governor

Upon the Peticion of Dr. John Des Jardins making request
that I would give him my Graunt for a certaine Trace of Land,
lyeing in St. Jones Creeke in Apoquemini in this River, heretofore graunted by Patent to one Dr. [blank] Wale[2], but
(as is by him alleadged) is elapsed and escheated by the death
of the said Dr. and his son to become at my disposall. To the
End the said Land may not lye vacant, but that some good Improvement may bee made thereon, I have thought fitt to graunt
the Petitioners Request, and if within the space of one yeare
and six weekes or such reasonable time as the Law doth direct,
no Relacion of the deceased shall appeare and make lawfull
clayme thereunto I shall graunt a Patent of Confirmacion for
the same. Given under my hand at Newcastle in Delaware River
May 15th 1675.

[Endorsed:] No. 26 A Graunt to Doctor John Des Jardin for
             some Land at Apoquiminy. 15th May. 1675.

---

1. Other transcription in NYCD 12:527.

2. This is possibly George Whale Sr. who was granted 400
    acres of land on St. Jones' Creek in 1671. See DYR:148
    for the confirmation of this patent.

20:65b   [PETITION OF MRS. PETERNELLA CARR GRANTED][1]

By the Governor

Upon the Petition and Request of Mrs. Peternella Carre on
the behalfe of her selfe and Children, that her husbands[2] debts
may bee paid out of the Estate hee left here and that the Remainder may bee at the Petitioners disposall for the releife of
her selfe and children, I doe consent to and hereby Graunt what
is in the said Peticion desired, That is to say, Thatt all
lawfull debts being first paid, the Residue shall remaine to
the use of the Petitioner and Children. To which End I have
ordered the sheriffe to take off the Attachment or warrant of
Seizure layd thereon by my order, the patriculars in the
peticion relating to Accounts and Charges etc. are to bee
determined by the Court.[3] Given under my hand at Newcastle in
Delaware River the 15 day of May 1675.

[Endorsed:]   No. 27 Governors Graunt to Mrs. Carre, on behalfe
of her selfe and Children. 15th May 1675.

---

1. Written in the hand of Matthias Nicolls.

2. Capt. John Carr.

3. This last sentence beginning with: To which End...,
   is crossed out.

20:65c   At a Court at Peter Rambo's May. 17. 1675[1]

Present

Peter Cock	The Governor[2]
Peter Rambo	The Secr.[3]
Izrael Helme	C. Ed: Cantwell
Laes Andersen	Mr. Gab: Minvielle
	Mr. Rich: Cornell

The matter under Consideracion was the Scandalous
buisnesse of James Sandylands, and Laurens Hulst.

It was ordered That James Sandylands pay the summe of
300 g and Laurens Hulst 200 The one halfe to bee towards the
building of the new Church at Wickakoe, and the other to the
sheriffe.

Sandylands putt off from being Capt. The Lt. Hans Juriansz
in his place - John Prince Lt. Jonas Keene, Ens.,

[Verso:]   To send a patent to C. Cantwell for Andries Boone
alias Swenske. for a plot or parcell of land amongst
others, scituate lyeing and being in Kinsesse[4]

conteyning by Estimacion ten acres or thereabout bounded upon the South and East by the
Kill, by the land of Swan Gunnersen on the West
and the land of Andrees Dalbo upon the North
with Commonage etc.

Taken out of his bill of sale from Peter Andersen, who
had Patent for this and other land from Coll: R. Nicolls
Jan: 1st. Anno 1667.

[Endorsed:]   James Sandylands and Laurence Hulst fined for
              misbehavior at Peter Rambo's In Delaware.
              May. 17. 1675.

---

1. Written in the hand of Matthias Nicolls. Partly
   transcribed in NYCD 12:527.

2. i.e., Edmund Andros.

3. i.e., Matthias Nicolls.

4. i.e., Kinsessing.

20:66   [PETITION OF THE LUTHERANS AT SWANWYCK AND
         CRANEHOOK][1]

To His Noble, Right Honorable, Major Edmond Andros, Governor-
General of all his Royal Highness', James Duke of York and
Albany etc., Territories in America.

The undersigned petitioners, the community of the unaltered Augsburg Confession, called the Lutheran by people
living on the South River, do declare and make known, with all
due reverence, that the petitioners made an humble request to
his Right Honorable Lord on the 13th of May anno 1675 together
with a document drawn up in the Council at New Castle on the
10th of December anno 1672, in which they divided the river
into two parishes, so that all that is above the Verdritige
Hoeck shall be and remain in the pastorate of Magister Jakobus
Fabricius, which the petitioners' pastor suggested and with
all due humility requested and petitioned that his Noble,
Right Honorable Lord would please to confirm such a document
and division for the glory of God and good order. Whereupon
the petitioners anticipated a favorable reply and recommendation and had also hoped that they would obtain the same
through Capt. E. Kantwel, but since the hasty journey and many
troubles of his Noble, Right Honorable Lord have hindered it,
so that they, the petitioners, do not know to what they shall
have to conform, the petitioners come once again to his Right
Honorable Lord with the humble request, if it pleases, to
confirm the document and division together with their pastor
Magister Jakobus Fabritius and to endow the petitioners with a
favorable reply, doing which they shall remain his Right

Honorable Lord's subjects and intercessors with God.

Done at New Castle   The Community of the unaltered
the first of June   Confession of Augsburg on the
anno 1675   South River belonging to the
                             Churches of Zwaenewyck and
                             Kraenhoek

                    [Signed:] Henrich Janssen
                               Hendrick *Hi* Jansen van Breemen
                               Harman Jansen
                               Piter Volker
                               Peter *Pᶜ* Classen
                               Peter *₰* Witten's mark
                               Corn. Janssen
                               Pieter *₮* Maaslandt
                               Jan *β* Barends
                               Sibrand *₳* Jansen
                               Hinrich *₰* Fransen
                               Willem Jansen
                               Jan Jansen
                               John Nohmers
                               Clos *⊦* Andressen
                               and all the others

[Endorsed:] No. 7 N. Castle in Delaware 1st. of June 1675
             Petition of Luterians Church

---

1. Other translation in <u>NYCD</u> 12:529.

20:67   [ORDER TO CONSTRUCT DIKES AT NEW CASTLE][1]

     Whereas it has been ordered by Gov. Edm. Andross,
Lieutenant General of all the Duke of York's dominions in
America, that the marshland situated on the northside of New
Castle on the Delaware River, belonging to Capt. John Carr,
should be appraised by four impartial persons appointed by the
Magistrates;[2] they have therefore unanimously selected Mr.
Pieter Aldericks, Mr. Johannes de Haes, Mr. Pieter Cock and
Mr. Lars Andriessen, who after inspection judged the marshland
to be of no value.

     Whereupon the aforesaid Magistrates met today and having
decided that the Governor's order to construct a highway can
not be carried out unless an outer-dike with sluices is first
built along the water, they therefore order herewith that each
and every male, who belongs to the district of New Castle,
shall begin work next Monday on the aforesaid outer-dike and
continue to work until the aforesaid outer-dike has been completed. They who work more than their share shall be paid for
their extra work by those who neither work nor hire laborers.
The inhabitants of New Castle shall work on it <u>pro rata</u>, head
for head, just as much as the country people, or pay

proportionally. Furthermore, it is so ordered that Martin
Gerritsen, Pieter de Wit and Hendrick Sybrants shall be, by
turns, officers and commanders of this project and construct
the aforesaid dike ten feet wide at the bottom, five feet high
and three feet wide at the top, providing it with well-made and
strong sluices. The country people shall thereafter not be
obligated to work on the aforesaid outer-dike or sluices
(without being paid for it), but on the other hand, the inhabitants of New Castle shall from time to time be obligated
to keep this outer-dike and sluice in repair under the condition that they shall also derive the profits from the aforesaid marshaland and have it as their own. The aforesaid Magistrates have also decided it to be in the public interest that
the outer-dike, which runs along Mr Hans Block's marshland,
should be repaired and strengthened. We therefore order
herewith that the aforesaid dike, as the other, shall this
time only be repaired and built up by each and every male who
lives in the district and under the jurisdiction of New Castle,
but that thereafter the aforesaid dike and sluice shall be
maintained and from time to time kept in repair by the aforesaid Mr. Hans Block or his heirs.

The laborers shall be divided into three parties by the
aforesaid three officers and each party shall be under the
command of its officer and work for two days at the dike.
Whosoever should refuse to come to work in his turn, or to
send a laborer in his place, shall be obligated to pay
immediately to the aforesaid officer the sum of ten guilders
in sewant for each day missed.

All of the aforesaid work must be completed and finished
to specifications within six weeks under penalty of defaulting
three doubled payments which shall have to be advanced for it
according to law. Thus done and publicized in New Castle this
4th of June anno 1675

                    [Signed:] Ed. Cantwell
                               H. Block
                               John Moll
                               Dirck Albertsen
                               [   ]³

[Endorsed:] No: 5 [   ] N. Castle the Courts order
             in relation to meadow and hy wayes⁴

---

1. This document has suffered extensive damage in several
   places. Material in the damaged portions has been recovered from 20:71 which is a contemporary copy of this
   document. Other translation in NYCD 12:530.

2. See 20:64 for a copy of this order.

3. A portion of the document is torn away below the
   signatures. There is an indication that several
   signatures have been lost, although 20:71 lists only
   the four names given above.

4. 20:71 carries the endorsement: No. 10 Order of the
   Court to make a dike etc. for a Hye Way. Both endorse-
   ments are written in English in the hand of Matthias
   Nicolls.

20:68   [DECLARATION OF THE MAGISTRATES OF NEW CASTLE
        CONCERNING A RIOT OVER THE CONSTRUCTION OF THE
        DIKES][1]

                            Declaration of the undersigned con-
                            cerning what happened June 4th last
                            in the rioting of the town's
                            people due to the construction and
                            repair of two outer-dikes.

    As soon as we had read and made public the order[2] con-
cerning it, John Ogle belligerently stepped forward (in church)
and said: "We neither intend to build Hans Block's dike nor
the other dike." Capt. Cantwell answered: "You John Ogle are
an Englishman and it does not become you to make such commotion
among so many people," and he (Cantwell) took him by the arm
and shoved him out of the church. Whereupon a certain Mathys
Smith angrily said: "The man speaks the truth and what he
says we all say," along with more foul words. Capt. Cantwell
called for the Constable to put him in the stocks, but since
the constable was not at hand and Mathys Smith continued with
his foul language, Capt. Cantwell was forced to strike him
with his cane. Then Magister Jacobus Fabritius shouted out
contemptuously: "The man is right, he speaks the truth, if he
has to go into the stocks then I want to go too," adding more
foul words unbecoming of a priest. Since the constable was
not present, we decided to prevent futher trouble by having
the aforesaid John Ogle and Magister Fabritius put aboard the
yacht. On the way to the yacht, when Capt. Cantwell tried to
grasp the unwilling priest by the arm, he swore and cursed:
"The devil take you if you lay hands on me," adding more
blasphemous words. In the boat he continued to use his foul
mouth so that some people who had gathered near the boat
shouted: "Seize it, seize it,"[3] while some milled around with
swords and clubs. Since it appeared as if a great disorder
was about to erupt, we resolved, at the request of several
people, to have the aforesaid John Ogle and Magister Fabritius
brought back ashore.

    A few days after we had had the confirmation of our order
put up on the church, I, Hans Block, met John Ogle on the
street and spoke with about the recent mutiny, perpetrated by
him and others. He said: "If the Finns had been drunk not
much good would have come of it." I replied: "There is now a
confirmation of our order posted on the church." Whereupon he
retorted: "I think as much of your order as this dirt on the
street," kicking the dirt with his foot.

                            [Signed:] H: Block
                                       John Moll
                                       Derck Albertsen

[Endorsed:] No. 12 A declaracon of the Magistrates of New
             Castle about the Dykes. June 4, 1675

----

1. Other translation in NYCD 12:531.

2. See 20:67 for this order.

3. i.e., the boat, which was to depart for New York.
    c.f., 20:74.

20:69   [PETITION OF THE INHABITANTS OF NEW CASTLE ABOUT
         THE CONSTRUCTION OF DIKES][1]

To the Right honorable major Edmund Andross Capt. Generall off
all his royall highnesses Territories in American and governor
of New Yorke.

                         The humble petition of the In-
                         habitants under the government of
                         Newcastle, humble shewith,

        Thatt whereas your petittioners att a publiqe meeting in
the towne of new Castle bearing date the 4th day of June 1675
by order of the shirriff and majestrates of this towne, to dispose of a percele of morash or flye formerly belonging to Capt.
Carr and through the said flye to make two dickes or highways,
one for the Concernes of the King and publiqe, the other for
Conveniency of the towne, all which your petittioners Condisend
to, butt nott any way willing to repaire the Dick which belongs
to the flye of Hans Block without the privelige thereoff, itt
being the said Hans his owne, and therefore belonging to him
to make good the dick; the whole Company of the inhabitants
or the most part, making the parties named John Ogle, and
Domine Fabricius theire speakers, thatt they were willing to
repaire the Kings high waye the Flye; as also to make and
secure the Dick for a foott passage over by the river side with
a soficient sluice to draine the water outt of the flye, butt
nott to be slaves to Hans Blocks perticular Intrest, for which
cause not onely one butt all in whose behalfe these whose
names are under written Complaine, that theire speakers were
sorely beaten, without cause, as we all hope your honor will
take Cognesens off, for not Condisending to make up the flye
of Hans Block which is nott a publiqe butt privett Concerne,
Comitting them likewise withoutt any Just Cause of offence,
onely speaking for the rights and intrests belonging to us,
which with our moneye according to your honors grant wear
willing to purchas, and god sending us helth to maintaine the
said Dikes, The Flye being by your honors apprizers accounted
of no vallew, yett According to your honors order in Newcastle
we humble acsept your honors pleasure therein, and are willing
to maintaine both ways, so that we may have the privelige of
the Comonage,

                         And your petittioners shall for
                         your Honor Ever pray as in duty
[Signed:]   his   bound
Liftenant Tho: T Jacobson
            marke

        his
Jacob ✠ Johnson Ensigne   his
      marke   Capt. Evertt ✠ Hendrikson Eck
                                        marke
both for the whole Company   for the hole Company of
of Cristena Creek,   Crane hooke

[Entitled:]   The petittion of the Inhabitants under the
              Government of Newcastle.

[Endorsed:]   No. 8 The subscribers to be questioned at the
              next generall Court att Delawarr. June 1675.[2]

---

1. Other transcription in NYCD 12:532.

2. Endorsement and order written in the hand of Matthias
   Nicolls.

20:70   [MAGISTRATES' JUSTIFICATION FOR CONSTRUCTING DIKES][1]

    Reasons which induced us to order all the inhabitants of
the district of New Castle to help construct both of the
outer-dikes.

First: In order to obey the Hon. Lord General's order to make
            roads from village to village where no wagon or cart
            road can be made unless all the aforesaid outer-dikes
            and sluices be made in order to stop the water.[2]

2nd: There are few here who have the knowledge for such work,
            especially among those living in New Castle, and they
            had to pay the laborers a daily salary of 30 or 40
            guilders for their work so that those who wanted to
            work gained much by it, and no one lost more than 5 or
            6 hours' time on the city's dike and 3 or 4 hours'
            time on Mr. Hans Block's dike.

3rd: All inhabitants, country-people and strangers would
            have to go 5 or 6 English miles through the woods in
            order to go as far as Zwaenwyck which is now not more
            than one English mile away since Mr. Hans Block's dike
            has been built. Even if the dike had not been built
            he still could have made his hay as is done in other
            marshes which have no dikes around them; nevertheless
            Mr. Block assumed the expences of 16 parts for the
            construction of his dike, excluding 1/4 part of the
            same dike which had already been built, and he also
            assumed the expences of building the sluices and all
            the appurtenances thereto, so that the mutineers had
            not the slightest reason or cause to question it or
            excuse for their absurd and foul behavior.

4th: There were severall private persons who offered Mr.
            Block to work a day or more on the dike which runs in
            front of his marsh because they did not want to go
            through the mire where various people have now and then
            experienced peril and danger; so that the community in
            general is not at fault as much as the ringleaders of
            the mutiny.

5th: In case of war with the Indians or other enemies,
            especially in the winter when one is unable to travel

by water, it would be very dangerous to go 5 or 6
English miles through the woods to assist our nearest
neighbors, or they us; besides, we daily require one
another's assistance in various necessary matters.

We request the Hon. Lord General earnestly to consider the
aforementioned, referring ourselves to his Honor's sound
judgment, and to decide whether we have given the community
the least lawful cause to resist our order and to mutiny.

                              [Signed:] H. Block
                                         John Moll
                                         Derck Albertsen

[Endorsed:]   No. 11 The magistrates of Delawares reasons about
              the repairing or mending the Dyke in Dutch.
              1675

---

1. Other translation in NYCD 12:533.

2. See 20:64 for a copy of this order.

3. i.e., Swanwyck.

20:71   [CONTEMPORARY COPY OF 20:67]

20:72   [SIGNED COPY OF 20:73]

20:73   [PROTEST OF THE INHABITANTS OF NEWCASTLE AGAINST
          THE BUILDING OF HANS BLOCK'S DIKE][1]

Honorable Gentlemen of the Council of New Castle:

      Pursuant to the permission given to us by your Honors to
submit our complaints and desires in writing, we protest, with
all due reverence, against being obliged to help build Mr. Hans
Block's dike and have resolved not to do it, having no reason

for it, unless we should be expressly ordered to do so by the Honorable General. We therefore all desire and humbly request also to have a copy of it so that we may act accordingly.

Concerning the marshland formerly belonging to Capt. Carr, we are ready to help build the dike together with the inhabitants of New Castle on the condition that we shall have a hereditary right to use a portion of the marshland and we will keep our part in repair. We request of your Honor to grant us a delay to do the aforesaid work until the grain is in the ground. Requesting herewith a favorable recommendation, we remain, etc.

New Castle 5 June 1675

[Signed:]   Jacop van der Veer
            Evert Eck ♯ his mark[2]
            Tomas Jacobsen T his mark
            Matihas Matihason Defo[   ][3]
            Jacob Janssen ✝ his mark
            Martin ✗ Gertsen his mark
            John Ogle
            John ⬥ Breadborne his mark
            Pieter Jegou

[Notation:]   The petitioners are commanded to obey our previous order immediately and in case of refusal the High Sheriff shall have the construction done at their doubled expense according to the Lord General's definitive order.

                   by the Court ordered[4]
                   [Signed:] Will. Tom

[Verso:]   Domine Fabricius and Ogle to bee sent for here and the other here subscribed to bee questioned and sentenced at the generall Court at Delaware.[5]

[Endorsed:]   No. 9 N. Castle in Delowor 5th of June 1675
              Petition to the Court in oposition to order.

---

1. Damaged portions of this document have been recovered from the signed copy (20:72), which lacks the court order, the order on the cover-fold, and the endorsement; the signatures of Jacob Janssen and Martin Gertsen also do not appear on this copy. Other translation and transcription in NYCD 12:534.

2. This is Capt. Evert Hendriksen Eck. c.f., 20:69.

3. NYCD 12:534 has Deforest as Matthias Matthiassen's surname. The final letters of the name have been lost due to a tear in the document. The name Matthias Matthiassen de Vos appears throughout NCCR and it is probable that de Vos was a variant form of Deforest in Delaware.

4. The preceding notation is translated from Dutch. This phrase is written in English in the hand of Wm. Tom.

5. This order which appears on the cover-fold is written
in the hand of Matthias Nicolls, as is the following
endorsement.

20:74   [WILLIAM TOM TO GOV. ANDROS CONCERNING THE
OPPOSITION OF THE INHABITANTS TO THE CONSTRUCTION
OF THE DIKES][1]

Right Honorable, these are to informe your honor that
according to order wee nominated fower good men to value the
valley belonging to Capt. Carr by name Mr. Peter Aldricke Mr.
Johannes de Haiz[2] for the Towne and Mr. Peter Cock and Mr.
Laus Andreeson to that purpose who viewing the said valley[3]
returned that itt was not worth any thing by the reason of the
greate reparacions and the yearely charge for maintenance of
the same thereto belonging Whereupon the Court did order[4]
having reguard to your honors instruccions in making High waies
betweene Towne and Towne which could not possibly be done untill the foote way by the water side was repaired that all the
Inhabitants which in the Jurisdiccion of this Towne [   ]
the repayring of the same the Towne paying double to [   ]
Outlivers and after such reparacion done the Towne to [   ]
itt for the future upon there owne charge And likewise upon
[   ] request of Mr. Hans Block for assistance in repairing his
Ditch itt being the Common and neerest foot way from this
Towne to Swanwick Crane Hooke and parts adjacent he likewise
obleging himselfe and his heires for the future to maintayne
itt upon his owne charge which said foote way is so necessary
and convenient as well for this Towne as the Outlivers themselves that itt cannot well be left unrepaired for that they
and the Towne people must goe five myle about or by water if
either of them have occasion but to buy or sell one pound of
butter or any other such small necessaryes or else wade up to
the middle in water and mudd somme having fallen into the perill
of there lives and losse of what they had about them all which
wee beeing gathered together and duely considering the greate
occasion and necessity of repairing the said way likewise itt
not being above two dayes worke for [   ] third of the people
who were ordered to worke in three companyes [   ] three
severall Overseers And the people of Swanwick and others there
by living having as much occasion for the way as wee and
be[   ] in number almost a full third of the three being willing
to ass[   ] alone that Ditch but the other also for there
necessary re[   ] likewise considering that the [   ] of
the [   ] bee of noe effect onely for the securing the
Ca[   ] an order that all the Inhabitants as above
[   ] meete [   ] Towne the fowerth of June instant
there to heare read our determinacion[5] which was accordingly
done in the Church but after the reading and [being opposed
the][6] wee returning from the Church by somme of this Towne and
a number of the Inhabitants from without in such a mutinous and
tumultuous manner being led on by Fabricius the preister Jacob
Vander Veere John Ogle Peter de Witt[7] Barnard Egburt Thomas
Jacobsen Iuryan Boatesman Math[   ] Smyth Evert Henrickson and
severall others somme having swords some pistolls others clubs

with them such dispitefull language saying they [   ] make
neither the one nor the other that they could not longer be
forborne insomuch that Capt. Cantwell by our consente calling
for the Constable layd hold of the preister and Ogle and sent
them on board the Sloope with intencion for Newyorke to your
honor but the tumult thereupon arising upon there going on
board comming and somme crying fatt them on fatt them on[8]
being most drunke and wee not Knowing to what height itt might
comme they being in such a humor still crying one and all wee
were inforced to send for them from on board and discharge
them which said mutinous way of procedings wee hope your honor
will not allow of and impossible for us to gett [   ] Justice
according to the best of our Knowledge when all our accions
shalbe disputed by a plebeian faccion which will not onely
force us to leave the bench but will expose the Country to
greate charges when upon every occasion there frenzicall
braynes pleases what wee determine there according to your
honors order and instruccions must be sent to yorke contrary
to the same instructions and order the Sweeds and Fynnes being
such a sort of people that must be Kept under else they will
rebell and of that nation these here are the worse sort as by
instance the Long Fynne for which wee referr your honor to
Capt. Niccolls then president[9] if this be not remedyed and a
free Court of law according to instruccions noe man Knowes
his owne and trade must dye when noe man is sure of his owne
estate witnes former examples as Mazinello[10] John of Leyden
Jack Cade and Wat Tyler the de Witts and in these parts since
our comming the insurreccion att New yorke[11] in the time of
Generall Niccolls for remedy of which wee wholly rely upon
your honors order in this materiall affaire Mr. de Haies[12]
will wayte upon your honor about eight or tenne dayes hence by
whome wee desire your honors order and answer who was then
present the next morning the mutineers brought in there request[13] to us which wee send to your honor to consider of
which our answer under the foote there of further wee believe
if Capt Cantwell had not seized upon the bodyes of the principall and beaten one of the principals itt would have pre-
ceeded to bloudshed if your honor thinkes itt fitt that two
fyls of Soldiers may be sent hither to ly in this river to
keepe the people in awe and us in security This our narration
and remonstrance wee present to your honor expecting an answer
by Johannes or sooner if occasion offers for if itt be not
done before the Harvest itt cannot be done then we remayne
Right Honoble your honors humble Servants
                              by order of the Court
                              [Signed:] Will. Tom
Newcastle upon Delaware
this 8th day of June 1675

[Addressed:]   For the Right Honorable Major Edmund Andros
               Generall of all the forces of his Royall Highnes
               in America and Governor of Newyorke these pre-
               sent in

[Endorsed:]   No. 6 N. Castle Delowor 8th June 1675 from justices
               or Court of the place

[Notation:]   The Domine and Ogle sent for by speciall warrant[14]
               to Nyorck the others [   ] be bound over to
               Answer att the next generall Court att Delaworr
               [   ][15]

1. Other transcription in NYCD 12:535.

2. i.e., Johannes de Haes

3. i.e., "marshland." cf., Dutch vly derived from valley,
    which appears in 20:69 as flye.

4. See 20:64 for a copy of this order.

5. See 20:67 for the text of this determination.

6. The words within brackets were marked for insertion at
    this point without allowing for any alteration of the
    sentence structure.

7. Peter de Witt is crossed out.

8. William Tom's rendering of Dutch: Vatt hem aen,
    meaning: "seize it," i.e., "seize the sloop," which
    appears in 20:68.

9. Capt. Matthias Nicolls was president of the Court of
    Assizes during Gov. Lovelace's administration. See
    20:4 for the charges against the "Long Finn."

10. Tommaso Aniello, known as Masaniello, was leader of a
    revolt in 1647 against Spanish rule in Naples.

11. Reference to the 1667 uprising of the Dutch inhabitants
    of Kingston against the English occupation.

12. i.e., Johannes de Haes.

13. See 20:72 for this petition.

14. See NYCD 12:538 for a transcription of this warrant.
    A copy of the original has survived in Miscellaneous
    Records 3:123 in the Colonial Documents at the New
    York State Library.

15. The final three lines of this notation by Matthias
    Nicolls are too faded for accurate transcription.

20:75   [PROTEST OF THE CRANE HOOK CONGREGATION AGAINST
         JACOBUS FABRICIUS][1]

             Laus Deo Semper

                              The 14th of August 1675

We Swedes and Finns,

    Belonging to the Crane Hook church, understand that the
Dutch priest has very sinisterly and without our knowledge
[   ] to the Honorable General [   ] our church and the
[   ] him, which was never granted him by General Lovelace unless the community consented to it; and what reason
should we have thereto since neither we nor our women and
children can understand him. We therefore request that the
Honorable Mr. Cantwell humbly petition the Honorable General
that we be permitted to keep our church with our own priest for
our edification as we have had up until now. If the Dutch
priest wants to preach, let him remain in his own area at
Swanwyck and preach to the Dutch.

                        [Signed:] Hendericus Lemmens

As deacons of the church

done himself Olle ⚡ Torsse
done himself Jan ⚲ Matson
done himself Sammel ⚶ Peetersen
done himself Mons ⚔ Pauwelson

For the whole congregation

[Endorsed:] No. 2 From Cranehook Church. Against Domine
             Fabricius Aug. 4 1675.[2]

_____

    1. Other translations in NYCD 12:539 and in Crane Hook on
        the Delaware by Jeannette Eckman p. 62; the latter
        features a photocopy of the original document.

    2. This last line of the endorsement beginning with
        Against is in the hand of Matthias Nicolls.

20:76   [WM. TOM TO GOV. ANDROS CONCERNING MRS.
          PETERNELLA CARR]

Right Honorable

    I was desired by Mrs. Carr her husband[1] not being att
home to write to your honor about her estate for the payment
of debts and she hopes your honor will not cutt her short of
any part of itt which wilbe the ruine of her and her children
tis true there has beene noe improvement upon that part of the
land for when the estate of Van Swearing[2] was given by patent
by the Right honorable Collonell Niccolls he had not the
meanes to settle itt att present for want of Stock but when
his beasts increased his resolucion was to seate had not the
unhappy change comme[3] as for improvement noe man has done itt
with there valleyes[4] in the river yett hope to hold them by
there respective patents excepting Hans Block and your honor may

well Know that although but small falls so heavy upon him that
he was inforced to crave the assistance of commons in his
reparacion the land is valued att 2000 lb. though more worth
but the Towne att the vendue making of itt out that itt would
be very prejudiciall if bought by [   ] particuler person the
vendue was stopped att that somme referring itt to your honor
hoping that the Towne in generall being better able to pay
then shee and her children to loose your honor will be pleased
to order that the Towne may pay her what was bid for itt and
then Keepe itt for a Towne common this is her request to me
and further I have not to say but that I am

Newcastle upon   Right Honorable your honors
Delaware this 10th of   most humble servant
August 1675.   [Signed:] Will. Tom

[Addressed:]   for the Right Honorable Major Edmund Andros
               Commander in Cheife of all the forces belonging
               to his Royall Highnes in America and Governor of
               New York these present in

[Endorsed:]   18th of Agust 1675 Mr. Tom from Delawar in
               behalfe of Mrs. Carr.[5]

---

1. This must be a reference to Peternella's second husband
    George Oldfield since Capt. John Carr died sometime
    between April 10th and May 15th 1675. Wm. Tom continues
    to use her first married name probably for adminis-
    trative reasons or from habit.

2. i.e., Gerrit van Sweeringen.

3. Probably a reference to the recapture of New Netherland
    by the Dutch in 1673.

4. i.e., marshland.

5. Endorsement written in the hand of Matthias Nicolls.

20:77   [CERTIFICATE OF JOHN CARR'S INDEBTEDNESS TO
        DR. HENRY TAYLOR][1]

    These are to certify all whom it may Concerne That to my
Knowledge Capt. John Carre was endebted unto Dr. Henry Taylor
at the surrender of this place to the Dutch for a pipe of
Madera wine and other matters The particulars whereof I cannot now remember amounting to the summe of 25 or 26 lb. which
hee promist to pay before me and gave a Note of his hand for
the same to the best of my Remembra[   ][2] In testimony whereof
I have hereunto set my hand this 15th day of Sept. 1675

                    [Signed:] M: Nicolls

[Endorsed:]   No. 25 Copie of a Certificate given to C.
              Cantwell for Dr. Taylour, about C. Carrs debt to
              him Sept. 15. 1675.

_____

1. Written in the hand of Matthias Nicolls.

2. the same to the best of my Remembra[   ] replaces: to
    returne good payment in wheate or the value, which is
    crossed out.

20:78   [MAGISTRATES TO GOV. ANDROS CONCERNING AFFAIRS
        AT NEWCASTLE][1]

Right Honorable

    Capt. Cantwell has recd. your honors letter with the two
warrants[2] for the apprehension of Magister Fabricius and Ogle
which are executed and they upon there Journey for New yorke
the others bound over to the next Generall Sessions. according to order as for that part of your honors letter concerning
Capt. Carrs valley[3] itt was never improved [   ] least itt
is our humble desire the fort lying [   ] may be removed [   ] making of a Court house and that
somme other conveni[   ] may be made by itt for a prison both
being very necessary for this Towne and river and where itt
stands rather detrimentall the otherwise to the place that itt
may be done att the publicque charge of the whole river and
bay itt being a generall concerne that there may bee somme
taxe layed for the expences of the High Court and low Courts it
formerly being one sch.[4] of Wheate for the High Court and one
sch. of Rye for the Low Courts all which is left to your honors
discretion That there may be more Magistrates named in this
Towne for the compleating the bench Mr. Moll being to goe to
Maryland where his busines will Keepe him most part of the
Winter Fop Outhout When there is Ice in the river cannot comme
over[5] Mr. Chew living so farr as Apoquermoin[6] not to be relyed
upon the same reason for Hans Block in fowle weather he being
ancient so as none to be relyed upon but Capt. Cantwell and
Dirick Albertsen who will make a slender Court that your honor
would be pleased to send over a new law booke and if to be
gott somme other paper bookes for the Keep[   ] the records
in order none being here to be purch[   ].

    as for the businis of [   ] itt in
open Court and can find noe reason of altera[   ] our in-
ducements thereto being these first the goods were left by
Laurensen[7] in the custody of Johannes de Haiz to be delivered
to Tarkinten[8] he to Dispose of them as he pleased noe man
having power to call him to account the Chest marked with his
name J: T: he being looked upon as the owner that procured him
creditt here which otherwise he had not had so that if any
person send goods out of Maryland or elsewhere into these
parts for the procuring of Corne provisions horses as commonly

they doe wee looke upon the bringer to be the immediate owner
of the said goods and lett the party trusting have a care who
he trusts or if he imbezells he can call him to account and
not the buyer and indeed itt would be a little preposterous
when any person commes proffering [   ] sale or exchange
to aske him are the goods your owne or how came you by them or
other such questions wee thinking itt is enough goods being
brought out of another government by a house Keeper to us
Knowne has power to dispose of the same without any other
questioning the as is he dayly practised these may itt please
your honor are our reasons for our standing to our former
sentence yett in that and all ther things Leaving itt to
your honors more serious consideracion who wee must and ought
to obey and remayne

	Right Honorable
Newcastle upon Delaware	your honors most humble
this 18th August 1675	Servants
[Signed:]	H: Block
	John Moll
	Derck Albertsen

[Addressed:]   For the Right Honorable Major Edmund Andros
                 Commander in Cheife of all the forces belonging
                 to his Royall Highnes in America and Governor of
                 New yorke these present in per Capt. Cantwell

[Endorsed:]   No. 3 18th: of Agust from the magistrats of
                 Delaworr Concerning Capt. Carrs meadow the re-
                 moving the blockhouse to be a Court house and
                 prison and Concerning Lourenson, or tarqitons
                 goods. Aug 18: 1675.[9]

---

1. This letter is written in the hand of William Tom.
    Partly transcribed in NYCD 12:539.

2. See Miscellaneous Records 3:123 for a contemporary copy
    of these warrants, which are transcribed in NYCD 12:
    538.

3. See Miscellaneous Records 3:122 for a contemporary copy
    of this letter dated July 28, 1675. Printed in PA 5:672.

4. An abbreviation of schepel.

5. Fop Outhout was living at this time on the east-side of
    the river in a settlement now called Salem, N. J.

6. i.e., Apoquemini.

7. i.e., John Laurensen.

8. i.e., John Tarkinten. See 20:52 for depositions in
    this matter.

9. Endorsement written in the hand of Matthias Nicolls.

20:79   [MEMORANDUM BY MATTHIAS NICOLLS CONCERNING LAND
         PURCHASED FROM INDIANS][1]

                         Land purchased by the Governor for
                         and on the behalfe of his Royall
                         Highnesse from the Indyan Pro-
                         prietors.

A large Tract of Land lyeing on the West Side of Delaware
River neare the Falls, as by the Deed bearing date Sept. 20th.
1675 doth appeare. There was payment made for the same in
Wampom and Goods to the value of [left blank   ]

Another Trace of Land at Muskitoe Cove, on the Northside
of Long Island, for which likewise payment was made to the
value of [left blank   ]

The Charge of both the Purchases being computed at...
...100 lb. 10 s. 00

---

1. Other transcription in NYCD 12:541. See PA 5:673 for
    the deed to this land.

20:80   [MEMORANDUM BY MATTHIAS NICOLLS CONCERNING A
         LAND TRANSACTION WITH INDIANS ON THE DELAWARE][1]

Sept. 23rd 1675.

         The Indyan Sachems Mamarakickan and Auricktan with
[   ]ko[   ]ewan, and Naneckos: having [   ] for the
sale of their la[   ]side of Delaware River
[   ] next [   ] cold spring [   ]
the Falls, and at [   ] as the other is [   ]
oods backward without [   ] the Island below and
above the Falls [   ] that compasse excepting one Island
commonly called Peter Alricks Isl.
This day appeare to confirme it.
The sale to bee made to the Governor [   ] the behalfe of
his R. Hs.
The Deed of sale was signed and sealed by the Indyans, and they
had their payment the F[   ][2] the Howes and 5 Guns excepted
which are to bee brought to them by C. Cantwell.

[Endorsed:]   Sept. 23 1675 The Indyans of the Falls at
              Delaware.

---

1. See 24:139 for another memorandum by M. Nicolls re-
    lating to a meeting with these sachems on Sept. 22,
    1675. These two documents were apparently folded to-
    gether at one time since they both have suffered
    identical damage.

2. Possibly "firkin," i.e., a barrel or cask. NCCR:99 in
    a 1677 letter from Gov. Andros to the court at New
    Castle repeats these items as: "Fyve Gunnes thirty
    Hoes and one ancor of Rume..."

20:81a   [LIST OF PERSONS AT WHOREKILL][1]

    [   ] of the persons young and old who are
here at Sekonnessinck or WhoreKill

[   ]nus Fredricks Wiltbanck, his wife, two sons, one
    servant...5
[   ]der Moelsteen,[2] his wife, two sons, one servant.......5
[   ] Wolgast, his wife, one son, one servant...............4
Willem Klasen, two daughters, one child.......................4
Jan Kipshaven, his wife, one daughter.........................3
James Weedon, his wife, 1 daughter, 1 son, 4 servants.........8
John Rods, his wife and five children: 3 sons and
    2 daughters...7
Daniel Brun, his wife and his partner John Colleson...........3
Jan Michiels, Antony Pieters, Abraham Pieters, Pieter Hansz..4
Pieter Gronendick, Antony Hansen, Herman Cornelissen..........3
Hendrick Drochstraeten..1
                                                             ──
1671 the 8th of May   Total souls   47

Capt. Martyn Cregier's sloop the Bedfort is still here........5
As well as Pieter Alrichs' small boat from New
    Castle with 2 persons.....................................2
                                                             ──
                                                              7

                          [Signed:] Helmanus Fr. Wiltbanck

[Entitled:] List of persons at Sekonnessinck.

[Endorsed:] [   ] at the Whore[   ] 16[   ][3]

───────────────

1. See 21:104/105 for a 1671 list of inhabitants in
    settlements from New Castle northward. Other trans-
    lation in NYCD 12:522.

2. i.e., Sander or Alexander Molestine.

3. Endorsement in the hand of Matthias Nicolls.

20:81b   [PETITION OF THE MAGISTRATES OF THE WHOREKILL
          TO APPEAR AT ASSIZES CONCERNING CHARGES MADE
          AGAINST CAPT. CANTWELL][1]

To the Honored Councell the Humble petition of
the Magistrates of the Whorekill.

In all Humble manner .
          Sheweth That your petitioners have Received from Capt.
Nicolls Secretary your order And alsoe notice from Capt. Edmund Cantwell to Appeare these Instant month of August Before
your Honoreds to make good wat wee acquainted his Honor the
Governor by a Letter sent from us the last yeare which hath
been your Honoreds opinion to Understand as an Information or
Charge Laid against Capt. Cantwell if so then your petitioners
Doe Humble Crave that your Honoreds Be pleased to Referr the
said matter untill next Assizes when as then wee or any of us
shall Willingly appeare to Answer if Capt. Cantwell will stand
upon his Vindication and more make appeare as wee have Exprest
against him to the which Impossibillities of passages these
time of the yeare are not to be had and alsoe the great
hindrances of our Concernes and occasions at these presents
would greately Damnifie us for which your petitioners Humble
Request your Honoureds to Referr the Cause untill the Assizes
aforesaid being soe neare at hand
                              And your petitioners Shall in Duty
                              pray

                    [Signed:]   Helm. Wiltbanck

[Endorsed:]   Mr. Helmanus Wiltbanck to the Councell about
              Capt. Cantwell[2]

───────────────

1. Other transcription in NYCD 12:523.

2. Endorsement in the hand of Matthias Nicolls.

20:82   [ARMEGART PRINTZ TO SAMUEL EDSALL REQUESTING
         ASSISTANCE][1]

Mr. Samuel Essiel

    It troubles me that I find it necessary to bother you
again in this matter wherein you have always given me assistance.
It is then my humble request, if it pleases, that you assist
me once again by presenting these documents together with the
enclosed letter to Governor Andris. Inform him that they were
not accepted here by Mr. Kentwel[2] and the Honorable Magistrates.
When I presented them to Kentwel he told me that I should take
them to the court and if they certified them then he would get
my money for me. They told me, when I took them there the 1st
of March, that they could do nothing because the judgment had
been handed down so long ago in New York. For this reason I

have been forced to trouble you. With regard to the payment
for the goods about which you spoke, I shall send it with
Captain Kriger. I would have sent it with Piter Groennendyck,
but he had already departed when I received your letter.
Herewith I commend you to God and remain, after cordial
greetings

                       Your faithful friend

Done at   [Signed:] Armmegartt Printz
Prinsdorp the 3rd of March 1675/6

[Addressed:]   Mr. Sammuel Essiel present at Nu Jorck

[Endorsed:]   1675/6 Delaware Jeuffr. Pappegay Receits of
              Tobacco by C. Carre[3] left by Sam. Edsall etc.[4]

---

1. Translated from the Dutch in which it was written for
    Armegart Printz.

2. i.e., Capt. Cantwell

3. See 20:42a for these receipts.

4. Endorsement is in the hand of Matthias Nicolls.

20:83   [PETITION OF WILLIAM HAMILTON AND WILLIAM
          SEMPILL CONCERNING WEIGHTS USED IN TRADE
          AT THE WHOREKILL]

                        To the Right Honorable Major Ed-
                        mond Andros principall and Cheiffe
                        Commander of all the forces of his
                        Royalle Heighnes in America, and
                        Governor of New Yorke the humble
                        petitione of William Hamilton and
                        Wm. Sempill:

        [   ]eth: That your petitioners the last sommer in
June came from New York[ ] with a considerable Cargo in to this
parte of your honors government of delouare with intention to
dispose of ther said Cargo to ther best advantage and the good
of the Inhabitants, And being strangers and unwilling to rune
into any premunire ther your petitioners applyed themselves to
Capt. Edmund Cantwall for Informatione as to the weights and
missors in this pleace who informed them that it then was and
ever had bein since the reduce[   ] by the Honorable Collonell
Nicolls the Custome of the pleace to [   ] dutch weight and
missur and if any for ther conve[ ]iencie [ ]d receave by
Stilliards, yett the debtor to make further [ ]llowanc[ ] to
dutch weight upon Confidence of which report your peitioners
disposed of a good part of ther above mentioned Cargo in and
about the Hourkill expecting to have ther pay in dutch weight

a[   ]ng to usance and sold ther goods according But [   ]ing
[   ]nd ther pay they your petitioners cold [sic] receave
n[ ] excep[   ] would receave English weight and tear, whereupon your petitioner wer enforced to arrest som[   ] ther
debtors to the Court in the Hourkill held the 13th d[   ]
167[   ] Court did then award against your petitioner
[   ] pay in English weight [   ] ruine
and [   ] ther greate dammage, after which [   ] Cantwell and Mr. William Tome running doune to the Ho[   ] and
Capt. Cantwell haveing occassione to call a speciall court
[   ] which was ther held the 19th day of March 1676 your
petitio[   ] then a[   ]ne did petitione the Courte for your
releife about [   ] did order to be referred to your honor
as by [   ]rdors of Courts may appeare, Now so it is
M[   ] your honor it being by the last ordor of Courte
refe[   ]onor That your Honor will be pleased to right
[   ] in ther aggrevances according to your Honor[
        ] the same caise to Capt. Collier, a copy of wh[   ]
your honor letter your petitioner are readie to [   ]¹

> Your petitioners shall as in
> deuty bound for ever pray etc.

[Endorsed:]   [   ]cion to the Go[   ] [   ] Mr.
              Wm. Hamilt[ ] [   ] about Engl. or D[   ]
              Weight at the Whor[   ] delivered mee by Capt.
              Br[   ] April 18th 16[ ]²

---

1. See Miscellaneous Records 3:252, which is transcribed
   in NYCD 12:578, for the Governor's order on this
   petition.

2. Endorsement in the hand of Matthias Nicolls.

20:84   [CAPT. CANTWELL TO GOV. ANDROS CONCERNING
        AFFAIRS ON THE DELAWARE]¹

N: Castle 11 of May 1676

Right Honorable

        The eight of this instand I Recd. your honnors Letter of
the 19 of Aprill where out I understand your honnors safe
arival from albany and the wellstand² of the indyans in them
partes I tanke god wee are as well and our indyans as Civell
as ever I Know them to be and as wee Can perseave no ill intent for They follow theire planting and honting as They use
to Do other years:

        I have had no Time ever sence the indyans Came from
honting to go to the fales to take possestion of that Land
that your honnor bought the Last Summer³ the Reason is Mr.
Blockes⁴ Death and Mr. Molls⁵ being from home but now with

the first I shall goe and take possestion of it, for planters
I give them as much incouragement as Lyes in me and shall observe your honnors orders about the fees it thus[6] very much
discourage the people that theire pattents thus[7] not Com out
all the people from the whore Kill and bay Did exspect to have
theire pattents with the Returnes of the Justices from our
generall Court it being ended this day I hope your honnor will
be plesed to order that they may be sent with the bearer Mr.
Cock and also order to Lay out the bounds at the Hore Kill for
there are already people in Dispute where they Live and under
whoes Government the Indyans Declares how farr the Dutch has
had the Land to the Southward of the Hore Kill summ people are
Doutfull it might Ly under Baltemore and will not take it up
when the pattents Coms from yorke I shall go to the Hore Kill
and with your honnors order Ly out the Line and the people may
Know how far to take up Land the indyans sayes that the Ducth
[sic] When they had bought the Land they Did sett up summ
thing which I supose may be the armes and summ indyans thus
promisse to shew the verry place[8] There was a great affront
this spring given to the imperor of those indyans a very
suttle fellow and one who bears the greates Command and Keepes
his indyans in the greates aw in this parte of the world,
the abuse was given by one Peter Smith[9] about bying summ skins
from him Capt. Crygier Can tell your honnor how it Came to
passe such fellows might be the occation of sheading much
blood who coms there for one month or two and Care not what
happens to the people when they are gon I Knew noting of the
businesse whilest hee was here or else would have called him
to accont for so Doing and to give the Sachem sattisfaction for
the abuse which I hope your honnor will be plesed to Do those
that others may take notice of.

The Susqehanno which I formerly writt to you of is as
yet here in the River and thus intend here to abide I have
ased all men no[ ] to speake with him and have inquired for
him by the indyans They all Deny him to me by Reason summ
people has tould the indyans that I would bind him and send
him to your ho[ ] not withstanding I tell them [ ] the
Contrary when I go to the fales I Do intend to speake with
him by one meanes or other in the mane while I shall end and
Ever Remaine

                         Right honnorable your honnors
                         moste homble and faithful
                         servant
                         [Signed:] Ed. Cantwell

[Addressed:]   For the Right honnorable major Edmond Andross
               Esq. Generall of all his Royall highnesse forces
               in america and Governor att new yorke present

[Endorsed:]   C. Cantwell to the Go: Newcastle May 11th 1676.[10]

---

1. Other transcription in NYCD 12:545.

2. Possible use of Dutch welstand meaning: "well being"
    or "welfare."

3. See 20:80 for a memorandum concerning this land
    transaction at the Falls.

4. i.e., Hans Block.

5. i.e., John Moll.

6. i.e., does

7. i.e., does

8. Probably a reference to the Dutch colony of Zwaenendael
    located in the area of present-day Lewes, Delaware
    which was destroyed by the Indians in 1632.

9. i.e., Peter Groenendyck who used the alias Smith.
    cf., 21:31.

10. Endorsement in the hand of Matthias Nicolls.

20:85   [CAPT. CANTWELL TO GOV. ANDROS CONCERNING A
         SESSION OF THE HIGH COURT AT NEW CASTLE][1]

Right Honorable

        On Tuesday last being the nyneth of May the high Court
sate in this Towne which continued wedensday and thursday
untill noone att which weere present all the Magistrates
above and two from the Hoerkill where they amongst other things
did order (the wolves being so overfrequet and doing such
dayly damamge both to sheepe and cattell and hogs) that any
person should bring in to any of the Magistrates of this river
or bay any wolveskin or heads upon the Certificate for the
said Magistrate the party or partyes so bringing itt or them
should have for each the somme of forty guilders to be payd
out of the next publicke leavy after the procuring of the said
Certificate and also considering the charges which may arise
by that and also that of the High Court which now must by
consequence greater by reason of the farr distance to the
Hoerkill and the dangerousnes of the bay did unanimously
order that a letter should be written to your honor to desire
that there might be a publicke leavy per pole for the defraying
such publicke and other incident charges as may arise as is
the custome in our neighbor province of Maryland or else that
your honor would be pleased to order somme other more convenient way this being the request of the whole Court I represent
to your honor and remayne

                            Right Honorable
Newcastle the 13th of   your honors humble
May 1676   servant
                            [Signed:] Ed. Cantwell

[Addressed:] For the Righ Honorable Major Edmund Andros
              Commander in Cheife of all the forces belonging
              to his Royall in American and Governor of New
              Yorke these present in.

[Endorsed:] Capt. [   ]ntwell [   ] Newcastle
             May.13.1676 To the Go[   ][2]

1. This letter is written in the hand of Wm. Tom.
    Other transcription in NYCD 12:546.

2. Endorsement is in the hand of Matthias Nicolls.

20:86   [LIST OF PATENTS SENT TO CAPT. CANTWELL][1]

Ent. x   Thomas Spry. 160...............................1 1/2
Ent. x   William Roods. 600.............................6
Ent. x   Hen: Ward. 446.................................4 1/2
Ent. x   Hanse Petersen. 157 1/2........................1 1/2
Ent. x   Charles Petersen. 266..........................2 1/2
Ent. x   Ann Wale. 300..................................3
Ent. x   Jacob Young. 1280..............................12 3/4
Ent. x   Bernard Egberts. 300...........................3
Ent. x   James Crawford. 210............................2
Ent. x   John Ogle. 300.................................3
Ent. x   Morris Listen. 150.............................1 1/2
         ⎧Peter Bawcom.⎫
Ent. x   ⎨Rich. Blinks.⎬ in one. 600....................6
         Fran: Neals.[2]
Ent. x   George More. 280 acres.........................2 1/2
Ent. x   Hermanus Woolbanck.[3] 800.....................8
                                                    57: 3/4

[Notation:]   Patents sent to C. Cantwell at Delaware by
              C. Cregier Apr. 1676

[Endorsed:]   14 Patents sent to Delaware by C. Cregier
              Apr. 19th 1676 Ent. /

1. The abbreviations for "entered" with check marks before
    the names, together with the notation and endorsement,
    are all in the hand of Matthias Nicolls. The first
    column of figures records the number of acres in each
    patent while the second column indicates the bushels of
    winter wheat to be paid as quit-rent. Confirmations of
    these patents appear in DYR.

2. This name is crossed out.

3. A frequent variation on Helmanus Wiltbanck's name.

20:87a   [CONTEMPORARY COPY OF 20:87b]

20:87b   Delaware Patents[1]

x Wm. Stevens 600 acres by the bay called York.
x Wm. Ford Duck Creeke 800 acres
x Wm. Sharpe Duck Creeke 500 acres
x John Morgan Duck Creeke: 300 acres
x Wm. Simpson Called Simpsons Choice 400 acres
x John Webb 300 acres
x Wm. Willoughby 200 acres
x John Scott for 400 acres called Thusk
x George Axton: 200 acres
x Peter Cock 650 acres called Quessawominck[2]
x Laurentius Carolus 350 called Tackquirasy
x Lawrence Cock Erick Cock
x Michael Nielson Otto Ernest Cock } 1600
x Goner Rambo and Peter Nielson
  Walraven Johnson defox[3] }   570 acres
  Charles Rumsy
  Richard Scaggs 300 acres
  John Nomers White Claye fall 540
  Wm. Marriott 100 acres
  Peter Peterson and Gasper Fish 500 acres called Pimmeepahka[4]
  Erick Mallock Olle Nielson Christiana
   Thomason: 950 acres called Towocawoninck
  Peter Thomason white Clayes Creek 220 acres
  Peter Dalboe 300 acres
  John Moll a Lott in new Castle
  Edward Man 500 acres
  John Denne 200 acres called Westmorland
  Henery Stevenson John Richards 600 acres called Bacthellors
   Harbor
  John Briggs 400 acres called Aberdeane
  Peter Bawcom 200 acres
  Thomas Phillips Jones Creeke 600
  Robert Francis Jones Creek 400 acres
  Francis Neale Jons Creek 400 acres
  Peter Perry 200 acres called Abergav[eny][5]
  John Stevens 1300 acres
  Robert Dicks 1200 acres called Gocester[6]
  Charles Jansen, Olle Raws Hanse Olleson
  Olle Nielson Hanse Hopeman
  John Hendrickson: 1000 acres
  Peter Alricks 560 acres called Groeningen
  Abraham Enloes 170 acres called Abrahams delight

---

1. This list of patents is one of two copies, the other
   being 20:87a. 87b has suffered minor damage, whereas
   87a has been torn in half with the loss of one inch
   from the top of the lower half. The transcription in
   NYCD 12:544 follows 87a which has lost the names
   between Peter Nielson and John Nomers.

2. Quessanawominck in 87a.

3. Appears most frequently as Walraven Jansen de Vos;
   cf., NCCR:407 for a reference to this patent in which
   the Dutch version (i.e., vos for "fox") appears.

4. Pimmeepaka in 87a.

5. Recovered from 87a.

6. Glocester in 87a.

20:88a   [LIST OF DELAWARE AND STATEN ISLAND PATENTS][1]

Delaware Patents. sealed the 24 July 1676

Mr. John Moll at Newcastle	100 acres
Henry Stricher Whorekill	600 acres
Capt. Cantwell	900 acres
Timothy Love Rehobay Creeke	411 acres
John King Whorekill	900 acres
Randall Revill Whorekill	900 acres
Robt. Winder Whorekill	1100 acres
Daniel Harte Whorekill	500 acres
Laers Cornelys: a small lott New Castle	
John Moll a lot in New Castle	
Abraham Coffin	800 acres
John Roods Whorekill	350 acres
Henry Smith Whorekill [this entry is cancelled]	3000 acres
Daniel Brown Whorekill	400 acres
Alexander Molestedy[2] Whorekill	411 acres
Abraham Clemens and Otto Wollgast Whorekill	600 acres

These 15 Patents were dadet 25 of March
16[76 81 bushel and 1/2 quit-rents.][3]

Oct. 13 4 Patents for Esopus delivered to George Hall and an
order for the Fines etc. of the Yorckmen at Sopez.[4]

Staten Island Patents

Capt. Wm. Dyer for Little Oyster Island
Capt. Dyer 245 acres woodland 35 acres of Meadow upon Staten
     Island
George Cummins 88 acres
Jaques Guyen 178 acres
Louis Lackman 98 acres

Richard Cornhill 160 acres Southside of fresh Kill with 20
   acres of fresh and salt Meadow
Elias Doughty upon Karles Neck 160 acres and 12 acres of Salt
   Meadow and 8 of fresh in the Cove to the north of Ceder
   point.
Thomas Wandall upon Karles Neck 160 acres 12 acres of Salt and
   8 of fresh in the Cove
John Fitzgerald 88 acres
John Hinchman 80 Acres and [   ]
Richard Harvy upon Long neck 80 Acres with [ ] acres of Salt
   Meadow and four of fresh
Richard Stillwell 100 acres with 12 acres [   ] and 8 of
   fresh meadow
John Edsall 80 acres 6 acres of salt and 4 acres of fresh
   meadow
Francis Charteir 80 acres fresh kill 6 acres of salt and four
   of fresh Meadow
[blank]⁵ Turcoate Eighty acres 6 acres of salt and four of
   fresh Meadow
Caerston Johnson 80 acres 6 acres of salt 4 of fresh
   Meadow
John Casee 80 acres 6 acres of salt 4 of fresh Meadow
Capt. Thomas Lawrence 160 acres 12 acres of salt and 8 acres
   of fresh Meadow
Capt. Wm. Lawrence 160 acres 12 acres of salt and 8 acres of
   fresh Meadow
Richard Doodyman 80 acres 6 acres of salt and 4 of fresh
   Meadow
Paulus Regreene 80 acres 6 acres of salt and 4 of fresh
   Meadow
Peter Bileau and 2 sons 270 acres
John Garretson 80 acres 6 acres of salt and 4 of fresh
   Meadow
Joseph Thorne 80 acres 6 acres of salt and 4 of fresh
John fitz Gerritt 80 acres 6 of salt Meadow and 4 of fresh
Robt. Ryder 80 acres 6 of salt 4 of fresh Meadow
Gideon Marlett and 2 sons 243 Acres with 13 acres of salt
   Meadow
Samuell Leet 160 acres 20 acres of fresh and salt Meadow
Andrew Cannon 80 acres 6 of salt and 4 of fresh Meadow
Elias Puddington 80 acres 6 of salt 4 of fresh Meadow

Delaware Patents⁶

A Confirmacion to Capt. Edm: Cantwell of 900 Acres of Land
   in Apoquiminy.
Henry Smith 3000 Acres upon Prime creeke near the Whore Kill.
John Roods 350 Acres upon the Whore Kill.
A Confirmacion to Capt. Edm: Cantwell of 800 Acres nigh the
   head of Apoquiminy creeke.
John Moll 100 Acres behind the Towne of New Castle.
A Confirm: to John Moll of a lott in the Towne of New Castle.
A Confirmacion of two peices of Land near Turkey Island to
   Laers Cornelessen
A Confirmaction to Daniel Harte of 500 Acres in Prime Creeke.
Robert Wi[ ]der⁷ 1100 Acres in Fish Creeke.
He[ ]y Stri[ ]her⁸ 60 Acres at the Whore Kill.
Randall Revill 900 Acres in Slachters Creeke.
John⁹

1. This document comprises two 14 1/2" by 6" leaves which
   are identical in size to 20:87a/b and 88b. The leaves
   have been cut in half and later taped together. A
   transcription of the upper half of the first leaf
   appears in NYCD 12:544.

2. i.e., Alexander or Sander Molestine.

3. The material within brackets has been recovered from
   NYCD 12:545.

4. This memorandum, which is the only entry on the lower
   half of the first leaf, is written in the hand of
   Matthias Nicolls.

5. Turcoate's given name is also omitted in the return of
   survey for his land (CLP 1:70). Miscellaneous Records
   3:205 has a copy of a pass which was issued to a Jean
   Turcoat in August 1676. He is described as: "a French
   Man belonging to this Government." Printed in PA 5:682.

6. This list appears on the upper half of the second leaf
   and is written in the hand of Matthias Nicolls.

7. Robert Winder. See first list for Delaware in this
   document.

8. Henry Stricher. See first list for Delaware in this
   document.

9. Either the remainder of this entry has faded away or
   this list was left incomplete.

20:88b   Delaware Patents June 5th 1676.

Herbert Craft 300 Acres in Duck Creeke[1]
William Troth two hundred Acres in Bawcom Briggs Creeke.
Francis Whittwell 400 Acres in Duck Creeke called Broobshay.
Henry Palmer 400 Acres in Duck Creeke
Nicholas Bartlett 400 Acres in Duck Creeke
Brian Omella 200 Acres in Drawers Creeke called South Side.
Stephen Durdene 400 Acres in Duck Creeke.
Francis Wittwell 400 Acres in Duck Creeke called White hall.
Oliver Melinton and George H[artle 400][2] Acres in Duck Creek.
[Samu]el Barbery 20 Acres [in Bancom B]riggs Creek[3]
Morris Lester 400 Acres in [Duck Creek][4]
Percifell Wosterdell, John B[arker] [blank], James Williams
   and [Edward] Williams 1200 Acres in Blackbird Creeke.[5]

James Wallem a lott in the Towne.
Henry Parker a lott in the Towne.
Edward Southeron 400 Acres in Pagan creeke.
George Young 300 Acres neare the Whore Kill.
Evan Salisbury 300 Acres in St. Georges Neck
John Pitt 500 Acres in St. Georges Neck.
John Scott 400 Acres at the first dividing of St. Georges Neck.
Olie Francen, Marcus Lourenson, and Niels Nielson 700 Acres
    about two Miles from Verdrietyes Hoock.
Wm. Currer and Wm. Goldsmith 600 Acres in St. Georges Neck.
John Avery 300 Acres neare the Whore Kill upon Rehobah's
    bay.
Wm. Waring 322 Acres neare the Whore Kill upon Rehobah's
    creek.
John Edmonson a Confirm: for 800 Acres of woodland and some
    meadow in Christina Kill.
Henry Peddington 400 Acres upon Rehobah creeke.
Wm. Tom 132 Acres at the Whore Kill.
Alexander Molestedy[6] 80 Acres at the Whore Kill.
Simon Judd 50 Acres at the Whore Kill.
John Kephaven[7] 69 Acres at the Whore kill.
Hermanus Woolbanck[8] 134 Acres at the Whore kill.
Robert Tallant 200 Acres by Black bird creek.
John Ashman and Samuel Jackson 300 Acres in Cedar Creek.
[Ed]ward Swandall 200 Acres in Bla[ck Bird Creek][9]
[two lines obliterated   ]
John Woodhas 400 Acres in Du[ck Creek][10]
John Ashman and Sam: Jackson 400 Acres in Cedar Creek.
Thomas Bromell 300 Acres in Black bird Creek.
Thomas Cocks 300 Acres in Black bird Creek.
John Woodars 400 Acres in Black bird Creek.
A Confirmacion of Lott in the Towne to Hendrick Jansen.
A Confirmacion to Edm: Cantwell and Johannes de Haes of two
    pieces of Land by New Castle the one of 50 Acres, the
    other of 100 Acres.
Brian Omella 200 Acres in Drawers Creek called Diason.

[Endorsed:] Delaware Pa[   ] sent by Dr. Lockart in Geo:
             Davis his Ketch. June 9th 1676. 42 patents.[11]

---

1. This entry is written in the hand of Matthias Nicolls.

2. Recovered from DYR:97.

3. Damaged portions in this entry have been recovered from
   DYR:86.

4. Recovered from DYR:87.

5. Damaged portions in this entry have been recovered from
   DYR:87, in which Wosterdell is recorded as "Woodersell"
   and the name "John Street" appears after Barker's name.

6. i.e., Alexander or Sander Molestein.

7. i.e., John Kipshaven.

8. i.e., Helmanus Wiltbanck.

9. Damaged portions recovered from DYR:90.

10. Recovered from DYR:86.

11. Endorsement in the hand of Matthias Nicolls.

20:89   [GOV. ANDROS TO CAPT. CANTWELL CONCERNING
           INDIAN AFFAIRS][1]

Capt. Cantwell

     I received your Letter concerning the comming in of the
Susquehanna Indyans about a weeke agoe, and having Considered
thereof, doe thinke it convenient that you encourage them
therein, till when not to promise or engage any thing to
them, you may acquaint them, that if they desire it, I will
endeavor a Composure of all things in Maryland, and perfect a
peace with the Maques and Sinnekes;[2] After which they may returne back to their owne land, as they shall thinke good.

     If the said Indyans doe comply herein, you are to give mee
notice of it, and doe the like to the Government of Maryland
and let them Know that I have given you order so to doe, and
doe thinke it the greatest service I can doe them, so to take
off the Indyans, least goeing to the Maques and Sinnekes, they
might induce them to make in reades upon the Christians, which
none of us could remedy.

     Upon the said Indyans comeing in, you are to let mee Know,
where they are most inclinable to goe for their present being
either at the Falls or the midle of the River.

     yours of the 6th instant I recd. thi[ ] morning, wherein
I understand [   ] upon the receit of Mr. Augustine He[ ]mans[3]
letter of the suspicion of a fam[ ]lyes being cutt of by the
Indyans, you shott three great Guns and sent for 4 men out of
each Company which gave an Alarum throughout the River, wherein
you did very ill upon so slig[ ] Grounds to bee so rash,
however you ar[ ] not to bee caresse;

     If you have not already you are to send to the Susque-
hanneh Indyans to Know their Intents about their coming in,
which if they will not, you are to bee carefull, as I advertised you before, not to promise them any thing, It being
not proper, as not in our power, If they shall come in, they
must live peaceabley as the rest of the Government doth, and
then shall bee lookt upon and cared for accordingly, I am

                          your affectionate friend
Aug. 11. 1676   E. A:[4]

[Endorsed:] No. 45 A letter sent Capt. E. Cantwell by order
             of the Go: and Councell. Aug. 11. 1676.

----

1. Written in the hand of Matthias Nicolls.

2. i.e., Mohawks and Senecas.

3. i.e., Augustine Herrman.

4. Initials of Edmund Andros in the hand of Matthias
    Nicolls.

20:90   [AUGUSTINE HERRMAN TO CAPT. CANTWELL ABOUT
        SURVEYOR'S FEES AND RUN AWAYS][1]

Capt. Cantwel

The Survayors Fees are for the first hundred 100 lb. tobacco
The resurvayes   ⎫ for the second   "   50 lb.
are dubbled and   ⎬ for the 3rd   "   25
the Pattant 320 lb.   ⎭ for the 4th. and so for every hundred
                         more 12 lb. with 10 lb. for the
                         Plotting and 10 lb. the warrant
But as to the appraisment off Daniel Makery Estate, whether
you can make the appraizers take the things, I can not tell,
and must bee informed by Bether Lauresen[2] but iff the Stear
should not bee found and delivered I suppose you need not
answer for.

    I wish you a happy Journey to New Yorck with a safe re-
turn, present my respect to all Friends there, especially to
his Honor the Governor and Capt. Nicolls,

    The 3 run awayes from Virginia where run a way from my
son Caspar and met with Mr. Stiles and Mr. Whart[3] 6 mile this
side New Castle, from whence they brought them along with
them to my house, but wee trusting to their promes, gave us
the slip next Mourning, iff per chaince you should meet with
them set them to worck at New Castle, Not els then rest
                         Your Friend and Servant
                         [Signed:] Augustine Herrman
August 27. 1676.

[Addressed:]   These For his Honored Friend Capt. Edmd. Cant-
               well at New Castl

[Endorsed:]   Surveyores the fees in Mariland from Mr. Harman
               27th agust 76.[4]

_____

1. Partly transcribed in NYCD 12:555.

2. i.e., Peter Laurensen.

3. Possibly Samuel Stiles and Henry Ward.

4. Endorsement in the hand of Matthias Nicolls.

20:91   [COPY OF A DECLARATION CONCERNING MRS. BLOCK'S
         RIGHT OF WAY THROUGH CAPT. CANTWELL'S PASTURE][1]

     Wee whose names are here under subscribed, doe with all
humble Reverence Attest and declare to all whom these may
Concerne; That Mr. Hans Block (Deceased) in his lifetime had
and Enjoyed a free way for his Cattle and fetching of wood in
the woods, (through the land which is now Capt. Cantwells
pasture) without the hindrance or mollestacion of any person
whatsoever, untill the sayd Capt. Cantwell (by his fence made
the Last Spring) did hinder the widdow of the sayd Mr. Block,
of the sayd way and outlet for her beasts, which is to her
very great Dammage: This wee, having been neighbours to the
sayd Mr. Block and Knowing all the actings Concerning the
sayd Land, doe upon our owne Knowledge attest and Declare to be
true : In witnesse whereof wee hereunder set our hands this
second day of September 1676:

                         Oly Toorson
                         Peter De Witt
                         John Barnson
                         Henry Johnson
                         Peter Matthiason

_____

1. Other transcription in NYCD 12:555.

20:92   [COPY OF A DECLARATION BY MARTIN GARRETSON CONCERNING
         MRS. BLOCK'S RIGHT OF WAY THROUGH CAPT. CANTWELL'S
         PASTURE][1]

     These may Certifie all whom it may Concerne that I Martin
Garretson was Imployed by Mr. Hans Block (Deceased) to make
a way from his Plantation over the valley and Creuple[2], into
his Bakward Land which Lyeth behinde the sayd valley and
Creuple; but Could not make the said way sufficient for Cattle
to goe over; by Reason of the Rottenness of the ground, being
a Quaking mire which hath noe foundation for a way; And I doe
further declare, upon my owne Knowledge, that the sayd Mr.
Block hath (for Eleven yeares past) had a free way for his
beasts and fetching of wood in the woods, (through the Land
which is now Capt. Cantwells pasture) without any hinderance
or Mollestacion of any one whatsoever, untill Capt. Cantwell
took away the priviledge of the sayd way and out=drift, from
the widdow the sayd Mr. Block which is to her very great
Dammage she having noe other to drive her beasts into the
woods nor fetch her fewell Except farr about by the Sweeds
This I doe attest and Declare to be true : In witnesse whereof
I have hereunder set my hand this 4th day of September 1676:

                         Martin Garretson

_____

1. Other transcription in NYCD 12:556.

2. From Dutch Kreupelbosch: "thicket."

20:93   [PETITION OF HENDRICK JANSEN VAN BREMEN ABOUT
         A JUDGEMENT AGAINST HIM]

                              To the honorable Major Edmond
                              Andros, Governor under his Royal
                              Highnesse James Duke of Yorke and
                              Albany of all his Territoryes in
                              America

The humble Peticion of Hendrick Janssen van Bremen.

     Sheweth with all Submissions your honors Peticioner living
about three miles from new Castle upon a plantacion, that a
while agoe having beene troubled with Mr. William Tom two
horses (wherefore very aftime[1] complained) by their spoyling
of his corne, which has redounded to your honors Peticioner
great damage and Losse. In which Case though your honors
Peticioner aftime complained and used his best meanes possible,
could have no redress: that at Last by vexacion and unaware
your honors Peticioner did shut one of them with some shot
which afterwards was found dead in the woods.

     Whereupon your honors Peticioner hath beene called in
question, and though having excused him selfe of the remedy-
less vexacion of the said horses was neverthelesse condemned
at last to the summe of seven hundred guilders with an
execucion thereupon, which perhaps is served before this time.

     The abovewritten matters being so, First the damages
suffered by them 2 horses, supposed to amount to about fl000:
and this Last sentence with Charges to f700:, it's to your
Peticioner a great burthen, not being able to suffer any such
fine; neither possible to pay it; except by selling all his
house stuffe and cloathing and so to leave his wife and Children Script naked.

     Therefore it's your honors Peticioners humble Request,
that the abovesaid Sentence may bee Lenifyed; your honors
Peticioner not being able to beare it. And finding no other
wyse to Satisfye Something on that matter; that if your honor
bee pleased to accept of his Service at new Castle for the
Space of three yeares or there about as a souldier for to make
an end of the premises; your honor may command him; or else to
mitigate the matter so, that your honors Peticioner may bee
able to beare it, and not to bee putt unto an utter ruine.
Your honors Peticioner expecting a comiseracion of the Premises
                         Shall ever pray[2]

[Entitled:]   The humble Peticion of Henry Janssen van Bremen.

[Addressed:]   To the honorable Governor Andros

[Endorsed:]   No. 42 Hendrick Jansen van Bremens papers.
              About the sentence for Killing Mr. Toms horse.
              1676.[3]

_____

1. i.e., aftimes: "often."

2. See Miscellaneous Records 3:198 for the Governor's
    order on this petition. Printed in PA 5:679.

3. Endorsement is in the hand of Matthias Nicolls.

20:94   [NOMINATION LIST FOR MAGISTRATES IN DELAWARE][1]

1 Mr. John Moll
2 Mr. Henry Ward
4 Mr. Jacob Young
5 Mr. John Paul Jaquett
3 Mr. William Tom
   Fof Authout[2]
   Gerett Otho

                                Whorekill
Peeter Cock   defer'd till Mr. Avery[3]
Peeter Rombout[4]   or in all
Israell Helme   Hermanus Wildebonck[5]
Laes Andrisen
Woole Swaine
Ernestus Otho[6]

                  Nominated Sept. 1676

[Endorsed:]   Nominacion of Magistrates Sept. 1676. Delaware.
              At Newcastle and up the river

---

1. Document is written in the hand of Matthias Nicolls.
    The first group of nominations is for New Castle, cf.;
    NCCR:4; the second group is for Upland, cf., UCR:35.
    cf., also 20:95. See Miscellaneous Records 3:213 for a
    copy of the commission for the magistrates at Upland.
    Other transcription in NYCD 12:559.

2. i.e., Fop Outhout.

3. i.e., John Avery, who was commissioned Captain of the
    militia at Whorekill in October 1676.

4. i.e., Peter Rambo.

5. i.e., Helmanus Wiltbanck.

6. i.e., Otto Ernest Cock. Cf., UCR:37-38 for this
    version of his name.

20:95   [JUSTICES NOMINATED FOR NEW CASTLE][1]

[   ] or Justices of Newcastle

Mr. John Moll
Mr. John Ward[2]
Mr. Jacob Young[3]
Mr. William Tom   Gerret Otto
Mr. Fof Outhout
Mr. Johañes de Hãse   To bee Capt.

        Capt. Edmd. Cantwell to be sheriffe or scout and act
acordingly for the due Execution of the lawe.

        The Magistrates or oficers above in the river to be con-
firmed for a year longer or further order.

                            354: 2:4
                             55:17:8
                            410:00:0

[Endorsed:] No. 43 New Magistrates nom[   ] of Delaware.
             Sept. 26. 1676.

---

1. Document is written in the hand of Matthias Nicolls.
    cf., 20:94. Other transcription in NYCD 12:560.

2. Probably an error by M. Nicolls for Henry Ward. cf.,
    20:94.

3. This name is crossed out.

20:96   Severall matters presented to the Governor by
           Capt. Cantwell with the Answers thereunto[1]

1. That there may bee an order
    for payment of the publick   A Rate to bee levyed as
    Charge at Delaware and for   at Albany.[2]
    the Interpreters

2. That the Patents for Del-
    aware may bee signed and   To bee sent to the Courts
    sent.

3. An order about the Fees   To bee as in Maryland.
    for Surveying.

4. An order for seating of   To bee ordred by the Courts
    Lotts and Land.   and settled according to
                                    Law.

5. Court Orders to bee put   According to Law.
    in Excucion.

6. To nominate new Officers   Already done and shall bee
    For the Courts   sent.

7. Some Order about the Susque- } To bee consider'd and shall
   hannah Indyans. } bee sent to immediately.

8. About Anthony Bryans } xReferr'd to the Court to
   Land. } certify to the Go: for his
                approbacion.[3]

9. An order for the money } To bee paid as directed by
   paid Mrs. Pappegay. } the Law and former orders.

10. Some order for the payment ⎫
x   of Capt. Cantwells Account ⎪
    for the public about the ⎪
    Indyans etc. in Go: Love- ⎪
    laces time. ⎪
                       ⎪
11. Capt. Cantwells Account ⎪ An account to bee given of
x   with his Honor for sever- ⎪ the Revenue both old and
    all disbursments. ⎬ new and if short for the
                       ⎪ publick Expence, A Rate
12. Cloath for 4 Indyans ⎪ shall bee allowed as at
x   employed, 12 Ells duffells ⎪ Alb:[4]
    promis't. ⎪
x   Lausa Cock for service. ⎪
x   The Governors Expences at ⎪
    Peter Rambo's. ⎭

13. Hendrick Sybrants peticion } Referr'd to the Court there.
   about Mr. Tom }

14. About Souldyers, shott or } To give a particular
   bullet for the Fort, and } Account of Guns, stores
   a Flagge. } etc.

15. Francis Stevens peticion } Graunted.
   for Goods seized. }

16. A patent for Capt. Cantwell } Answer'd.
   and Mr. De Haes for Land on }
   the East side. }

17. Some Order about Major Fen- } An order, none to bee
   wycks granting of Land. } granted by him.

18. About liberty for Mr. Izrael }
   Helme, to make use of his } Not granted.
   distilling Kettle. }

[Endorsed:]   No. 41 Copie of answ. to C. Cantwells proposalls,
         given him Sept. 27. 1676.

---

1. Document is written in the hand of Matthias Nicolls.
   Other transcription in NYCD 12:560.

2. This answer is crossed out.

3. This answer is crossed out.

4. This answer replaces the following which is crossed out:
   An account to bee given in the Revenue at Delaware both
   old and new and if short a Rate as at Albany with
   approbacion.

20:97   A Pattent for a Parcell of Land at Delaware
         Granted unto Daniel Whitley[1]

Edmond Andross Esq. etc. Whereas there is A Certain parcell of Land which by my Order hath been Layd out for Daniell
Whitley Called by the Name of the Grove Scituate Lying and being in a Creeke Called Saint Johns Creeke at the head of the
said Creeke and on the West Side of Dellaware Bay, begining at
a poplar marked Tree and Runing South East along the Creeke
Side One hundred and fifty Pearches to a Black Wallnutt marked
Tree, and from thence Southwest three hundred and twenty
pearches to A Bounded Red Oak and from thence Runing Northwest
One hundred and fifty pearches to a Bounded Red Oak and from
thence to the first bounded Poplar by the Creeke side three
hundred and twenty pearches Northeast, Containing and Layd out
for three hundred Acres as by the Returne of the Survey under
the hand of the Survey or Doth and may Appear Know Yee etc.
Dated [blank   ]

     Secretary's Office New York April the 29th. 1746 I do
hereby Certify the aforegoing to be a true Copy of the Record
thereof Remaining in this Office in a Book of Patents begun in
the year 1666 p. 161 And I do further Certify that the Record
of the patent succeeding the aforegoing bears Date the first
day of December 1675.

                          [Signed:]   Jno. Catherwood Secry.

[Endorsed:]   Copy Patent to Daniel Whitley probably about
               1665.[2]

---

1.   This is a copy made from the original patent. See
     Book of Patents: 1666-1679 volume four for the ori-
     ginal record. See also DYR:181 for a transcription of
     this patent from Delaware records. Other transcription
     of this document in NYCD 12:567.

2.   According to the preceding certification the year
     should be 1675.

20:98   [RULES OF GOVERNMENT FOR THE DELAWARE SETTLEMENTS;
         ORDER ON CAPT. CANTWELL'S APPLICATION FOR A PATENT][1]

                         Edmund Andros Esq. Seigneur of
                         Sauzmarez Lieut. and Governor
                         Generall under his Royal Highnesse
                         James Duke of Yorke and Albany
                         etc. of all his Territories in
                         A[merica:]

     Whereas the last yeare at my being at Delaware, upon
applicacion of the Inhabitants representing that my Predecessor Go: Lovelace had begun to make a regulacion for the
due administracion of Justice, according to the Lawes of this

Government Pursuant to which I did appoint some Magistrates and
make some rules for their proceedings the yeare ensueing or
till further Order In which Having upon mature deliberacion by
the advice of my Councell made some alteracions, they are to
remaine and bee in force in forme following:[2]

1. That the booke of lawes Establisht by his Royal Highnesse,
and practiced in New Yorke, Long Island, and Dependences, bee
likewise in force and practiced in this River and Precincts,
Except the Constables Courts, Country Rates and some other
things peculia[r] to Long Island, and the Millitia as now
Ordered to remaine in the King, but that a Constable in each
place bee yearely chosen for the Preservacion of his Majesties
Peace with all other Power as directed by the Law.

2. That there bee three Courts held in the severall pa[rts of
the River] and Bay as formerly To witt one in the Towne, on[e
above at] Uplands another below at the Whorekill.

3. That the said Courts consist of Justices of the Peace,
whereof three to make a Coram, and to have the Power of a
Court of Sessions and decide all matters under twenty pounds
without Appeale, in which Court the eldest Justice to preside,
unlesse otherwise agreed amongst themselves,[3] above twenty
pounds and for crime Extending to life, Limbe or Banishment,
to admitt appeale to the Court of Assizes.

4. That all small matters under the value of five pounds may
be determined by the Court without a Jury Unlesse desired by
the Partyes as also Matters of Equity.

5. That the Court for Newcastle bee held once a Month, To
begin the first Tuesday in each Moneth, And the Court for Uplands and the Whorekill Quarterly and to begin the second
Tuesday of the Moneth.

6. That all Necessary By Lawes or Orders (not repugnant to
the Lawes of the Government) made by the said Courts, bee of
force and binding, for the Space of one whole yeare, in the
severall places where made; They giveing an Account th[ere]of
to the Governor, by the first Convenience, And that n[o] fines
be made or imposed but by Order of Court.

7. That the Severall Courts have power to regulate the Court
and Officers Fees, not to exceed the Rates in the booke of
Lawes, nor to bee under halfe the Value therein Exprest.

8. That there bee a high Sheriffe for the Towne of Newcastle,
the River, and Bay; And that the said high Sheriffe or Marshall
being a fitt person, and for whom hee will bee responsable, to
be approved by the Court, But the Sheriffe as in Engl., and
according to the now pra[ctice] on Long Island, to act as a
principall offic[er for] the Execucion of [the Lawes] but not
as a Justice of Peace or Magistrate.[4]

9. That there bee fitting Books provided for the Records, In
which all Judiciall Proceedings to be duely and fairely Entred
as also all Publick Orders from the Governor, And the Names of
the Magistrates and Officers Authorized, with the time of
there Admission: The said Records to bee kept [in] English,
To which all persons concernd[5] may have free Recourse [at]
due or Seasonable time.

10. That a fitt person for Clarke when vacant bee recommended
by each Court to the Governor for his Approbacion in whose
hands the said Reccords to be kept.

11. That all writts, Warrants and Proceedings at Law sha[ll]
bee in his Majesties Name, It haveing been practiced in [the]
Goverment ever since the first writing of the Law book And
being his Royall Highnesses speciall pleasure and order.

12. That No Rates bee imposed or Levyed of Money Made within the Town of Newcastle River or Bay, by any, under what
denomination soever, without the Approbacion of the Governor,
Unlesse upon extraordinary occasion, in Case of Necessity,
of the which the Governor to have a present Acco[mpt sent
him.] That upon the Levy of any Rates, there bee a F[aire
accompt] Kept, both of the Receipts and disburstments, whi[ch
accounts] to bee given into the next Generall Court there to
bee past, and then sent to the Governor for his Allowance Untill which not to bee deemed a Sufficient discharge,

Whereas by this Regulacion there are no Overseers
appointed, nor Constables Courts, but all matters to be determined by the Justices I doe therefore recommend the Composure
or referring to Arbitracion of as many matters (particularly
under the Value of five pounds) as may properly bee Determined
that way: Provided it may bee by the Consent of Partyes.

That any person desiring Land, make applicacion to the
Court in whose bounds it is, who are requir[ed to] sitt once
a month or offener if there be[e occasion] to give order
therein, and certify [the Governor for any land nott taken upp
and Improved,] fitt proporcions not exceeding 50 acres per
[head unlesse] upon extraordinary occasion where they see good
Cause for [itt,] which Certificate to bee a sufficient
authority or warrant for the Surv[eigor to] Survey the same,
and with Surveyors returne to bee sent to N. Y. for the
Governors Approbacion.

That in the Certificates bee specifyed how much Upland
and Meadow, with due regard that each may have a proporcionable
share according to the place they are in.[6]

Given under my hand and Seale in New Yorke the [blank][7]
day of September in the 28th. yeare of his Majesties Reigne
Annoque Domini 1676.

In answer to C. Edm: Cantwells and Mr. Joh: de Haes
applicacion for a Patent for the within mencioned land.

Having heard some rumors that my Lord Berkly hath disposed of his Right to some other persons and that it is approved of by the Duke, I forbeare to give a further Graunt or
patent till the Certainty bee knowne, but doe recommend Capt.
Cantwells and Mr. de Haes right to the Justice of such whom
it may concerne to confirme this title. Given under my hand in
N. Y. this 27th day of Sept. 1676.[8]

[Endorsed:]   Orders to bee observ[ ] in Delaware, sent by
             Capt. John Collyer Sept. 27. 1676.

1. Other transcription in NYCD 12:561. Transcriptions of contemporary copies of the final draft appear in NCCR: 5 and UCR:39. This document represents an engrossed draft which Matthias Nicolls saw fit to revise extensively. All revisions are written in his hand. The bracketed material has been recovered from the copy in NCCR.

2. The original preamble is crossed out and is printed in the appendix to this volume. This revised preamble appears on the reverse of the last leaf of the MS.

3. This phrase: unlesse...themselves, is marked for insertion at this point.

4. This sentence beginning with: But the Sheriffe..., is marked for insertion at this point.

5. This word is marked for insertion at this point.

6. These final two paragraphs are marked for insertion at this point, replacing: That this Regulacion bee of force for the space of one whole Yeare after the date hereof or till further Order, which is crossed out.

7. This space left for the day appears in the NCCR and UCR copies as the 27th.

8. This order appears on the reverse of the last leaf below the revised preamble. It represents a first draft of an order which is to be sent to Capt. Cantwell and Johannes de Haes and bears no relationship to the preceding orders. See 20:96, No. 16, for a reference to this order.

20:99   [MEMORANDUM OF ORDERS ON PETITIONS FROM WHOREKILL]

Memorandum

Upon the peticion of Peter Bawcom, The Governor Recommends the buinesse to a friendly Composure, or the Law.

Upon the Peticion of Joshua Barkstead, The Governor Orders, if the Land were not possessed, afore, It is to be enjoyed (if surveyed for and Setled) by the Peticioner, of which a returne to be made by the Magistrates of Whorekill by the first Convenience in Order to a Confirmacion according to Law.

Upon the Letter of Wm. Winsmore, The Governor Referrs it
to the Court of Whore Kill to examine and report the matter
to him with all Just favour to the peticioner, if the matter
he writes about be justly stated by him in Order to a
Determinacion.

Upon the Peticion of George Young, According to law and
practice referred to the Court at the Whorekill.

[Endorsed:] No. 40 The Governors Answer to severall peticions
and letters from the Whorekill. Oct. 28. 1676.[1]

---

1. Endorsement in the hand of Matthias Nicolls.

20:100 [THE MAGISTRATES OF NEW CASTLE TO GOV. ANDROS
ABOUT MUNICIPAL AFFAIRS][1]

Right Honorable Governor

Sir Wee your Honors Humble Subjects, being Commissionated
by your Honor to bee Magestrats for the Towne and Jurisdiction
of New Castle, do find owr selves oblidged, (for the Best of
the Towne and Inhabitants) Humbly do present to your Honor the
hereafter mentioned particulers for which wee desire his
Honors favorable Grant, and order;

1. That your Honor will bee pleased to send the Lawbooke, of
his Royall Highnesse, Corrected of all such Lawes and orders,
as do not properly Concerne this River, Your Honor being
pleased, to make mention of the same att his being here;

2. Itt prooves verry Burthensome to those who belong to the
Company of the Militia of this Towne (who for the most part
Live out of it a myle 3 or 4) to come and watch in the forth,[2]
and therefore Suppose itt to be better (if his Honor thinkes
fitt) that some small number of souldiers were Kept (it being
not only for the Ease of the People, but also for the Reputation of the Government and Concidering that this is a
frontier place) as itt was in the tyme of Your Honnors predecessors and do find that severall of the Inhabitants would
Incline to pay towards their maintainance then to be Constrayned to watch themselves;

3. That your Honor will bee pleased to bestow on us a Lesser
Seale for the office. There being necessity in severall
Respects for the same, and Cheefly in sending papers or In-
struments to the Neighouring Collony, who have a Seale in
Every County Given them for the Lyke Purpose;

4. There being no prison for the securing of debtors,
fugitieves and malefactors, who often make theire Escape for
want of the same, Wee therefore desiere his honors order for
the Errecting of a prison, which wee Immadgine woulld bee

Convenientt to stand in the forth, and that your Honor will Lykewyse prescrybe what allowance prisoners shall have, and by whome to bee paid, alsoo that the Sherrife may bee Responsable in Case of Escapes;

5. There was by the Last Generall Court here an order made, allowing 40 Gilders for Every woolfs head to be Levyed from the Publicque, of which said order wee Inclosed send his honor a Copy desiering your honors approbation uppon the same, severall of the Justices, and others haveing Laid out monny on the said Account, and Lykewyse, further desire his Honors order Impouring us to Rayse a Levy for the defraying of small publicq Charges, Itt being now the tyme of payment, and whereas it often happens that fynes are Imposed by the Court, uppon perticular persons, wee Lykewyse desire his honors grant, that all such fynes may henceforth bee Converted, for the defraying Publicq Charges, in Repairing of the forth, Building of a Prison, or the Lyke (allowing the Sherrife out of the same what your Honor shall thinke fitt) as also that all fynes heretofore Imposed, and not as Yett paid may bee Lykewyse Converted to the same use.

Lastly and Cheefly wee are Constrayned to tell Your Honor, that Incase sloops and vessels bee henceforth permitted to go upp and downe the River traeding with the People, and getting all the Reddy pay (as they now do) that this place will in short tyme bee dedersted[3] and come to nothing, (which then will make this River as Bad as Maryland) for Sir the merchants and traeders here duely and dayly supplying the people their wants in the Summer trust to bee paid att the Cropp, of which they are Putt by, by the said sloops and vessels, who as itt appeareth Little Reguard the 3 per C?[4] Custome, as now the Ketch and sloope are both gon upp the sloope (takeing the opportunity of Capt. Coliers going to Maryland and our Clarke whome hee had deputed in his absence, going but 2 or 3 dayes to Conduct him) went up the River without Clearing or paying any Customes; all which and the Lyke doth quite disharten the People and New Commers here; Wherefore wee in all humility Intreat your honor (Concidering the necessity for itt) to prohibit the going of all sloops and vessels, upp and downe the River and Bay on the said accompt, as it was in the tyme of your Honors predecessors, and Lykewyse that this Towne as being the only medium and best place may bee the only place of Loading and unloading, and Keeping of stores for all merchants, and that Your Honor will bee pleased that a publicq weighouse and Store house may be Erected, which will verry much Encouradge treadsmen and merchants to Resort hether, and the place will not only be populated but also the whole River will thryve by itt;

Uppon the aforesaid Particulars wee Humbly Intreat his honors favorable answer and approbation, so far as your Honor in his wisdome shall think fitt

New Castel   Remaining
November 8th 1676   Right Honorable Sir
                             Your Honors Most Humble
                             and faithfull Servants
                             [Signed:] John Moll
                                        Henry Ward
                                        Will. Tom
                                        Foppe Outhout
                                        Jean Paul Jacquet
                                        Gerret Otto

[Endorsed:]   No. 38 8 of Nov. 1676 Proposals from the Court
              of Delawar[5]

---

1. Other transcription in NYCD 12:563. Transcription of
   the court's copy in NCCR:21. See 20:102 and 20:103
   for reply to these proposals.

2. i.e., fort.

3. i.e., deserted.

4. The abbreviation apparently is intended for Cw. or Cwt.
   meaning "hundred weight." In 1683, for example, the
   custom duty in New York was set at 40 shillings or
   2 pounds per hundred weight.

5. Endorsement in the hand of Matthias Nicolls.

20:101   [SURVEY-RETURNS FOR DELAWARE][1]

Surveys recorded July 13th 1676

1. Edm. Andros Esq. etc.

     Whereas there is a certaine Tract of land called Marities
Hooke lyeing and being on the Westside of Delaware River, the
which by vertue of a warrant hath been layd out for Charles
Jansen, Olle Rawson, Olle Nielson, Hans Hopman, John Hendrickson and Hans Olleson, The said land being bounded as followeth
vizt. beginning at a small point of Highland within the mouth
of Naamans Creeke, and from thence running North and by west
one hundred twenty and three perches and North two hundred
perches, bounded with the Creeke to a Corner marked white Oake
by the Creeke side, at the mouth of a small branch, and from
thence East and by North, (bounded with the said branch, and
with a lyne of markt Trees from the head of the branch to a
corner markt spanish Oake standing by a small Run), three
hundred and eighty perches, from thence North North East
(along the Run) thirty two perches to a Corner markt white
Oake standing at the side of Maritiens Creeke, at the lower
side of the mouth of the said Run, and from thence downe
severall Courses of the Creeke to the Maine River side and
from thence downe along the River side to the place of beginning at the mouth of Naamans Creeke; Conteyning and layd out
for one thousand acres of Land, As by the returne of the survey under the hand of the surveyor doth and may appeare Now
Know yee etc. Quitt Rent 10 bushells. blanck date

2. Edm. Andros Esq. etc.

     Whereas there is a certaine Tract of land called
Groeningen lyeing and being on the West side of Delaware River
and on the North East side of St. Augustines Creeke the which

by vertue of a warrant hath beene layd out for Mr. Peter
Alricks, the said land beginning at a corner markt black Oake,
standing on the nearest point of Woodland, unto the said
Creeke by the River side, and from thence running North East,
Ninety foure perches, North Easterly thirty [blank] seventy
eight perches, North North East fifty two perches North East-
erly fifteene [blank] seventy perches and North East and by
North one hundred Eighty and six perches (bounding upon the
Maine River) unto the Mouth of a small sprout or Creeke called
litle St. Georges Creek which divideth this from the land of
Mrs. Anne Wales, and from thence west forty perches, South
West and by West, One hundred fifty and three perches, and
North Westerly seventy three [blank] One hundred forty and six
perches (bounding upon the said Creeke or sprout to Mrs. Wales
line of markt Trees, crossing the said branch and from thence
West South West along the said Mrs Wales line of marked Trees,
One hundred forty and two perches, to her upper Corner Tree
being a white Oake standing nigh unto the head of a swamp,
which proceedeth out of the Northerne branch of St. Augustines,
and from thence downe along the severall Courses of the said
branch and Marsh to the first mencioned black Oake Conteyning
and layd out for five hundred and sixty acres of land As by
the returne of the survey under the hand of the surveyor doth
and may appeare, Now Know yee etc. Quitt Rent five bushells
and a halfe   blanck date

3.   Edmund Andros Esq. etc.

     Whereas there is a certaine parcell of land called
Abrahams Delight lyeing and being on the West side of Delaware
River and on the North side of St. Augustines Creeke, next
adjoyning to Mr. Peter Ardricks[2] the which by vertue of a
warrant hath beene layd out for Abraham Enloes, The said land
beginning at a Corner marked white Oake standing on a point
in the first forke of the said Creeke, and from the said Oake
running North East sixty eight perches, North sixty foure
perches, North Westerly fifty eight [blank] two hundred
twenty and three perches (bounding on the Northerne branch)
to a corner white [sic] marked white Oake standing on a small
point betweene the two head branches of the said Northern
branch from thence South and by west by a line of markt Trees
sixty and two perches to a corner markt white Oake standing
at the East side of the head of a swamp, which proceedeth out
of said Maine branch of St. Augustines Creeke, and from thence
downe the severall Courses of the said swamp and Creeke to the
first mencioned white Oake, Conteyning and layd out for one
hundred and seventy Acres of Land, As by the returne of the
survey, under the hand of the Surveyor doth and may appeare:
Now know yee etc. Quitt Rent one bushell and a halfe:
blanck date

4.   Edm. Andros Esq. etc.

     Whereas there is a certaine parcell of land called
Drummers Neck, lyeing and being on the West side of Delaware
River and on the North West side of Apoquemini Creeke, the
which by Vertue of a warrant hath beene layd out for Maurice
Daniel, the said land beginning at a corner markt white oake
standing on a point by the said Creeke at the upper side of
a branch which at the Mouth thereof divideth this from the
land of Bernard Hendrickson, and from the said Oake running up
the branch North, North West forty perches, and then North
West by the said Bernards line of markt Trees, foure hundred

and Eighty preches to a corner markt Hickory, from thence
Southwest by a line of markt Trees sixty perches to a corner
markt Red Oake, being the upper corner tree of a parcell of
land formerly granted to Jacob Fiaen,[3] from thence South East
by the said Jacobs line of marked Trees foure hundred perches
to a Swamp, And then downe the Swamp South South East sixty
perches to the aforesaid Creeke, and finally downe along the
Creeke to the first mencioned white Oake, Conteyning and layd
out for one hundred and ninety acres of land, As by the returne of the Survey under the hand of the surveyor doth and
may appeare, The said land having beene formerly graunted by
Patent unto John Bradburne, bearing date June 17th 1671, and
by him diserted, Now Know yee etc. Two bushells etc. Quit
Rent, blanck date

5.   Edm. Andros Esq. etc.

Whereas there is a certaine Tract or parcell of land
called the good Neighbourhood, lyeing and being on the West
side of Delaware River, and on the North East side of St.
Augustines Creeke the which by vertue of a warrant hath beene
layd out for Casparus Herman, the said land beginning at a
Corner markt white Oake standing on a point at the upper side
of the mouth of a branch or swamp, etc. from thence running
North and by East up the said Swamp, and (from the head thereof) by a line markt Trees one hundred and fifty perches to the
land of George Axton nigh unto a corner marked Hickory standing a litle out of the lyne by the head of a small swamp, and
from thence West, North West by a line of markt trees three
hundred and seventy perches to a corner markt white Oake
standing on a Levell and from thence South west and by South
(by a line of markt Trees) three hundred perches, to a
corner markt Maple, standing at the North side of the maine
branch of St. Augustines Creeke, and from thence downe along
the said branch and Creeke to the first mencioned white Oake,
Conteyning and layd out for three hundred and thrity acres
of land, As by the returne of the survey under the hand of the
Surveyor doth and may appeare. Now Know yee etc. Quitt Rent
three bushells. blanck date

6.   Edm. Andros Esq. etc.

Whereas there is a certaine parcell of land called Calton
lyeing and being on the West side of Delaware River, and on
the North side of a Branch of black Bird Creek, that divideth
this from the land of [blank   ][4] the which by vertue of
a warrant hath beene layd out for John Barker, the said land
beginning at a corner markt Hickory, standing at the side of
the said branch by a Beaver dam, It being the upper corner
Tree of the land of John Hartop, and from thence running North
by the said Hartops line of marked Trees, two hundred forty
and six perches to a corner markt white Oake, from thence west
by a line of markt Trees, one hundred and fifty perches to a
corner markt Gumme Tree standing on the side of a [blank][5]
from thence South by a line of markt Trees two hundred and
thirty perches to a corner markt Maple, standing at the side
of the said branch, and from thence downe along the Run of the
said branch to the first mencioned corner Tree, Conteyning and
layd out for two hundred and twenty acres of land, as by the
Returne of the survey under the hand of the surveyor doth and
may appeare: Now know yee: Quitt Rent 2 bushells blank date

7.   Edm. Andros Esq. etc.

Whereas there are two certaine parcells of land, lyeing
and being on the westside of Delaware River betweene the land
called Pimepahka and the land of Towocawoninck the which by
verture of a warrant have beene layd out for Michael Fredericks,
Two hundred acres (part thereof) beginning at a corner markt
black Oake by the River side, which divideth this from the
land of Peter Peterson and Gasper Fish, and from the said Oake
running North, North west by their line of marked Trees three
hundred and twenty perches, to their upper corner bounded Tree,
being a black Oake, and from the said Oake West South West by
a line of marked Trees one hundred perches to another corner
markt black Oake, and from thence South South East, by a line
of markt Trees three hundred and twenty perches to a corner
markt white Oak standing by the River side, and from thence
East North East along the River side to the first mencioned
corner Oake; And the other hundred acres the residue of the
said land, beginning at a corner markt Beech, standing on a
small point at the mouth of Sissowokissinck Creeke, and from
thence running East North East forty perches, and North East
and by East one hundred and fourteene perches (by the Riverside)
to a corner markt black oake at the side of a small Creeke,
and from the said Oake North North west by a line of markt
trees, two hundred and sixty perches to a corner markt white
Oake standing by the main run of Sissowokissinck Creeke and
from the said white Oake, downe along the said R[iver] and
Creeke (dividing this from the land of Towocawoninck) to the
first mencioned Beech Tree Conteyning and layd out for three
hundred acres of land, As by the returne of the survey under
the hand of the Surveyor doth and may appeare, Now know yee
etc. Quitt Rent 3 bushells blanke date

8.   Edmond Andros Esq. etc.

Whereas there is a certaine parcell of land called point
Pleasant, lyeing and being on the West side of Delaware River,
and on the lower side of Nishambanack Creeke, about a mile and
a halfe up the said Creeke, the which by vertue of a warrant
hath beene layd out for Francis Walker and Dunk Williams, The
said land beginning at a corner markt black Oake, standing on
a Point, at the mouth of a small branch or Run and from thence
running North west along the Run forty perches, to a corner
markt white Oake, standing by the Run side, and from that
Oake North by a line of markt Trees three hundred and sixty
perches to a corner markt white Oake standing on a Levall and
from that Oake East North East by a line of markt Trees two
hundred and forty perches, to a corner markt Birch Tree,
standing at the side of the Maine Creeke, and from thence down
the severall Courses of the said Creeke to the first mencioned
corner Oake, Conteyning and layd out for the quantity of foure
hundred and fifty acres of land, As by the Returne of the
Survey under the hand of the surveyor doth and may appeare
Now Know yee etc. Quitt Rent 4 bushells and halfe: blanke date

10.   Edm. Andros Esq. etc.

Whereas there is a certaine parcell of land called
Quessinawominck lyeing and being on the West side of Delaware
River, the which by vertue of a warrant hath beene layd out
for Peter Cock, The said land being bounded as followeth, viz.
Beginning at a corner marked redd Oake, standing by a piece
of meadow ground, being a bounded Tree of the land of

Shakhamexunk, and from the said Oak running North North west
by Shakhamexunks line of marked Trees, three hundred and fifty
perches, to a corner marked white Oake, being the upper corner
bounded Tree of the said land of Shakhamexunk and from thence
East North East by a line of marked Trees, one hundred and
fifty perches to a corner marked black Oake stand [sic] nigh
unto Quessinawomink Creeke side opposite to the mouth of Taw-
acawonink Creek, and from thence downe the severall Courses
of the maine Creeke to the Maine River side, and from the
mouth of Quessinawomink Creeke, downe by the River, and by the
side of the first mentioned corner Oake, Conteyning and layd
out for six hundred and fifty acres of land together with the
Meadow ground thereunto adjoining, As by the returne of the
survey under the hand of the surveyor doth and may appeare:
Now know yeet etc. Six bushells and halfe Quit Rent   Blank for
date

11.   Edm Andros Esq. etc.

Whereas there is a certain parcell of land called Teck-
quirassy, lyeing and being on the west side of Delaware River
being the land where Olle Stille formerly dwelt the which by
vertue of a warrant hath beene layd out for Mr Laurentius
Carolus; The said being bounded as followeth viz. Beginning at
a corner marked Poplar standing nigh unto the old landing
place in Olle Stilles Creeke, and from the said poplar running
along by the Swamp side (which lyeth along by the River) North
Easterly sixty two [blank] one hundred forty foure perches,
North East Eighteene perches North Easterly sixty two [blank]
ninety eight perches to a corner makred Maple, standing by
the Swampe side, and divides this from the land of Niels Matson
and from the said Maple North west by a line of marked Trees
dividing this from the land of the said Niels, three hundred
thirty and eight perches, to a corner marked red Oake standing
on the Ridge between the aforesaid Creeke and a Creeke called
Crum-Kill and from the said Oake South west forty six perches
by a line of marked Trees, to a corner marked red Oake standing by a small piece of Marsh at the side of Olle Stilles
Creeke and from thence downe the severall Courses of the said
Creeke to the first mentioned poplar, Conteyning and layd out
for three hundred and fifty acres of land together with the
meadow Ground there to adjoining, part of the said land having
beene formerly granted by patent to the said Laurentius Carolus,
As by the returne of the Survey under the hand of the Surveyor
doth and may appeare, Now know yee etc. Quitt Rent 3 bushells
and halfe A blanck for the date.

12.   Edm. Andros Esq. etc.

Whereas there is a certaine parcell or Tract of Land
called Shakhamexunk, lyeing and being on the Westside of Delaware River, the which, by vertue of a warrant hath beene layd
out for Laurence Cock, Erick Cock, Michael Nielson, Otto Ernest
Cock, Goner Rambo and Peter Nielson, the said land being
bounded as followeth, viz. Beginning on a small point at the
mouth of a Creeke called Cohocksinks Creeke, and from thence
running betweene the East and North East along the Riverside
(according to the severall Courses thereof) to a Corner marked
red Oake, standing by a piece of Meadow Ground, and divideth
this from a Tract of land called Quessinawomink belonging to
Peter Cock, the distance from the mouth of the said Creeke to
the said Oake in a direct line, being nine hundred and twenty
perches and from the said Oake North, North West by a line of

marked Trees, dividing this from the said land of Peter Cock,
three hundred and fifty perches, to a corner marked white Oake,
standing by a small Swampe or Creuple nigh unto the highway
and from that Oake West North west, by a line of marked Trees
six hundred and twenty perches, to a corner marked Maple,
standing at the side of the Run of the West most branch of
Shakhamexunk Creeke, and from thence up the severall Courses
of the said Run to a corner markt white Oake standing in the
Swampe at the North East side of the Run, and from that Oake
West South west by a line of marked Trees, two hundred and
twenty perches, to a corner marked Oake, standing at the North
East side of the Run or maine branch of Cohocksinks Creeke,
And from thence downe the severall courses of the said Creeke
to the place of beginning, Conteining and layd out for sixteene hundred acres of land together with the Meadow Ground
thereto adjoyning, besides the watry and sunken land therein
conteyned, six hundred acres thereof having beene formerly
graunted by Patent unto Peter Cock and one thousand acres the
Residue being new Land, As by the returne of the Survey under
the hand of the Surveyor, doth and may appeare: Now know yee
etc. Quitt Rent 16 bushells   a blanck for the date.

...the dividing of the aforesaid two branches and from
the said point up the western branch (which divideth this from
the land of George Axton) to the place of beginning; Conteyning and layd out for one hundred acres of land, As by the
returne of the survey, under the hand of the surveyor doth
and may appeare. Now know yee etc. Quitt Rent 1 bushell
blanck date.[6]

17.   Edm. Andres Esq.

Whereas there is a certaine Tract of land called Pimmeepahka, lyeing and being on the West side of Delaware River
and on the lower side of Pimmeepahkas Creeke the which by vertue of a warrant hath beene layd out for Peter Peterson and
Gaspar Fish, The said land being bounded as followeth, viz.
Beginning at a corner marked black Oake standing by the River
side, nigh unto the lower End of a piece of meadow ground and
from the said Oake running North North west by a line of
marked Trees three hundred and twenty perches to another corner marked black Oake standing about twenty perches from the
Northward side of a small Swamp, and from that Oake East North
East by a line of marked Trees three hundred and sixty perches
to a corner marked white Oake, standing on the bank of Pimmeepahka's Creeke, about thirty perches about the highway, and
from the said White Oake downe the severall Courses of the
said Creeke to the Maine River side and from the mouth of the
said Creeke downe along the River side to the first mencioned
black Oake, Conteyning and layd out for five hundred acres
of land together with the meadow ground thereto belonging, the
said land being part of a Tract of land formerly granted by
patent to Andrew Carr, As by the returne of the Survey under
the hand of the Surveyor doth and may appeare: Now know yee
etc. Quitt Rent 5 bushells. blanke date.

18.   Edm. Andros Esq. etc.

Whereas there is a certaine tract of land called Towo-
cawonink lyeing and being on the west side of Delaware River,
between two Creeks, the one called Quessinawomink, the other
Sissowokissink the which by vertue of a warrant hath beene layd
out for Erick Mallock, Olle Nielson and Christian Thomason,

The said land being bounded as followeth, viz. beginning at
the River side at the West side of the Mouth of Sissowokissink
Creeke and from thence running up the said Creeke North Westerly
thirty [blank] two and twenty perches North and by East twenty
eight Perches North North West one hundred and twenty perches
(bounded with the said Creeke) to a Corner marked white Oake
standing at the side of the Run of the said Creeke by the
mouth of a small branch, and from the said Oake by a line of
marked Trees West three hundred thirty six perches to a Corner marked white Oake standing on the side of a Knowle on the
Eastward side of a branch or Creeke called Tawocawonink Creeke,
being a branch of Quessinawomink, and from thence downe the
severall Courses of the said branch and maine Creeke to the
River side, and from the mouth of Quessinawomink Creeke along
by the River side to the place of beginning, Conteyning and
layd out for Nine hundred and fifty acres of land, together
with the Meadow Ground thereto belonging, The said land being
part of a tract of land formerly granted by patent unto Andrew
Carre, As by the returne of the Survey under the hand of the
Surveyor doth and may appeare: Now know yee etc. Quitt Rent
9 bushells and a halfe blanck date

19. Edm. Andros Esq. etc.

Whereas there is a certaine parcell of land lyeing and
being on the West side of Delaware River upon a branch of
Christina Creeke called White Clayes Creeke, above the fall
thereof, on the upperside of the land of John Nomers, the
which by vertue of a warrant hath beene layd out for Peter
Thomason, the said land being bounded as followeth vizt.
Beginning at a Corner marked Gum Tree, standing at the south
side of the Maine Run, and from the said Gum running South by
a line of marked Trees, dividing this from the land of John
Nomers twenty Perches, to a Corner marked white Oake, And from
the said Oake South West and by West by a line of marked Trees,
two hundred Perches to a Corner marked white Oake, standing
betweene two small Swamps or Creuple, And from that Oake
Northwest and by North, by a line of marked Trees one hundred
and eighty Perches to a Corner marked white Oake standing on
a piece of high ground on the North side of the said Run, And
from that Oake North East and by East, by a lyne of markt
Trees two hundred and twenty perches to a Corner marked Hickory,
and from the said Hickory South East and by South, by a lyne
of marked Trees, one hundred thirty six perches to a Corner
marked white Oake standing on a high bank at the North side
of the aforesaid great Run being the upper Corner Oake of the
Land of the aforesaid Nomers and from thence South Westerly
foure [blank] slanting over the Run and bounding on the
land of the said Nomers thirty two perches, to the first mencioned Gum Tree. Conteyning and layd out for two hundred and
twenty acres of land, As by the returne of the Survey under
the hand of the Surveyor doth and may appeare: Now know yee
etc. Quitt Rent 2 bushells blank date

20. Edm. Andros Esq.

Whereas there is a certaine parcell of land lyeing and
being on the west side of Delaware River and on the East side
of the Schuyle Kill, the which by vertue of a warrant hath
beene layd out for Peter Dalboe, The said land being bounded
as followeth viz. Beginning on a point by the Upperside of a
Rock at the Mouth of a Deep branch, nigh and by the dwelling
house of the said Dalboe, which said branch divideth this

from the land of Peter Rambo, And from the said point running
by the side of the said Kill or Creeke, North Easterly thirty
[blank   ] fifty six perches North Easterly Eighty five
thirty two perches, East and by South fourteene perches, South
East thrity six perches East...[7]

---

1. Partly transcribed in NYCD 12:547. Some of these surveys appear in WWS and DYR. Matthias Nicolls, in whose
   hand the surveys are written, consistently left a blank
   for the word "degrees," whereas it does appear in WWS
   and DYR. Pages are missing from this copy book which
   contained surveys No. 9, 13, 14, 15, and portions of
   16 and 20.

2. i.e., Peter Alrichs.

3. i.e., Jacob Fiana. cf., NCCR:21.

4. For this omission WWS:76 has: "Capt. Matthias Nicolls
   and Mr. Tho: Lovelace."

5. For this omission WWS:77 has: "Poquoson."

6. Only this fragment of survey No. 16 has survived.
   See WWS:51 for the complete survey.

7. The final pages are missing. See WWS:47 for the
   complete survey.

20:102   [COUNCIL MINUTES RELATING TO JOHN FENWICK
         AND DELAWARE AFFAIRS][1]

                              At a Councell held in New York
                              November 20th 1676.

Entred in the Councel booke. The answer to the proposalls to bee in the Common booke of Entryes.[2]

Severall Letters being read concerning Major John Fen-
wicks actings in New Jersey on the East side of Delaware River
by his granting patents for Land, and refusing to obey the
Governors speciall warrant etc.[3]

Resolved, It importing his Majesties service, and good
and quiet of those parts and Inhabitants, That hee bee sent
for with the first Convenience hither, and if there bee occasion
that the Commander and Magistrates at Delaware doe use force
for seizing and sending him.

That there being no Lawfull Authority for Major Fenwycks
giving forth patents for Land, Its not thought fitt to returne
back those sent hither, But the persons who have paid their
moneys for them, may have their Remedy at Law for the same,

against the person that gave them.

Upon the Complaint of Jean Paul Jaquet, That hee hath
beene dispossest by Major Fenwyck of some Land on the East
side of Delaware River, Ordered, That the said Jean Paul
Jaquet bee repossest of what land hee was in possession of on
the Eastside of the River, at the last comming in of the English Government, The which the Court is to take Order about,
and if occasion the Commander at Delaware is to assist them.

In answer to the Proposalls sent by the Magistrates of
Newcastle for my Approbacion.⁴

1. To the first, That one of his R. Hs. Lawbookes shall
bee sent them.

2. To the second, That the Inhabitants of the towne of
Newcastle and within a Mile thereof, doe keepe watch, but that
none bee obliged to come to the watch farther. The other part
of the Proposall about Souldyers to bee sent thither, To bee
taken into farther Consideracion.

3. To the third, About a public Seale, Care will bee
taken against the next yeare, In the meane time to make use of
their owne Seales, as is usuall for Justices of the peace
every where.

4. Allowed That a prison bee built in the Fort, and the
Sheriffe to bee responsable for prisoners; For the allowance
or Fees to bee directed by the Law booke, with regard to former Custome and practice.

5. That order made about killing of Wolves, to be confirmed for the present yeare, and till further order.

6. Fines to bee granted to the Court for the present
yeare, and for the two yeares last past, to bee applyde for
publick uses, For the which the Sheriffe and Receiver or Receivers to bee called to Account, and pay in the same to the
Courts order, who are to make a Returne to the Governor how
disposed of.

The Sheriffe for his paines in Collecting or levying the
same, to have 5s in the pound, and for extraordinary Charge,
to bee farther allowed by the Court, as there shall bee cause.

That towards the farther defraying of public Charges in
the Towne of Newcastle as also up the River and in the Bay,
there bee a Levy made of one penny in the pound upon every
mans Estate, to bee tax't by indifferent persons there unto
appointed by the respective Courts and by the severall Courts
to be disposed of accordingly whereof an account to bee given
hither.⁵

7. That former Orders prohibiting Sloopes and Vessels
goeing up the River above Newcastle to trade bee duely observed as heretofore.

And that A weigh-house bee allowed of, for which a sworne
officer to bee appointed.

[Verso:] A Copie of the Go: Letter sent to Newcastle
No: 23.1676.

I have received your Letters[6] by the expresse sent hither
with several other papers and writings, relating unto Major
John Fenwycks actings[7] on the Eastside of Delaware River by
his granting patents for Land, and refusing to obey my speciall
warrant etc.[8] as also your more peculiar affaires. Whereupon
having taken advice of my Councell It is Resolved, It importing his Majesties service, and the good and quiet of these
parts and Inhabitants, That Major John Fenwyck bee sent for.
etc.[9]

[In margin next to letter:]   This entred in the Councell booke.

[Endorsed:]   No. 39 Answer Delaware buisnesse Nov. 20. 1676.
    Councell.

----

1. This document is written in the hand of Matthias
   Nicolls. Other transcription in NYCD 12:565.

2. These two notations were written between the heading
   and the first paragraph at a later date. The heading
   above and the following paragraphs concerning John Fenwick are crossed out. This was apparently done after
   the minutes had been entered in the Council Book, see
   Council Minutes 3 (part 2):133 for this entry; the
   remaining uncancelled minutes, which concern the proposals, were then to be recorded in General Entries.

3. For a copy of this special warrant dated Sept. 25, 1676
   summoning John Fenwick to appear before the council in
   New York see Miscellaneous Records 3:231. In PA 5:688.

4. See 20:100 for these proposals from the magistrates of
   New Castle. cf., 20:103 for a draft of a reply to
   these proposals and NCCR:37 for a transcription of the
   final draft which was sent to New Castle.

5. This paragraph is marked to replace the following order
   which is crossed out: For a Levy 1d in the pound Towne
   River and bay, all the Courts to bee acquainted with it,
   for publicke charges.

6. See 20:100 for this correspondence.

7. The phrase in New Jersey, which follows actings, is
   crossed out.

8. See F.N. 3.

9. See 20:103 for a draft of this letter to the magistrates of New Castle. For a transcription of the final
   draft sent to New Castle see NCCR:37.

20:103   [GOV. ANDROS TO THE MAGISTRATES OF NEW CASTLE
          ABOUT JOHN FENWICK AND MUNICIPAL AFFAIRS][1]

Gentlemen

        I have received your Letters[2] (by the Expresse sent hither)
with severall other papers and writings unto Major John Fenwycks actings on the Eastside of Delaware River by his granting
Patents for Land, and refusing to obey my speciall warrant
etc.[3], As also touching your more peculiar affayres; Whereupon
having taken advice of my Councell,

        I have thought fitt, (It importing his Majesties service,
and the good and quiet of those parts and Inhabitants,) That
Major John Fenwyck bee sent with the first Convenience hither,
and if there bee occasion, That the Commander, and you the
Magistrates doe use force for seizing upon and sending him.

        And there being no Lawfull Authority for his giving forth
Patents for Land, those sent hither are not to bee returned
back for the present, But the persons who have paid their
moneys for them, may have their remedy at Law, against the
person that gave them, before hee depart out of Custody.

        As for Jean Paul Jaquet who hath beene dispossest of some
Land on the Eastside of Delaware River of which hee was in
possession at the Last comming in of the English Government,
hee is to bee repossest and you are to take order about [sic],
and if occasion the Commander is to assist therein.

        In answer to your Proposalls, one of his Royall Highnesse
Law Bookes shall bee sent you by the first opportunity.

        The Inhabitants of the Towne of Newcastle, and within a
mile thereof, are to Keepe watch, but none are obliged to come
to it further. As to the Proposall about souldyers to bee sent
for it, the same shall bee taken into farther Consideracion.

        For a publick seale Care will bee taken against the next
yeare, In the meane time you are to make use of your owne
seales, as is usuall for Justices of the peace every where.

        You may cause a prison to bee built in the Fort, and the
Sheriffe is to bee responsable for prisoners; For the allowance or Fees, you are to bee directed by the Law booke, with
regard to former Custome and Practice.

        I doe confirm the Order made about Killing of Wolves, for
the present yeare, and till further Order.

        As to Fines I doe grant them to the Court for the yeare
currant and for the two yeares last past, since the English
Government, to bee applyde for publick uses; for the which the
Sheriffe and Receiver or Receivers are to bee called to account,
and pay in the same to the Courts order, who are to make a Returne to the Governor, how disposed of. The Sheriffe for his
paines in collecting or Levying the same, to have five shillings
in the pound and for extraordinary Charge, at Newcastle up the
river or into the Bay, to bee farther allowed by the Courts as
there shall bee cause.

        And likewise towards the farther defraying of public
Charges in the Towne of Newcastle, as also up the River, and in

the Bay, a Levy is to bee made of one penny in the pound upon
every mans Estate, to bee tax't by indifferent persons thereunto appointed by the respective Courts, and by the said Courts
to bee disposed of accordingly, whereof an Account to bee
given hither.

The former Orders Prohibiting Sloopes and Vessells goeing
up the River above Newcastle to trade, are duely to bee observed as heretofore, and Care to bee taken that none goe up.

And a weigh-House is likewise to bee built in the Towne
of Newcastle, for the which you are to appoint an Officer to
bee sworne thereunto.

This is all from -

Nov. 23rd 1676.
                To the Magistrates of Delaware

[Endorsed:]   No. 44 An answer to the proposalls sent from
              Delaware. Nov. 23rd 1676.

---

1. Other transcription in NYCD 12:566. The final draft of
   this letter appears in NCCR:37. The following transcription represents the revised draft incorporating all
   corrections, deletions and insertions made by Matthias
   Nicolls on the manuscript. The unrevised version is
   printed in the appendix to this volume. See 20:102 for
   the council minutes upon which this letter is based.

2. See 20:100 for this correspondence.

3. For a copy of this warrant dated Sept. 25, 1676 summoning John Fenwick to New York see Miscellaneous
   Records 3:231. Printed in PA 5:688.

20:104   [ASSIGNMENT OF AN ISLAND IN THE DELAWARE BY
          SAMUEL EDSALL TO GEORGE HEATHCOTE][1]

      Where[   ] Edsall of this City hath assigned all
[   ] title and Intrest over to me George Heathcote, of an
Island called by the Ingin name of Sankhikins, Lyinge in
delaware nere the falls, these are to sertyfie whom it may
conserne That I doe acknowledge to have but one halfe of the
said Iland properly belongeinge unto me, and that is in Consideration of Charges of gettinge the whole Iland Confirmed to
me by the Duke of Yorke, and That I give the said Edsall, the
same Confirmemation [sic] derived from mine, soe gott of the
duke for his halfe, and forty pounds more Currant p[   ] New
yorke, for my halfe, beinge in full for it, [   ] said
Confirmation of the dukes Cannot be procuered, Then [   ]
Agreements to be voyd not withstandinge, and the [   ]
retorne to Samuel Edsall [   ] first, in wittnes [   ]

they have [   ] theire hands and [   ] the second
[   ] [   ] [ ] the yeare one thousand six honndred
[   ]

Signed sealed and   [Signed:] Samuell Edsall
delivered before
[Signed:] Guilain Verplanck
Clement Sebra
Robert Roberts

---

1. Other transcription in NYCD 12:570. cf., 20:137.

20:105   The Survayer Fees in the Province of
          Mariland by Act of Assembly[1]

Item   For one hundered one pownd per Aker if the Plot be between one hundered and tow hundered then for the first one
hundred as A for said for all Above halfe A pownd of tobako per
Aker, if between tow hundered and five hundered then for the
first tow hundered as A for said, And for all Above A quarter
of A pownd per Acker, if it be between five hundered Acker
[   ] Thoussand Aker then for the first five hundered Akers
As A for said and for all A bove on Pownd of tobako for every
ten Akers, for entereing the Survay uppon the booke five
Pownds of tobako, for discribing A Plott of the Plott of the
Grant if it be A hundered or under ten Pownds of tobako if
Above five for every hundered Akers besides thees Fees the
Survayer may demand for goeing or coming if twenty mills and
under forty Pownds of tobako if Above twenty mils forty eight
Pownds of tobako the Partie or Imployer is to [   ] boot and
hands in Caisse he cannot goe [   ] by Land and victalls
out And whome etc.[2]

[Verso:] From Mr. Aug. Hermans
          The Surveyors Fees[3]
For the first 100 acres   100 lb. Tob.
For the 2nd   "   "   50   "
For the 3rd   "   "   25   "
For the 4th and so for every }
          100 more   }   12   "
with for the plott   10   "
     For the warrant   10   "

[Endorsed:] The Surveyors Fees in Maryland To bee observed in
             Delaware. 1676.

---

1. This document is written in the hand of Augustine
   Herrman. cf., 20:90 and 20:106.

2. See 20:106 for the sense of this last line.

3. This schedule of surveyor's fees including the endorsement is written in the hand of Matthias Nicolls.

20:106   [COPY OF THE SCHEDULE OF SURVEYOR'S FEES IN
          MARYLAND][1]

The Surveyor Generall and his Deputies Fees

To the Survey of 100 acres or under one lb. of tobacco per acre. For any quantity above 100 acres and under 200 acres for the first 100 as before and halfe a lb. of tobacco per acre for the rest. If between 200 acres and 500 acres, then for the first 200 acres as before and a quarter of a lb. of tobacco per acre for all above. For every Platt allowing two Platts for every Survey, (that is to Say) one for the Party and another to be entred upon the Surveyors booke 10 lb. of tobacco, for the first 100 acres or under and after the rate of 5 lb. of tobacco per Cent for all above the first hundred.

For Journy Fees if the Place be distant from the Surveyors house 20 miles or under, 40 lb. of tobacco if above 20 and under 40 miles then 80 lb. of tobacco if above 40 miles and under 60 then 120 lb. of tobacco and soe pro rato, the Party finding boat hands and necessary Provisions.

For every Certificate of Survey be the quantity more or less 5 lb. of tobacco. For the Resurvey of 140 acres or under made with Circumferenter and Chaine or other necessary Instrument 400 lb. of tobacco.

For the Resurvey of any Quantity of Land above 140 acres Double the Fees above Specified for Survey in all Respects.

The above said Fees amongst other Acts made at a Generall Assembly held at St. Maryes the 15th of May 1676 was allowed to the Surveyor Generall of this Province of Maryland and remain of record in the Secretaryes Office upon Record.

                         John Blomfeild Cl, Cons.
                         and Cur. Province[2]

[Endorsed:] 1676 Mariland 15th of May Surveyeors fees[3]

---

1. cf., 20:90 and 20:105 for related documents.

2. i.e., Clerk of the Provincial Council and Court.

3. Endorsement is written in the hand of Matthias Nicolls.

20:107   [ORDER OF JUSTA ANDERSON ON MR. BLACKWILL FOR
          PAYMENT OF A DEBT]

Mr. Blackwill

        To be pleased to pay unto this bearer Mr. Robart Huchesone
the summe of Thirty seven gulden and Tenn stivears which is
dew to mee which you tould me I should have it by James
Williames but I cant get it of him I wrott to by Simon Gibson
but he Could see you So having Noe more but this my Notte
shall be youear disch[ ] with his resight from youer Loving
frend

                            [Signed:] Jestoe Andersone
New Castle
Feb. the 18th 1676/7

[Verso:][1]

Ralfe is Dr.   29. 18.
[ ]se - 12 botles   Ralfe Hucheson
Clarke   3   "   Dr. to Mr. Moll on account
Will   1   "   To: 6 qts. of madera
the Smyth 1   "   1 qt. ditto To Fr. Whitwell
your Selfe 5 "   30: To 3 pints ditto
Salter   1   "
Ralfe is Dr.
50 qt. Claret
26 qt. of Sack
Billop 2 qts. of Claret

---

1. These two accounts, which appear on the reverse of
   Anderson's order, are written in a second hand.

20:108   [MATTHIAS NICOLLS TO THE MAGISTRATES OF WHOREKILL
          ABOUT LAND GRANTED TO WILLIAM PLAINER][1]

Gent.

        By Informacion from Mr. Peter Groenendyke (the bearer
hereof) to the Councill, That a certaine piece of Land granted
to Wm. Plainer, whereof hee was in possession twelve months,
was by misinformacion or mistake afterward given and granted
by patent to Randall Revell, who neither sought after nor ever
had pretence to the same, Concerning the which no order being
left from his honor, It will bee convenient to let the matter
rest as it is untill his Returne, and in meane time Wm. Playner
not to bee dispossest, This I give you as the opinion of the
Councell, being
                            Gent. your humble servant
Feb. 20. 1677   [Initialed:] M. N.

For the Magistrates at the
Whorekill.   These

[Endorsed:] A Letter to the Magistrates of the Whorekill by
             order of Councell. Feb. 20 1677

---

1. For related documents see 20:88a and 20:118 a/b.
    Other transcription in NYCD 12:571.

20:109   [HELMANUS WILTBANCK TO GOV. ANDROS ABOUT
          AFFAIRS AT WHOREKILL][1]

Richt Honorable Gouverneur

     Yours receaved the 18th of this Instend month wear in wy
unterstand your great Cear en deligenth af us wich wy durender[2]
to your Honor menny tanks wear in wy doe inform your Honor that
wy ar in good Helt Likeweise thear is good Hops af succes an
sittuatie[3] af this pleats by menny persons both out Virginia
en Merrylandt en heave also receaved ohn halfe barrel af pou-
der which youe thet sent by your schaloep en given alsoo menny
tancks to your Honor for your good Instruction en schal mack
as good jus af them as possibelly Lays in our pour en schyl[4]
how that your Honor thet deseir af accasion thet requier a
piloot for your Honors Schaloep thear was non Keapabele her
en your Honors Schloep meester thet not much question gohin
wel Wy doe here a fulger[5] raport from the Commin people in
merrylandt that the Lord Baltimore thus ar inmagine to heave
this pleats again but wy doe weafet(?) en wy thacht[6] fit to
give your Honor notis af at Lickeweis her is dayly severul
persons Commin out Virginia which brings news that the rebellien
thus Continuen stil against thear gouverneur en gouverment en
Lick to be wors which is agreat dashartening to al payes en
sober meyndeth people Not els but your Honors Servant to
Commaund and pray for your Honors good Helt en succes in your
gouverment
                              [Signed:] Helm. Wiltbanck
1676/7 this 26th of Feb.
at the Whorkil
[P.S.]
Her is present news out af accumacko[7] that thear is tree
fregats is [sic] Com in and that the heave brought the Contre
tow a paes again en moor that [   ] lord Baltomore heave gott
agrant from His Majesty [   ] his Land en that the seam scud[8]
follow fourtnicht [   ] the fregats thet seth outh

[Addressed:] These For the richt Honorable gouverneur Ed.
              Androsz At Ny Jorck

[Endorsed:] [   ] Whorekill Feb. from Mr. Wiltbanck
             Magistrate[9]

---

1. Helmanus Wiltbanck's spelling reflects a heavy Dutch
    accent and Dutch spelling conventions. N.B. thet = "did"
    and thus = "does." Frequently final th = "t" or "d"

and t = "th." Other transcription in NYCD 12:571.

2. i.e., "do render."

3. Extention of Dutch situatie: "lay of the land," to mean "settlement."

4. i.e., "skill."

5. i.e., "fuller."

6. i.e., "thought."

7. i.e., Accomack, Virginia.

8. i.e., "...the same should..."

9. Endorsement in the hand of Matthias Nicolls.

20:110   [NO CALENDAR ENTRY AND NO DOCUMENT]

20:111   [COURT ORDER FOR THE RESURVEY OF LAND
          PURCHASED BY JOHN STEVENS][1]

                    At a Speciall Court held for the Whorekill
                    the 19th Day of March 1676/7.

                     Mr. Helm. Wiltbanck
Justices {Mr. Edward Southrin } Mr. Alex Molestine } Present
          {Capt. Paul Marsh   } Mr. John King   }

John Stevens petitioner
     Granted unto John Stevens purchaser of the Land of Perry
     William Willoughby and Robert Dicks that the said persons
     Lands So purchased by the Said John Stevens shall bee
     Resurveyed according to pattents for the proper use of the
     said John Stevens with an addition of Six hundred acres
     thereunto Adjoyning and the said Assignment by the said
     Reservey from the afore said persons unto the said John
     Stevens shall bee Authentyque in Law.
                    Vera Copia
[Signed:] Test: Cornelis Verhoofe Cl. Co. Whorekill

[Endorsed:] A copy of ann order of Corte March the 19 1676/7.

_____

1. Other transcription in NYCD 12:572.

20:112   [DEPOSITIONS OF WITNESSES IN THE CASE BETWEEN
          DOM. LAURENTIUS CAROLUS AND HANS PETERSEN][1]

Aprill the 3rd. 1677.   New Castle

      The following wittnesses were sworne in Court in the Case
depending betweene Lace Carolus Plt. and Hans Peterson Deft.

      Pelle Hendricx sworne in Court declares that about 2 Jeare
sence this deponant came over from Craynhoeck, as when Hans
Peterson desiered this deponant to come and Looke on a mare
of about 3 Jeare, to see whether the said mare had any brandmarke but the deponant Comming Could see no brandmarke, and
sayeth that hee did not see Hans marke the said mare in the
Eare, but about 3 or 4 dayes after hee did see the said mare
markt in the Left Eare.

      Christina the wyfe of Pelle Hendricx sworne declareth,
that about 2 Jeare sence Hans Pietersen desiered this deponant
and hur husband to help them dryve up an unmarkt mare, which
the deponant did, and haveing drove the mare in the stable;
Hans Peterson said: I will now goe to the Commander Capt.
Cantwell to get order for the markeing of the mare, and Returning againe hee said I have now obtayned Leave to marke the
said mare, but the deponant did not see him marke the said mare;

      Margrieta Poulsz sworne declares that about 2 Jeare sence
Hans Pieterse did dryve a Certaine Mare in this deponants
Cowe Stall where the said mare stood one night and the depon-
ant sayes that the said mare was then now markt;

      Jan Jansen sworne declares that the mare of Lace Carolus,
about 4 Jeare sence did get a foale att Marretiens Kill where
shee then did Run the whole sommer and winter, and afterwards
the mare did Run to Marretiens hoek where shee then with hur
said foale Run all the next Sommer, about which tyme the mare
dyed, and the foale Run away all the winter but in the sommer
next the said foale came againe and was seen att Verdritige
hoek, where Lace Carolus markt the same;

      Hendrik Jansz being sworne declares that being about one
Jeare sence in the Schillpatts Kill; hee heard Christina the
wyfe of Pelle Hendricx and Margreta Poulsz say, that they had
holp Hans Pietersz dryve in the stable an unmarkt mare and
that the said Hans did not then marke the same; but about 2 or
3 dayes after Hans had tould them that hee had markt the said
mare which they then alsoe did see to bee markt but were not
by when Hans markt the same;

      Jacob Clementsz being sworne declares that next harvest
tyme come twoo Jeare, this deponant was in the doare of the
forte att Verdrietige hoeck, and did see in the said house a
mare which was not markt, which mare Dom. Carolus sayes to bee
his mare;

      Oele Oelsen being sworne declares that about twoo Jeare
agoe hee was in the house att Verdrietige hoeck, and did see a
mare in the said house, but could not see any marke about hur
Eares att which tyme shee was there markt for Dom. Carolus.

      Jacob Martense being sworne declares, that Comming from
the t'Church att Craine hoeck, hee saw the mare of Dom. Carolus
at Verdrietige hoeck but was not markt untill afterwards by

his the said Dom. Carolus order;

Hendrik Nealson being sworne declares that about 2 Jeare
sence Dom. Carolus came to this deponants house att Verdrietige
hoeck, where then did Run an unmarckt mare, which the said
Dom. Carolus said to bee his mare; and was markt by his order
by Jacob Martensz his Clark.

Justa Poulsz being sworne declares that about twoo Jeare
sence this deponant did help Hans Pietersz dryve a Certaine
unmarkt mare into the stable of the said Hans, att which tyme
Hans Pietersz went to the Towne and sayed that hee would goe
and get Leave of Capt. Cantwell to makre the said mare, and
Returning againe hee said; I have obtayned Leave of Capt.
Cantwell for to marke the Mare and about twoo or 3 dayes after
this deponant did see the mare marckt with a small Cropp in the
Left Eare, but did not see Hans Pietersz marke the same;

Oele Oelsen being sworne declareth that hee was with in a
house Lenght of the Mare att Verdrietige hoeck but could not
see that the said mare had any marke;

Carell Pietersen being sworne declareth that hee the
deponant now about twoo Jeare agoe did see att Verdrietige
hoeck a mare but Knowes not whoes mare shee was or whether shee
had any marke;

Poull Moensen being sworne declares that about 2 Jeare
agoe hee Saw at Verdrietige hoeck a mare which as much as the
deponant Could see had no marke neither doth hee know whoes
mare shee was;

Neales Nealson being sworne declares that next harvest
tyme come twoo Jeare this deponant did dryve by the order of
Dom. Carolus a mare with his horses in at Verdrietige hoeck
which mare the deponant could not see that had any marke but
was by order of the said Dom. Carolus (who Claymed hur) markt
att Verdrietige hoeck.

Oele Fransen sworne declareth that hee Knowes nothing of
the mare in Controversie;

> A True Coppy of the Depositions
> by the Wittnesses declareth and
> sworne in Court the 3rd of aprill
> 1677; att New Castle.
> Exam. per mee
> [Signed:] Eph: Herman, Clarke

[Endorsed:]   [   ] Laurentius Carolus
                [   ] Hans Petersen
                Proceedings at the Court of Newcastle about a
                Mare. 1677.

---

1. For related documents see 20:113, 20:119 and 20:124; as
    well as NCCR:73 and 88, and UCR:74. The plaintiff in
    this case is Laurentius Carolus Lokenius, pastor or
    domine of the church at Crane Hook.

20:113   [PLEADINGS IN THE CASE BETWEEN DOM. LAURENTIUS
          CAROLUS AND HANS PETERSEN][1]

                                        Att a Court held in New Castle
                                        Aprill 3 and 4th. 1677.

              Mr. William Tom   ⎫
Present   Mr. Fopp Outhout   ⎬ Justices
              Mr. Jean Paul Jacquet ⎭
              Mr. Gerret Otto

Dom: Lace Carolus   Plt.
Hans Pietersen...   Deft.

        The Plt. declares that the deft. Contrary to the Know-
ledge or without the order of the Plt. did take up a mare of
your Plt. which Run in the woods, with intention as your Plt.
doth Really thinke to defraud your Plt. of the said mare,
Challenging your Plts. mare for his owne, altough [sic] it can
bee prooved by several witnesses; the mare properly belongeth
to [your] Plt., and that your Plt. Caused the mare to bee
marked with his owne marke, there never being any other marke
on the said mares Eeares, but what was put on by the order of
your Plt. and that the said Mare hath ben Knowne to bee your
Plts. ever sence it was a filly notwithstanding which the deft.
still Challenges the said Mare as his owne and would if it Lay
in his pouwer defraud your Plt. of the said mare exposing by
his unlawfull demands your Plt. to great Cost and trouble,
Wherefore your Plt. humbly Craves of this worshipfull Court
that hee may have an order peaceably to Enjoy the said mare
being properly his owne as alsoe that the deft. may Render him
sattisfaction for the Trouble hee hath ben Exposed unto
through his occasion with Costs of suitt.

        The deft. being an Illiterate person did humbly desier
that Capt. Cantwell might speake for him there being no other
attorney but what the Plt. Imployes, [which] the Court grant;

        Whereuppon fifteen Witnesses be[ing] sworne and Examined
in Court,[2] and [uppon] the Plts. Request a Jury Empann[elled:]
The Court did find uppon due Examin[ation] of all the said
wittnesses before the Jury was sworne, that the Plt. had no
Cause of action unlesse the Plt. brings better proofe to proove
his declaration;

                    Vera Copia Exam. Per
        [Signed:] Eph: Herman, Clark

_____

    1. See NCCR:73 for a transcription of the original record
        from which this copy was made. For documents related
        to this case see 20:112, 20:119 and 20:124; as well as
        NCCR:88 and UCR:74. Damaged portions have been re-
        covered from NCCR.

    2. See 20:112 for these depositions.

20:114   [COPY OF COURT PROCEEDINGS CONCERNING THE
          WIDOW BLOCK'S RIGHT OF WAY][1]

                              Att a Court held in the Towne of
                              New Castle the 3 and 4th of aprill
                              1677.

Uppon the Peticion of Capt. Cantwell and Joh: d'Haes
sheweing that they had bought in open vendu a peece of Land
formerly belonging to Capt. John Carr for the summe of 1250
gilders without any Clayme of any of the Neighbours to the
Same which said sale was Confirmed by the Right honorable
Governor, as by the Pattent may apeare and the Peticioner
haveing fenced the same notwithstanding which the fences are
dayly pulled downe Mistris Bloke[2] dryving hur Cattle in the
Peticioners Land, Saying Itt is the way to the woods and that
they the Peticioners could make appeare that Neither by the
Dutch or English Government any way was allowed, only by
sufferance The said Peticioners desiering that they might bee
maintained and have an order quietly to possess their said
Land, or in case Mistris Bloke can make apeare any Clayme to
the same, the Peticioners are willing to Joyne Issue with hur
Either here or before his honor the Governor att New Yorke etc.

     Mistris Bloke producing in Court an order of Councell
touching the said way, and Capt. Cantwell and Mr. d'Haes their
Pattents etc. The Court doe answer that they deare not breake
Either of his honors orders but Refer the Case bake to his
honor the Governor to determine, and that the partees in the
meane tyme prepair themselves to Informe his honor about the
same;
                              By order of Court
                         [Signed:] Eph: Herman, Clarke

[Endorsed:] The widdow Blocks papers from Delaware about an
             Outdrift etc. Apr. 1677.[3]

----

1. For a transcript of the original court proceedings see
    NCCR:78. See 20:91, 20:92 and 20:116 for related
    documents.

2. i.e., Mary Block, the widow of Hans Block.

3. Endorsement in the hand of Matthias Nicolls.

20:115a   [CERTIFICATE ALLOWING CAPT. ISRAEL HELME
           TO BUY LAND][1]

     These are to certify, that when the unpurchased Land ad-
joyning to that which hath been bought by the Governour near
the Falls, shall bee purchased, his honor hath graunted that
Capt. Izrael Helme shall have two hundred Acres thereof, the
which the Surveyor is to Lay out for him.

By Order of the Governor

New Yorke
Aprill the 6th 1677.

[Endorsed:]   No. 54 A Certificate by the Go. order for C.
              Izrael Helme for 200 Acers at Delaware Apr. 6.
              1677

---

1. Other transcription in NYCD 12:572.

20:115b   The dimensions and bounds of Prime Hooke
            neare the Whorekill[1]

Beginning at a bounded white Oake standing upon the point,
running up the Creeke, for breadth W. and by S. 1000 perches,
to a bounded red Oake standing by the side of a Cypres Swampe,
from thence N. and by W. 480 perches to a bounded red Oake
standing by the side of Slaughters Creeke, from thence E. and
by N. 1000 perches downe the said Creeke to a bounded Poplar
standing by the Marsh. Then downe the said Marsh S. and by E.
480 perches to the first bounded white Oake standing upon the
point by the aforesaid prime Hooke, Containing and layd out
for 3000 Acres.

[Verso:] Newyorke the 10th Aug. 1687 These are to certify that
upon request of Matthias Nicolls who was Secretary for the
above said Province in Gov. Lovelaces time I searched the old
papers filed in the office and found the within written in
file No. 55.

                     Wittnesse my hand
                     [Signed:] David Jamison[2]

[Endorsed:] The dimensions of Prime Hooke in the Whorekill.
             Mr Hen. Smith[3] 1677

---

1. Other transcription in NYCD 12:573; See DYR:115 for
   confirmation. Written in the hand of Matthias Nicolls,
   except for the certification by Jamison on the back.

2. David Jamison was Deputy Provincial Secretary; M.
   Nicolls retired as Provincial Secretary in 1680.

3. i.e., Henry Smith the recipient of the grant. cf.,
   DYR:115.

20:116   [PETITION OF MARY BLOCK CONCERNING HER RIGHT
          OF WAY]1

Right Honorable

    Mrs. Block came by me2 and desired me in her behalf to
write to your honor about her way into the woods for which she
had a former order3 from your hand and Councell bearing date
the fowerth of August 1676 though her way still denyed which
being so much to her detriment she was enforced to make her
addresse to the Court here and brought in severall attestacions
into the Court that to the furthest of there Knowledge and time
of being here the way not onely for her but the rest of her
neighbors was never stopped untill the new fence made by Capt.
Cantwell as by a copy of there attestacions the originill
being att New yorke already by Capt. Niccolls may appeare yett
Capt. Cantwell and Johannes de Haiz comming into the Court and
producing a patent under your honors hand and seale for that
land which she verily believed your honor was misinformed in
the Court being very tender to breake any the least of your
honors orders did referre itt to your honors further determinacion hoping your honor will bee pleased to peruse her
attestacions which if not enough she will make itt good by all
the neighbourhood the copy of which order of Court is here
likewise sent with this inclosed now may itt please your honor
after your honor has perused her papers to send your order with
the first for now grasse beginning to comme she shall be ruined
in her stock if debarred of her way and must be forced to sell
them and leave her plantacion in which doing your honor will
obliege her to bee

	Right Honorable
Newcastle 11th of Aprill	your honors most humble
1677	Servant the mark of
[Signed:]	Mary *MB* Block

[Addressed:]   For the Right Honnorable
                Major Edmon Aandross
                Govener att New York4

[Endorsed:]   No. 54 4th aprill 1677 from Newcastle of Mrs.
               Block for a way. An order sent.5 1673 to 776

-----

1. For related documents see 20:91, 20:92 and 20:114.

2. i.e., William Tom, in whose hand the letter is written.

3. See Council Minutes 3 (part 2): 110 for this order of
    council which allowed Mary Block "convenient outdrift"
    for her cattle.

4. Address is written in a second hand.

5. Endorsement is written in the hand of Matthias Nicolls.

6. File reference.

20:117   [SURVEY OF LAND AT CEDAR NECK FOR CAPT.
          NATHANIEL WALKER]¹

                                          May 11th Anno 1677

     Laid out a parsell of Land for Capt. [Nath.] Walker
Called by the name of Cedar neck Scituated upon the South
westernmost Creek of Rehoba Bay Beginning near the head of said
Creeke at a marked Redd oake standing [by] a Branch proceeding
from the said Creek [and] from thence South by East to a
marked white oake standing by a small bay or pann being Betweene the beatch of the [seaside] and the aforesaid white
oake and from thence [north] East by East binding upon the
aforesaid bay or pann four hundred and fourty pertches onely
proceeding a small narrow Slip of Land in manner of an Island
from the maine woods adjoyning to the beatch aforesaid about
a quantity of thirty acres then from the Extent of the Said
North East by East Course being at a small Inbyte of marsh
Running from thence north East one hundred and [eighty] pertches unto the aforesaid Beatch [by the sea]side [and Northwest binding and] adjoyning upon the said Beatch fourty pertches then from the said Beatch Southwest by west [to] a
marsh proceeding from part of the aforesaid Rehoba Bay and
from thence to a point of the [said] Bay northwest then from
the Said point West to another pointe Sixty pertches And from
the said point north west to another pointe Laying upon the
mouth of a River proceeding from the aforesaid Rehoba bay now
Called Indian River And from thence South West binding upon a
Little Creeke one hundred and Eighty five pertches to a marked
white [oake] standing neare the head of the said little Creeke
and from the said white oake Running south by East two hundred thirty and six pertches to the first bounded Redd oake
Including Containing and [Layd] out [for] six hundred and
eighty acres of Land as [by the survey] thereof may appeare.

[   ]²   [Signed:] per Cornelis Verhoofe

[Endorsed:]   [   ] for Capt. [   ] Walker.
          May [ ] 1677. Respited.³ A patent drawne the
          22nd day of Oct. 1679.⁴

     _____

     1. Other transcription in NYCD 12:574. NYCD follows
         O'Callaghan's Calendar which contains several inaccuracies
         for this entry: Nath. Carr instead of Nath. Walker
         and Cruder's Creek instead of Cedar Creek. The Calen-
         dar also has an incorrect date for the patent drawn on
         this survey. See 21:37 for the patent which was drawn
         up according to this return of survey; for other related
         documents see 21:16, 21:76 and 21:79. Damaged portions
         have been recovered from 21:37.

     2. Several short lines defective at this point.

     3. See 21:76 for reference to this respite.

     4. Endorsement is written in the hand of Matthias Nicolls.

20:118a   [SURVEY OF LAND ON SLAUGHTER CREEK FOR
           RANDALL REVILL][1]

                August the 3rd day Anno 1675.

     Survayed for Randel Reavill, A tract of land lying Upon
Slouhters Creeke Neare to the Whore Kill, beginning at a
bounded White Oake standing at the point of a mash[2] runing Up
the Creeke for breadth west and by south foure hundred and
fiftie peartches to a bounded popler Standing by the Creeke
And from thence to a bounded read Oake standing in the Woods
North by west Three hundred and Twentie peartches from thence
east and by north foure hundred And fiftie peartches to a
bounded Chest-nut standing by the side of a mash then downe
the saide Mash south and by east Three hundred and Twentie
peartches to the first bounded White Oake standing Upon the
point Containing Nine hundred Acres.
Per Order of Capt. Edmond Cantwell
Survayer generall, Survayed by me.
                         [Signed:]   William Taylor

[Endorsed:]   Randall Revill Entred.

---

  1. Other transcription in NYCD 12:537. For related
     documents see 20:88a, 20:108 and 20:118b. See DYR:115
     for confirmation.

  2. i.e., marsh.

20:118b   [COURT PROCEEDINGS CONCERNING A PETITION OF
           WM. PLANER FOR LAND GRANTED TO RANDALL REVILL][1]

                At a Calld Court Held for the Who[   ]
                the 14th Day of May Anno 167[ ].

            ⎧ Mr. Helm. Wiltbanck ⎫
Com: ⎨ Mr. Edward Southrin ⎬   present
            ⎩ Mr. Alex. Molestine ⎭

     Whereas it Appeares to the Court by suffic[   ] Evi-
dencies produced by William Planer the petitioner In the
Craveing his Just Right and title of a parsell of Land setled
by the aforesaid petitioner Containing nine hundred acres of
Land Situated at Slater Creeke[2] the which said Land one Randell
Revell hath Recovered a pattent for the Same and by the Examination of Evidencies produced by the aforesaid petitioner the
Court have Apprehended and Considereth the Said Cause and find
by theire opinium [ ] the Said petitioner Being wronged by
the Surveyor his unjustness and ought to possess and Enjoy the
said quantity of nine hundred acres of Land hee the petitioner
being setled upon and th[ ] the Right and title of the aforesaid Randell Revell may bee Disanulled which whole matter the
Court find Convenient to Referre for a Determination unto the

Honorable Governor his Approbation.

Vera Copia

[Signed:] Test, Cornelis Verhoofe Cl. Cur. Whorekill[3]

[Endorsed:] Wm. Planer his Coppy of order of court.

From Mr. Peter Groenendyke.

---

1. See DYR:115 for confirmation of Randall Revill's patent.
    For related documents see 20:88a, 20:108 and 20:118a.
    Other transcription in NYCD 12:574.

2. i.e., Slaughter Creek.

3. i.e., Witnessed by Cornelis Verhoofe, clerk of the
    court at Whorekill.

20:119   [COURT PROCEEDINGS AND VERDICT IN THE CASE
           BETWEEN DOM. LAURENTIUS CAROLUS AND HANS
           PETERSEN][1]

                              Att a Court held in the Towne of
                              New Castle begun the 5th and Con-
                              tinued the 6th and 7th of June
                              Anno 1677;

            Capt. John Colier Commander
            Mr. John Moll   ⎫
            Mr. William Tom   ⎪
Present   Mr. Fop Outhout   ⎬ Justices
            Mr. Jean Paull Jacquett⎪
            Mr. Gerret Otto   ⎭

Dom: Laurentsius Carolus Plt.
Hans Peterson.......... Deft.

     The Plt. declares for a mare by this deft. unjustly de-
tayned from the Plt. whereby the said deft. did expose this
Plt. to great Trouble Costs and Charges att Uppland Court,[2]
with a fyne of one hundered and fifty gilders to the Sherrife
besides the damadge as to the plts. Credit and Reputation etc.
Wherefore the Plt. desiers that hee may have sattisfaction in
Equity from this deft. for the slander hee hath Lay'd uppon
his Credit and Reputation, as also for all the Costs fines and
t'Charge hee hath ben Exposed unto by the unjust dem[ands] of
the said Hans Peterson in Uppla[nd] Court, as also that hee may
have a peaceable Enjoyment of the said mare which the said
deft. so unjustly Challengeth as his owne; etc. with Costs of
Suit;

Jurymen   The defts. answer being heard; The Court thought
Walter Wharton good (uppon the Plts. Request) to Referr the
Tho. Morse   Case to a Jury. Whoe brought in their Verdict

```
John Siericx       vizt. Wee find for the Plt. against the deft.
Hend: Williams     with 400 gild[ers] zewants vallu for damadge
Henry Jones        and all Costs of suit, and wee doe Lykewyse
William Orian      find that the mare which the Plt. Caused to
Gerret Smit        bee marked is his owne.
Broer Sinnexe
Hans Muller
Peter Maesland
Ambroos Backer
John Boyer
                   The Court ordered Judgement according to
Verdict; Vera Copia Exam: per
```

                    [Signed:] Eph: Herman, Clark

---

1. See NCCR:88 for transcription of the original record
   from which damaged portions in this document have been
   recovered. For related documents see 20:112, 20:113
   and 20:135. See also Miscellaneous Records 3:257 for
   the Governor's order dated July 28, 1677 which suspended
   execution of the judgement and ordered all court proceedings be sent to New York. Printed in PA 5:692.

2. See 20:124 for a copy of these court proceedings.

20:120   [COURT ORDER CONCERNING THE RECORDS OF
          WILLIAM TOM][1]

                    Att a Court held in the Towne of
                    New Castle Begun the 5th and Con-
                    tinued the 6th and 7th of June
                    Anno 1677;

     Mr. William Tom the former Clarke brought in Court twoo
small old Pa[per] Bookes, the one sowed with sheets toget[her]
most of his owne hand wryting, saying that the same were the
Records of the former proceedings here, which the Court delivered into the Custodie of the now Clark etc. But after the
said Record being Examined and Complaint of the Insufficiency
thereof made to the Court by Mr. Henry Ward; The Court did
think good to seale them upp, delivering them into the hands of
the Commander; to bee sent to his Honor the Governor for his
further order therein.
                    By order of the Court above said
                    [Signed:] Eph. Herman, Clerke

[Endorsed:] No. 49 Delowarr by the order of Court about
             records etc.[2]

---

1. See NCCR:82 for a transcription of the original record.
   Other transcription in NYCD 12:575.

2. Endorsement is written in the hand of Matthias Nicolls.

20:121   [NEW CASTLE COURT TO GOV. ANDROS ABOUT
          MUNICIPAL AFFAIRS][1]

Right Honorable Govenor;

Sir   In answer to your Honors Letter bearing date the 6th of
aprill[2] Last past wee humbly Reply; - about the watching

That there is none Lives neare the Towne but Swanwike
and in case they are Exemted from watching and warding most
part of the Towne will fly theither to bee free from the same
and t'Cheefly those whoe are no housekeepers; So that the
Strenght of the Towne may thereby mutch decrease: Wee therefore
humbly In treat your honor to furnish us with a small number
of souldier[s] to watch the forte whoe may bee serviceab[le]
uppon all occasions to the Commander and Court; as formerly itt
hath ben allowed of by your honors predecessors for wee humbly
Conceive that there is no Keeping of a forte without Souldiers,
and that it is better to have no forte, then a forte without
some to Keep it;

And whereas your honor hath ben pleased to admitt of a
Levy by the Pole, wee find that the same can not bee Laid
without a generall meeting or high Court of all the Justices
once a Yeare; whereof in our former Letter bearing date the
8th of february[3] wee have made mention of to your honor Wee
therefore humbly desiere that his Honor will take the same in
Conciederation and that the same meeting or Generall Court May
begein in September next; So that those whoe have Long Sence
disbourst their monny for the publicq account may Know where
to bee Repaid; for without the same no person will for the
future bee willing to disbours for any publicq account, and if
So no worke-men will bee to bee had, and no publicq workes go
forward; And as for a Treasurer wee appoint Mr. John Moll,
and Intreat his honor to nominate the Treasurers fees;

Wee Likewise humbly desier that the sending of the Lawbooke may not bee forgot, there being Great occasions for the
same.

Wee further Returne his honor humble thankes of the
Gracious Act of granting the fynes for the Lessening the Levys
but wee feare itt will bee verry difficult to Collect unlesse
your honor Resolves to send soldiers to assist the Sherrife in
the Execution thereof; The People fyned haveing formerly
Showed their Mutenous actions.

As to Letters of administracion wee shall follow his
honors Instructions; For Vendu Master wee nominate the Clarke
Eph. Herman, but In Regard the trouble in Collecting of the
debts by reason of the distance of the peoples Liv[ing] is so
great, wee suppose itt would bee Convenient to Raize the salary
to above Six per Cento;

The Dyke and Sluce being by a Storm Lately broke and
mutch out of Repair Capt. Colier and Capt. Cantwell have therefore Ingaged the payment for the Remakeing of the Same againe
the t'Charge thereof amounting to about 800 gilders, for the
Repaying thereof The Court have ordered that the Burgers In
Gennerall bee Called together and that those whoe will pay
pro Rato towards itt To have their parts but those whoe Refuse, to Loose their Commonadge.

As to the departing of persons without a passe, wee shall
Endeavour to observe his honors orders and make the people
accquainted therewith;

And as to the Liberty Given to Sloopes for the goeing upp
the River for Receiving former debts etc. wee suppose they will
never bee without that presence; and about the Indians wee
Refer ourselves to what Capt Colier hath writt to Your Honor
about the same. So Praying for his honors health and Prosperity; Wee Remaine Right Honorable Sir

N. Castle June
8th 1677.

Your Honors Most humble
Subjects and Servants
The Justices of the Court
att New Castle.
By order of the same
[Signed:] Eph. Herman, Clarke

[Addressed:] To the Right Honorable Mayor Edmund Andros Esq.
and Governor Generall under his Royall Highnesse
These
In New Yorke

[Endorsed:] [ ]5 [ ] June 1677 from the Court of
Newcastle in Delawarr.[4]

---

1. See NCCR:99 for a transcription of the court's copy of
this letter. Other transcription in NYCD 12:575.

2. See NCCR:98 for a transcription of this letter which
was read in court, and 20:142 for notes from which this
letter was drafted.

3. See NCCR:65 for a copy of this letter. Also 20:142.

4. Endorsement is written in the hand of Matthias Nicolls.

20:122 [HELMANUS WILTBANCK TO GOV. ANDROS ABOUT
AFFAIRS AT WHOREKILL][1]

Right Honorable

Whereas I am Informed Lately very Creditable that those
of Mary Land have Surveyed Sum Inconsiderable quantity of
Land the Certaine quantity unknown but Supposed to bee Severall

thousand acres the which Land Lyeing within the Limitts of
these government As I Can produce by an Instrument In Writting
made Between the Christians and the Indians In the first setlement of these place being then bought and paid for, as the
Writting more at Large may manifest Being to the Southward of
the Whorekill Creek about the Distance of 18 or 20 miles But
to the northward of the Supposed Cape Hinlopen[2] and the Extended
Limitts according to the aforesaid writting Being Called
Assawoma InLett Conveniently at the Sea board Side wherefore
I have already acquainted severall persons that what Incouragement priviledges and Assistance Can or may bee procured from
your Honorable shall not bee wanting if that any persons are
willing to Setle there In those partes aforesaid Under the
protectie of these his R. Hs. Dominacion for to proceed as
speedly In the proceedings of Setlement unto the utmust Extent
of the Limitts of the government The most part of these
magistors[3] are at present absent and about her owne occasions[4]
that noe posibillity Could permitt to make any further Conclusion there of for which I thought fitt to make your Honor
acquainted thereof it Should be needfull that your Honor
would Be pleased to Consider thereof Shall not further InLarge
at present onely Remaine In Duty

Whorekill June   Your Honors Humble Servant
11th Anno 1677   [Signed:] Helm. Wiltbanck

[Addressed:] To the Right Honorable Governor Edmond Andross
              Esq. Seigneur of Sausmarez
                                        Present at
              N. York
                        These
              per Capt. Cryger

[Endorsed:] No. 51   [   ] June 1677 from Whorekill[5]

---

1. Other transcription in NYCD 12:576.

2. This is a reference to Indian River Inlet which was
    sometimes called the False Cape because of its con-
    fusion with Cape Henlopen.

3. i.e., Magistrates.

4. i.e., "...about their own business...," which may be an
    example of Dutch interference in Wiltbanck's English:
    her is Dutch haar meaning "their"; or he may have in-
    advertently left out the t in ther, i.e.,
    "their."

5. Endorsement in the hand of Matthias Nicolls.

20:123   [CAPT. COLLIER TO GOV. ANDROS ABOUT WM. TOM'S
          RECORDS][1]

Honored Sir   New Castle the 12 June 1677

    My last to Your Honor was per Capt. Thomas De Lavall who
sayled from hence the 30th of May; This opportunity presenting
by Land have sent your Honor the Records of this Place Kept in
Mr William Tom his time they being ordered by the Court to be
delivered to mee as appeares by the Inclosed;[2] Mr Tom have not
anything to say for himselfe (onely) that when your Honor was
here you did then promist to send him bookes from York they
not coming must take the Records as they are.

    The Newes from Maryland is that wee have warrs with France;
Mr Shakerly wilbe ready to sayle from hence Thursday next; All
things here are in Quietness (God be thanked) I take leave and
remaine

                        Sir Your faithfull Servant to Command
                        [Signed:] John Colier

[Addressed:]   For the Honorable Edmond Andross Esq. Generall
                and Governor of his Royall Highness his Territory
                att Fort James in New York
                                these present

[Endorsed:]   1677 No. 53 Delawar 12 of June from Comander
                with an order of Court of records to be sent
                but none brought.[3]

---

1. Other transcription in NYCD 12:577.

2. For this court order see 20:120.

3. Endorsement in the hand of Matthias Nicolls.

20:124   [COURT PROCEEDINGS IN THE CASE BETWEEN HANS
          PETERSEN AND DOM. LAURENTIUS CAROLUS][1]

                    14th March 1675

[   ] Peterson plt.
[   ]entius Carolus deft.

    The plt. complaynes against the deft. that about Aprill
last hee had and was possessed of one mare which was but his
proper goods and the said mare running out of his possession
as above he the deft. finding the said mare running in the
woods tooke or caused to bee taken up the said mare and marked
her with his the defts. owne marke with intension to defraud
the plt. of his said mare to his greate damage wherefore he

prayes he may have his said mare with the cost.

The deft. replyed and said itt was his owne mare he marked
and not belonging to the plt.

The Court having heard the cause and both parties being
unprovided with witnesse did jointly move respite till next
Court for further proofe.

13th of June 76

Both plt. and deft. appearing and there witnesses saying
little materiall to the property of the mare itt was referred
to a Jury by name (Mr. Walter Wharton foreman   Wm. Monntague
Dunck Williams   Francis Walker   Olla Raysen   Peter Dalbo
Olla Neilsen   Jonas Neilsen   Peter Johnson   Mathias Holsteyn
Laurence Cock and Wm. Oryon) who all being sworne returne by
the foreman in writing as followeth [   ] if unmarkt horses
and mare belong to the King [   ] but whether
I   ] find not [   ] Capt.
Cantwell satisfying them out of the law booke did order [   ]
deft. to deliver the said Mare and bee fyned 150 g. with the
cost.
                    Vera copia [Signed:] Will. Tom
11th July 1676

[Endorsed:]   proceed[   ] about [   ] in the Court
               [   ]wcastle. 1677. No. 61[2]

---

1. For related documents see 20:112, 20:113 and 20:119.

2. Endorsement is written in the hand of Matthias Nicolls.

20:125   [CAPT. CANTWELL TO JOHN STEVENS CONCERNING
          LAND AT WHOREKILL][1]

          N. Castle the first of august 77.

Mr. Steevens Sir

     This Day I Received yours of the 18 Day of July where out
I understand that John Edmondson thus still Keepe a Passe
about your Land and that he should tell you that the governor
should Com here this month I here no such thing nor will he be
here [ ]am sure you may give him Leave to talke if the[ ]
should be any need to [ ]devou[ ] as for seating it [   ] his
honors order to seat the fir[ ] year and effect in three
years my Kind Love to yourselfe father and mother and wife and
I shall Remaine
                    Sir your assured Lo. freind
                    [Signed:] Ed. Cantwell

[Written in margin and on back:]   you need nott fear that
h[   ]onor will give two pattents for one peace of Land [   ]
most send or goe to the whore Kill and gett your certificatt
signed under the Court hand and mention the other three pattents in the Certificatt and the Date of the pattents but
Leave the place for the Date open till it Com to mee I would
send you the Certificatt you sent mee but I Cannot find butt
Mr. Avery will give you a Co[   ] of it
                            Vale
                  [Signed:] Ed. Cantwell

[Addressed:]   To Mr. John Steevens att his plantation in
               Little Creeke
                        These

---

1. Other transcription in NYCD 12:578. See DYR:113 for
    confirmation of John Stevens' patents.

20:126a   [COURT ORDER IN THE CASE BETWEEN EDWARD SOUTHRIN
          AND JOHN ROADES][1]

     Whereas: Mr. Edward Southrin plt. and John Roades Deft.
these Day Before mee appeared to Implead and Deft. the Complaint made by the plt. against the Deft. but upon alligations
of Fellony made by the plt. against the Deft. therefore I
order that the plt. shall put in Sufficient Bayle to prossecute and Answer all Lawfull Dammages unto the Deft. at the
next Court of Sessions for the WhoreKill and the Deft. to Remaine In prison without bayle or maineprise this the 16th Day
of August Anno 1677

                              Helm. Wiltbanck
                        Vera: Copia
[Signed:]   Test. Cornelis Verhoofe Cl. Co. Whorekill

---

1. See 20:128 for the decision in this case.

20:126b   [JOHN STEVENS TO CORNELIS VERHOOFE ABOUT HIS
          LAND PAPERS][1]

[Mr. Corn]elias Verhufe

     pray deliver unto the barer h[ere of] the Coppy of my

surtifi[cate that John Auere][2] did give you of mine it [is
1200 acres] of Land you will see by Capt. Cantwells Letter[3]
hou it should be that hee may carrie it to Captin Cantwell that
I may have my pattin made and in so doein you will oblidge mee
who is your Loveing friend

August the 19th 77   [Signed:] John Steevens

---

1. Other transcription in NYCD 12:582. Damaged portions
   have been recovered from NYCD.

2. i.e., John Avery.

3. See 20:125 for this letter.

20:127   [COMPLAINT OF JEAN ERSKINE AGAINST JOHN MOLL
          AND WILLIAM SEMPLE][1]

     Thatt whereas your petittionors hussband was formerly a
souldier under the Comand of Collonell Richard Nichols who
Came into thes parts to subdue the Duch nation to his majestes
obediens, and eversince hath lived in thes River of Dellaware:
behaving himselfe as a subject oft[2] to do till god was pleased
to take him outt of the world. Now thus itt is may itt please
your honor that your petittionors husband going in a cannew
in Cristena Creeke the 23rd day of october last past to fech
nessesary provitions for the Relife of himself and family was
acsedentally drownded. so that your petittionor with fowre
children was left husbandless and fatherless: being broctt[3]
to a misserable low Conditton by the loss of her said husband.
Nottwithstanding which Mr. John Moll and Mr. Will. Semple unto
home[4] your petittionors husband was indebted; did (before ever
that your petittionors husband was found and interd or ever
that your petittionor had gotten a letter of administration or
before any demand was made of the sayd debtts) Attach all the
Cropp of Tobakow that was upon the plantation of the deceased
which was a forty foott Tobakow house full and Rehung: setting
the Broad arrow upon the Tobakow house Dore: so that your
petittionor Durst nott medle with or handle the Tobakow: that
was in The Tobakow house: so that Itt was all or most part
spoyled to The greatt loss of your petittionors [   ] that
should hav[   ] further: after the said Moll and Semple
did understand that the said [   ]ow was damnified they proceded further in Rigor againstt your P[   ] To attach both
her movabels and Chattell so that by execution (as they [   ]
your petittionors Cows that was to give milk for her selfe and
4 children was all taken away: and when your petittionor was
att Courtt the above said Mr. Moll sent his servants unknowne
to your petittionors house who withoutt any officer, either
Constable or sheriff, did enter into the house of your petit
tionor, and Take away with them for the use of there said Mr.
such houshold goods as they best liked nott leaving your
petittionor so much as a pott or Kettell or dish to dress or

eatt victualls in, or so much as a paile to fech water in, in
so much that your petittionor with her 4 children was forced
to deserte theire said habitation; and to be maintained by
the charity and almes of other good people who for gods sake
hath since January last past maintained your petittionor and
her children with dyett who of necessety else must have per-
ished, wherefor your petittionor humbley prays of your honer
that she may have sattisfaction Rendered her for the loss of
her Tobackow: as also that your honor would be pleased, to
Consider the misserable Condittion of your petittionor, and
Her fatherless children: and your petittionor for your Worships shall pray as in duty bound etc.

[Endorsed:] Serjt. Erski[   ] Wid: Complaintt. 1677.[5]

---

1. For Matthias Nicolls' rough draft in response to this
   petition see 21:30. The final draft of this response
   is transcribed in NCCR:252.

2. i.e., ought.

3. i.e., brought.

4. i.e., whom.

5. Endorsement is written in the hand of Matthias Nicolls.

20:128   [DECISION OF THE COURT IN THE CASE BETWEEN
          EDWARD SOUTHRIN AND JOHN ROADES][1]

                        At a Court held for the Whorekill
                        the 12th Day of Sept. Anno 1677

           ⎧ Mr. Helm Wiltbanck ⎫
Com.   ⎨ Mr. Alex. Molestine ⎬ present
           ⎩ Capt. Paul Marsh   ⎭

Edward Southrin plt. ⎫
John Roades Deft.   ⎭

     Whereas the plt. making nothing Appeare upon the Charge
of Felloney Laid against the Deft. the Court finding the
matter to bee noe Cause of action and the plt. to pay Cost of
Suite Alias Execution.
                      Vera Copia
[Signed:] Test. Cornelis Verhoofe Cl. Co. Whorekill

[Endorsed:] [   ] of Whorekill Edward Southron [   ]
             John Roads Deft.
             60[2]

1. See 20:126a for a court order in this case.

2. Endorsement is written in the hand of Matthias Nicolls.

20:129   [JOHN AVERY TO GOV. ANDROS CONCERNING HIS
           INABILITY TO APPEAR IN NEW YORK FOR A CASE
           BETWEEN PETER GROENENDYCK AND HENRY SMITH][1]

My Lord

  I Am At p[ ]t In A very wecke Con dishon And have
[ ] ben out of my hous this sicks wekes but [ ]ns[2] And still
have A fever Every day In [ ] much I Can not goo on hundred
yardes from my hous If it woold save my Life The holl Pepell
of the Plas Knous It your ouner Knous the Thing That I Am
brout thether Is nothing Consarnin me but [ ] lies betwen
Peter Groondicke And do[ ][3] Smith And Allsoo what I did
was to the be[ ] of my Knouledg not having Any Conserns
with on of them more then the other [ ]oo humbelly Craven
your ouner to Consder my Condishon I shall Ever Remaine your
ouners most humbel servant

dated this 10th day of   [Signed:] John Avery
september 1677.

[P.S.]
My Lord

  The intent of mister Smit[ ] was to have Com with me
In my bot[ ] And had it not ben for mister Hallman[ ]
Willbanck[4] for he toulld me he was in Tended to Com to the falls
in his oun bot which was the ocashon I Left him be hind me
This Is very sertin I shal Ever Re man your ouner most humbele
servant.

       [Signed:] John Avery

[Addressed:] This for The Rit ounerabele Edmand Andros
     governer Generall of his Roiall hines Is
     Teritoris in America.

[Endorsed:] No. 40 Whorekill 10th Sept. 16[ ] from Capt.
    Avery.[5]

---

1. Other transcription in NYCD 12:582.

2. Probably ons for "once."

3. Probably doctor; Henry Smith was a "chirurgeon" from
    Somerset County, Maryland. In Council Minutes 3 (part
    2):32 his name is recorded as Dr. Henry Smith.

4. i.e., Helmanus Wiltbanck.

5. Endorsement is written in the hand of Matthias Nicolls.

20:130   [HELMANUS WILTBANCK TO GOV. ANDROS ABOUT
          AFFAIRS AT WHOREKILL][1]

Honorable Sir   Whoorekil Sept. 18th Anno 1677

     Whereas by accidentiall of sum sicknes of body by feavor
and ague and lamenes of my one Legg Cannot by no possebillity
appeare at the Hig Court of assizes please your Honor to pardon mee Have but this onely to say for my selfs that upon the
Relations of Peter Gronendick in the matters between the said
Gronendick and Henry Smit I apprehend and understood at that
time with rest af the Jury buth Gronendick afterwards goth
Abraham Clement with a petition that wy migt Recalle oure verdict and Gronendick spoocke him selfs to mee s'umtimes whit
treatning that the Jury hath given his mony away and further
sayeth that of soo bey[2] wy would petition to the Court I may
heave Rehearing this would bee the easest way and the Least
chardge and so I taght the Jury may have him done wrang not
noyng and of soo bie the Court would give rehearing what is
that to the Jury and the Jury being from thear oath and the
writtens out af thare aknowlege which being to mee understanding
to have Rehearing or a Reaxamination as being not perfect to
Distinguisch the Circumstanges of many Englisch woords or
speatches by which Referr my selfs unto your Honors favor
forther aquainthing your Honor of one Major John West out of
accumack in Virginia whom hath writ unto mee about a Considerable quantity of Land for him selfs and sum partners of
him which Land being Just to the Noortwaard of the supposed
Cabo Hinlopen seperating it selfs from the said Cape with one
Inlett and a Creeck Comly Called by the Indians assawamon
the which I have mensioned unto your Honor In my former Letter[3]
that they of merryland have made sum Certaine Survays by thiere
pretended Right the which said Land the said Major West affirmes
by his letter to settle Imediatly In his R. H. right soe he
the said major well may obtaine good Incorredgement and bee
protected by your Honor hee being a very able person with a
vast Estate to which end I have answered his Lines that what
soever previlidges and Incorredgement might or Could bee
Expected from your Honor should not be wanting therfore of
your Honor pleased to Express any particulars In such a Concerne to Setle the utmost bound and Limits of the gouverne-
ment Refer the same unto your Honors wisedome and discretion
ottherwise it is lickly to bee setled by them of merryland
these winter as farr as I can understand One favor shall request of your Honor that Whereas it was your Honors pleasur
the last yeare to deputed mee for on of the magistrates for
these parts which now the time of Limitation thereof being
Expired therefor hertely begg your Honor may be pleased to
discharge mee by Writ of Ease Shall Humble thanck your Honor
for the same Being but little learnet and weake of appre-
hention and understanding of the Lawes have no more at present to acquaint your Honor onely take leaf to Conclude and
Remaine with all due Love and Respect

Your Honors Humble
Servant to Command
[Signed:]   Helm. Wiltbanck

[Addressed:]   To the Right Honorable Major Edmund Androsz
Gouverneur Generall of all his R. Hig. His
Territories in America Etc.
New Jorck

[Endorsed:]   No. 50   1677 Whorekill 15th Sept. from the
Magistrate.[4]

---

1. Other transcription in NYCD 12:582.

2. i.e., if so be.

3. See 20:122 for this letter.

4. Endorsement is written in the hand of Matthias Nicolls.

20:131   [CAPT. CANTWELL TO GOV. ANDROS ABOUT AFFAIRS
AT NEW CASTLE]

N. Castle the 26 Day of Sept. 1677

Right Honorable

These are to give your honor account of one Symon Gibson
who was indicted here in Court and fond gulty by the Jury and
ordered by the Court to be sent to new yorke which I have Don
with the vessell of Capt. Crygier the proseeding and his tryall
here I also send your honor inclosed after he was fond gulty by
the Jury and Commited to prison I seased and toke his goods
in to Castody till I Do here and understand your honors pleasure: Capt. Nicolls writt me that your honor scruples signig
of pattents which the Certificatts has not bene Confirmed here
in Court to the best of my Knowledge ever sence your honor
gave that order which was when I was Last att yorke there has
not bene any sent but was Confirmed and signed by the Judge of
the Court as your honor may see by summ Certificatts now sent
with this vessell: I hartely begge and Desire of your honor
to order my payment that I may once Com out of Debt att yorke
I am ashamed to be so Longe there ingaged if your honor will
be pleased to order upon the Levey or any other way your honor
shall tenke mete[2] I was intended to waett upon your honor with
these vessells but my sonn being taken very sick henders me at
the present to Com and Kisse you honors hand I shall not att
present in Large only my honorable servis to your honor and
Lady and I shall ever Remaine
Right honorable your honors
faithfull Servant
[Signed:]   Ed Cantwell

[Addressed:] To the Right Honorable Major Edmound Andross Esq.
Generall of all his Royal Highnesse forces in
america and Governor att Forte James att New
Yorke. Present

[Endorsed:] C. Cantwell the Sheriffe of Newcastles Letter,
sent with the proceedings against Sim. Gibson.
past. 1677.[3]

---

1. See NCCR:104 for these proceedings against Simon Gibson.

2. i.e., think meet.

3. Endorsement is written in the hand of Matthias Nicolls.

20:132 [THOMAS WELBURNE AND WM. ANDERSON TO GOV.
ANDROS ABOUT IRREGULARITIES IN DELAWARE][1]

Honorable Sir

Not to obtrude your more weighty affaires the inclosed is
a remonstrance of our agrievances which we have presented to
the Court at the HoareKill they having thereunto a Certifica[   ]
to your Honor anexed to shew the verity of the Same, our
great damage and disapointments in being letted from Seating
and bringing families to the Same; desire your honors to doe
[   ] Justice in the Concerne and give of such Countenance as
we [   ] others may not be disincouraged to inh[   ]
[ ]ccasioned by the partiall doings and [   ] of your officers for want of [   ] Ubiquity not doubting but we shall
receive all Just Satisfacion when your honor has once well
weighed the premises we subscribe our selves

Hoarekill   Your Honors most humble and
Oct. the 13th 1677   obedient Servant
                             [Signed:] Tho. Welburne
                                        Wm. Anderson

[Addressed:] To the Honorable Major Edmond Andross Esq. Lt.
and Governor Generall under His Royall Highness
overall His Royall Highness His Teritoris in
America
This Present

[Addressed:] To the Honorable Anthony Brockholds Esq.
Governor of New York
These present[2]

[Endorsed:] From the [   ]trates of the [   ]kill to the
Go[   ] about some abuse of C. Cantwells concerning some Surveys.

Oct. 13th 77 Received March 28th per [   ]ter

Groenendyke   An order May 1st 1678.[3]

---

1. See 21:33 for related documents.

2. This letter was redirected to Capt. Brockholls who
   served as Deputy Governor while Governor Andros was in
   England. See 27:130 for a note on the redirection of
   this letter.

3. Endorsements are written in the hand of Matthias Nicolls.

20:133a/b   [COURT PROCEEDINGS CONCERNING THE   1
             SETTLEMENT OF FRANS BARENTSEN'S ESTATE]

                          Att a Court held in the Towne of
                          New Castle the 7th and 8th dayes
                          of November Annoque Domini 1677.

     Hans Petersen preferring in Court a Peticion sheweing,
that there is in his hands belonging unto one Frans Barentsen
whoe dyed, without any heir in Maryland twoo young steers, six
schipple of wheat and a screw gun for which the peticioner
bille is still out in the hands of Charles James in Maryland,
And that the said Frans Barentsen did owe and was to deliver
the Peticioner 75 gilders with twoo paire of shoes and stockings
att the Receipt of the said Steers,   Sheweing further that
Capt. Christopher Billop, now demands of the Peticioners said
Steers with the wheat and gun; The said Peticioner humbly
desiering that the Court would bee pleased to order to whome
hee shall Receive his Remaining 75 gilders with the shoes and
stockings.

     The Court answer that their opinion is (sence the said
Frans Barentsen dyed without any kindred and Consequently his
Estate fallen to the King) That whome his honor the Governor
shall bee pleased to order to Receive the above premisses from
the Peticioner the same then to bee a Lawfull delivery, and
that the same person whoe Receives ought to Cleare the Peticioner
and save him harmlesse of future trouble about the same.
                          Vera Copia Exam. per
                     [Signed:] Eph: Herman, Cl.

                          Att a Court held in New Cas[   ]
                          the 7th and 8th of May 1678.

Capt. Christopher Billop in   }
the behalfe of his Royall Highnesse }   Plt.

Hans Petersen[2]...................   Deft.

The Plt. delcares that this deft. stands indebted unto
one Frans Barentsen whoe dyed Instate in Maryland without any
heir by foure severall bills the following summes to witt 15
schipple of barly 16 sch: of wheat twoo young oxen, and a
screw gun, desires that this Court will bee pleased to passe
Judgement against the deft. to pay the said debts unto him,
hee haveing sufficient power to Receive the same etc. The
deft. sayes to owe no more then the 2 young steers and six sch:
of wheat, hee haveing paid the screw gun to Capt. Colier,
delcares further against the Insufficiency of the bill of the
barly, and that the figure of one in the other bill of the
wheat is putt before the figure of six after hee signed etc.
and sayes further to have ben alwayes willing to pay what he
owes provyded hee might not pay itt in his wrongh.

The debates of both partees being heard and itt being
alledged by severall persons in Court that Frans Barentsz declared before his decease that hee had a brother alyve in
Europe whoem hee Expected into this Country, The Court therefore thought itt fitt first to send their former opinion to
his honor the Governor, or The honorable Counsill att New
Yorke and to take their order what they shall bee pleased to
doe in the buisnesse the more sence some of the bills are
found to bee not sufficient as they ought to bee, The deft.
being still willing to pay what heretofore hee aknowledged
to bee Indebted;

A true Coppy out of the Records
Exam. per
[Signed:] Eph: Herman, Cl.

[P.S.]
The worshipfull Court have given the same order as above
in the other twoo Actions Entered by Capt. Billop in the behalfe above said against Hans Mulder and Poul Moens.[3]

[Entitled:] Frans Barentsz

[Endorsed:] Order of the Court at Newcastle about Frans
Barents [   ]eased November 7 and 8
May...7 and 8[4]

---

1. See NCCR:154 and 199 for transcripts of the original
    records from which these copies were made.

2. In NCCR:199 Petersen's name is followed with the alias
    Patascus.

3. See NCCR:200 for the court record of these two suits.

4. Endorsement is written in the hand of Matthias Nicolls.

20:134   [PETITION OF THE INHABITANTS AT UPLAND TO
          FORM A TOWN BELOW THE FALLS][1]

To the Worshipfull Court of Upland

Israell Helm, Laurens Cock, Moens Cock, Andries Benckson,
Swen Lom, Ephraim Herman, Caspar Herman, John Dalboo, Jasper
Fiske, Hans Moensen, Frederick Romey, Erik Mulk, Gunner Rambo,
Tho. Harwood, Erik Cock, Jan Cock, Peter Jockum, Peter Cock
Junior, Jan Stille, Jonas Neelsen, Oele Swensen, James Sander-
lin, Mathias Mathiasse de Vos, William Orian;

Doe most humbly Shew to your Worships:

That they the Peticionors being all Inhabitants and for
the most part borne and brought up in this River and parts
Have a great Inclination (as well for the strength of the
River as for the Convenience of travelars and otherways) to
settle together in a Towne att the westsyde of this River Just
Below the faalls, Doe therefore humbly Request this worshipfull Court to move the Case to his honor the Governor that they
the Peticionors may have Each of them In Lotts Laid out one
hundered acres of Land with a fitt proportions of marrish as
alsoe that a fitt place for a Towne may bee Laid out, In the
most Convenient place thereabout with such priviledges and
Libertys for their Incouragement as shall bee thought fitt and
that the same may bee Confirmed unto them by his honor the
Governor and the peticionors will forthwith seate accordingly,
and shall for your Worships Ever pray etc.

[Verso:]   Att a Court held att Upland November the 13th 16[ ].

The Court answer that they will send the Peticionors
peticion to his honor the Governor and withall Moove and Request the Governor In the peticionors behalfe
                              By order of Court
                         [Signed:] Eph. Herman, Cl.

[Endorsed:]   A Request to the Court at Upland in Delaware with
              the Answer about Land at the Falls. Nov. 13
              1677[2]

---

1. See UCR:74 for transcription of the original court
    record from which this copy was made. Other tran-
    scription in NYCD 12:586.

2. Endorsement is written in the hand of Matthias Nicolls.

20:135   [SETTLEMENT OF A CASE BETWEEN DOM. LAURENTIUS
           CAROLUS AND HANS PETERSON][1]

                              Att a Court held at Upland In
                              Delowar River By his Majesties
                              Authority, on Teusday the
                              13th of November 1677;

              Mr Peter Cock   ⎫
              Mr Peter Rambo   ⎪
Present.   Mr Israell Helm   ⎬   Justices
              Mr Lasse Andries   ⎪
              Mr Otto Ernest Cock ⎪
              Mr Oele Swensen   ⎭

     Hans Petersen and Dom. Laurentius Carolus declared that
they had this day mutually agreed about their processe of the
mare, in manner following vizt. That Each of them was to pay
halfe of all the Charges which had acrued by said processe
and that Dom. Laurentius was to pay over and above the said
halfe the summe of twenty anf fyve Gilders; and Hans Petersen
declared that hee would have nothing m[ore] to doe with said
Mare;

     The Court did order that their said agreement [shoul]d
bee soe Recorded;
                              A True Copy out of Upland
                              Court Records Exam. per mee
                       [Signed:] Eph. Herman, Cl.

[Endorsed:]   [   ] Carolus out of Up[   ] Records
               the 13th November 1677.[2]

_____

1.   See UCR:74 for transcription of the original court
     record from which this copy was made. For related
     documents see 20:112, 20:113, 20:119 and 20:124.

2.   Endorsement is written in the hand of Matthias Nicolls.

20:136   [LIST OF PATENTS SENT TO DELAWARE IN 1677][1]

Thomas Davis...[003][2]
James Wells.. 004
Daniell Whittly...................................... 003
Christopher Jackson.................................. 003
John Stevens... 012
John Cornelius....................................... 003
Cornelius Verhoofe................................... 001
John Allard[3]....................................... 004
Abraham Clement...................................... 004
Edward Fourloung..................................... 004
John Anterey... 003
Robt. Brasidy Junior................................. 003

```
Wm. Prentice.............................................. 004
John Liming.............................................. 003
John Otten.............................................. 003
Richard Brasey..........................................[ 003 ]
James Lille.............................................[ 003 ]
Robt. Brasey Senior.................................... 008
Sander Molestine...................................... 000
[Elias Coudrey]4.......................................[      ]
Jacob Seth.............................................[ 005 ]
Wm. Warren.............................................[ 003 ]
Henry Stretcher........................................[ 004 ]
James Peddy............................................[ 006 ]
Wm. True...............................................[ 003 ]
Samuell Styles......................................... 004
John DuPre............................................. 010
Thomas Davis........................................... 003
Edward Cooke5.....30................................... 003
John Kirke............................................. 008
Richard Hill........................................... 010
Walter Lewes........................................... 003
Samuell Styles and Robert Trayly...................... 007
Wm. Borton............................................. 010
Hubertos Frances....................................... 004
Robert Hart Junior.....37.............................. 005
```

[Endorsed:]   List of Patents sent to Delaware by Cornelys
              Cregier in Capt. Cl[   ] Nov. 21st 1677[6]

---

1. Other transcription in NYCD 12:586. O'Callaghan's Calendar entry for this document has an incorrect date and
   description, both of which NYCD follows. Confirmation
   for these patents appear in DYR. cf., 21:17 for a
   later list.

2. This column of figures indicates the amount of quit
   rent due in bushels of wheat. The amounts in brackets
   have been recovered from DYR.

3. This name appears as Alward in 21:17 and Allward in
   DYR.

4. This name is situated at a fold in the document and
   has since been torn away. NYCD has Elias Coudrey
   which may be a mistranscription for Josias Cowdery
   whose name appears in DYR; 21:17 also lists a patent
   for Josias Coudrey.

5. Does not appear in DYR.

6. Endorsement is written in the hand of Matthias Nicolls.

20:137   [COPY OF AN ASSIGNMENT OF AN ISLAND IN THE
          DELAWARE BY SAMUEL EDSALL TO GEORGE HEATHCOTE][1]

          Know all men by these presents that I Samuell Edsall of
the City of New Yorke for and in consideration of the Sume of
one hundred Pounds Current Money of New England to Me in hand
Paid by George Heathcote of the County of Middlesex in England
Marriner doe hereby Give Grant Alienate transport assigne and
Sett over from mee and My heires unto the said George Heath-
cote his heires and assignes all My right title Claim and
Intrest to the Within Mentioned Island In Delaware river Called
Sankhikans Granted Me by Pattent from Governor Richard Nicolls
as is there in Sett forth To have and to hold the said George
Heathcote his heires and Assignes Unto the proper Use and be-
hoof of the said George Heathcote his heires and assignes for
Ever In Testimony whereof I have hereunto Sett My Hand and
Seale in New Yorke this 29th day of January in the 29th Year
of his Majesties Reign Annoque Domini 1677[2]

Signed Sealed and   Sam: Edsall
Delivered in Presence of
Wm. Williams
James Mathews

[Entitled:]   Edsalls Assignement of an Island in Delaware to
               Heathcott

[Endorsed:]   Copy

———————————————

1. cf., 20:104. Other transcription in NYCD 12:570.

20:138   [CIVIL AND MILITARY APPOINTMENTS FOR WHOREKILL][1]

Whorekill
                    A List of Magistrates and Officers have
                    Being [sic] Depu[   ]

[   ]   Capt. Paull Mash Lieut. and President of the
November   Court.
                    Mr Helmanus Wiltbanck Justice Sheriffe and
                    Collector
                    Mr Alexander Molest[ ]de Justice
                    Mr John Kiphaven Justice
                    Mr Otto Wolgast Justice
                    Mr Daniell Browne Under Sheriffe and Const[   ]

1675
June 25th   Mr John Avery Lieut. and President of the
                    Court
          4   Mr Edward Sout[ ]in Justice
          3   Mr Alexander Molestede Justice, wish nott[   ]
                    Mr John Kiphaven Justice, well to take
                    Mr Otto Wolgast Justice, good ordinary plan[   ]

Mr Daniell Browne Under Sheriffe and Constable
Cornelis Verhoofe Clerke Deputy Surveyor and
Coll[   ]

167[ ]
January 4th   Mr Daniell Browne being Discharged of the
C[   ] office and Simon Paling Ellected
in the [   ]

Dito   Jury of Inquest as followeth
Helmanus Wiltb[   ] foreman   William Prentic[ ]
Abraham Clement [   ]   Simon Paling
John Collissen   Robert Murdic[ ]

[   ] 5   Capt Paull Mash   wis[ ] poor
[   ]   [   ]
               [   ]
               Mr. Josuah Backsteade
       1   Helmanus Wiltbanck
               Robert Hart,   Honest poor man
               Abraham Clement petit,   dead
       7   John Rods
       6   John Barckstead   dead

[Endorsed:]   List of Mag[   ] [   ] officers [   ]
               at [   ]orekill [   ] 1677 and 1678

_____

1. Other transcription in NYCD 12:588. The comments and
figures before and after the names as well as the final
two names are in the hand of Matthias Nicolls.

20:139   [NOMINATION LIST FOR OFFICES IN DELAWARE][1]

   N. Castle   for the Whore Kill
1 Mr. John Moll   Henry Smith
   Mr. Henry Ward   John Avery
   Jacob Younge   Edward Southren
   James Walliam   John King
   Marten Roseman   Pawell Mash
   Gysbert Derikson   Sander Mallesten[2]
   Henrik Johnson   Harmanes Wildbank
   Samuell Land   Thomas Phillips
   John Cann
4 Fop Outhout
   Johannes Dehaes
   Olle Torrsen
x3 William Tom
x6 Paull[3] Jaquett
5 Walter Wharton
7 Gerett Otto
2 Peeter Aldricks

1. Other transcription in NYCD 12:589. The final three
   names in the New Castle list as well as the numbers and
   marks before them are in the hand of Matthias Nicolls.

2. i.e., Alexander Molestine.

3. The original given name of John appears under Paull
   which was written in pencil by Matthias Nicolls.

20:140   [EXTRACTS FROM GOV. ANDROS' LETTERS CONCERNING
          SLOOP TRAFFIC ABOVE NEW CASTLE][1]

                          An Extract out of a Letter sent
                          by his Honor the Govern[or] to the
                          Commander and Court att New Castle,
                          dated 23rd of November 1676.

   The former orders prohibiting Sloopes and vessells going
up the River above New Castle to traede, are to bee duly observed as heretofore, and Care to bee taken that none goe up;

                          Extract out of a Letter sent by his
                          honor the Governor to the Court
                          above said dated Aprill the 6th
                          1677.

   Liberty is Granted for Sloopes etc. going up the River
as formerly for this Jeares Effects or former debts;

                          These are true Coppies out of the
                          Records Exam. per mee
                          [Signed:] Eph: Herman, Cl.

[Endorsed:] An Extract out of Delaware Records sent by Capt.
             Billop arrived Apr. 29, 1678.[2]

1. For the letters from which the extracts were taken see
   20:103 and NCCR:98 respectively.

2. Endorsement is written in the hand of Matthias Nicolls.

20:141   [EXTRACTS MADE BY MATTHIAS NICOLLS FROM COUNCIL
           MINUTES CONCERNING SLOOP TRAFFIC ABOVE NEW
           CASTLE][1]

At a Councell held in N. Y. May 1st 1678

        Upon the desire of C. Christopher Billop Commander of
Delaware to bee directed about sloopes goeing up the River
above Newcastle for which a [tempor]ary permission had beene
granted by the Gov.

        Ordered That the time granted by the Gov. being expired,
The former Orders not to goe up to bee observed.
                              By order of the Councell

At a Councell held in N. Y. May 1st 1678

        The answer of C. Edm. Cantwell to the Justices of the
Whorekill about abuse in altering some surveys.

        The answer from Capt. Edm. Cantwell sent to the Sec.,
wherein hee justifyes himselfe as to the Complaint made against
him by the Justices of the Whorekill, about abuses pretended
in altering some Surveyes,[2] hee intimating likewise his Intent
to bee here this Spring. The same being read and taken into
Consideracion.

        Ordered etc. as in the Councell papers

[Endorsed:] Order of Councell. Delaware May 1st 1678.

----

    1. Other transcription in NYCD 12:593. For the council
        minutes from which these extracts were made, see
        27:84/85.

    2. See 21:33 for this complaint.

20:142   [THE MAGISTRATES OF NEW CASTLE TO GOV. ANDROS
           ABOUT MUNICIPAL AFFAIRS][1]

                              New Castle F[eb. 8th 1676/7]

Right Honorable Sir

        Wee have Received your Honors Gracious answer dated the
23rd of november Last past[2] to ours of the 8th of the same
month,[3] and do hereby Returne your Honor humble thankes for his
Readdinesse to Impro[ove] all opportunitys for the good of the
River and in perticular of this place, whereof wee are dayly
made more sensible. In further answer to the same, order is

taken for the Errecting of a prison, and a weighouse; To bee
built with all possible Epedition; about [the] watching of all
those within a myle of the T[owne
None to watch or ward   wee] Reply, that some of those of
in the town or fort but   Swanwike [wil fall] within the
such as live in or neare   myle, and others their neigbours
the town unles on alarmes   [without,] although they Live but
or Extraordinary ocasions.   next doore, which [will cause]
                               discontent, the one haveing with-
in a [small matter] as far to goe as the other; wee the[refore
desier] his honors further order therein;

As to the Levy of a penny in the [pound which your honor]
was pleased to allow; The people [live so far] distant and
their Estates for the most [part soe] Inconciederable; that
                               wee can find no [Convenient] way
Levyes to bee by the pole   to discover the vallue of their
as usuall notice being   said [estates, and if discovered
first given of the summe   to bring itt in a valluable
then a responsable Tre[surer] [manner] to Receive; But if your
to bee appointed who is to   honor will bee p[leased to] al-
bee accomptable [and to]   low of a Levy to bee Laid by the
cleare every yeare.   Pole, as [those of] Virginia and
                               Maryland doe and have Continu[ed]
itt for so many Jeares, not finding out a more Easier and
better way; then the Levy can bee Easier made and Received;

The [Sas]quehannos have not ben in Towne but passing by on
the bakes[side,] went upp the River; if they had desiered any
thing they should have ben treated according to your honors
order;

Wee hope your honor will bee pleased to Remember our
                               former Peticion about the sending
A lawbooke shall be sent per   of sould[iers,] The lawebooke
the first Convenience. The   and Seale; here Inclosed wee
past and next yeares fines   send your Honor a Coppy of the
(the Sheriffes allowance ex-   form[er fynes] as also of the
cepted) graunted for publick   fynes sence Capt. Coliers
charges so to Lessen the   Co[mming.]
Rate.

Wee also now present his Honor with the hereafter mentioned perticulars, humbly desiering his honors order and approbation for the same;

1. That your Honor will bee pleased so far to Impouwer the
                               Commander Capt. Colier, or the
The severall Courts [may] at   Court, that wills may bee
a Session take proofes and   prooved before them and Letters
[Se]curity and grant admini-   of administration Granted Ac-
stracion of Wills [but if]   cordingly; with setlement of the
above 20lb. to [Re]mit the   fees for the Estates of the most
same here [to] the Secretarys part of the People in these
office to [bee] Recorded.   parts, are too Inconsiderable,
                               that otherwyse the Charges and
Expenses of going to Your Honor att New Yorke for to obtane
the same; may Proove much to the hinderance of such Estates;

2. Wee desier his Honor to nominate some fitt person for
                               Vendu Master In the River, or
[The] Court to recommend [one Else to Impoure the Court to
for Vendu-Master who must]   do the Same; Itt haveing

give [security and accompt] once [a yeare then to bee] recorded. [The fees to bee six per Cento] besides [the Cryer and no other] Charges always ben a Custome here; and often occasion Requiers the same;

3. That the Valley above the Towne Lately belonging to Capt. Carr, and by your honor Given to the Towne for a Common; may bee a Stinted common to bee shut up the first of may, and opened againe [the] Last of July; and that Every Individuall Burger have his Equall Sheare therein, and their parts being Laid out by the Surveigor, then to draw Lotts for theire Sheares, and no man to put in more then one other; Lykewyse that all [The Commons to bee Regulated by the Court as Equally as may bee, also the maintaining the] dykes [sluce and fence, till further order.] persons who shall bee Concerned in the said Common, bee obliedged to maintaine the dyke and fence with the sluce in Keepeing itt in Repayre, and if any openly Refuse, them to Lose theire said Commonadge;

4. That an order may bee set forth In the River and Bay, forbidding all persons, not to Transport or set over; or Lend a Vessel to any Strainge person, to goe over to the Eastsyde of this River w[itho]ut a ticket from a Magestrate; as also servants; uppon penalty that Every such person so setting over or Conveiging any person who shall bee fugitieve and in debt, bee Lyable to make good the debts; and if a servant, to make good the Tyme of his servitude to the master; Your honor may bee pleased to Concider, All persons in Delaware river or bay leaving the Government to sett up theire names where they live and in Newcastle and this City according to Custome [in t]hese parts, in default [there]of and any assisting [thier dep]arture, to bee [Lyable to] the penalty, [and any servant] prison [or Criminall Run]ning [away to bee purs]ued by [hue and Cry as is] usuall. that if such order bee not made, (when the alteration of the Government Commeth on the other syde) wee shall not bee able to keepe any servant on this syde;

And Lastly, that your Honor will bee plea[sed to] admitt of a Generall Court or meeting of a[ll] the Justices; as heretofore (if but only for [the] makeing upp of the Levys, Collecting of Genera[ll] Revenues and other publicq and Gennerall afair[es)] which if your honor Thinkes not Convenient to [bee] that then Your honor will prescrybe us a way The levy by the pole in the severall Jurisdictions ansers the next particular [as to publicq Charges.]4 how, that, that which is alreddy In Generall do[ne] shall bee stated and devyded, and also how [the] Levys or other Gennerall Taxes yet to Come shall bee ordered and devyded

Uppon a[ll] the aforesaid Perticulars wee humbly desier his honors favorable order and Constructio[n,] Wee being Reddy to observe his honors o[rders] and to use all possible Endeavours for [the good] of the River and advancement of the People [over] whome your honor hath putt us who [are]

Right Honorable Governor
Your honors Most [humble]
Subjects and S[ervants]

The Court of [New Castle in]
Delowar,
By order of the [same]

[Signed:] Eph. Herman, [Clarke]

[Notations by Matthias Nicolls below signature:]

Liberty is granted for sloopes etc. goeing up the River
as formerly for this yeares effects or former debts.

5 Guns, 30 hoes and 1 ancker of Rume the remainder of the
pay for the land at the falls to bee forthwith paid them,
The remaining part of the Land betwixt the old and new purchase as also the Island called Peter Alricks or so much as is
not already purchased and the Indians will part with to bee
bought of them, for which C. Izrael Helme is to enquire for
the Owners and if they will be reasonable to bring them to the
Commander and Court at Newcastle for agreeing and [con]cluding
and Confirming [a] bargaine thereof.

If the above unpurchased Land bee bought the Surveyor
may lay out 200 acres forr Izrael Helme.[5]

[Addressed:]   To the Right Honorable Mayor Edmund Andros Esq.
and Governor Generall under his Royall Highnesse
Att New York

[Endorsed:]   No. 47 8th feb. 1677 propositions from the Court
of New Castle in delaworr. Answered the 6th of
April[6] To bee recorded with the within of Nov.
20th.[7]

---

1. Other transcription in NYCD 12:590. A transcription of
the court's copy of this letter appears in NCCR:65.
Damaged and missing portions of this document have been
recovered from NCCR. Marginal notations which were
made by Matthias Nicolls in response to the various proposals are indented in the text. The damaged portions
of these marginal notations have been recovered from
NCCR:98 which is the letter form of the orders that
were sent to New Castle in response to the various proposals.

2. See 20:103.

3. See 20:100.

4. This phrase in brackets appears in NCCR but not in the
marginal notation.

5. This final notation does not appear in NCCR.

6. See NCCR:98.

7. See 20:102.

20:143   [EXTRACTS FROM COUNCIL MINUTES CONCERNING AFFAIRS
          IN DELAWARE][1]

                              Att A Councill May 1st 1678.

          Capt. Billops Proposall about Sloopes going up the River
The time being Expired the former orders not to goe up to bee
Observed,

          The Other part of his Letter about the Goods landed by
the Mary of Leverpoole pretended to bee seized by Capt. Billop
for which they offer to pay the Custome, to bee left to Capt.
Dyre to answer.

          Capt. Mannings Peticion for [payment of] the ballance of
his Sherriffaltyes [account it be]ing fully advised according
to the Go. Order.

          To be refferred till the Governor returne which is in a
short time expected when the Councell will recommend it to
the Governor.

[Endorsed:] Order about Sloopes Going up Delaware River etc.
             May 1, 1678. 20.

---

1. See 27:84/85 for the council minutes from which these
    extracts were made. Damaged portions have been re-
    covered from this source.

20:144   [COURT PROCEEDINGS IN A SUIT BETWEEN JOHN
          SHACKERLY AND HENRY SALTER][1]

                              Att a Speciall Court held in the
                              Towne of New Castle Upon the Re-
                              quest of Mr. John Shackerly
                              May the 9th 1678.

                    Mr. John Moll   ⎫
Present.   Mr. Fopp Outhout   ⎬ Justices
                    Mr. Jean P. Jacquet ⎪
                    Mr. Gerrett Otto   ⎭

John Shackerly Plt.⎫ In an action of the Case for the perfor-
Henry Salter Deft ⎭ mance of a Bargaine of some plate by the
                      Plt. bought of the defts. wyfe.

          The debates of both partees being heard and Henry Salter
not giving any Reason why John Shackerly Should nott make oath
to the Bargaine, The Court thought fitt to put the said Plt.
(The deft. Refusing) to his Oath, whoe declared that hee Bar-
gained and absoluthly bought of Anna the wyfe of Henry Salter,
Six Spoones, Twoo small Trensier Salts and one parrenger all
of Silver, for fyve Shill. Six pence an ounce, but for Costs

of the fashion itt was Referred to Henry Salter whoe was Lykewyse to bring itt downe to New Castle, and that hee the said
Shackerly was to pay the overplus which was above his freight
Either to Capt. Billopp upon account of the defts. Customes or
in Melasses att first Cost in New York, And Henry Salter Con-
fessing in Court that his wyfe would have had him bring downe
the Plate but that hee would not alledging that hee did thinke
to pay John Shackerly in some other pay, and itt being alsoe
Evident by the Confession of the said Henry Salter as otherwayes, that his wyfe doth frequently as mutch as himselfe use
to make bargaines and Buys and Sells goods where of hee the
said Salter allowes.

The Court therefore doe order the said deft. Henry Salter
to deliver the Plate and Receive his Remainder of the pay
according to Bargaine and hee to pay Costs;

By order of Court

[Signed:] Eph: Herman, Cl.

[Entitled:] Jo: Shackerly

---

1. See NCCR:209 for a transcription of the original court
record from which this copy was made.

20:145/146   [TESTIMONY OF CAPT. CANTWELL, FOP OUTHOUT,
MICHAEL BARON, REYNIER VAN HEYST AND
JOHANNES VAN IMMEN ABOUT JOHN FENWICK][1]

Att a Court held in [Towne of
New Castle] 9th day of May
[Anno 1678]

Edmond Cantwell Dec[lares that hee being] in N. Salem
(alias) Swa[mptowne the 30th day] of April 1678, where Ma[yor
John Fenwike had] ordered a meeting of the Inhabitants of the
East[syde] of [this River,] hee the said Fenwike did the[n a]
point [some] officers vizt. Samuell Hedge Surveigor Gen[erall]
James Nevell to Secretary, Samuell Winder Register, and declared that hee would nominate and appoint other officers att
his Leasure and Caused his said Secretary to Read severall
papers, as his Mayesties Pattent to his Royal Highnesse, and
his Royal Highnesses to the Lord Berckley, and a Coppy (as hee
said) of the Lord Berckelys to him the said Fenwike with
severall other papers which the attestant did not minde, and
after the Reading of all these papers hee the said Fenwike demanded in his Mayesties name the suppreority and the submission
of the People there as his Right and propriety, after his demand hee brought a Paper upon the Table in the forme of an
oath or some such thing, which severall of his People or
officers sighned, after they had don, I tould him that the most
parte of the People that was there, did not know what was Read,
hee answered mee that they [Co]uld Kn[ow] well a noff to take
away his Land, I alsoe [tould] him that there was a small

Levy Laid by [the Court] upon the People on that syde hee said
the [Court] had no power to Lay no Levy on that syde [and]
said whoesoever did pay any Levy should forfeit their Lands and
priviledges, I asked him if hee would beare them out and sa[ve
them] harmlesse, hee said hee would [Give under] his hand to
answer itt before The [King,] and sayed that the People should
sta[nd in their] owne defence if any boddy ca[me to] demand
itt, and alsoe did forbi[dd] Justice Outhout not to act any
thing [in the] behalfe of the Court of New Castle upon the for-
feiture of his Estate, I tould him that his honor the Governor
had Commissio[nated] him the said Mr. Outhout, and was still
pleased for to Continue him, hee said the Governor had nothing
to doe on that syde, and that hee meaning himselfe was Subject
to [noe] man but God and the King, hee alsoe [said] that hee
would doe nor act nothing [without] the advyce of his Counsill
which hee would nominate verry suddenly, with sever[all] more
Speeches which the attestant doth not now Remember;

Justice Fop Outhout declares to have [been] present with
Capt. Cantwell and to have heard In Substance the same that is
her[eabove] declared by the said Capt. Cantwell;

Mr. Machiell Baron and Reynier van [Heyst] Sworne In
Court declare in substance to ha[ve] heard and seen the same
as hereabove by Capt. Can[twell] is declared;

Johannes van [Immen sworne] in Court declares [that being present at the house of] one Gillis Gi[ljamsen att the
East syde of this] River, Some [tyme in the Laest of the month]
of Aprill Laest past [att] which [tyme Mayor] John Fenwike
came [there whoe] demanded whey the deponant and [the rest]
that were there did not come att New Salem as others did to
aknowledge him (meaning himselfe) to bee Lord and Proprietor
of the place Upon wich they answered him saying how [th]ey
could owne him, so long as they paid Levy to witt 12 1/2
gilders per head att New Castle Court, where upon hee the said
Fenwike Replyed saying that all those whoe paid the same
should never Injo[y] a foot of Land on the Eastern Shoare And
further sayeth not

These aforestanding Testimonys
are True Coppies out of the Records
Exam. per

[Signed:] Eph. Herman, Cl.

[Entitled:] Testimonys Conserning Mayor Fenwike etc.

[Endorsed:] The Deposi[   ] of Capt. Edm. Cantwell and
others about Major Fenwick before the Court at
Newcastle May 9th 1678.

---

1. Other transcription in NYCD 12:592. See NCCR:206 for
the transcription of the court record from which the
missing portions have been recovered. These testimonies were enclosed with a letter dated May 9th 1678
from the Magistrates of New Castle to the Governor.
See NCCR:208 for the transcription of the court's copy
of this letter.

20:147   [MATTHIAS NICOLLS TO THE JUSTICES OF NEW
          CASTLE ABOUT FENWICK AND OTHER MATTERS][1]

Gent.

     Yours of the 9th instant[2] arrived here the beginning of
the weeke, which having not the hap to find the Go. returned,
was communicated to the Councell: Upon Consideracion of the
new Alteracions made by Major John Fenwyck on the East side of
the River, and perusall of the Testimonyes[3] and Informacions
given concerning the same, They have thought good to make the
inclosed order, which they desire you will doe your part to
see put in Execucion, if occasion, but with as litle mischeife
as may bee, Capt. Billop is written to likewise concerning it.

     The matter of Frans Barentsz[4] was not well represented by
C. Billop to C. Brockholes who supposing the accident of his
death was very lately and is being likewise intimated, that
hee having no heyre, the Estate hee left did belong to the
Duke as an Escheate, Hee gave order to C. Billop to secure
what hee had and give account of the same but upon farther
Informacion that the said Frans Barentsz dyed severall yeares
agoe, and that the Court hath formerly taken Cognizance of the
said Estate and the Go. having likewise beene made acquainted
therewith They doe not thinke fitt that Capt. Billop should
any farther concerne himselfe therein, but that you prosecute
what you had begun, and give account thereof to the Go., If
the deceased had a brother as is suggested, hee can have no
pretence after the disposall of it otherwise, a yeare and six
weekes being past and no clayme made, which is the time
limited by the Law.

     Here hath beene an addresse from Capt. Cantwell in the
name of his son,[5] resigning all the Right title and Interest
his said son might have to any of the Estate of William Tom
deceased by vertue of his will and desiring it may bee sold at
a publick vendue for the paiment of his Just debts, but that
hee may have preference before the rest of the Creditors next
to Capt. Delavall who hath judgment and Execucion against the
said Estate The Councell doth thinke it reasonable that the
said Estate belonging to Mr. Tom, bee sold for the payment of
his debts, but are not willing to alter the Course of the law,
which gives directions how debts shall bee paid That is
Statutes and Judgments first, then bonds and specialtyes, after
that booke debts, and other Clay[mes.] If any thing shall
after that bee left the son of C. Cantwell may have it.

     The sooner Mr. Toms Estate bee sold the better after some
weekes notice, For the Complaints made by the Commonalty
against the Commander C. Billop wee are not willing to enter
me[dle] therein, the rather for that you signify your resolucion to send some of your bench to the Go. after his arrivall (which wee expect daily) to treate with him about that
and other materiall Concernes This having as neare as may bee
answered the particulars of your Letter, I take leave and
remaine
          Gent.
                         your most humble servant
May 25, 1678   By order of the Councell
                         [Initialed:] M. N. Sec.

[Endorsed:] A lettre by order of the Councell etc. May 25, 78
             To the Justices at Newcastle in Delaware.

About Major Fenwyck C. Billop and other
particulars.

---

1. Other transcription in NYCD 12:595. See NCCR:220 for
   the transcription of the final draft of this letter.

2. See NCCR:208 for the court's copy of this letter.

3. See 20:145/146 for these testimonies.

4. See 20:133a/b.

5. See 20:152 for this petition.

20:148a   [COURT ORDER CONCERNING A SUIT BETWEEN
            HELMANUS WILTBANCK AND JOHN ROADES][1]

                          At a Court held for the Whorekill
                          the 11th day of June Anno 1678

                Mr. Helm. Wiltbanck Concernd:
[Com.] ⎰Mr. Henry Smith   ⎱ Mr. Edward Southrin   ⎱present
       ⎱Mr. Alex. Molestine ⎰ Mr. John Roades Concerned⎰

John Roades plt.....⎱
Helm. Wiltbanck deft⎰

     By Reason of the Death of Mr. John Backstead and absence
of Capt. Paul Marsh there was not magistors for a Court therefore by Consent of both parties and the magistors it is Referred to the next generall Assizes at New Yorke for tryall.
                          Vera Copia
[Signed:]   Test. Cornelis Verhoofe Cl. Co. Whorekill

[Entitled:]   Order of Court of Whorekill
              John Roades plt.
              Helm. Wiltbanck deft.

---

1. Other transcription in NYCD 12:597.

20:148b/149   [EXTRACTS BY MATTHIAS NICOLLS FROM COUNCIL
               MINUTES CONCERNING FENWICK, WILLIAM TOM'S
               ESTATE AND OTHER MATTERS][1]

               At a Councell etc. June 18, 1678

The matter of the Letters[2] Received from Delaware Magistrates at Newcastle and the Commander concerning Major Feen-
wyck etc. The former Orders[3] being taken into Consideracion
and the positive direction sent, the which they Neglected, The
Councell doth not thinke fitt to alter anything of their former
Orders being fitt, but leave them to answer their Neglect to
the Go., who is daily expected, and all the prejudice or mischeife that may happen thereby, to lye at their Doores.

The matter concerning Wm. Toms Estate. The former Order
of sale to bee followed, An Administrator that gives security
of the Creditors, of which C. Cantwell may bee thought convenient his son being Executor by will.[4]

To mind the Court for their so sudden giving Judgment for
a stranger without proofe, when so many other Creditors in the
Colony.

Upon Mr. Halls death at the Esopus, The Sheriffe or
Schouts place being vacant Mr. Wm. Asfordsby thought convenient
to bee in his place, till the Go. further order, and John Ward
to write the Passes as formerly.

[Endorsed:]   [   ] June 18 1678.

_____

1. Other transcription in NYCD 12:597. See 20:150 for the
   letter that is based on these minutes.

2. See NCCR:225 for the court's copy of the letter concerning John Fenwick.

3. See NCCR:222 for the transcription of these orders.

4. See NCCR:225 for the query from New Castle to which this
   paragraph responds.

20:150   [MATTHIAS NICOLLS TO THE COURT OF NEWCASTLE
           CONCERNING FENWICK AND WILLIAM TOM'S ESTATE][1]

Gent.

Yours of the 5th[2] by the return of the Expresse sent to
you by the Councell arrived here the beginning of the weeke,
but your answer seem very litle satisfactory to any particular
they writte about; As to the Order sent concerning Major
Fenwyck,[3] the Councell then did thinke, and upon serious

perusall of the same againe, doe find that it was absolute and
full, It expressing that in case of his Refusall to act in
assuming a power to Government to himselfe or denyall to come
to New Yorke upon your summons according to his parole that
then the Commander and you the Magistrates were to use force
to secure his person and send him hither, so you needed not any
new Result to bee directed to your selves along, (it being
thought fitt to direct it to the Commander also) more absolute then the former, which the Councell thinke sufficient, so
shall not alter anything therein, but leave your to answer your
Neglect to the Go. who is daily expected, and all prejudice or
mischeife that may happen thereby, to lye at your doores, they
having done their duty.

For the buisness of the Estate of Mr. Wm. Toms deceased,
The Councell likewise thought they had exprest themselves
very plaine as to the sale of that Estate to satisfy Creditors
as the Law directs, but thinke it very unreasonable to exclude
Capt. Delavall from his Judgment because Mr. Tom did it in his
will,[4] unlesse Errors can bee proved in it, or that it was
illegally obtayned, The strict nicety of his body being taken
in Execucion, being not thought sufficient to debarre the
Creditor of his just debt, where Effects can bee found to make
satisfaction, neither hath it ever beene practized in these
parts, though in England it may, where the Restraint of
prisoners is much more strict, and of another manner then Mr.
Tom's ever was, who in a manner had as much liberty after as
before the Execucion layd on him;

The Councell doth also very much admire at the Courts so
sudden giving judgment against the Estate of the deceased for
a stranger of Maryland concerning 2000 and odd hundred weight
of Tobacco upon so slender proofe (as they are informed,) which
may defeate many others within the Government who can it may
bee proofe their debts more substantiall, Upon Consideracion
had hereof and your desire of more positive and absolute
Orders therein the Councell thinke it convenient that one of
the Creditors doe administer upon the Estate of the said Wm.
Tom and in regard of the Resignacion of any Interest in the
Estate of the deceased, by C. Edm. Cantwell, on behalfe of his
son to the prejudice of the Creditors by vertue of the Will
made by the said Mr. Tom, wherein his son is named Executor,
They are of Opinion that the said Capt. Cantwell is the
fittest person to have the same who upon giving security to
administer according to Law, and returning a Certificate thereof may have letters of Administracion from hence, so to pay
the debts and put an Issue to that buisnesse, as is usuall in
such Cases;

Thus having not farther at present, Conclude and remaine.
                                            Gent.
N. Y. June 21st 1678

[Endorsed:] Copie of a letter to the Justices of Newcastle
             from the Councell June 21, 1678

---

1. Other transcription in NYCD 12:598. See NCCR:236 for
    the transcription of the final draft of this letter.

2. See NCCR:225 for the court's copy of this letter.

3. See NCCR:222 for this order.

4. See 20:151 for a copy of Wm. Tom's will.

20:151   [A COPY OF WILLIAM TOM'S LAST WILL AND
          TESTAMENT]

Copia

          IN THE NAME OF GOD amen, This third day of the month of
January in the Jeare of our Lord and savior Jesus Christ one
thousand six hundered seventy and seven, I William Tom of New
Castle in Delowar Gentlm: being Sike and weake in boddy but
of good and perfect memory thenkes bee to Almighty God, therefore doe make and ordayne this my present will and Testament
in manner and forme following: That is to say first I bequeath
my soull and spirit into the hands of almighty God my heavenly
father my Creator and Redeemer, my mortal boddy in hope of a
Joyfull Resurect: I Committ to the Earth to be burried in
decent Christian manner: and touching the distribution of all
my worldly Estate goods and t'Chattles I dispose thereof as
followeth:

          First I will that all such Debts as I Legally owe shall
bee truely and honestly paid out of my said Estate only Ex-
epting the debt I am bound to pay to Capt. Thomas DeLavall for
which I declare to bee and Dye a Prisoner; and after that I
doe give will and dispose of the Remainder of all my Estate
goods t'Chattles and unto Richard Cantwell my Godson to him
his heirs or assignes for Ever, hereby declaring the said
Richard Cantwell to bee my only heire and Executor of all the
premisses abovementioned; And In Reguard that hee the said
Richard Cantwell is Yett in minority and not Capable to Execute
this my Laest will and Testament, I doe therefore hereby desier
ordaine and appoint the worshipfull Court of Justices of this
Towne of New Castle to bee his overzeers and Guardians of and
over the premisses untill hee the said Richard shall bee Come
to adge and no Longer and further I doe hereby Revoake and
disanull all former wills and Legacies by mee made or Intended
before this date, In wittnesse and Confirmation hereof and of
this my Laest will and Testament, I have Confirmed this with
my hand and seale In the presence of Mr. John Moll Mr. Walter
Wharton and Gisbert Dircks the day and Jeare abovesaid;
                              (subscrybed)
John Moll   Will: Tom L. S.[1]
Walter Wharton
Gysbert Dircx

[Entitled:] Copie of Mr. Thoms Will.

_____

1. i.e., <u>locus</u> <u>sigilli</u>: "the place of the seal."

20:152   [PETITION OF CAPT. CANTWELL CONCERNING
          WM. TOM'S WILL AND ESTATE][1]

                              To the Honorable the Deputy
                              Governor and the honorable
                              Counsill In New Yorke;

The Humble Peticion of Edmund Cantwell

Humbly Sheweth.

        That Mr. William Tom Late of this Towne of New Castle
deceased by his Laest will and Testament[2] bearing date the
3rd of Jannuary 1677/8 did make and bequeath all his Estate,
Goods and Chattles Lands and Tennements unto your Peticioners
son Richard That is to say all that should bee Left after his
Just debts Should bee paid, with Exclusion of the debt of
Capt. DeLavall as by said will more att Large doth and may_
Apeare, Now Soe itt is that the said Capt. DeLavall by his
attorney John Addams desiering of the worshipfull Court of the
Towne of New Castle, that hee might have his former Execution
Renewed against the goods and Estate etc. of the said Mr. Tom
for the payment of his debt;

        Itt is therefore the Earnest desire of the Peticioner
that the said whole Estate Reall and personall of Mr. Tom
aforesaid may bee appraized or publicqly Sould and that out of
the produce thereof the said Capt. DeLavall may bee first paid
and that the Remainder bee for payment of the other debts the
Peticioner as one of them desires the preferrence The Peticioner
being alsoe willing and Ingageing In his Son Richards Behalfe
to desist of all benefitts and proprietys comming to his said
son by the said Will, and that the said Testament bee disannulled and Canselled;

        Upon which Your honors humble Peticioner desires Your
honors answer and Remains

                              Your honors Most humble
N: Castle the 10th   Subject and Servant
of May 1678.
                              [Signed:]   Ed Cantwell

[Endorsed:]   Capt. Edm. Cantwells peticion to the Dep: Go: and
              Councell about Mr. Toms Will and Estate.   May 10.
              1678. Newcastle.[3]

_____

1. The petition is written in the hand of Ephraim Herman.
    For the reply to this petition see 21:32.

2. See 20:151 for Wm. Tom's will.

3. Endorsement is written in the hand of Matthias Nicolls.

20:153 [COURT PROCEEDINGS AGAINST WALTER WHARTON
FOR MARRYING HIMSELF, AND OTHER OFFENCES][1]

Att a Court held In the Towne
of New Castle By his Mayestis
Authority June the 4th and
5th 1678.

Mr. Walter Wharton being heretofore by the Minister Reader
and t'Church Wardens presented for marrying himselfe or being
married directly Contrary to the Knowne Lawes of England and
alsoe Contrary to the Lawes and Customes of this place and
Province, as alsoe for Promissing of Lands and Entring the
same in his booke before that the persons for whome hee did itt
had any grant or order of Court for the same, And the said Mr.
Wharton not appearing in three following Court dayes, And to
the End the Reproach may bee taken away from the River and
that such notorious breatches of the Lawes and disorders may
for the future not passe unpunnished Especially in persons of
Lesser qualitys whoe if this of Mr. Whartons (whoe is in
Commission and beares the office of a Justice of the peace
ougt to give good Examples to others) had not ben Reguarded
migt att all tymes herea[fter] bee held for a bad president;
The Court doe therefore thinke itt necessary, Humbly for to
offer the Premisses to the Judgment of his Honor the Governor,
for to Inflict such punnishment as his honor in his wisdome
shall think fitt and Expedient;

A True Copy of o[   ] the
Records Exam. per
[Signed:] Eph: Herman

[Endorsed:] To bee out of the Commission[   ] Justices and
Left to the Law.[2]

---

1. Other transcription in NYCD 12:596. See NCCR:210 for
   the transcription of the original from which this copy
   was made.

2. Endorsement is written in the hand of Matthias Nicolls.

20:154 [COURT PROCEEDINGS AGAINST WALTER WHARTON FOR
BEING ABSENT FROM COURT][1]

Att a Court held In the Towne of
N: Castle June the 4th and 5th 1678

Mr. Walter Wharton being Comissionated one of the Justices
and members of this Court and hee haveing not appeared in fyve
months or ordinary following Courtdayes for to help to doe and
attend the publicq and Country Buisnesse as others the Justices
and members of this Court from tyme to tyme doe; the Court
therefore in Reguard that hee the said Mr. Wharton during the
tyme of this his absence has not ben out of the precincts of

this River and Bay; Doe therefore thinke itt fitt that hee for
an Example to others bee fyned according to the Expresse Lawes
of the Government the Summe of Ten Pounds, And doe hereby
Condeme him the said Mr. Wharton in the said fyne of Ten
pounds with the Costs:

                    A True Copy out of the Records
                    Examined per mee
                    [Signed:] Eph: Herman, Cl.

[Endorsed:] No. 4 Mr. Walter Wharton

---

1. Other transcription in NYCD 12:596. See NCCR:215 for
   the transcription of the original from which this copy
   was made.

20:155   [COURT PROCEEDINGS CONCERNING MAJOR FENWICK][1]

                    Att a Meeting of the Commander and
                    Justices held in the Towne of New
                    Castle July 17th 1678.

The Letter from the Honorable Councill[2] Read and the
buisnesse of Mayor Fenwike taken into Consideracion by the
Commander and Justices of this Court, and Capt. Billop sig-
nifying that att his Laest being over att Salum the Laest
weeke, that then Mayor Fenwike was willing to answer the
honorable Councills order att New Yorke, and that hee will surrender himselfe att New Yorke according to his Parole; Resolved
and ordered by the Commander Joyntly with the Court that Mayor
Fenwike in case hee will Give under his hand by a Letter to
the Counsill that hee will not act by assuming any power of
Government to himselfe on that syde of the River or any where
Else, and that hee within the space of Twenty dayes promises
to make his personall appearance att New Yorke according to
his Parole that then hee bee Left there but In case of Refusall
and that hee doth not send a sattisfactory Answer, That then
the said Commander together with the high Sherrife Presse and
take with them so many of the Militia as they think fitt and
with them seize the said Fenwiks person and send him to New
Yorke without delay according to the order of the honorable
Counsil.

                    A true coppy out of the Records
                    Exam. per
                    [Signed:] Eph: Herman, Cl.

Followeth the Letter sent to Mayor Fenwike

Mayor Fenwike

Sir

        Capt. Billop Signifying to us that you have altered your
former Resolucion and that now you are willing to answer the

order from the honorable Counsill of New Yorke, and that you
will goe and there surrender yourselfe according to your Parole,
Now therefore if you will forbeare the assuming any power of
Government to yourselfe, and within the space of 20 days will
apeare in New York and there surrender yourselfe according to
your Parole then Signify soe mutch in a Letter under your hand
to the honorable Counsill in New Yorke, and send the same
Letter open to us under a Covert by this bearer that soe wee
may bee possitive of your Resolucion Remaining Sir

<table>
<tr><td></td><td>Your affectionate frinds</td></tr>
<tr><td>N: Castle</td><td>(was signed)</td></tr>
<tr><td>July 17th 1678.</td><td>Chris Billop</td></tr>
<tr><td></td><td>John Moll</td></tr>
<tr><td></td><td>Peter Alrichs</td></tr>
<tr><td></td><td>Fop Outhout</td></tr>
<tr><td></td><td>Jean Paul Jacquet</td></tr>
<tr><td></td><td>Gerret Otto</td></tr>
</table>

Memorandum in answer to the above Mayor Fenwike sent a Letter
to the Counsill and one to the wryters of the above, which
both are yett in the hands of the Commander.

[Endorsed:] [   ] the Co[   ] at Newcastle about Major
             Fenwick July [   ]³

---

1. Other transcription in NYCD 12:599. See NCCR:237 for
    the original records from which this copy was made.

2. See 20:150 for this letter.

3. Endorsement is written in the hand of Matthias Nicolls.

20:156   [THE COURT OF NEW CASTLE TO MATTHIAS NICOLLS
          ABOUT JOHN FENWICK AND WM. TOM'S ESTATE]¹

Honorable Sirs

    Your Letter of the 21th of June Laest² wee Received In
answer; To which wee Reply, that the occasion of our wryting
alone the 5th of the same month³ (in which to our Sorrow your
honors Reply to Receive so Little Satisfaction) was not that
wee desiered to bee only Conserned without the Commander, But
That which was writt Then Conserning Mayor Fenwike, wee had
out of the mouth of the said Commander, (who mutch takes the
part of and is agreat frind to the said Fenwike) and his not
signing of the said Letter was by Reason the other perticulars
therein mencioned Conserned him nott;

    By the Inclosed Coppies⁴ your honors will see what Result
hath ben tacken by the Commander and us sence the Receipt of
Your honors said Letter, and sence the Commander and high
Sherrife have fetched the said Fenwike to this Towne and although itt was supposed to be a more securer and better way

to send him by waeter in this Sloope, Yett the Commander thinkes
it best to send him by Land; which hee Lydewyse hath obligeth
to doe;

     As to Mr. Toms Estate Capt. Cantwell offers security, and
Intends to Come to New Yorke himselfe to take out Letter of
administracion and as to the Judgement so suddenly Given as alledged the same was for Twoo Bills which were divers tymes before Confessed by the deceased, and those of Maryland make no
difference in the Lyke Cases with us, but Suppose there will
bee Little Left after Capt. Delavalls debt is paid; so haveing
no more att present Remaine
                              Honorable Sirs
New Castle   Your honors most humble Sub-
July 24th 1678.   ject and Servants
                              The Court of the Towne of New
                              Castle;
                                  By order of the same
                              [Signed:] Eph: Herman, Cl.

[Addressed:] To the Honorable Capt. Matthias Nicolls [   ]
              the Rest of the Honorable Council New Yorke
              These

[Endorsed:] A Letter from the Court of Newcastle
             July 24th 1678. 39.⁵

----

1. Other transcription in NYCD 12:600. See NCCR:239 for
   the court's copy of this letter.

2. See 20:150 for this letter.

3. See NCCR:225 for the court's copy of this letter.

4. See 20:155 for these copies.

5. Endorsement is written in the hand of Matthias Nicolls.

20:157   [PETITION OF JOHN HILLYARD CONCERNING LAND
         IN WHOREKILL]¹

To the Right honnorable Sir Edmon Andros govnore of New Yorcke.

     The humble peticion of John Hillyeard Humbley Sheweth
that wheare as youre peeticinor obtanned a warrant of the worshipfull courte of the Whorekill too Eight hundred accores of
Land in the prosinckes of Dellayway bay wheare upon youre
peeticionor sould his Land and cattill at a verey under Rate
by Reason of the greate distance I lived from youre honners
goverment and in october last I adventred with Three of my
fammiley in a verrey small boat through the mane sea and came
to the Whorekill Wheare finding noe survayore mayde my addresse
to the courte who ordred Cornelous Verhoofe Clarck to the Court

to Lay out my Land I heareing theare was plentey of Land in
Duck Creeke and noe man theare settled went theare and finding
Land built a house and Clearred ground and by the courtes
order Cornelous Verhoofe came to Duck Creeke the twentey
fourth day of December Last and Layd out my Land and was ordred by the court to give Mr. Walter Whorton the survayer an
account of what hee had done in the Laying out the Land now
soe it was that Mr. Whorton did not come doune from New Castill
till feebrarey following and hee putting in at St. Jones
Francis Whitwell in formed him that I was settled upon his the
sade Francis his Land as indeede it doth appeare by a pattin
hee hath for fower hundred accores in the verey place that I
have setted and planted uppon now soe it was that in Jennarey
Last yeare peeticinor wanted profidgion and other nessesareyse
weent doune by sea with his boate and handes to Marey Land to
fetch providgion and the wintter prooving harde could not
accomplish to arrive at Duck Creeke bee fore the second day of
march following now I be[   ]ech youre honner to Considder the
proceedinges beetwene Ienewarey and march Mr. Whorton as afore
sade arriving at St. Jones in febrarey and understood what
Cornelous verhoofe had doone not withstandinge suravyed and
Layd out for the sade Francis Whitwell one thousand accores
of Land² which was the verrey Land which was Layd out for mee
and an other man by the courtes order and this was done in
feebrarey following after my settlement youre peeticinor not
knowing of theare proseedinges till hee had transportted his
whole fammiley beeing Elleven Soules having fower soones and
one daughter I with my fammeley arrived at my house at Duck
Creeke as I supposed the 2 day of aprill Last but was forwarned
of the Land by the sade Whitewell and hee produced a pattin
for fowre hundred accores wheare I was seatted wheare upon I
was forced to beecome his tennant for this yeare now my humble
peticion to youre honner is that I may have my Land which hee
hath survayed from mee which I had parte of beeside the fower
hundred accores of his which I must surrender for mine was
Eight which I hope youre honner will grant mee out of the
thousand hee is but a single man and hath bee sides that thousand accores fower other seates of Land namely two at St. Jones
containing sixe hundred accores and two at Duck Creeke contaning
Eight hundred accores one wheare I live called white hall and
an other called Seewelles Point and trewly theare commeth
severall men who would gladley settell but that the Land is
ingroced into such menes handes that thay must Ether bey or
goe without I humbley beechech [sic] youre honner to considder
my condission my servantes gooe free and If I have not the
Land adjoyning whear I had Rite beefore the sade Whitwell it
will ondoe mee to Remove agane If youre honner would bee
pleased to Let mee have youre order how to proseede by the
bearrer youre peeticinor shall as induty bee Ever bound to
pray July the 30/78

[Entitled:] John Hillyard his peeticin.

---

1. Other transcription in NYCD 12:600.

2. See DYR:181 for Whitwell's patent to this land.

20:158   [PETITION OF GEORGE MERTEN CONCERNING LAND
           IN WHOREKILL][1]

To the Right honnerable Sir Edmon Andros Govenor of New Yorck.

The humble peticion of George Merten humbley sheweth that
wheoras youre peeticinor obtaned a warrant for fower hundred
a[ ] of Land of the Worshipfull Court of the Whore Kill and
by Reason y[ ]ure pe[   ] was Reddey to settell and Could
not tell wheare the survayer was the Courte [   ] Cornelous
Verhoofe to Lay out my Land which was done by him the verrey
day [   ] John Hillyard his Land[2] was Layd out and Joyning to
the sade Hillyard his L[   ] the sade Whitwell including youre
peticinors Land in to his Thousand a[   ] mensioned in John
Hillyard peticion youre peticinor hath built and plant[   ]
and is threatned to bee disposesed by the sade Whitwell hee
having an in [   ] in the survayer hath a setificate Returned to new yorck for the t[   ] accores Called Whitwell
his Chance[3] theare Came three poore men to Loocke [ ] Land
and the sade Whitwell would sell them the a fore thousand
accores for [   ] thousand poundes of tobaco perswading them
theare was none to bee [   ] they would bey I humbley
desire youre honner not to thinck this a fi[ ]ion [   ] of
aney mallis but the verrey truth to the great discoridgment of
many people who would gladly seate in youre province and
farther youre peeti[   ] desireth youre honner would bee
pleased to grant him a order the p[   ] Injoyment of his
Land by the bearrer and Lickwyse order the sur[   ] to Lay
out the sad Hillyard his Land and mine for oure Case is al-
licke [   ] peticinor shall as in duty bee Ever bound to
pray July the 30/78

---

1. Other transcription in NYCD 12:601.

2. See 20:157 for Hillyard's petition concerning his land.

3. See DYR:181 for Whitwell's patent.

20:159   [MINUTES OF THE COURT OF NEWCASTLE CONCERNING
           MATTERS TO BE LAID BEFORE GOV. ANDROS UPON
           HIS RETURN FROM ENGLAND][1]

By the Court of the Towne of N: Castle

Itt being taken into Consideracion that Severall necessary
buisnesses Relating to the welfare of this Towne of New Castle
and the parts adjacent ought to bee demonstrated to his Honor
the Governor att his arrivall from England, as alsoe Severall
priviledges and other good and benefitiall orders and grants
ought to bee Requested att his honors hands; The Court have
therefore thought best to the End itt may bee well presented
and his honor made acquainted with all material passages here
and a Result and answer from his said honor the Governor

obtayned; To desire Impower and depute Mr. John Moll one of
the members of this Court; In the behalfe of the said Court
to Effect and accomplish the abovesaid, and humbly to shew and
att Large demonstrate the hereafter mencioned particulars as
followeth vizt.

1. To Desire and humbly Request his honor the Governor to
   grant us Leave and permission to obtayne and have an
   orthodox minister, to bee mayntayned by the gifts of the
   free willing givers.

2. To desire of his honor that a double number of magestrates
   may bee ordayned, and to present as the fittest persons
   vizt. Mr. Johannes Dehaes Mr. William Semple Mr. Abram Man
   and Mr. Hendrik Williams - and that A Coroner may alsoe
   bee appointed;

3. To Intreat his honor to send us the New corrected Lawbooke
   and seale for the office as heretofore promissed;

4. Whereas the Land of Capt. Car deceased Ly[ing] betweene
   Mr. Toms Plantation and This [Towne] was formerly Kept up
   in the vendu, for [the] Towns use, and whereas the Towne
   h[ave nott] as Yett proffered any monny for itt, [There-
   fore] to desire his Honors orders to seel the said Land
   [publicqly] and further to know what Tytle shall [bee
   given] to the purchazers;

5. To make his honor acquainted that the [Surveigor] Mr.
   Walter Wharton neglects his o[ffice] surveiging to the
   great obstruction a[nd hinderance] of Severall People, as
   well within the Ju[risdiction] of Upland as this Court,
   and that the [Rate allowed] to bee paid for his Surveiging
   fees far Exceeds [the] Maryland Rate, which much dis-
   courages the Pe[ople,] Therefore to desire that the fees
   may be Equali[zed with] Maryland fees; And Cheefly [to
   make] his honor acquainted how that to the Gre[at blame]
   and Shame of the government hee the said Mr. W[harton]
   hath married himselfe, and further [that] hee promisses
   Lands to people and Enters [the same] in his Surveigors
   booke before that the pers[ons] have any grant or order
   of the Court, and [takes] bills under the peoples hands for
   the same, [all which] This Court by an order bearing date
   4th [of June] Laest² have Referred to the Censure of his
   [honor the] governor; And more That hee h[ath forced] one
   man in Maryland to assigne his Pattent to him only for
   surveigors f[ees] Whereby twoo familys are hindered of
   [settling] which said Land hee the said Surveigor hath
   sould.

6. That his honor will bee pleased to Establish [waights] and
   measures, and that a gage bee ap[ointed in this] River for
   all Coopers to make the [Tobbacco hoghsheads.]

7. To make his honor acquainted how That Mayor Fenwike forbids
   the People of the Eastsyde of this River to pay their pro-
   portion of the publicq Rate Layed Laest Yeare for the Paying of the woolfs heads and that hee the said Fenwike
   threatnes the People with Ruine incase they pay any, and
   that hee the said Fenwike now has Laid a tax himselfe:
   Therefore to know wheather the People there shall pay any
   of the said tax, and how for the future this Court shall
   act and behave Themselves towards the said Eastsyde;

8.   To shew how that dayly Severall People doe mutch Com-
     playne, that their old debts due unto them out of the
     Publicq are not paid, To desire his Honor, to Consider
     the Poore People that some way may bee found out for
     their Sattisfaction Either by the Lotts of Land Yett to
     bee Granted in this Towne, or otherwyse as his honor
     Shall think best;

[9] To Know his honors will and pleasure, whether a Levy or
     tax may bee Laid for the paying the debts made during
     the tyme of this Government Conserning the forte and the
     Lyke etc;

[10] To Know whether houses and Lands of persons deceased or
     Runaway, are Lyable and may bee publicqly Sould for the
     paying the Partees Just debts, Incase the personall
     Estate falls short; and how the Court shall act in that
     and [the li]ke buisnes[ses.]

[11] That Liberty of traede may bee granted us with The neig-
     bouring Collony of Maryland for the supplying us with
     negros, Servants and Utensils without wich wee can not
     subsist, and alsoe that Liberty may be granted us for
     our owne Vessells which wee may gett, to Enter and Cleare
     the same here, without Touching att New Yorke in case wee
     might send Them for England Barbados and other p[laces]
     wee observing the acts of Parliment;

12. To Represent and make his honor acquainted [with] actions
     and proceedings of the Commander Capt. Billop here sence
     his honors departure, to [the end] that the poore People
     may not bee oppressed, a[nd that] the Court may know for
     the future the Rig[ht] meaning and Extent of the Com-
     manders [Commission] The t'Cheef of which said Commanders
     acti[ngs being] breefly mencioned, vizt.

     1: That the said Commander att his first Com[ming]
     here and all along hath publicqly blamed [and] de-
     famed the governor, and alsoe That hee [the said]
     Commander Contrary to his duty Stands up [for and]
     holds with Mayor Fenwike, which hath so ama[zed the]
     Inhabitants of the Eastern shoare that some of [them]
     know not whome to Obey;

     2: To Know whether the said Commander hath [power]
     over the Court to Command them and the Lyke [as hee] in
     Severall Speeches hath declared;

     3: To take a Coppy and to present to his [honors] view
     what in the Records the 8th of March[3] La[est is] En-
     terred downe Conserning said Commander.

     4: To desire his honor to Explaine whether [hee the]
     said Capt. Billop hath acted Lawfully to take [Poore]
     peoples goods out of their houses, which they [had]
     gott out of Maryland for old debts due for [Cattle]
     sold to the Marylanders, and without an[y forme] of
     Lawfull proceedings, to keepe the same [goods and]
     Convert them to his owne use, The perso[ns from] whome
     hee hath taken said goods being Las[se Dalbo] Jan
     Boelsen Andries Boen etc., and [humbly] to Intreat his
     said honor in the behalfe of [the poore] People that
     that and other the Lyke buisnes[ses may] bee Examined

and the goods Returned [to them.]

5: And Laestly, To make his honor acquainted that hee
the said Commander hath from tyme to tyme taken up and
made sale of unmarkt hoghs horses and mares, as alsoe
of Stray markt horses; for Instance one hors of doctor
Tymen[4] one of Caspares Herman, one markt mare taken out
of Capt. Cantwells Pasture and sould to Mr. James
Coursey in Maryland for 1200 lb. of tobacco and
severall hoghs had of doctor Tymen and Jan Staalcop
To the End his Royall highnnesse may have his due out
of the above said Creatures And further to desire his
honor to know whether the said Commande hath power to
grant Lycenses for marriage, as to severall persons
hee hath done, where by the Common Course of 3 pro-
clamations in the Church or beannes[5] setting up is
Laid aside;

Given under our hands In New Castle
this 17th of July Anno 1678;
[Signed:] Ed. Cantwell
           Jn. Moll
           Pieter Alrichs
           F: outhout
           Jean Paul Jacquet
           Geret Otto

By order of Court
[Signed:] Eph: Herman, Cl.

---

1. Other transcription in NYCD 12:606. See NCCR:232 for
   the court's copy from which the missing portions have
   been recovered.

2. See 20:153 for this court order.

3. See NCCR:194.

4. i.e., Tymen Stiddem.

5. i.e., banns.

NEW YORK
HISTORICAL MANUSCRIPTS:
DUTCH

Volume XXI

Delaware Papers, 1664-1682

21:1a   [JOHN BRIGGS TO ANDREW BOWDLER ABOUT PAYMENT
          OF A DEBT]

Mr Androwe Boudler

        Sir whare ass I have gaven my Mother a letter of Aterney
I ould [sic] desier you to make Satfshon [sic] to her ore if
you Cann make Satfshon in the hands of my Freind John Shakerly[1]
you will Oblege youer freind and his Recaite Shall bee youer
descharge for the same

                              Sir youer to Comand

                              [Signed:] John Brigs

Horkill the 10th of July 1679

_____

    1. This note is written in Shackerly's hand.

21:1b   [JOHN SHACKERLY TO JOHN BRIGGS ABOUT DISPOSAL
          OF CORN; BRIGG'S REPLY THERETO]

        [   ] Sente to you by John Boyer [   ] [   ]ells
of Ingan Corne and whatt [   ] [   ] have a Cashon for
the Plantashon Pray Keep and the Rest lett my Nabo[ ] which
are my Custemers have. I sh[ ] if god willinge bee with
you within fue dayes which Corne is Desposed of Lett Edward
Pecke Enter in to my Booke : my Kinde Love to yo[ ] Mother
and Wife Nott Ellce att Present butt ame youer

                          Asshored Freind
                          [Signed:] John Shakerly

[P.S.]
Allie [   ]bereth her
Kind Love to Her Husband
N. Castell the 24th 1679

My Sarves to Mr. Whittell[1] and desier [   ] my [   ]
Redey and if hee hath aney more then what is Recei[   ] to Let
mee have itt.

[Addressed:]   To Mr John Briggs att St Jones [   ] per John
                 Bouear[2]

[Verso:]
Mr. Shakerly

        Sir I have receved your Letter from John Boyer and the
Corne which you sent me which I have noe Occation for itt and
If you had Left itt when you ware att the Creeks mouth I would

[ ] don [   ] Indever [   ] to your Advantaige for[ ] att
present I have noe occation for itt So [   ] with my respects
to you and your wife I rem[   ]

                              [Signed:]   John Brigs

----

1. Probably Francis Whitwell.

2. i.e., John Boyer.

21:1c   [AN ACCOUNT AGAINST JOHN SHACKERLY]

New Castile the [   ] 1679

     Jno. Shakerly Dr.

To Butter... 00:12:06
To 19 lb. of bread and 2 bunches to twine........... 00:07:09
To 1 barrell Mollasses.............................. 03:05:00
To 5 lb. of Suger delivered per order att times[1].... 00:02:06
To 2 qts. Rum delivered per order................... 00:04:00
To goods delivered the Shoomaker.................... 00:12:06
To 6 hows and 5 Axes att 3s per..................... 01:13:00
To 22 1/2 yds. Crocus att 12d per yd................ 01:02:06
                                              Sum   07:19:09

     Ditto Cr.

By 57 Skiples wheat.................................. 07:02:06

                                         Due..   00:17:03

To 2 pr. Shoos Peltery   00:16:00
                                                     01:13:03

     PER WB[   ][2]

----

1. Possibly a reference to Tymen Stiddem.

2. Remainder of signature has been cut away.

21:2   [AN ACCOUNT AGAINST JOHN BRIGGS]

John Briggs   Dr.

To 1 dozen of porangers att	Tob[1]....................	72
To 2 Large Cittells.....att	....	56
To 2 Culenders.........att	....	50
To 2 Brode pints.......att	....	14
To 2 qt. pots..........att	....	18
To one large Saspann....att	....	12
To one Lampe...........att	....	14
To one flower box.......att	....	8
To 2 gratters..........att	....	12
To one dripinge pann....att	....	18
To 3 Large puden pan....att	....	36
To 2 smaller ditto......att	....	20
		330

1. i.e., tobacco, indicating that payment was to be made in
pounds of tobacco or the value thereof.

21:3a   [DISCHARGE OF A DEBT BY JOHN SHACKERLY][1]

Received this 18th of Feb. 1678/9 From John Shakerly,
Full Satfashon [sic] for one gra[ ] Horse Bridell and Sadell
delivered and Paid To the Said Shakerly att the Horkill in
Delawar bay I Say Received Per

[Signed:]   Richard Higinbothom

Testes
[Signed:]   Will Masten
            Ralph Hutchinson

1. Receipt is written in the hand of John Shackerly.

21:3b   [AN ACCOUNT AGAINST JOHN SMITH]

Uplands 3rd of March 1678/9

Loving friend John Smith acording to thy order I have
hear sent the[1] down by my Friend John Shackerly an anker of
wine which comes to 20 Skiples of wheat and 6 gilders of Cask

```
                                                      gld. st.
all which amounts to one hundred and six gilders.......106= 00
which I would desier the to pay to this bearer John Shackerly
Pray faill not and in soe doeing the wilt obledg thy
```

                              loving Friend
                       [Signed:] John West

_____

1. i.e., thee.

21:4   [NO CALENDAR ENTRY AND NO DOCUMENT]

21:5a   [DISCHARGE OF A DEBT FOR ALEXANDER MOLESTINE]

Mr. Sander Maulstene   N. Castle the 14 May 79

     Pray you pay to the bearer hereof Mr. John Shackerly: the
ten minckskins which you owe mee For the Rume which you had of
mee when I was In your parts pray you Fail not and this noat
with his Receipt shall bee your discharge From

                          Your Friend and servant
                       [Signed:] John Addams

21:5b   [AN ACCOUNT OF SUSANNA GARLAND AGAINST JOHN
         SHACKERLY][1]

                         Hoerekill the 3rd of Feb. 1678/9

                                                        tobacco
        Mr. John Seekerly[2] for punch[3]..............   010
8   ditto   3 pints of rum......................... f024 1/2
    ditto   1 quart for Sammel Styls............... f020
    ditto   3 pints of rum......................... f022 1/2
            3 pints of vinegar 1 1/2 pounds of sugar f015

```
                                                       tobacco
 9  ditto   one pint of rum........................ f007 1/2
    ditto   Sammel Styles one quart................. f020
            one half pint of rum.................... f005
    ditto   one bowl of punch⁴...................... f028
10  ditto   part of a bowl of punch⁵................ f010
            Sammel Styles 1 quart................... f020
    ditto   one bowl of punch....................... f028
            Sammel Styls 1 1/2 pints................ f015
12  ditto   2 quarts of rum......................... f030
    ditto   one quart for Sammel.................... f020
            one pint of rum and sugar............... f010
    ditto   part of a bowl of punch................. f014
14  ditto   one gallon of rum....................... f060
            Sammel Styls 3 quarts................... f060
15          6 pints of rum.......................... f045
            7 pounds of sugar....................... f040
                   [Signed:]  Susanna Gorland       441 1/2
```

[Entitled:] Susanna Garland

---

1. This account is translated from the Dutch which exhibits considerable English interference.

2. i.e., John Shackerly.

3. Written: pons.

4. Written: een boly pons.

5. Written: paer van een boly pons.

21:6   [NO CALENDAR ENTRY AND NO DOCUMENT]

21:7   [HELMANUS WILTBANCK TO MATTHIAS NICOLLS ABOUT
        SURVEYS AT WHOREKILL]¹

Honored Sir

        I Recd. yours from [blank] of May the 18th Day of June
Relating to the Surveyors and Surveys in our partes I Know not
who are Surveyors onely by the Returne of the Surveys to the
Court to home them signed the which the quantitys granted to
the pertier² if noe Grievances are Entred against as for the
Just[   ] of the Same according to act the Court not being

skillfull alsoe the Copia of order from the Conncell Concerning
the Cause of Capt. Cantwell to the which I have Inclosed this
petition please to present it to the Conncell I hope to [   ]
at York the next Assizes if god willing then may Discourse
farther with you about aney Concernes as may Require have not
farther to Inlarge at present then Remai[   ]
                              Sir Your Most Humble Servant
Whoorkill   [Signed:] Helm. Wiltbanck
the 4th of S[   ]tember 1678

[Addressed:] These for Capt. Matthias Nicolls
              Secretary Ny Jorck

---

1. Other transcription in NYCD 12:602.

2. Possibly Wiltbanck's spelling of "petitioner."

21:8   [EDWARD SOUTHRIN TO GOV. ANDROS COMPLAINING
       ABOUT JOHN AVERY][1]

                    To The Honorable Edmond Andros Esq.
                    Capt. Generall of All his Royall
                    Hignnes territories In America

        Whereas it was your Honors good pleasure to put and Con-
s[   ] mee though a person unworthey of soe high a Callinge
to bee a magestrate at the Whorekilles In which office and
Calling I have Indeavored by the help of g[   ] to Discharge my
Concience before god and man to the best of my Skill and Knowledg without favor or Affection to any person and for soe doeing I have Receiv[   ] many Abusess both from Mr. John Avery and
Mr. Henry Smith and for noe other Cause nor Reason as I Know
of but for Doeing my office which I humble Conseave to bee my
Duty to Doe When Lawfull Called there to by any of his magesties Subjects and not to bee Called Roague and beggerly Roague with many Such Like abuses Speatches Saieing Sarra[2] you
pretty full Loasy Raskell Lett mee know you Ever grant any
Atteachment or warrants againe and you had better behanged and
if the Governor doth Lett Such pettifull Raskels to bee In
Commission I will not Sitt for I hold it beneath mee to Sitt
with Such a pettyfull fellow as thou art It is not onely mee
but others of the Commission when they will not bee Comformable
to his unreasonable will for Mr. John Kiphaven because hee
would not Draw him a Bottell of Rom for a Indian hee had hired
on the Sabbath Day In the Like termes and for noe other Cause
that I Know of unreasonably abused by Mr. John Avery And as
for Mr. Henry Smith his abuses to the Court and the book of
Lawes are not Inferior to the Rest: for if wee Doe act any
thing Contrary against Mr. Smith his will then wee are Called
Roagues and a Confeaderet with Roagues and with other treathning
words which as I humbly Conseave not to bee omitted therefore
thout it my duty to Informe your Honor with it for if I Issue
forth a Sommons or a warrant In his magesties name to warren

In any persons who are Liveing In Mr. Smith his house Either
the warrant is not Excecuted or if Excecuted not obeyed for hee
doth pretend they are his Servants and not to Answer noe
warrant or Summons without his Leave but I Humbly Conceave
though they where Mr. Smith his Servants which I know not Such
thing for to my knowledg they were both freeman not Long Since
yet they where as Lyable to his majesties Lawes as Mr. Smith
or any other person if they bee good Subjects this being part
of the Errigular proceedings I humble beseech your Honor to
give mee the patient parsell hearing hereof for Should I take
a penn man to writt all it would weary the hand of a good
penn man to writt and your Honors Eares to heare an Like your
Honor I have Send all the proceedings that I have Done In my
office and place which I hope your Honor will peruse and find
whether I have deserved these abuses or no and wholy Rely upon
your Honors good pleasure Either to Justifie mee or Condem mee
as your Honors wisedom Shall thinck fitt soe hoping your Honor
In your good time will Rectifie Both these and all others
misdemanors by whoesoever Committed one thing I humble begg
of your honor not [   ] I am worthy to give advise but onely
begg it of your Honor Both for the good of The people and the
good o[ ] the place that your Honor will bee pleased to Constitute Sum wise Discreete Sober minded Gentleman that m[   ]
Lead the people into o bidience for the Savety of a King or
Cheife governor Consiste In obidient people for hee that Knows
not how to obey neither Knowes not how to Command for which
Cause I humbly Beseech your Honor to make Choyse of a Cheife
Commander according to your Honors Discretion for this partes
And that your Honor will bee pleased to Discharge mee from this
and all other offices of trust which is the Humble Request of
your Honors Servant to Command Soe hopeing your Honor will Be
pleased to pardon my Boldnes and make the best Constructions of
these my Rude lines I am and Ever Shall Remaine as In duty
bound your Honors Humble Servant Soe wishing all health and
happiness to Attend your honor Both in this Life and the Life
to Com which is the prayer of him who is your Honors Humble
Servant to Command

From the Whorekill   [Signed:] Edward Southrin
Sept. 18th Anno 1676

[Addressed:] To the Honorable Edmond Andross Esq. Capt.
              Generall of All his Royall Highnes Territorius
              In America At N: Yorck present

[Endorsed:] A[   ] peticon from Mr William Southrin from
             Whorekill Sept. 18, 1678[3]

---

1. This petition is written in the hand of Cornelis
   Verhoofe. Other transcription in NYCD 12:603.

2. i.e., sirrah.

3. The endorsement, which is in the hand of Matthias
   Nicolls, errs in the name and date.

21:9   [PETITION OF LUKE WATSON FOR A LICENSE TO
         GATHER STRAY HORSES AT WHOREKILL]

                              To the Right Honorable Sir Edmond
                              Andros Knight and Governor Generall
                              of all his Royall Highness his
                              Teritories in America etc. The
                              Petition of Luke Watson Humbly
                              sheweth

     Whereas there are Running in the woods several horses and
Mares which noe man Lyes Claim unto and there being noe person
as yet as we Know of that is Impo[   ]ed by your Excellency
to take the same into his Custody, Now your Supplycants humble
Request is, that your Excellency would Grant him your Lycense
to Range the woods and Take into his Custody all strayes, and
alsoe all shipwracks if any shall happen, with in the Whorekill County, for which your Petitioner shall be at all times
Ready to give an account of and shall as in duty he is Bound
Continually pray for your Honor etc.

[Endorsed:]   A peticon from Luke Watson about an order to
              take up stray horses about the Whore Kill Oct
              7th 1678 Recd.[1]

---

1. Note that the date on the endorsement by Matthias
    Nicolls indicates when the petition was received in New
    York.

21:10   [PETITION OF LUKE WATSON FOR LAND AT WHOREKILL]

                              To the Right Honorable Sir Edmond
                              Andros Knight Governor Generall of
                              all his Royall Highness his Teri-
                              tories in America, The Petition of
                              Luke Watson Humbly
                  sheweth

     Whereas your Petitioner Removed himselfe and his Family
from Elizabeth Towne to the Whore Kill with in this Goverment
at which time not finding any Land Convenient but what was before Taken up though not Improved soe that your supplycant
was forced for his present settlement to pass his Bill unto
Mr. William Tom for the summe of 5000 lb. of Tobaccos for 132
Acres of Rough Land which Land was never before seated nor
Improved and being since Informed that your Excellency doth
not allow of the sale of Lands before Improvement is made on
it and that your Petitioner did seate and manure the same,
Now your Petitioners humble Request is that his obligation to
the said Mr. Tom may [   ] and That your Petitioner may
have [   ] his own name for the said 132 [   ] of
Land, for the which your Supplycant shall as in duty hee is
bound, Continually pray for your Honor etc.

[Endorsed:] A peticon from Luke Watson for some Land at the
             Whorekill. Oct. 7th 1678 Recd.[1] Mr. Tom's

---

1. Note that the date on the endorsement by Matthias
   Nicolls indicates when the petition was received in
   New York.

21:11   [PETITION OF HENRY STRETCHER FOR LAND AT WHOREKILL]

To the Right Honorable Sir Edm: Andros Gov. of all his Royall
Hyghnes Territoryes in America

        The Humble petition of Henry Stretcher sheweth that your
petitioner being A trades man and being att the Whorekill
desirous to Live as neare to the towne as I could for the conveniency of following my trade: your petitioner could not take
up Any land there Abouts: by reaso[ ] most of the land neare
unto the towne was claimed by Helmanus Wilbanke of whom I was
forced for my necessity and conveniency to follow my trade to
buy a tract of Land: But sence I post by bill your petitioner
hath bin informed that your honors order is that noe man shall
make sale of Land that he hath not seated

        Therefore your humble petitioner craveth your honors order
unto the serveyor: to servey itt for your petitioner that hath
seated built and planted upon itt and now Liveth with my family
upon itt: neither hath the said Helmanus Renewed his grant
which is of Above seven years standing: and hath bin given
sence unto on Mr. Jenkins that Liveth in Maryland as A bribe
for releasing him the said Helmanus out of prisson after he
had bin in pr[   ] severall dayes for speaking treason
Agains[ ] our Governor Lord the King:

        The premisses considered your humble petitioner craveth
your honors graunt of the said relapsed Land and your petitioner
as in duty bound shall ever pray etc.

                        [Signed:] Henry Strecther

[Endorsed:] A petition from [   ] Henry Stretcher about land
             at the Whore Kill Oct. 7th 1678 Recd.[1]

             Helmanus Wiltb:
             land, but not improv'd

---

1. Note that the date on the endorsement by Matthias
   Nicolls indicates when the petition was received in
   New York.

21:12   [PETITION OF CORNELIS JOHNSON FOR LAND AT WHOREKILL][1]

To the Right Honourable Edmond Andrewes Esq. Gouerner Generall
Under his Moste high and Sacred [ ]aiesty Corlus King of
Brittany and his Royall highness James Duke of Yorke and albany
over all his terytorys In Ameryka

The humble petetion of Cornelis Johnson

        Your honours petetioner humbly sheweth as he was Latly
A[ ] Inhabeter In Verieny[2] and Distytute for want of Land and
hearing [ ] Land to be taken up In your honourable goverment
Caused your pete[ ] [ ] Come up and Coming up to the
Whourkill and finding no surueyers was [ ]nt[3] to Anunplus[4]
but still Resallving to trance porte my famely [ ] Harrymainus[5] being a inhabetor In the place and aquainted with the
Land that was Clear and your petetioner not nor yet the Laws
and Customs of the place Harrymainus agreed with your petetioner
to Live upon A peice of Land for three year which he had no
right too and after your petetioner had maid a large plantation Harrymainus sowld it to a marylander for a great quan-
tety of Tobacko being seated and might Ly for the futer so
Harrymainus Knowing his tightle being weak Came over to the
plantation and bounde[ ] Two Trees by the vetue [sic] of a
owld paten from gouerner Lovlis [ ] A peice of Land Lying
In another Creik so your petetioner finding the plantation
to be the Dukes Land and Harrymainus having Sowld it was unwilling to Survey it so your petetioner being [ ]willing to
Lous his Labour which he had Dun and the housen he had bulte
got it surueyed and now Harrymainus being the [ ]eidge of
the Corte threatens to take away plantation and hous[ ] by
Reson of Contract allthough he hath not fullfilled any
[   ]tickle and it the Dukes Land Which enbowldeneth me
to [   ]aint your honour with it hoping for Right and [ ]
your petetioner shall be ever bound to pray for Youre honours
Hapyness

[Endorsed:]   A peticion from Cor: Jansen for land at the Whorekill Received by mee Oct. 8th 1678

                Hermanus Witb:
                land, but not improved[7]

_____

1. See DYR:48 for Cornelis Johnson's return of survey dated
    January 15th 1676/7.

2. i.e., Virginia.

3. i.e., sent.

4. i.e., Annapolis.

5. i.e., Helmanus Wiltbanck.

6. i.e., judge.

7. Endorsement is written in the hand of Matthias Nicolls.

21:13   [COPY OF A WARRANT FOR THE ARREST OF HENRY SMITH]

By the Governor

These are in his Majesties name to require you to take
into your Charge and Custody the body of Henry Smith of the
Whorekill and him safely to keepe untill hee give security
to the value of five hundred pounds to make good or prosecute
a Charge[1] given this day under his hand in this place against
Helmanus Wiltbanck and Edward Southrin Justices and Cornelys
Verhoofe Clarke of the Court at the Whorekill, This is to say
[   ][2] Helmanus Wiltbanck as guilty of felony, bribery,
and treasen Edward Southrin for being foresworne and guilty
of Witchcraft, and Cornelys Verhoofe to have falsifyed the
Records as in the said Charge is more particularly Sett forth[3]
and for soe doeing this shall bee your warrant; Given under my
hand in New York this 8th day of October 1678.

By order of the Gov. Councell

[Initialed:] M N[4]

To Mr Thomas Ashton
Sheriffe of this City of New Yorke.

[Endorsed:]   Copie of the Mittimus for Dr. Henry Smith at the
              Whorekill Oct. 8th 1678

---

1. See 21:23/24 for these charges.

2. The word charging has been crossed out; the word which
    replaces it has been lost due to a tear in the document.

3. This sentence beginning with: That is to say...,
    is marked for insertion at this point; it replaces the
    original insertion which is crossed out and reads as
    follows: for employing Indyans to Kill Cattle and
    bring him the hides, breech of the Sabboth, and employ-
    ing his servant to take away the said Smiths Loggs and
    planck unlawfully.

4. Initials of Matthias Nicolls in whose hand the warrant
    is written.

21:14   [PETITION OF THOMAS SPRY FOR THE RETURN OF
          A COLT]

To the Right Honorable Sir Edmond Andross Knight Barron,
Govornor Genrall of all his Royal Highness his Teritories in
Amerika, The petittion of Tho: Spry Chyrurgion,

Humble Shewith,

Thatt Whereas your petittioner was bayle To the Sheriff of New Castle for the appearance of Mr. George Oldfeild att a Court held in the Towne of New Castle in the month of Sept. 1677[1] and for want of the said Oldfeilds Appearance was in the month of Jan. 1677/8[2] Condemned By the Courtt then held in New Castle to pay the said debts for which the said Oldfeild was arested which amounted to the summ of 6700 lb. of Tobakow and upwards besids the Costs of Suitt, now your petittioner having Layne seven teene weeks in prizon under two executions, as the high Sheriff Capt. Cantwell Can attest, and forced to pay the said Debts, the said Oldfeild in partt of payment of your petittioner and for the troble and losse he sustaind sould and made over som horses and mares, Amongst the which there was, a yearling Coultt of an Iron gray Collor which belonged to One of the mares, as severall Can attest which Knew both mare and Coult butt by reson that the same Coult was unmarked, Captt. Christopher Billop challenged the said Coolt for the King and ordered itt to be marktt, and did forthwith sell itt befor your petittioners face to John Ogle Although your petittioner and others told him itt belonged to your petittioner and the mare then att thatt Instant owned the said Coult, wherefor your petittioner humble prays of your honor To Consider his Condittion and losse he hath ben att, and that your Honor would order him to Injoye his owne Coultt which is yett Runing with the mare unmarkt though sould and your petittioner for your honor shall pray as in duty bound:

[Entitled:]   Tho. Sprys petittion.

---

1. See NCCR:120 for this court proceeding.

2. See NCCR:173 for this court proceeding.

21:15   [NOMINATION LIST FOR MAGISTRATES AT WHOREKILL
        WITH THE LIST OF THOSE NAMES SELECTED][1]

Whorekill		
	John 4 Kiphaven [ ]ish nott rite	o
	Helmanus Wiltbanck rites	x
att Whorekill	Lucas 5 Watson - - rites	o
planters	Alexander 3 Molestein - nott	o
att Rehoba	John Hagester a Cooper rites	
att Rehoba	Capt. John 1 Avery planter rites	o
[ ]outh of Rehoba	Robert Bracy planter - nott	
[ ] mile from town	Otho Wolgast rites	o
St. Joneses	Francis 2 Witwell a planter rites	o
head of Whorekill	James 7 Wells planter - rites	
att Ceader Creek	Alexander Draper planter nott	
att Rehoba	Charels Johnson planter nott	
[ ]le of Whorekill	Edw. Southeron planter rites	x
town	Cornelis Verhove planter rites	x
town	Henery Smith planter [ ] rites	x
St. Joneses	John Brigs planter - nott	
St. Joneses	Josua Barckstead whimsicall - rites	

att Rehoba   John 6 Rods planter rites o

                    John Avery
                    Francis Whitwell
                    Otto Wolgast[2]
                    Alexander Molesteyn
                    John Kiphaven
                    Luke Watson
                    John Rodss
                    James Wells

[Endorsed:] Names out of Who[   ] the Magistrates were
             chosen at the Whorekill. Oct. 1678.

---

1. Document is written in the hand of Matthias Nicolls.
    The numbers which are affixed to certain names indicate
    their rank after selection. The circles apparently
    represent preliminary selection while the x's denote
    rejection.

2. This name is crossed out.

21:16   [COPY OF A LETTER FROM MATTHIAS NICOLLS TO THE
        COURT AT WHOREKILL CONCERNING NATHANIEL WALKER'S
        LAND]

                    N. Y. Oct. 11. 1678.

Gent. Severall matters in your parts having beene represented
to the Go: His honor hath been pleased to order mee to acquaint
you with his mind therein.

        There was[1] produced a Judgment from your Court in a Case
depending betweene C. Nath:[2] Walker and Mr. Edward Southerne
where the said Southerne was cast and Judgment past against
him for the quantity of 1147 lb. of Tobacco with Cask, but
could obtayne no Execucion whereupon I am to acquaint you that
Execucion is the life of the Law, and do[ ] so naturally follow
Judgment that without grosse Errors appeares therein it ought
not neither can it bee denyde to any.

        The next matter was a piece of land layd out for C. Nath:
Walker by Cor: Verhoofe, May 11. 1677 ca[   ] by the name of
Cedar Neck scituate upon the south wester most Creeke of Rehobah Bay and Conteyning 680 - acres as by a dra[   ] there of
may appeare.[3] It is the Go: order that hee shall have the
said land, after it having beene certifyde by your Court that
it is not already granted or posses[   ] by any other, upon the
returne whereof hee may have a patent for the same.

        There is one thing more About a piece of land at the
Whorekill possest betweene Capt. Nath: Walker and Capt. John
Wyneder of Somerset County in Maryland for which there is a

patent in the name of Robt. instead of John Wyneder, the which
is to bee rectifyde, the land is called Wyneders Neck lyeing
by Broade Kill betweene the said Kill and Prime Hooke, Containing in the patent 1000 acres, and a certaine Isl. lyeing
at the bottome of the land of about 100-acres the which was
surveyd for part of it and is said to bee proper for none else,
Notwithstanding the which one Henry Stretcher having a Grant
from the Court for about 600 acres in no certaine place, hath
pitcht upon this 100 acres Isl. as part of his Complement the
same not being particularized in C. Wineders patent, although
as it were adjoyning to it, being onely divided by a slip of
Marsh, the which if enjoyed by Stretcher will redound much to
the prejudice of said C: Walker and John Wineder It is the
Go. pleasure that the Isl. shall [   ]long to John Wineders
patent and the said Stretcher is to take up his land in some
other place all together and not by parcels or piece meales.[4]
This is all I have in Charge to deliver to you So remaine
                              your very humble servant

                                        M. N.

For Mr. Helmanus
Wiltbanck and the rest of
the Justices of the Whorekill
[   ] Delaware bay.

[Endorsed:] Copie of a Le[   ] for C. Nath: Wats[   ] to
             Mr. Helmanus Wiltbanck and Court [   ] [   ] Kill
             Oct. 11 1678

             with some other particulars.

─────────────────

1. There was replaces the following lines which are crossed
   out: Capt. Thomas [sic] Walker having made Applicacion
   to the Go. concerning some particular affaire hee hath
   in your parts, in which he hath desired directions and
   Releife, I am ordered by his honor to represent the
   same unto you, in manner following; The said Capt.
   Walker...

2. Walker's given name has been corrected by writing Nath.
   over Thomas.

3. See 20:117 for return of survey.

4. See DYR:76 for a 1681 return of survey for this land.

21:17   A List of patents in the [hands] of Capt.
        Edmond Cantwell at Newcastle[1]

	Acres		Ac [ ][2]
Rich. Hill.	1000	Cornelius Verhoofe	[100]
James Wells.	400	Daniel Whitley	[300]
Robt. Hart junior	500	John Cornelys	[300]

	Acres		Ac[ ]
Rich. Brasey.	300	John Alward[3]	[400]
John Antry	300	Wm. Prentice	[400]
Sander Molesteyn	50	John Lining[4]	[300]
Robt. Brasey sen.	800	Josias Coudrey[5]	[700]
James Lille	300	Edward Forlong	[400]
John Johnson	400	Robt. Brasey jun.	[300]
Jacob Seth	500	Robert Frazer	400
William Warren	300		
Henry Stretcher	400		
James Pedy	600		
William True	300		
Samuell Styles	400		
John Dupre	1000		
Thomas Davis	300		
Edward Cooke	350		
Walter Lewis	300		
Sam: Style and Traley	744		
John Kirke	800		
Wm. Borton	1000		
John Otter	300		
Abrah: Clement	400		
Thomas Davis	500		
Christopher Jackson	300		

[Endorsed:] A list [   ] pat[   ] at the Whorekill, in
             [   ] hands of Capt. Cantwell or his Attorney
             these

             Given mee by Luke Wattson[6] in Oct. 1678.

---

1. Written in the hand of Matthias Nicolls. Other transcription in NYCD 12:605. cf., 20:136.

2. The amount of acres in this column is mostly lost.
   Figures in brackets have been recovered from DYR.

3. 20:136 lists John Allard.

4. 20:136 and DYR:170 have John Liming.

5. See 20:136, F.N. 4.

6. i.e., delivered to M. Nicolls by Luke Watson.

21:18 [NOMINATION LIST FOR OVERSEERS IN SALEM WITH
        THE LIST OF THOSE NAMES SELECTED][1]

Wm. Pen[n-ton]		William Penton	x 1
James Nevell	quaker	ser	
George Deacon	quaker		
Edward Broadway	quaker	x 4	
Samuell Hedge	H shiref[	]	

```
John Smith    quaker   Cons
Edw[   ] Wade   quaker   x 6
Richard Hancock   surveor

Michiell Baron   x 3
Edward Chamnis
Richard Guy  x  quaker  2
William Malster  x 5
```

```
                    William Penton
                    Richard Guy
                    Michiel Baron
                    Edward Broadway
                    William Malster
                    Edward Ward[2]
```

[Endorsed:]   Names of persons at Salem or Swampetown where
Major Fenwyck satt downe. Given in by Mr. Malster.
Oct. 25, 1678.

---

1. Other transcription in NYCD 12:608. This document represents a list of names submitted to Matthias Nicolls
   upon which he made corrections, additions and comments.
   The first group of names is the original list in an
   unidentified hand. The four names in the second group
   were added by Nicolls in red pencil as well as the name
   of William Penton and the comments beside each name.
   Nicolls at first attempted to correct Penn by writing
   ton over the final n, but then apparently decided to
   rewrite the entire name to the right of it. The check
   marks indicate those names selected, and the numbers
   denote their rank which appear by the order of the
   names in the third group.

2. Note that Ward's name appears in the original list as
   Wade.

21:19   [PETITION OF CORNELIS VERHOOFE COUNTERING CHARGES
        MADE BY HENRY SMITH]

                    To the Honorable Major Edmond
                    Andross Esq. Signeur of Sanzmaress
                    Lieut. Capt. Generall of all his
                    R. Hs. Territories In America:

Humbly Sheweth -

     That where[ ] your petitioner was and hath been Deputed
Clerk of the Whorekill Court and alsoe Constituted Deputy
Surveyor By a Comission from Capt. Ed: Cantwell and your pe-

titioner having acted In those abovesaid offices to his best
Skill and understanding without any favor Affection or any
other falshood of what nature soever to any person or persons
that hath had any occasion to Imploy your petitioner but your
petitioner being ordered to Survey a small tract of Land upon
Pruime Hooke which was supposed to bee Cleare and without the
bounds of one Henry Smith his Land, your petitioner Comming
In Compangnie of the Said Henry Smith In the howse of Helmanus
Wiltbanck Being the 29th Day of Aprill Anno 1676: now last past
Whereas your petitioner Called the Said Smith by him selfe and
told [   ] said Smith that your petitioner being ordered to
Survey a Small [   ] upon Pruime Hooke neck the which
Being Suppos[ ] to be without his bounds of his pretended
Land and if In Case it would Injury the said Smith or that his
owne Survey was not yet Compleated that I would Advise him to
send up to New Castell unto Capt. or to the Honorable Gouernor
for I and more other[ ] person where Ready to goe up within
these 2 or 3 Deyes [   ] unto new Castell that In Such a way
hee might make a sto[ ] In the procedings otherwise I Could
not Refuse to make the aforesaid Survey being Charged and
ordered thereunto with that the Said Smith flyeing out In a
Rage and Impatient and told your petitioner hee would Break
him his Legges af In Case your petitioner Did Come there upon
Pruime Hooke to Survey any Land and Calling your petitioner
Knafe Roague with many more filty Abusefull Expressions the
which your petitioner Could not well bear and made S[ ]vriall
words and Speetches against the said Smith the which your
petitioner Cannot well Remember for which Cause and no other
that I Know of the said Smith Sended a Letter unto Capt. Ed:
Cantwell against your petitioner where of your petitioner Can
produce a Copia of the Said Letter where upon Capt. Cantwell
Stopped your petitioners proceedings In the aforesaid offices
untill your petitioner being Comdemned or Cleared and Charged
the Coart of the Whorekill to Examinen your petitioners Busenes and To punnish according to fact the which Being Examined
by the Said Court and Referred untill next Generall Court [ ]
Beholden at New Castell or Sooner if the Justices of the high
Court shall See fitt whereof your Honor and the Instruments
[   ] Defence to Cleare the articles Laid against your
petitioner are In Such nature that your petitioner hath
[   ] In Honor   [   ] and [   ] of your petitioner
to the Court whose [   ] and [   ] which your [   ]
shall [   ] your Honor and by the [   ]
         ] that the Whole matter of the Information Laid against
[ ] petitioner Shall appeare to bee soe small and Inconsiderate
Errour of Ignorance that it is not whorthy to bee Regarded for
which I hope and Doe not Doubt but that your Ho[ ] wil[ ]
Be pleased to pardon your petitioner of Such Ignorant Err[ ]
and Restore your petitioner if worthy Into his former offices
againe provided that your petitioner may by your Honors pleasure officiale as principall of or over the whole presinct of
the Whorekill In manner and form as followeth that the Inhabitants or any person or persons whatsoever taken up any
Land or Lands may be priviledged for paying [   ] Surveyor
for [   ] of the Survey[ ] and if then not yet
[   ] so bee compelled but for bearne and other years
[   ] a Reasonable Interest and the fourth yeare bee
Lyable to pay without Delay if it bee Required onely Som persons [   ] by the providence of god almighty or any other
accident [ ] fallen to poverty to bee favorable with them
onely Excepted persons of good Estates to make payment when it
[ ] Due or Som part thereof if your petitioners occasion
Req[   ] Because of need to Supply your petitioners necessity

which would bee the onely way for the Speedy Setlement of
th[ ] part of your Honors Government otherwise your petitioner
Doth no[ ] Desier to officiate at all if your petitioner Cannot by [   ] the Like meanes Doe the Contrey any good and
ga[   ] Love of the Inhabitants of the Same wherefore yo[ ]
Humbly Craveth your Honor will be pleased to take [   ]
petitioner Cause Into your Honors Serious Considerations and
[   ] your petitioner favorable for all persons whatsoever
are So[   ] unto Ignorant Errours and that your petitioner
may obtaine your Honors order to bee Cleared of the Information Laid against your petitioner by Henry Smith and alsoe
order against the said Smith for Scandilisen your petitioner
In his good name and Reputation and for Dammages Sustained
thereby which your petitioner values at one hundred pounds
Sterling money of England Besides Costs of Suites and other
Charges which hath not been onely the Lost of your petitioner
but a great deale of hindrance to the Contrey all because your
petitioner had sevriall tracts Land then to Survey [   ]
the which your petitioner by such meanes [   ] not perform
because being Stopped In such proceedings for the which your
p[   ] Doth not Doubt to Expect your Honors favorable
Judgment a[ ] [ ]der according to the meritts of the Cause of
your petitioner [   ] And your petitioner In Duty bound
Shall Ever pray

[Signed:] Cornelis Verhoofe

21:20   [CERTIFICATE OF RECOMMENDATION FOR CORNELIS
          VERHOOFE]

To the Honorable Governor

     These may Certifie your Honor that Cornelis Verhoofe [ ]
the best Surveyor in Delaware bay and best acquainted [   ]
the Lands that is Surveyed or unsurveyed and that all p[   ]
which Desiring Land bee hardly Satisfied untill th[ ] have
his Directions to our Certaine Knowledg.

[Signed:] Helms. Wiltbanck
John ⾦ Kipshaven

21:21/22   [COPIES OF WARRANTS ISSUED BY EDWARD
            SOUTHRIN AT WHOREKILL]¹

Whereas William Blackston hath made Complaint to mee that
William Caning standeth Indepted to him Elleaven Scepple of
Indian Corne and will not give him the said Blackston no pos-
sitive answer where or when to be paid and the said Kaning
Removeing out of the place Desireth an atteachment for the said
Corne.

These are In his majesties name to will and Require you
to Atteach the Corne of William Kaning and it In Save Custody
Keepe untill hee shall make good payment of Elleaven Scepple
of Sheld Corne to the said William Blackston and for soe Doeing
these shall bee your warrant given under my hand this 8th Day
of October 1675.
                                    Edward Southrin
To Daniell Browne Constable
for the Whorekill or his Deputy.

This is in his majesties name to will and Require you
William Prentice to make your personall appearance upon Sight
hereof before mee or sum other of his majesties Justices of
the peace for the Whorekill to Answer the Complaint of Ously
Briant there of faile not as you will answer the Contrary at
your perrill given from under my hand this 3rd Day of March
1675/6.
                                    Edward Southrin
To the Constable for the
Whorekill or his Deputy.

These are In his majesties name to will and Require you
William Prentice to Deliver to Usly Briant her goods you have
In pocession and alsoe her wages which is Due to her thereof
faile not as you will answer the Contrary at your perrill
given under my hand this 7th Day of March 1675/6
                                    Edward Southrin

By order of Mr. Henry Smith
Names of Evidences to be summoned in his majesties suite
Against Cornelis Verhoofe for sevrall misdemanors Done and
Commited by the said Verhoofe
            Peter Bawcombe ⎫ Thomas Philps and what Eviden[ ]
            Cornelis Johnson ⎬ hee shall give on account of Eliza-
            Henry Harmon   ⎭ beth Simpson and what Eviden[ ]
                                she can give on accout of
        ⎛ John King   ⎞   Thomas Morgan ⎞
        ⎜ Francis Megges ⎟   John Lemon   ⎟
        ⎨ William Kaning ⎬   John Oakey   ⎬
        ⎝ Henry Smith   ⎠   William Sharp ⎠

This are In his majesties name to will and Require you to
Sommon Peter Bawcombe to make his personall Appearance Before
his majesties Justices of the peace at the next Court to bee

held for the Whorekill being on twesday next the first of
August 1676 for to give In your testimoney of what you know
In an accion Depending Between his majestie and Cornelis Verhoofe hereof faile not as you will Answer the Contrary at your
perill Dated these 26th of July Anno 1676.

                                   Edward Southrin
To Daniell Browne Sheriffe
or his Deputy

        This are In his majesties name to will and Require you to
Sommons Cornelis Johnson and Henry Harmon to make their personall Appearance Before his majesties Justices of the peace
at the next Court to beheld for the Whorekill being next twesday the first of August [   ] to give [   ] theire testimony
what they Know for an accion Depen[   ] Between his majestie
and Cornelis Verhoofe thereof faile [   ] will Answer the
Contrary at your perrill given under my hand this 26th of July
Anno 1676.
                                   Edward Southrin
To Daniell Browne Sheriffe
for the Whorekill.

        This are In his majesties name to will and Require you to
Sommon Thomas Philps and what Evidences hee shall give on
account of to make his and their personall appearance before
his majesties Justices of the peace at the next Court to beheld
for the Whorekill being on tuesday next the first Day of august
for to give In your testimoney of what you Know In an accion
Depending Between his majestie and Cornelis Verhoofe hereof
faile not as you will Answer the Contrary at your perill
Dated this 26th Day of July Anno 1676.
                                   Edward Southrin
To Daniell Browne Sheriffe
or his Deputy.

        This are In his majesties name to will and Require you to
Sommon Elizabeth Simpson and what Evidences shee shall give on
account of to make her and theire personall appearance Before
his majesties Justices of the peace at the next Court to bee
held for the Whorekill for to give In your testimoney of what
you Know In an accion Depending Between his majestie and
Cornelis Verhoofe hereof faile not as you will answer the Contrary Dated this 26th of July Anno 1676.
                                   Edward Southrin
To Daniell Browne Sheriffe
or his Deputy.

        This are In his majesties name to will and Require you to
Sommon John King and Frances Megges to make theire personall
appearance before his majesties Justices of the peace at the
next Court to beheld for the Whorekill being next twesday the

first twesday of august to give In theire testimoney what they
Know In an accion Depending Between his majestie and Cornelis
Verhoofe thereof faile not as you will answer the Contrary at
your perrill given under my hand this 26th of July 1676.
                              Edward Southrin
To Daniell Browne Sheriffe
for the Whorekill.

        This are In his majesties name to will and Require you to
Sommon William Kaning to make his personall Appearance Before
his majesties Justices of the peace at the next Court to beheld
for the Whorekill being next twesday In august to give In his
testimony what hee Knoweth In an accion Depending Between his
majestie and Cornelis Verhoofe thereof faile not as you will
answer the Contrary at your perrill given under my hand this
26th of July 1676
                              Edward Southrin
To Daniell Browne Sheriffe
for the Whorekill

        This are In his majesties name to will and Require you to
Sommon Henry Smith to make his personall Appearance before his
majesties Justices of the peace for the Whorekill at the next
Court to beheld the next twesday being the first twesday of
august to give In his testimoney what hee Knoweth In an accion
Depending Between his majestie and Cornelis Verhoofe thereof
faile not as you will answer the Contrary at your perrill
given under my hand this 26th of July 1676
                              Edward Southrin
To Daniell Browne Sheriffe
for the Whorekill

        This are In his majesties name to will and Require to
sommon Thomas Morgan to make his personall Appearance Before
his majesties Justices of the peace at the next Court to be-
held for the Whorekill being on next twesday the first of
August to give In your testimoney of what you know In an accion
Depending Between his majestie and Cornelis Verhoofe hereof
faile not as you will answer the Contrary at your perrill
Dated this 26th Day of July Anno 1676.
                              Edward Southrin
To Daniell Browne
Sheriffe or his Deputy.

        This are In his majesties name to will and Require you to
Sommon John Lemon to make his personall appearance before his
majesties Justices of the peace at the next Court to beheld
for the Whorekill being on twesday next the first of august
to give In your testimoney of what you know In an accion Depending Between his majestie and Cornelis Verhoofe hereof faile
not as you will answer the Contrary at your perrill Dated

this 26th of July Anno 1676.

                                        Edward Southrin
To Daniell Browne   }
Sheriffe or his Deputy }

This are In his majesties name to will and Require you to
sommon John [Oake]y[2] to make his personall appearance before
his majesties Justices of the peace for the Whorekill at the
next Court to beheld the next twesday being the first tewsday
of august to give In his testimoney what hee knoweth In an
accion Depending Between his majestie and Cornelis Verhoofe
hereof faile not as you will Answer the Contrary at your perrill given under my hand this 26th Day of July 1676.
                                        Edward Southrin
To Daniell Browne Sheriffe
for the Whorekill.

This are In his majesties name to will and Require you to
Sommon William Sharp to make his personall appearance Before
his majesties Justices of the peace for the Whorekill at the
next Court to beheld the next twesday being the first twesday
In August to give In his testimoney what hee Knoweth In and
accion Depending Between his majestie and Cornelis Verhoofe
thereof faile not as you will Answer the Contrary at your
perrill given under my hand this 26th Day of July 1676.
                                        Edward Southrin
To Daniell Browne Sheriffe
for the Whorekill.

Evidences to bee summoned In his majesties Suite against Henry
Smith by order of Cornelis Verhoofe as follows.

Imper. {Peter Bawcombe}   John Lemon }
        {Alice Raymon   }   William True}
Sept. 8th Anno 1676   Cornelis Verhoofe

This are In his majesties name to will and Require you
to Sommon Alice Raimon to make her personall appearance Before
his majesties Justices of the peace at the next Court to beheld for the Whorekill and there to give In her testimony of
what shee Know In an accion Depending between Cornelis Verhoofe
and Henry Smith In his majesties suite hereof you are not to
faile at your perrill given from under my hand this 8th of
Sept. Anno 1676.
                                        Edward Southrin
To Daniell Browne Sheriffe
for the Whorekill.

This are In his majesties name to will and Require you to
Sommon John Lemon and William True to make theire personall
appearance Before his majesties Justices of the peace at the
next Court to beheld for the Whorekill and there to give In
theire testimoney of what they Know In an accion Depending
Between Cornelis Verhoofe and Henry Smith In his majesties
suite hereof they are not to faile at theire perrill given
from under my hand this 8th of Sept. Anno 1676.

                                    Edward Southrin
To Daniell Browne Sheriffe
for the Whorekill.

        Whereas this Day being the 13th of Sept. Anno 1676 Cor-
nelis Verhoofe hath made his Complaint before mee that whereas John Lemon and William True where summoned to the last
Court Being the 12th of the said Sept. and not appearing at
the said Court to give In theire testimoney as Require by the
said Summons and therefore Desireth warrant to Answer the said
Cornelis Verhoofe his Complaint.

        These are therefore In his majesties name to will and
Require you John Lemon and William True to make your personall
Appearance on Sight hereof before mee or sum other of his
majesties Justices of the peace to Answer the Complaint of the
said Cornelis Verhoofe hereof your are not to faile at your
perrill as you will Answer the Contrary given from under my
hand this 13th of Sept. Anno 1676.

                                    Edward Southrin
To the Constable }
for the Whorekill}

[Entitled:] Mr. Edward Southrin his Busenes to Derect unto
             the Governor.

[Endorsed:] From Whorekill in deloworr.

             Copies of Warrants in the difference betweene
             Mr Smith and Cor. Verhoofe. Whorekill.[3]

---

1. These copies of warrants are written in the hand of
    Cornelis Verhoofe. Although O'Callaghan enters 21:21
    and 21:22 separately in his calendar they represent one
    set of copies from the Whorekill records which were
    sent together to New York.

2. This name is recovered from the list of people to be
    summoned which appears in this document.

3. Endorsement is written in the hand of Matthias Nicolls.

21:23/24   Charges made by Henry Smith against divers
            persons on the Delaware[1]

first as for Curnelinus Verhoof is A person that hath bin
found Guilty of keeping fals records as alsoe A sabbeth
Breaker and A person that hath onlawfully executed the office
of both Maiestrat and Sheriff as hath bin made appeare in
Coart

        And as for Mr. Helm: Wylebanke[2] he hath bin Charged with
imploying of Indians to kill Catle and to bring him the hides
and to signe attachments upon the Sabbath day and cause them
to be executed as soone as the people came out of the meeting
house: suffer the Indians to work in his corne feild upon the
sabbeth day; imploying his servant to take Away my loges and
planke onlawfully

        for declaring in the yeare 1676 That how the prince of
Orring[3] had bought New Yorke with its territoryes of his
Maiesty: and that afterwards his Maiesty would not let the
prince have itt but there was a friggett come out of holland
to New Yorke who brought Newes that if his Maiesty would not
lett the prince have itt by fayer meanes: he would have itt
by force: but there was few Knew of itt but himself and some
particuler persons in New Yorke; and that the Helmanus was
for[ ]rly apprehended for treason spoken Against his Maiesty
for which was smothered up and sett att Liberty by giving one
Jenkins[4] A bribe That the said Helmanus with others did hold
a coart: after he had adiorned the coart for a month without
sumoning or giving notis unto those persons your honor had
added as Maiestrats unto them the ould commissoners.

        [ ] for Mr Sowtherne he is on[5] that declareth himself
[ ] have familliarity with develes and that the said [ ]ow-
therne hath severall times proffered to swere [ ]hose things
he could not in honesty swere, the things being fals; but when
required to give in his attestation in what he knew concerning
the difference betweene the subscriber and Peter Grundick[6]
according to your honor and the assizes order he refused to
doe itt; but att last in comtempt to [ ]e coart Rashly
snatched up the bible and swore by [ ]he Living god that all he
Knew was sowrne to allredy in A paper the secritary had; the
which thing was not soe found at the assizes; and none other
satisfaction would he give to the coart; the said Sowtherne
hath given passes to A murderer and others that hath bin committed by Lawfull [ ]uthority; alsoe hath caused A pore mans
corne to [ ] [ ]aken Away from his and his wife and children
[ ] without any try[   ] proceedings in law; with many
other proceedings contrary to Law.
                                [Signed:] Hen Smith
[ ]tober 167[ ][7]

[Endorsed:] [   ] Charge against Hel[ ]nus Wiltbanck
             etc. 1678

_____

1. This heading was written by a second hand, possibly in
    the 19th century.

2. i.e., Helmanus Wiltbanck.

3. i.e., Orange.

4. Francis Jenkins, a justice of the peace in Somerset
    County, Maryland.

5. i.e., one.

6. i.e., Peter Groenendyck.

7. October 8, 1678. See 21:28 for a reference to this
    document.

21:25   [EXTRACT BY HENRY SMITH FROM COKE'S INSTITUTES] [1]

Sir Edw. Cookes [2] In the 3rd part of the institutes of the
                Lawes of England Concerning high treason;
and other pleas of the croune and Criminall Causes there is
these words Amongst others, viz.

e l.E.3   e   if Any of the Kings·Councell or his ministers
  Stat.2   doe exact A bond of any of his subiects to come to
  Ca.15   the King with force and Armes etc., when they should
f Nota   be sent for, such writings are to the Kings dis-
               honor, for that Every man is bound to doe to the
King as his Lieg Lord, f   all that appertaineth to him without any manner of writing (note the generallity heareof) and
such writings are to be Cancelled [as] by the act appeareth.

     Heare upon (by authority of this Parliament) these Con-
clusions doe follow: First, [whatso]ever any subiect is bound
to doe to the King as to his Leige Lord, noe bond or writing
[is to be exacted] of the subiect for doeing thereof.
[Secondly, whatso]ever bonds or writings are to the Kings
[dishonour, are] Against Law. [Thirdly, whether such] bonds
or writings be ma[de to the King] or any other, the bonds or
[writings] be voyde.

[Verso:] Sir Edw. Cooks opinion in 3rd part of his institutes.

[Endorsed:] A paper produced by Mr. Henry Smith before the
             Go. extracted out of my L. Cooke Institutes.
             Oct. 24. 1678 [3]

1. The following extract was copied from chapter 69 of
    The Third Part of the Institutes of the Laws of England
    by Sir Edward Coke. The damaged portions have been
    recovered from page 149 of the fourth edition (London,
    1669). The lower case letters e and f refer to mar-
    ginal notes in the Institutes which were also copied
    by Henry Smith in the margin of his extract.

2. This note was written in the margin by Henry Smith to
    identify his source.

3. Endorsement is written in the hand of Matthias Nicolls.

21:26   [PETITION OF HENRY SMITH ABOUT GIVING SECURITY
          IN HIS SUIT AGAINST HELMANUS WILTBANCK AND OTHERS]

To the Ri[   ] Honorable Sir Edm. Andros Gover. etc.

    The [   ]ble petition of Henry Smith

Sheweth That your pet. was Comitted by your Honor untell he
should give security to the value of 500 lb. to prosecute Helm:
Wiltbanke, for treason, fellony and bribery, and Edw: Sowtherne
for witchcraft and perjury, and Curnel: Verhoof for falsifying
his records, as by the Mittimus;[1]

    That your pet. did give A paper under his hand in order
to your Honors satisfaction, the which your Honors petitioner
is Redy and willing to give security to prossecute the said
persons; as becomes his Maiesties subiect; as an Evidence for
his Maiesty whose Cause itt is and not your petitioners as
your petitioner humbly Conceives;

    And therefore prayes that his recognizance may be taken;
the time and place may be assertained for his appearance; where
hee needs not doute but your Honor will have the persons to answer for themselves according to his Maiesties Lawes and [   ]
with such Evidences as is conveni[   ] to prove their facts;

    And your petitioner shall pray etc.

[Endorsed:] A petition from Mr. Henry Smit to the Go. Oct.
             24nd 1678.

───────────────

1. See 21:13 for this mittimus.

21:27   [DECLARATION OF HENRY SMITH CHARGING H. WILTBANCK
          AND OTHERS WITH VARIOUS CRIMES][1]

Nov. 2nd 1678.

    Henry Smith declares that the time that Helmanus Wiltbanck
was questioned for Treason was when the Whorekill was under
Maryland, The persons that accused him were Dr. John Roades and
William Prentice, The accusacion was made to Mr. Francis Jenkins a Justice of peace in Maryland, who committed him to prison for the space of about a weeke, and as is reported here
was cleared by the said Jenkins by giving him a Bribe.

    That afterwards the said Mr. Jenkins was questioned for
taking a bribe to cleare the said Wiltbanck and taken into Custody as a prisoner by order of Dr. Roades on that Account, but
in a few dayes was release, Whereupon Dr. Roades came to the
above Mr. Smith complaining of the Fact, but hee having newly
had his writte of Ease, directed him to goe to my Lords to St.
Maryes, which hee did accordingly, But what the Issue of it
was there, hee knowes not.

As to the discourse of Edw. Southrins conversacion with the devill, Hee knows nothing but what hee and divers others have heard from his owne Mouth tal[k]ing often extravagantly in that nature.

As to Cor. Verhoofes being guilty of keeping false Records, The same hee saith hath beene proved in Court.

[Endorsed:] Henry Smiths Declaracion

---

1. Other transcription in NYCD 12:612.

21:28   [PETITION OF HENRY SMITH TO BE RELEASED FROM JAIL IN ORDER TO PROVE HIS CHARGES AGAINST H. WILTBANCK AND OTHERS]

To the Right Hon. Sir Edm. Andros Knight and Governor of New Yorke etc. the humble petition of Hen Smith

Sheweth   That your petitioner did in obedience to your Honors Command prefer unto your Honor the 8th of octo[   ] last past,[1] A writing or Charg Against Helm[   ] Wiltbanke, Edward Sowtherne, and Curnelius Verhoofe; for severall Misdemeanors Committed by them, as per writing more att Larg may appeare; and your petitioner being Committed by your Honor untell he should give security of 500 lb. to prossecute or make good the same accordi[   ] to the Mittimus;[2] the which your petitioner hath indevored to performe, but could not by reason of being A strainger in these parts, notwithstanding your petitioner hath A competent Estate farr surmounting the said some within this Goverment, Neither being Able to prove the said facts by Reason of the far distance of the Evidences from this place; where your petitioner is kept a prissoner, and the offenders being there att the Whorekill alsoe.

Your Humble petitioner Craveth that your Honor would be pleased to graunt him his Liberty, for want of which I am on Capable to prove the said facts; and alsoe on Capable of acting in My owne affaires to my great preiudise and hinderance; itt being the cheif time of the yeare for the receiving and [   ] in [ ]f debts that Lyeth in the hands of other [   ] and your petitioner as A Loyall subiect shall performe both redily and Willingly Any order or orders as your Honor shall Command him to performe in these parts to his Utmost power and Abillity according to Law, in the said premisses;[3]
And your petitioner as in duty
bound shall ever pray etc.

---

1. See 21:23/24.

2. See 21:13.

3. On Nov. 30, 1678 Henry Smith was sentenced by the Coun-
    cil. Since he was unable to prove his charges he was
    fined £10 with all costs to be paid to the Church or
    the poor. At the Whorekill he was required to post a
    £20 bond of good behavior until the next General Court
    of Assizes. See 28:32 for this order of the council.

21:29   [AN ACCOUNT BETWEEN HENRY SMITH AND PETER
        GROENENDYCK]

An Account of Charges that I have bin [   ] in the suite
depending in the assizes att New Yorke in the yeare 1677 and
1678 betweene Peter Grundick and the subscriber

[ ]tt	for Part of charges for fetch- ing A Shallup out of Maryland to the Whorekill	} 800 lb. tobaco
[ ]ember	for A boat and two hands to bring me to the fals;........	400
	for 39 dayes upon my voyage before I came home...........	1170
	for on Monthes dyet in New Yorke......................	0400
	paid Peter Grundick for my passage home.................	0106
[ ]78	for my boat and passage to the fales...................	0400
	for 22 dayes upon my voyage att 30 lb. per day...........	0660
	for my [ ]omedation att New York [ ]...............	0300
	for my passage home	0106
		4342 tobaco

Errors execepted per me
[Signed:] Hen. Smith

[Verso:] Nov. 1678

21:30   [MATTHIAS NICOLLS TO THE JUSTICES OF NEW
        CASTLE ABOUT THE COMPLAINT OF JANE ERSKIN][1]

Upon the Addresse and Complaint[2] of Jane the widow of
Serjeant John Erskin late of Newcastle in Delaware to the Go.
on behalfe of herselfe and Children, setting forth that suddenly after her said husbands death before any account was

taken of the Estate left by him, (hee dyeing Intestate) or any
Administrator appointed to take Care [thereof as] required
[by the Lawe] Mr. John Moll one of the Justices there seized
by attachment on a forty foot house of Tobacco which was
struck and lay in bulke but not stript, in the said house the
which continued so, but was neglected by the said Mr. Moll and
his Agents or the Under sheriffe who attacht it The widow not
dareing to meddle therewith the broad Arrow being put on the
house Untill the greatest part was lost being rotten and the
remaineder apprized at a small value was received by the said
Mr. Moll with divers household Goods and Utensils belonging to
a plantacion taken in Execucion for his debt[3] and upon another
Execucion obtayned by Wm. Semple her Cowes likewise were taken
away which proved very much to the prejudice and damage of the
said widdow and children; By the Governors order and direction
I am to acquaint you, that the proceedings herein have beene
very irregular, and that the Administracion (belonging to the
widdow if still refused by her) the Court ought to nominate one
or more responsable persons to administer and take that trust
upon them and to appoint a time for the Creditors to make their
Claymes so that Care may bee taken for the payment of their
just debts equally according to Law, which directs Judgments
and specialtys to bee first paid and other debts of bookes or
accounts afterwards, that is such Judgments and specialtys as
were obtayned in the partys lifetime with due regard to the
widdow and children but to take notice that all Estates of
houses or lands in this Country, are as lyable to pay debts as
moveables, So that the [persons whoe] have received any part
or proporcion of the said Goods or Estate upon pretence of
Judgments since [irregul]arly obtay[ned] are to redeliver the
same back to the widdow and the administrators to take account
thereof and if any damage hath happen'd to the Tobacco by
occasion of the Attachment, through the want of Care of the
Under sheriffe or those that employed him the same is by them
to bee made good; If the widdow desires to administer (for
whome it is most proper) the Estate will bee a good part of the
security and you will doe well not to bee hard with her for the
remainder It being supposed there is enough for the Creditors
and to Leave a Competence for the widdow and Children.

As to the difference betweene the said Widdow and Mr.
Ephraim Hermans as one of the Overseers of the children of
Martin Rosamond deceased, concerning a small Lott of land in
the Towne for which her husband had a patent and possest the
same for the space of neare fourteene yeares shee cannot bee
ejected out of her husbands right therein by an pretence of
former title, or later patent, but by due Course of Law.

[Endorsed:] To the Justices of the Court of Newcastle, about
the widdow Erskin. Nov. 6, 1678.[4]

---

1. This document represents the rough draft of a letter
    sent to New Castle. All insertions, deletions and
    corrections have been followed in this transcription.
    An uncorrected version of this document appears in the
    appendix. See NCCR:252 for the final draft of this
    letter from which all damaged portions have been
    recovered.

2. See 20:127 for Jane Erskin's petition.

3. The phrase: <u>for his debt</u> does not appear in the <u>NCCR</u>
    transcription.

4. <u>NCCR</u> transcription is dated Nov. 4th 1678.

21:31   [JOHN YEO TO HENRY SMITH CONCERNING SMITH'S CASE
         AGAINST H. WILTBANCK AND OTHERS; COPY OF A WARRANT
         TO SUMMON WITNESSES]

                                      Whorekill November the 14th 1678

Worthy Sir

        Yours of the 5th I Received the 7th Instant, in which you
desired me to minde Capt. Avery to sweare the Evidences, that
there depositions might be sent to you, in order to your desire I did (the same day) write a warrant, and Carried it myselfe to Avery and he signed it and Imediately I Ride with it
to the Sherieffe[1] who with all Expedition served it upon most
of the Evidences but the day before they were to appeare to
give in there Testimony, the said Avery came to your house and
did abuse me at a very high Rate and Thretning to send me to
Yorke to answer what I had done (viz) written a warrant which
did (as he sayeth) properly belong to the Clarkes office and
for bringing it him to signe, when he was as he pretendeth,
Drunke (to his Creditt be it spoken) at which time he absolutely
refused to Examine any evidence untell it were by Express Order
of the Governor notwithstanding the warrant was for them to
give in there Evidences in the behalfe of our Sovoraigne Lord
the King. And Avery did then take away the warrant and Toare
his name out of it Neither would he Returne it anymore to the
Sherife, but I (with much Intreaty and some thretning) gott A
Coppy of it Attested by the sherife A Coppy of which I have
sent you[2], Avery is very Greate with Helmanus[3] and there Gange,
there is never a Barrell the better Herring amongst severall of
them, they are very Briske againe Now Since the sloopes Brought
noe Order for there Coming to Yorck, and Now Helmanus sayeth
that all the men in the Countrey shall never gett him to Yorke;
and Avery sideing with them, you are daily abused and I am
Counted amongst them the worst of men Helmanus Cannot Leave his
Tricks yet for when Mr. Clarkes Goods came downe, out of 1/2
doz. Reape hooks he Borowed Six, for he left not one, he Kept
them severall dayes, till [   ] told Clarks servants that his
Master had them and [   ] and fetch said [   ]oks to them, he
hath alsoe lately Brought Hog [   ] alsoe he did one the
14th of the last Month declare before severall people that the
King did Allow both Dutch waights and measures to pass in this
Country but the Governor did Cheate the Countrey of it, with
other scurrolous speeches one the 26th of Oct., The day after
our Arrivall at the Whorekill Avery sold Cornelis[4] the Clarks
place[5] for one quart of wine at Mr. Vines his house and one the
Tuesday after he acted as Clarke at the Court I heartily Long
to see you here and then I doubt not but all will be well Mrs.
Smith presents her Affections to you, she is mightily troubled
at your absence I have seen very few women Grieve more for the
death of A husband then she Grieves for your Long absence Es-

pecially in that you Came not with the sloops. Thus not doubting but that you will in A short time [   ] all your Enimies
and Returne victorious I am Sir

                    Your Ready friend and servant
                        [Signed:] John Yeo

[Copy of the warrant sent with Yeo's letter:]

      These are in his Majesties name to will and Require you to
suppena and summon Mr. Peter Smith Alies Groundike⁶, Daniell
Browne, Rich. Patte, Mr. Alex. Molestaine, Mr. Otto Wolgast,
John Helliard, Tho. Skidmore, William Prentice, William Kenning,
Mrs. Elizabeth Roades widdow and Tho. Saxton to make there personall Appearance before me or some other his Majesties Justices
of this place in the County (Imediately upon sight hereof) to
give in there Evidences and to Answer to such questions and
Interogatories (against Mr. Helmanus Wiltbanke Mr. Edw. Southren
and Cornelis Verhoofe) as shall then be demanded in the behalfe
of our Soveraigne Lord the King, and be you there yourselfe
with this warrant, and Ready to answer to the like Intergatories
hereof you are not to faile Given under my hand this 7th day
of Oct. Anno 1678.
                    Signed by John Avery president
To Mr. Henry Stretcher
High Sheriff of the Whorekill
Or his Deputy These
Vera Copea per J. Y.

[Notes by John Yeo for Henry Smith written on the warrant:]

      I wish I knew your minde whether you will stay here or
not, for if you Resolve to stay I would Imediately putt the
Carpenters to worke about a house.
                    Yours [Signed:] J. Y[ ]

      there is A Carpenter at your house who is A handyman
      to Luke Watson he wants a sett of Tooles which (if
      you stay in those parts) and would assist him with A
      sett he would worke for you Cheaper then for any
      other man per [Initialed:] J. Y.

[Addressed:] To Mr. Henry Smith at Capt. Cregor his house
              present these in N: Yorke

[Endorsed:] Mr. John Yeo Minister of Whorekill to Dr. Henry
             Smith Nov. 14, 1678⁷

---

1. Henry Stretcher.

2. The copy of this warrant follows the letter.

3. Helmanus Wiltbanck.

4. Cornelis Verhoofe.

5. i.e., the office of Court Clerk.

6. i.e., Peter Smith alias Groenendyck.

7. Endorsement is written in the hand of Matthias Nicolls.

21:32   [MATTHIAS NICOLLS TO THE JUSTICES OF NEW CASTLE
         CONCERNING THE ADMINISTRATION OF WILLIAM TOM'S
         ESTATE][1]

Gent.

         Capt. Edm. Cantwell having made applicacion to the Go.[2]
to have lettres of Administracions on the Estate of William Tom
Late of Newcastle in Delaware deceased who in his last will
and testament[3] after just debts paid with exception to Capt.
Delawill[4], did give and dispose of the remainder of all his
Estate, Goods Chattells and Tenements etc. unto his Godson
Richard Cantwell the son of C. Edm. Cantwell as his hyre[5] and
Executor desiring, ordaining and appointing the Justices of
the Court at Newcastle to bee for the time being Overseers and
Guardians of the said Richard etc. untill hee should come to
bee of age, as in the said Will is more particularly sett
forth; And the said C. Cantwell having formerly made suite to
the Councell that the whole Estate both reall and personall of
the said Wm. Tom deceased might bee appriz'd or publickely sold
to satisfy the Creditors, hee the said C. Cantwell being willing and engaging in his son Richards behalfe to desist of all
benefitts etc. comming to his said son by the said Will, and
that the said Will and Testament might bee disannulled, and
cancelled, whereunto the Councell ordered me to returne an
answer to the Court to which I referre you.

         The Go. having now seene a Copie of Mr. Tom's Will, and
heare what C. Cantwell hath alleadged of his Resignacion of the
right of his son to the Will, whereby the trouble that would
have beene given the Court as his Guardyans will bee at an
End, doth recommend it to you to appoint one fitting to administer and if you approve of Capt. Cantwell who seemes to bee
the most proper and as wee thought was allowed of by you before, Its the Go. order that you admit him upon giving security
to administer according to Law and give an account thereof
here with the first opportunity and lettres of Administracion
may bee granted from his honor in the spring, but hee may have
liberty to act in sale or disposall of the Estate of the deceased and pay debts immediately. I have not further in
Charge as to this matter at present, but remaine
                         Gent.
                    your most humble servant.

[Endorsed:] A lettre to the Justices at Newcastle by order of
         the Go. N. Y. Nov. 19. 78 By Capt. Edm. Cantwell.
         about administracion on Mr. Toms Will.

---

1. See NCCR:251 for a transcription of the final draft
    of this letter.

2. See 20:152 for Cantwell's petition.

3. See 20:151.

4. i.e., Thomas De Lavall.

5. i.e., "heir."

21:33 [THE JUSTICES OF THE WHOREKILL TO GOV. ANDROS
CONCERNING THE ALTERING OF SURVEYS BY ED. CANT-
WELL AND THE PETITION OF THOMAS WELBURNE AND
WILLIAM ANDERSON COMPLAINING OF THE SAME]¹

Honorable Sir

Upon perusell of the petion [sic] of Thomas Welburne and
William Anderson: and Examination of Cornelis Verhoofe who did
Survey the Said Lands for the Said parties and give Certificates of the Same In Due time to Capt. Ed. Cantwell Surveyor
who Blotted out and obliterated the names of The Said Thomas
Welburne and William Anderson, without any Cause objection or
Remonstrance why hee did soe, and putt on his owne and friends
which Appeares to be done with his owne hands, where by it is
Evident to us, that the Said Welburne and Anderson hath been
much Injured and Abused by the Said Cantwell, Illeagally and
arbitrary actings, which if not discountenanced and Reproved
by your Honors Such presidence will for the future Retard and
hinder very much the peopling of the place But doubt not but
the parties above mencioned may and undoubtedly will Receive
Justice from your hands and their Right and Interest, which is
Affirmed for the Reall truth, by
[ ]horekill   Your Honors most humble Servants
[   ] [ ]3th 1677   [Signed:] Helm. Wiltbanck
Test[   ]   Edward Southrin
                                  Alex. ℳ Molestine his mark.

To the Worshipfull His majestis Justises of the peace for the
Whorekill The Humble peticon of Tho: Welburne marchant In the
behalfe of him selfe and partners, And William Anderson of
Accomak County in Virginia

Humbly Sheweth That your peticoners Being Desirouse to be
Intrested And have Free Houlde, In these parts, did in order
Thereunto Imploye Mr. Cornelias Verhoofe (Then deuputy Survayor
of these parts) to make Choyce off procewre and survaye, for
your peticoners Lands (According to pertickelar Instruckticons
to him given) for the which fees and Just Clames or disburst-
ment, wee ware to pay him and alsoe to performe what the Law
or Custome of the place Requires for seating etc. In Comply-
ance where unto (the said Verhoofe giving Advice hee had
ackted) we your peticoners had Layd or made provitions for
settling of familys and seating the same, But soone After wee
Reseaved farther Advice for the said Verhoofe, that When he
The said Verhoofe (Deputy Survayor) was to Returne Certificate of his Survays Into the Survayors offes, and thereby to
take out pattents According to the said survays made Capt.
Edward Cantwell Generall Survayor to whome the said Certificate ware Returnd, did Refewse to give The said deputy Re-
cepts for shuch [sic] Certificats Received, But on the Contra-
[   ] Raced oute the names of Thomas Welburne and partners
named In one Certificate, And placed In the place (or Interlined) his owne, Henry Streetcer and Abraham Clements names to
be owners of The same Lands, Calling the same by the former
name of Welburnes Wilderness, he the said Cantwell did Likewise Race out the name of Wm. Anderson oute of the other Certi-
fycate and in the steede thare of Interloyned the names of
Samuell Styles and Robert Trayly (still Retayning the name of
Anderson delight Expresst on the said Certificate) Notwithstanding survays for both seats of Land may and doth Appere in
the said Verhoofes Booke of survays made in the partes, By all

which means (and as wee Humbly Conceive Illegall proceedings)
we have bin Retarded for bringing Up of familys and stockes
to settle the same, hareing since Receaved Advice from the
said Verhoofe of the Before Res[   ] proseedings, which hath
and doth not [   ] Butt severall other Adventurors,
Whose Inclinacons ware to [   ] These parts and Cohabitt.

Your peticoners Doth Tharefore Humbly pray your worshipps
would please to Examine the nature of all proceedings in The
before Resited premises, And According to your worships Judgments give Approbacon and Certifye the same to the Honorable
Edmond Andross, Esquire and Governor soe that wee may be thare-
by the better Inabled To Recover our Just Right and Intrest
which being obtaing we shall Joyefully Imbrace and settle the
same acknowledging your prewdent Care in Justis, and for your
Worships Ever Pray etc.

[Endorsed:] A petiton to the Justices at the Wh[   ]
             [   ] [   ] Mr Anderson,
             [   ] to the Gov[   ] 1678.

             William Anderson [   ] survey, granted by [   ]
             Court at Whorekill to [   ] others, whose nam[   ]
             are put in the s[   ] Certificate [   ]
             patent extant upon [   ]²

---

1. Other transcription in NYCD 12:587.

2. Endorsements written in the hand of Matthias Nicolls.

21:34   [THE PETITION OF ANDREW POULSON FOR LAND ON
          APOQUEMINI CREEK]¹

To the Right Honorable Sir Edmond Andross, Knight Barron, and
Governor Genrall of all his Royall Highness his teritories in
America, The petittion of Andres Poulson:

Humble Shewith,

     That whereas your petitioner as a subject under his
majesties obedience Did obtaine a grant from the officers att
dellaware for a certine peice of Land in Apoquameni Creke in
Dellaware River for himselfe and famely to Seatt on, and with
all gott it survayed by Mr. Walter Wharton - then Survayor
Genrall and had a pattentt from Coll. Francis Lovelace for the
same Butt by reson of the Duch Taking of the River into their
goverm[   ] your petittioner was disapointed of seating the
said land, and taken f[   ] a spie and Clapt into prizon in
the towne of Newcastle, Now th[   ] is your petitioner having
som horses, mares, and Chatle here on the [   ] of Dellaware,
which since the Alteration of the Goverment was broug[   ] one
purpose, and with intention to seatt the said land and stock
itt if ha[   ] nott been Impeaded by Mr. Wharton, who gott the

pattentt by his threa[   ] Assigned to him from your pet-
tioner for the paymentt of the pattentt and survay of the said
land, when your petittioner was able to pay him butt Contrary
to his promise, hath sould the said land from your petittioner
without ever demanding his pay, and your petittioner being
redy and willing to seatt the said land Is hindred by the said
Wharton from seating, he thretning your petittioner that if he
seats he will turn him of the land againe your petittioner
Knowing no cause given him for the same, withoutt itt be for
the pattent and survaying of the land the paymentt of which
your petittioner hath often tendred him but he hath Refused to
Receive itt, thereby thinking to defraud your petittioner of
his land, Further more your petittioner hath a mare Runing in
the woods with two Coults by her side one of the last yeare
and the other of this yeare, which by reason your petittioner
hath ben impeaded they have been astray in the woods so that
the Coults ware unmarked, butt the mare owned The said Coults
as severall Can attest Notwithstanding which when the mare and
Coultts ware brought into newcastle, Capt. Christopher Billop
although told by several whose mare and Coults itt was (and
thatt they had seen the said Coutls suck the mare which belonged to your petittioner) Did Contrary to the knowledge of
your petittioner Cause the oldest Coultt to be marked for the
King and Imeadeatly sould the said Coultt to John Ogle which
is to the Greatt loss and hindra[   ] of your petittioner
being a pore man and having a great famely, whe[   ] for the
petittioner humble prays your honor to Consider his Condi[   ]
on both sides. so that he may nott be defrauded of his land
nor Cou[   ] butt may have an order from your honor peacably
and quietly to Inj[   ] them both

                         And your petittioner for your Honor[   ]
                         Shall pray as in Duty bound,

[Notation:] to be heard att Newcastle Court.[2]

[Entitled:] Andrew Poulsons Petittion to the Governor.

---

1. Other transcription in NYCD 12:613.

2. This notation is written in the hand of Matthias Nicolls.

21:35   [LEASE OF MATINICONK ISLAND TO ROBERT STACY][1]

    This Indenture made the 14th day of November, in the 30th
yeare of the Raigne of our Soveraigne Lord Charles the Second,
by the grace of god, of England, Scottland, France and Ireland
King, Defender of the Faith etc., Annoque Domini 1678, Beet-
weene Sir Edmund Andros, Knight, Governor, Generall under his
Royall Highnesse, James Duke of Yorke and Albany etc., of all
his Territories in America; for an on Behalfe of his Said
Royall Highnesse, on the one part, And Robert Stacy, one of

the Commissioners of the New Plantacion, in West New Jersey,
in Delaware River, on the Other part, Witnesseth, That the said
Sir Edmund Andros, for divers good Causes, and Consideracions,
him thereunto Especially moveing, hath Demised, granted, and
to farme lett, unto the said Robert Stacy his Executors,
Administrators and Assignes, all that Certaine Island Commonly
Called, or Knowne by the name of Matiniconk Island; in delaware
River, towards the Falls; together with all the Houseing Lands,
Pastures, feedings, Meadowes, and Appurtenances to the said
Island belonging or in any appertaining, now or lately in the
tenue or Occupacion of Peter Jegoe and Hendrick Jacobse, in
partnership, to have and to hold, the Said Island as alsoe the
Houseing and Appurtenances, unto the Said Robert Stacy, his
Executors, Administrators and Assignes, from and after the
first day of January next untill the terme of Seven yeares
Shall bee fully Compleated, and Ended, Hee the said Robertt
Stacy his Executors Administrators, or assignes, makeing Improvement on the Said Island and premises, and paying or
Causeing to bee paid yearly and every yeare thirty Bushells of
good winter Wheate, unto the said Sir Edmund Andros His Successors, assignes or Order at Upland, upon the twenty fifth
day of March annually, And in Default of payment, of the said
Summe thirty Dayes after it shall bee due, that then it shall
and may bee Lawfull to and for the said Sir Edmond Andros, his
Successors or Assignes, into the Said Island, and Demised premises, wholly to re=enter and the Same to have againe Repossess,
and enjoy, this Indenture or any thing Else to the Contrary,
in any wise Notwithstanding; Provided always And it is to bee
understood, that at the Expiracion of the said terme, if the
Said Robert Stacy his Executors Administrators or Assignes,
Shall Leave and goe off the said Island That Whatsoever Edi-
fices, Buildings, or Improvement thereof, hee the Said Robert
Stacy his Executors Administrators or Assignes, have or shall[2]
Cause to bee Erected, or done on the said Island for the Benefitt thereof, there Shall bee Such allowance given for the
same as Shall bee Adjudged by Indifferent Persons, In Testimony Whereof the Partyes aforemencioned to these presents have
Interchangeably Sett to their hands and Seales in New Yorke the
day and yeare first above written.

　　　　　　　　　　　　　　[Signed:]　Robert Stacy

Sealed and Delivered in presence
of, after the Interlineing of the
word, (shall) in the twenty
forth line,
[Signed:] Matthias Nicolls Sec.
　　　　　Ed. Cantwell

[Endorsed:]　The Counterpart of the Lease of Matineconck
　　　　　　Island from Sir Edm. Andros Go. under his R. Hs.
　　　　　　to Robert Stacy. Nov. 14th 1678.

---

1. Other transcription in NYCD 12:64. See PA 5:709 for the
   governor's order granting Robert Stacy possession of the
   island.

2. Interlined as noted below signature.

21:36   [PETITION OF QUAKERS SUPPORTING HENRY JACOBSEN'S
         CLAIM TO MATINICONK ISLAND]¹

Burlington the 5th of the 10th mo. 1678

        At the request of Henry Jacobs wee whose names are under-
written doe give this our testimony one his behalfe To the
[ ]overnor of yorke. The said Henry beeing tennant and in
possession [ ] the Island called Mattinnaconke, when wee first
came into this [ ]ntry, And behaved himselfe scivily and
fairely to us in our [ ] strangers [ ] alsoe was service-
able and helpefull to us at the [   ] land of the Indians, where many of us are [   ] beeing neere to the saide
Island of Mattinnaconke, and since [ ] of our settleing
beeing a neere neighbour to us, hath been [ ]dy to assist us
at any time one the account of the Indians, And wee [ ]eing
strangers in the Country, And unaquainted with the Indians
[ ]guage have often had occasion to make use of the afore-
saide [ ]enry amongst the Indians, whoe hath redily come to us
from [ ]me to time to serve us, and answre our request as
occations [ ]th requiered. And as equally concerned with
Peeter Jegoe [ ]d both tennants to the Governor for the Island
as afforesaide. and it hayeing soe fallen out of late that
another hath gott a graant² of the afforesaid Island which
Henry Jacobs and Peeter Jegoe are now in possession of. And
are very unwilling [ ] foregoe it beeing now in a way to Improve the land an to [ ] corne upon it they paying there
yearely rent according [ ] agreement. And that another should
soe come to sucseed that hath [ ]en received and Entertained
as a stranger in time of nessessity [ ]d by reson the men are
are soe dejected and discouraged in that [ ]ly are like to
bee put out of there place, wee can doe noe lesse [ ] give
our testimony as above written. And doe not question [ ]
the Governor comes to understand things throaghly [sic] but
that [ ] will sett all to write.

[Signed:]   T. Wright
Tho. Eves   William Woodhouse
Matthew Allen   Joshua Bore
Robert Powell   John Cripps
Samuell Lovett   Andrew Smith
William Brightwen   John Champion
Daniel Wills the younger   Thomas Kendall
William Clayton   Thomas Palmer
Robart Durham   Luke Brindley
Tho. Ollive   John Rogers
Daniel Wills   William Black
Wm. Peachee   George Elkinton
John Woolston   William Mattlock
Will. Clayton the olldur   Peter ℘ Stringham
Tho. Harding   his marke
Peter Heerisone

[Endorsed:]   [   ] [   ] the Go. [   ] [   ] Henry
          Jacobs of Matincom Isl.   Dec. 5th 1678³

_____

1. Other transcription in NYCD 12:615.

2. See 21:35 for Robert Stacy's lease to the island.

3. Endorsement is written in the hand of Matthias Nicolls.

21:37 [PATENT GRANTED TO NATHANIEL WALKER FOR LAND AT
       WHOREKILL][1]

SIR EDMUND ANDROS KNIGHT Seigneur Sauzmarez Leiut. and
Governour Generall under his Royall Highnesse James Duke of
Yorke and Albany etc. of all his Territories in America,
Whereas There is a certaine parcell of Land in Delaware Bay
Scituate, lying and being upon the South Westermost Creeke of
Rehobah Bay called by the name of Cedar Neck the which hath
beene Surveyed and layd out for Capt. Nathaniel Walker, by the
approbacion of the Court at the Whorekill as is by them certifyed, The said Land beginning neare the head of the said Creeke
at a marked Red oake Standing by a branch proceeding from the
said Creeke, from thence running South and by East to a marked
white oake standing by a Small bay or pond being betweene the
Beach on the seaside and the aforesaid white oake, from thence
North East and by East binding upon the aforesaid Bay or pond
foure hundred and forty perches, there only proceeding from the
maine woods ad=joyning to the Beach aforesaid a narrow Slipp
of Land in the manner of an Island being about the quantity of
thirty acres, Then from the Extent of the said North East and
by East course being at a Small piece of Marsh, running from
thence NorthEast one hundred and eighty perches, unto the
aforesaid Beach by the Seaside and Northwest binding and adjoyning upon the said beach fourty perches, Then from the said
Beach South West and by West to a Marsh proceeding from part
of the aforesaid Rehobah Bay and from thence to a point of
the said Bay Northwest Then from the said point West to another
point sixty perches and from that said point North West to
another point Lying at a mouth of a River proceeding from the
said Rehobah Bay now called the Indjan River And from thence
Southwest binding upon a Little Creeke one hundred Eighty five
perches t[o a ma]rked white oake st[anding] neare the head of
the said Little Creeke and [from th]e said white Oake running
South and by East two hundred thirty and six perches [to the
first] bounded Red oake Including and Containing Six hundred
and Eighty acres [of] Land by the draught thereof and returne
of the Survey[2] doth and may Apeare And whereas besides the
number of acres aforemencioned returned in the Survey there
is a certain Swamp lyeing in the midle of Cedar Swampe aforemencioned as also severall Sand Hills and Pines by the Seaside
with divers Slashes Marshes or broaken Land betweene the said
neck and the sea and Rehobah Bay and Likewise an Indjan Inlett to the Southward And it being certifyed from the said
Court at the Whorekill that the same is onely convenient for
Capt. Walker and that his Enjoyment there of can bee no Injury
or prejudice to any Towneship or particular person seated or
Inhabiting thereby, Know Yee that by vertue of his Majesties
Letters Patents and the Commission and Authoritie derived unto
mee under his Royall Highnesse I have given and granted and
by these presents doe here by give and grant unto Nathaniel
Walker his heires and Assignes the afore=recited parcell of
Land and premises with all and Singular the Appurtenances,
Together with the Swamp Sand Hills and Pines as also the
Slashes Marshes or broken Land and Indyan Inlett aforemencioned
To Have And To Hold The said parcell of Land and premises
together with the said Swamp Sand Hills and Pines as also the
slashes, marshes or broken Land and Indyan Inlett unto the
said Nathaniel Walker his heires and Assignes unto the proper
use and behoofe of him the Said Nathaniel Walker his Heires
and Assignes forever; Hee making Improvement thereon according
to Law, and yielding and paying therefore yearely and every
yeare unto his Majesties use as a Quitt Rent [blank] unto

such of Officer or Officers as shall bee Empowered to receive
the same at the Whore=kill Given under my hand and Seealed
with the Seale of the Province in New Yorke this [blank] day
of [blank] in the 31th yeare of his Majesties Raigne Annoque
Domini 1679.

---

1. Other transcription in NYCD 12:616.

2. See 20:117 for return of survey.

21:38   [CONFIRMATION OF A PATENT GRANTED TO RALPH
         HUTCHINSON FOR LAND FORMERLY BELONGING TO
         THOMAS YOUNG][1]

     SIR EDMUND ANDROS KNIGHT Seigneur of Sausmarez Leiut. and
Governor Generall under his Royal Highnesse James Duke of York
and Albany etc., of all his Territoryes in America. Whereas
upon a Certificate from the Officers at Delaware, of a grant
made by them unto Thomas Young his Heires and Assignes by the
Late Governour Colonell Francis Lovelace, bearing date the 16th
day of June 1671.[2] The said Land being bounded on the South
with a Swa[ ] running Westerly from the Bay side, on the
Southwest with the Land of Walter Wharton and [Tho]mas Merrit,
on the Northwest with a Line running [   ] East from a
Corner markt Oak [ ] the head of the said Merritts Land, to
the Bayside and on the [ ]st with the maine Bay, to the
mo[ ] the aforesaid Swampe, Containing According to the
Surv[ ] Quantity of foure hundred Ac[ ] Land which said
parcell of Land hath since beene purch[   ] William Young the
son and H[ ] Thomas Young aforemencioned by [   ]
Pat[ ] his name for his farther Confirmacion therein
[   ] by vertue of his [   ] Le[   ]tents and
the Commission and Authorite derived [   ] his Royall
Highnesse I H[ ] given Confirmed and Granted and by these
presents doe here[   ] unto Ralph Hutchinson [   ]eires
and Assignes the afore=recited parcell [   ] premisses
with all and Sing[   ] the Appurtenances, To Have And To
[   ] parcell of Land and premisses, unto the said Ralph
Hutchinson his heires and Assignes unto [   ]per use and
behoofe of him the said Ralph Hutchinson his heires and Assignes forever. [   ]aking Improvement thereon According to
Law; and yeilding and paying therefore yearly [   ]ry Yeare
unto his Majesties use as Quitt Rent, four Bushells of good
winter unto [   ] Officer or Officers as shall bee Empowered
to receive the same at the Whorekill; Given under my hand and
Seale with the seale of the Province in New Yorke the [blank]
day of [blank] in the 31st Yeare of his Majesties Raigne
Annoque Domini 1679.

Examined by mee
[Signed:] Matthias Nicolls Sec.

[Endorsed:]   [   ] Hutchinson [   ] Confirmation 1679

---

1. Other transcription in NYCD 12:616.

2. See DYR:150 for the confirmation of this patent.

21:39/40   [EXTRACTS FROM COURT RECORDS PERTAINING TO
            A SUIT BETWEEN THOMAS HARWOOD AND JACOB VAN
            DER VEER][1]

                                    Att a Court held in the Towne of
                                    New Castle by his mayesties Auth-
                                    ority this 7th of Jannuary anno
                                    Domini 1678/9.

            Mr. John Moll
            Mr. Peter Alrichs
            Mr. Gerret Otto
Present   Mr. Jno. Dehaes   Justices
            Mr. Abraham Man
            Mr. William Sempill

Thomas Harwood Plt.
Jacob Vanderveer Deft.

      The Plt. Demandes of this Deft. by account for sundry
goods and Commoditys sould and Delivered unto this Deft. the
summe three hundred ninety and three gilders In good and mer-
chandable winter wheat or Peltry of which said summe is Paid
341 gilders and ten stivers so that there Rests Due to Ballance
the Summe of fifty one gilders ten stiver for which hee Craves
Judgments with the Costs. The Deft. makes an obiection
against the Article of the Penniston in the account that the
same was overcharged and that the Pay has ben Reddy and sayes
that the same Plt. now allready is overpaid Etc. The Debates
of both Partees being heard and the Plt. heaving made Oath to
his account In Court, The Court doe order Judgment to bee
Entreed against the Deft. for the summe of 51 gilders and 10
stivers with the Costs of Court.

                                    a true Coppy out of the
                                    Records Exam. per
                            [Signed:] Eph. Herman, Cl.

Jannuary 7th 1678/9.

      Jacob Vander Veer was this Day by the Court bound In a
bond of tenn pounds To appeare att the next Court to bee held
in this Towne of New Castle on the first teusday of the month

of February[2] now next Enseueing to Answer to what shall then
and there bee alledged against him for a Certaine stone
fraudulently by him Putt into a bagg of Feathers sould and
Deliv[ered] unto Thomas Harwood the Laest Jeare which said
stone was now Produced In Court Etc.

Thomas Harwood swoorne In Court Declares that Laest
Jeare hee Receiveing a bagg of Fathers [sic] of Jacob Vanderveer weiging 21 lb. English waight In which bagg the Deponant
Comming therewith to New Castle found a stone of about 4 or 5
lb. waight which said stone was waiged and Delivered to him
for fethers [sic].

Mary the wyfe of John Can sworne in Court sayeth that
shee was present the Last Jeare when Tho. Harwood Came with
the bagg of Feathers from Jacob vander Veers and when the said
bagg was Emtyed there was found [in] itt a stone which the
Deponant beleeves to bee the Same or the Lyke stone now Produced in Court.

                          Vera Copia Exam. per
                     [Signed:] Eph. Herman, Cl.

                          Att a Court held in the Towne of
                          New Castle In Delowar by his
                          Mayesties Authourity this 4 and 5
                          of February 1678/9

          Mr. John Moll   ⎫
          Mr. Peter Alrichs ⎪
          Mr. Garret Otto   ⎬
Present   Mr. Johannes DHaes ⎪   Justices
          Mr. Abraham Mann   ⎪
          Mr. William Sempill⎭

     Jacob Vander Veer being Examined about the stone which
was in the feathers of him sould and Delivered unto Thomas
Harwood Did Deny to have Put the said stone In the Feathers.

     Jan Staalcop Sworne in Court De[clared] That Jacob vander
Veers Son Bri[nging] Least Jear a Bagg of Feathers to th[is]
Deponants house for Thomas Har[wood] The said bagg was weiged
by the Depona[nt] the waight thereof then did agree with what
the said Boy did Say that the Fathers [sic] had weiged att his
Fathers house and as soone as the Feathers were weighed the
servant of Thomas Harwood did bring them in the Cano, but
wheather the stone was In the Feathers or noe the Deponant
Cannot tell.

     The Court upon Examination of all the buissinesse Greatly
Suspecting that Jacob Vander Veer is Guilty of the Fact and
not being willing to Proceed to Judgment before that all Evidences were brought In Doe therefore order that Jacob Vander
Veer appea[re] att the next Court and then that als[oe]
appeare the person that was Thomas Harwoods servant Least
Jeare and that found the stone first in the bagg with Feathers
                          Vera Copia Exam. per
                     [Signed:] Eph. Herman Cl.

[Endorsed:]　An order of the Court of Newcastle.　Jan. 7th
1678/9.　about Capt. Jacob Vander Veer.[3]

---

1. See NCCR:273 and 290 for the court records from which
these extracts were made.

2. See the following extract for this court appearance.

3. Endorsement is written in the hand of Matthias Nicolls.

21:41　　[EXTRACT FROM COURT RECORDS PERTAINING TO A
　　　　SUIT BETWEEN JACOB VAN DER VEER AND THOMAS
　　　　HARWOOD][1]

> Att a Court held In the Towne of
> New Castle by his Mayesties
> Authority this [4th] and 5th dayes
> of February Anno Domini 1678/9.

Present

Mr. John Moll	
Mr. Peter Alrichs	
Mr. Garret Otto	Justices
Mr. Joh. Dehaes	
Mr. Abraham Man	
Mr. William Semple	

Jacob Vander Veer Plt.
Thomas Harwood Deft.

The Plt. Instead of bringing a Decleration haveing Entred
an Intangeled accompt without [any] summes Exprest of which
the Court [have] Past their Judgment the Laest Cou[rt] Day[2]
against this Plt. att this Defts. Sui[te] and this Plt. Likewise not Proovi[ng] what he brings In The Court th[erefore]
Do Judge this to bee a vexaious Su[ite] And order a non Suite
to bee Ent[erred] against the Plt. with Costs.
　　　　　　　　　a true Coppy out of the
　　　　　　　　　Records Exam. Per
　　　　　　　[Signed:]　Eph. Herman Cl.

[Entitled:]　Jacob V. Veer against Tho. Harwood.

---

1. See NCCR:290 for the court record from which this
extract was made.

2. See 21:39/40 for this judgment.

21:42   [DUPLICATE OF 21:43]

21:43   [EXTRACT FROM COURT RECORDS PERTAINING TO A
         SUIT BETWEEN THOMAS HARWOOD AND JACOB VAN
         DER VEER][1]

                              Att a Court held In the Towne of
                              New Castle By his mayesties
                              Authority this 4th and 5th dayes
                              of March Anno Domini 1678/9.

           Mr. John Moll   ⎫
           Mr. Peter Alrichs |
           Mr. Fopp Outhout |
Present   Mr. Garrett Otto   ⎬   Justices
           Mr. Joh. Dehaes |
           Mr. Abraham Mann |
           Mr. William Sempill ⎭

     Jacob Vander Veer being ordered the Laest Court to appeare
att this Court for to answer to the action of the stone which
was Put Into the Feathers by him sould and Delivered unto
Thomas Harwood and being three tymes Called did not appeare.

     Reynier Petersen Sworne In Court Decleared that Least
Jeare he being Servant To Thomas Harwood was with the said
Harwood att John Stalcops house In Cristina where att that
same tyme was brought by Jacob Vander Veers Son Some Corne and
A bagg of feathers and the Deponant being att the Canoe with
Jacob Vander Veers Sons taking the bagg of feathers out of
Jacobs Canoe and Putting the same In Tho. Harwoods Canoe Did
feele A stone in the bagg of Feathers and afterwards telling
his master when they Came to New Castle opening the bagg did
find the same stone in itt.

     All Circumstances and Evedences being taken in Considera-
tion the Court are of the opinion and Doe finde that the said
stone was fraudulently by Jacob Vander Veer or his order Putt
Into the Bagg of Feathers and with the same weiged and sould
for feathers and hee the said Jacob Perremtorily Refusing the
Laest Court Day to appeare att this Court Day all which and
other his Uncivill Carriadges Doe merit a Severe Punnishment: Yett the Court Considering the Poverty of him the said
Jacob Doe therfore onely Condem him to pay a fyne of twoo
hundred Gilders for the use and Repairing of the Forte to bee
Levyed upon the goods and Chattles Lands and tennements togeather with all Costs and Charges.
                         A True Coppy out of the
                            Records Exam. per
                      [Signed:] Eph. Herman, Cl.

[Endorsed:]   An order of the Court of Newcastle Mar. 4th 1678/9.
              about Capt. Jacob Vander Veere.[2]

1. See NCCR:301 for the court record from which this
   extract was made.

2. Endorsement is written in the hand of Matthias Nicolls.

21:44   [EXTRACT OF A LETTER SENT TO THE COURT BY
          MATTHIAS NICOLLS CONCERNING JACOB VAN DER
          VEER][1]

I am Likewise to Acquaint you that Its the Governours
pleasure in the Case betweene Thomas Harwood and Jacob Vanderveere concerning the Stone found or put into the Bag of
feathers[2] that there bee no further proceedings in your Court
on that Account, his Honor hath remitted the fine and a
st[ope] is to bee put to the Levying of the Charg[es,] the
whole case being ordered to bee heard in this place before the
Governour and Councell at the beginning of the month of October
next, when both Plt. and Deft. are to give their Attendance
here.

And as to the difference before your Court about the
pretence of Land betweene the said Jacob Vanderveere and his
Neighbour Dr Teeneman[3] the same is also to bee remitted here,
with all papers or proceedings relating thereunto by the first
oppertunitie for a finall Determina[tion.]

          Dr. Tymen Stiddem.
          Jacob Van der Veere.[4]

[Endorsed:]   Part of the Letter and order sent to Delaware
              about Jacob Vander Veeres and Dr Tymens buisnesse.
              The matter also between the said Van der Veere
              and Mr Harwood about the stone in the feathers.

1. This document represents an extract from a letter
   written by Matthias Nicolls to the court at New Castle
   dated May 19th 1679. The extract which is written in
   the hand of Ephraim Herman, pertains only to Jacob van
   der Veer. See NCCR:323 for the complete text of the
   letter.

2. See 20:39/40 and 20:43 for the court records concerning
   this case.

3. i.e., Dr. Tymen Stiddem. See NCCR:182, 291, 304 and
   329 for the court records concerning this case. See

also 21:71 and 21:72 for Tymen Stiddem's case and the
list of papers sent to Matthias Nicolls in this matter.

4. These names and the following endorsement are written
    in the hand of Matthias Nicolls.

21:45   [COURT'S TRANSLATION OF JACOB VAN DER VEER'S
        DECLARATION CONCERNING THOMAS HARWOOD'S ACCOUNT
        AGAINST HIM][1]

To the Worshipfull Court of New Castle

Jacob Vander Veer plt.
    against
Thomas Harwood Deft.

    The Plt. declars that this deft. hath Sould unto him the
Plt. 5 Ells of Penniston for the value of a bever.

    2dly the Deft. Sould this Plt. 5 Schipple of salt for 1
1/2 sch: wheat or 1 1/2 bever.

    3dly 1 piece of Linning for 20 Schipple of wheat which
hee the deft. hath Received.

    4thly about the duffells is noe difference.

    5thly 50 lb. of Shott, for which hee and my wyfe Shall
speake with the Deft. and for which hee hath Received the
feathers.

    6ly the Deft. Received in C[   ] 32 Ells of penniston
which I the same tyme bought againe of the Deft. for Red
duffills, 3 Els of duffills for 5 Els of penniston.

    7 hee the Deft. has Received of mee 24 drest dearskins,
halfe buke and halfe doew skins; Yett I kan not say Exactly
whether the halfe were bucks or dowes, neverthelesse itt were
all 24 good Skins at 6 for a bever, and hee discounts mee noe
more then f80 for the 24 skins.
                            (was signed)
                            Jacob Vander Veer
    [   ] the first[2]

[Entitled:] Jacob V: Veer against Tho: Harwood

---

1. This document represents the court's translation and
    phrasing of Jacob van der Veer's declaration which was
    originally written in Dutch. See 21:47 for this dec-
    laration.

2. The original declaration is·dated Feb. 1, 1679.
According to the account in 21:46 the date is in new
style.

21:46   [COPY OF THOMAS HARWOOD'S ACCOUNT AGAINST
          JACOB VAN DER VEER]

Dilwer River the 26, June 1676

Jacob Vandever is debitor to Thomas Harwood For Severall
goods Sould to him For to be paied in good winter wheate or
peltrey at or befoer the 20th of Dec. next Comeing the goods
is as Foloweth viz

```
For 40 ells Fine Lining¹ at 3 gild. is.............120:00
For 56 pounds Shott at 1 gild. is..................056:00
For 46 yards peneston at 8 gild. is................368:00
For 4 bushels Salt at 12 gild. is..................048:00
For 49 ells 1/2 duffels at 3 ells For
[   ] bever.........................    ..........408:06
For one barell with his Salt.......................008:00
For 12 pounds nailes at............................024:00
                              Suma is  1032:06
```

```
Contra is Creditor                                      gild.
May the      For 24 drest skinns at...................080:00
20th 77      For dufels to Indian and Shott...........025:00
             For 52 ells duffels: 3 for bever is......433:06
Dec. the     For 105 pounds Raw Skinns is.............087:10
  20th                                                 625:16

Aprill       For 25 ells dufells of Hen[ ]icakas
the 10th     Williamson at......................      200:00
  78         For 20 scivels² wheate at...............100:00
             For 3 ells dufels at.....................025:00
             For one bage Fethers together with a
             Stoane waying 21 lb. the Stoane and the    030:00
             bag being ducted³ Rest 15 lb. Fethers
             at 2 gild. per pound is 30 gilders
                                                       980:16
                              Rest due.....051:10
```

This is a true acompte Erors execpted by mee Thomas Harwood

This account Sworne unto in Court by Tho. Harwood Jann. 7th
1678/9 which attest. [Signed:] E. Herman, Cl.

[Entitled:] Account of Tho. Harwood against Jacob V. Veer
             1678/9.

---

1. i.e., linen.

2. i.e., skipples.

3. i.e., deducted.

21:47   [JACOB VAN DER VEER'S DECLARATION CONCERNING
         THOMAS HARWOOD'S ACCOUNT AGAINST HIM][1]

Mr Ephrahim Clerck[2]

   Please write down the declaration between me and Harwis[3]
as follows:

   1. I declare that he sold me 5 ells of penniston for
   the value of 1 beaver.

   2. He sold me 5 skipples of salt for 1 1/2 skipples of
   wheat or 1 1/2 beavers.

   3. 1 piece of linen for 20 skipples of wheat which he
   has received.

   4. There is no argument about the duffels.

   5. 50 lb. of shot which he and my wife shall discuss;
   for which he has received the feathers.

   6. He received from me 32 ells of penniston which I at
   the same time bought back from him for red duffels: three
   ells of duffel for 5 ells of penniston.

   7. He received from me 24 dressed deerskins: half buck-
   skins and half doeskins. I cannot say whether they were
   exactly halfe buck and half doe, nevertheless, all 24 were
   good skins: 6 for one beaver, and he credited me no
   more than f 80 for the 24 skins.

Christina February 1, 1679[4]   [Signed:] Jacob Van der Veer

[Entitled:] Jacob Van der Veer against Tho. Harwood.

----

   1. The following declaration has been translated from the
   Dutch original which was written and signed by Jacob
   van der Veer. See 21:45 for the court's translation
   and phrasing of this document. cf., 21:46 for Thomas
   Harwood's account.

   2. i.e., Ephraim Herman who was clerk of the court.

   3. i.e., Thomas Harwood.

   4. This date is new style.

21:48   [RECEIPT FOR JACOB VAN DER VEER'S PAPERS][1]

The Go. tooke Jacob Van der Veers papers of the Court at
Delaware between him and Mr. Harwood.[2]

                                 June 10th 1679.

[Entitled:]   Jacob Vander Veers papers.

---

1. This receipt is written in the hand of Matthias Nicolls.

2. See 21:39-47 for these papers.

21:49   [TESTIMONY OF JOHN ANDERSON AND CHRISTINA
              CARRLLSDOTTER IN THE SUIT BETWEEN JACOB
              VAN DER VEER AND THOMAS HARWOOD]

Becauce Jacob van Derweer have Dessiret testimony Concerning som trockencloatt,[1] Mr. Harworet[2] resewed[3] from heem,
and wy Kan nott Denay him the Same and the truth So Faare wy
Cnow theraff, that Mr Harwooret hath Come to our hous and
brogt tw[4] peases of trockenclott one read and one blow[5], and
wy Deseyread him to measuer the Same, and hee Dead[6] allsoo,
and wy ascke him iff itt was richt[7], he answert y.[8] and littell
teim theraffter hee Comming From Peter Coocks Tolld that he
have loockt ower his Aconnt and he wantet tree Ells, and
Further haveing nooe Knoulegh, that this is the truth are wy
ready to Confirme with our oaths and testeffy itt whitt our
hand.
Datum Christina the 16 Agusty Anno 1679

                          [Signed:]   John Anderson
                                  Christina Carrllsdotter[9]

[Endorsed:]   Jacob Van der Veere.[10]

---

1. Possibly a term used by Swedes for "duffel." cf.,
   21:50 where Anderson writes dyffels.

2. Thomas Harwood.

3. i.e., received.

4. i.e., two.

5. i.e., blue.

6. i.e., did.

7. i.e., right.

8. i.e., aye.

9. The Swedish patronymic for: Christina the daughter of Carl.

10. Written in the hand of Matthias Nicolls.

21:50 [TESTIMONY OF JOHN ANDERSON IN THE SUIT
BETWEEN JACOB VAN DER VEER AND THOMAS
HARWOOD][1]

All the Dealings that wy have haede, have y Declared For
the Corret att the Sandhoeck[2], that Mr. Harwordt have solld me
Fiyff Ells penneston For one bever and tree Ells dyffels For
one beaver, that this is the truth testeffey y whitt my one[3]
hand heer under ritten.
Datum Christina the 16 Agusty Anno 1679

[Signed:] John Anderson

Further Doe y testiffey that
y have boegt For twenty Schepell
Wheat one peas off Linnen.

1. A few lines have been lost at the top of this document
due to trimming.

2. Zand Hoek was the Dutch name for the neck of land upon
which Fort Casimir stood. The reference here is to the
court at New Castle.

3. i.e., own.

21:51 [PETITION OF ARNOLDUS DE LA GRANGE CONCERNING
TINICUM ISLAND][1]

To His Excellence Sir Edmund Andros Knight Lieut. and Governor
Generall under his Royall Highnesse of all his Territories in
America

The humble Petition of Arnoldus De La Grange Sheweth That
your Petitioners father Joost De La Grange heretofore of Delaware did agree with and buy of Juffro Armgart Prince Attorney

of her father Johan Prince then in Sweden a Certaine Island in
Delaware River, called Tinicum Island, together with the house-
ing and Stock there upon for the Sume of Six thousand
Gilders Hollands Money, upon Certaine Condicions in a bill of
Sale Sett forth past upon the 29th day of May 1662 before
Cornlis Van Ruyven then Secretary of this place, and the said
Joost De La Grange, your Petitioners Father being put into
possession of the said Island and premises, paid unto the Said
Juffro Prince or her Order, in part of the said Purchase the
one Moiety or halfe thereof, being three thousand Gilders
Hollands money (vizt) two thousand upon her Arrivall in Holland
which was upon the last day of July Following, and the other
thousand Gilders a yeare after, as appeares by the Acquittances
for the Same: That Afterwards upon the Death of the aforenamed Johan Prince the Father then in Sweden, there was a Stop
put to the payment of the Payment [sic] of the remaining three
thousand Gilders, untill a Full and new power Should Arrive
from the Other three Sisters of the said Juffroe Prince, alias
Pappegay, out of Sweden who were Copartners with her in the
Fathers Estate which never arrived that hee hath heard in his
Fathers time, whether ever it Came into these parts or no
your petitioner is Ignorant off, but in the meane time your
Petitioners Father Died, and Left Margarett his Widdow your
Petitioners Mother Invested of the premises, who a while after
was married to one Andrew Carr, that Came over with Governor
Nicolls, and upon his Request had the said Island to Tinicum
aforemencioned granted and Confirmed by pattent unto him and
Margarett his wife, by Governor Francis Lovelace, without any
reservacion, as by the Pattent bearing Date October 1st 1669
may appear[2], That Dureing the abode of your petitioners Mother
or father in Law on the said Island, they nor either of them
received any Disturbance by Law Suite or Otherwise, Concerning
the Same, nor till After the Departure of your petitioners
Father in Law for Holland which was above a yeare after his
mother went to Looke after an Estate befallen her there when
Capt. John Carr Attorney for your Petitioners Said Father was
First Summoned by the aforenamed Juffroe Prince alias Pappegay,
and Sued att a Sepciall Court held before [ ] Governor at
Newcastle, in Delaware and Afterwards by Consent Beetween them
put off to the Genrall Court of Assizes where Little Defence
was made the said Capt. Carr being also Absent Soe that hee
was Cast on the behalfe of your petitioners Said Father and
Mother and the Said Juffro Prince put in possession of the said
Island and premises (which were apprized very Low) and the Same
hath ever Since beene Detayned, and as your Petitioner is Informed, Since Sold to One Ernestus Otto much under the Value,
which will redound greatly to the Detriment of your petitioners
relacions, and perticularly himselfe, the Said Sume of money
or a good part thereof designed for his portion of his Fathers
Estate, without reliefe therein.

Now Your Petitioner haveing full power by procuracion from
his aforenamed Father in Law and Mother to Clayme their Rights
in the premises, wherein hee is Likewise So much Concerned
hath recours to your Excellence, desireing to bee heard in
Equity Concerning the Same (what hath past heretofore being
only at Common Law) humbly Imploring your Excellence will please
(though Ommitted before) to have Some regard to the three
thousand Gilders Soe Long Since Disburst, the Long Possession,
and Improvement made on the said Island for which if the entire Summe Agreed for were not paid to happened to bee by the
aforenamed Accidents, and also your petitioner desires that
Consideracion may bee had to the Lawes of England of which

hee is a Subject in Like Cases provided Viz that Definitive
Sentence Shall not passe against a man beyond the Seas, against
a femme Covertt³ whose husbands Neglect Cannot make her loose
her right, [   ] against an Infant under Age hee being un-
capable [   ] Non age, but now makeing his Clayme as
hei[   ] to his Father, which last is really your petitioners
Case and prays with hopes that your Excellence in your pru-
dence haveing Seriously pondred your petitioners request will
please to direct Some way for his reliefe herein either by a
hearing in Equity So that hee may bee reinburst his money or
that he may have the Advantage of preferrence So much haveing
beene already paid for the remaining part of the Agreement to
have the Said Island and premises, as it hath beene purchased
by the party in possession which to bee repaid him there haveing beene no pattent of Confirmacon from your Excellencyes
predecessor or yourselfe to any other person or persons for
the said Island; your petitioner haveing transported himselfe
and Family with Intent to remaine and abide in these parts
under your Excellenceys Goverment and protection for whose
prosperity Hee Shall.

As in duty bound ever pray etc.

[Endorsed:]   18 March [   ] Mr La Gra[   ] Petition of
              Ti[   ] Island⁴

---

1. Other transcription in NYCD 12:618.

2. See DYR:141 for the confirmation of this patent.

3. i.e., a married woman. The term is generally used in
    reference to the legal disabilities of a married woman
    as compared with the condition of a feme sole.

4. Endorsement is written in the hand of Matthias Nicolls.

21:52a   [RECEIPT OF JOHN STEVENS FOR QUIT RENT ON TWO
          PARCELS OF LAND]¹

    John Steevens is Debtor to Quit Rent of twoo parcells of
Land, as followeth vizt.

1679
March 25th   one Yeare quit Rent of 1200 acres
                Called Content, Lying in Duke   Bushs
                Creeke, In wheat..................... 12:

March 25   one yeare quit rent of 1300 acres
                Lying in a Little Creeke below
                Duke Creeke, Caled London. wheat...... 13
                             Wheat Bushels: 25:-

Received of John Steevens by order of the Right Honorable Sir
Edm. Andros, Governor Generall twenty and fyve Bushells of
wheat being Quit Rent Due for the twoo parcells of Land above
named, March the 25th 1679.

                              [Signed:] Eph: Herman.
25 Bush:

[Verso:] paid quit rent

------

1. Other transcription in NYCD 12:619.

21:52b   [FRAGMENT OF A MEMORANDUM BY MATTHIAS NICOLLS]

[Top portion destroyed   ]
bring his 2 [   ] here in [   ] the like for the
Indyans that were present with the Squaw when hurtt, and as
many others as were thereby, that Knew the Negroes.[1]

    An order to bee sent for Sloops to goe up the River at
Delaware.

    Mr. Norwood[2] about Staten Island.

[Endorsed:] [   ] Mar. 27, 1679.

------

1. Reference to the murder of an Indian woman by one of
    Capt. Wm. Laurence's negro servants. See 28:79 for the
    court proceedings in this case.

2. Andrew Norwood, surveyor of Staten Island.

21:53   [NO CALENDAR ENTRY AND NO DOCUMENT]

21:54   [JUSTICES OF NEW CASTLE TO GOV. ANDROS ABOUT A
        THEFT COMMITTED BY ROBERT HUTCHINSON][1]

                        New Castle Aprill the 23rd Anno 1679.

Honorable Governor

     Whareas Adam Wallis his Chest with Sundry goods whas well
Lockt and putt in the house off Robbert Hudjeson[2] came
from Maryland to fetch itt away and openinge off itt found the
said Chest had ben Broke open Lockt again and that there whas
taken out, viz; one Silver Tumbeler markt A.W. bought by him
for 50/ speci [mo]nny in N. Yorke Idem 2 Witte fustian Was-
coates and 2 pair [of br]idges ditto 1 doulis Schort 2 pair of
New Ledder Stockins [2 pair] off Worsted Stockins 1 pair of
New Schoes, almoost 2 lb. [of] Silck, 2 lb. off Cullerd thrid
2 Neckelosch[3] markt A.W. 3 [R]emnants off Linnen Closch 2 pices
off Cullerd felletinge[4] 1 lb. off Whyted Brown thrid 1 pair
New Gloves Sum Napkins and Sum [silver] Monney, etc. - 2 pair
off Sliefs[5] and 1 Scholder Knott.

     After 3 Strickt Exsaminations the said Robbert Hudjeson
has Confest before [us] What hee had Stolen Outt off the Said
Adam Wallis his Chest all the particulars heere above Mensionet
[Ex]cept the Silver [mon]ny.

     Search being made there is found in the house off the
[said] Robbertt Hudjeson off the goods heer above spessified,
viz, One Silver Tumbiler markt A.W. 16 1/8 yds. off a Kjnde
[of] Locquerom Linnen 10 1/4 yds. off brote Ham. Linnen[6]
[3 3/8] yds. off Indifferent fyne Schiftinge Linnen, 2 fustian
Wascote 1 pair Bridges ditto, 1 doulis Schort 2 pair off Sleefs
1 pair off Ledder Stockins, 1 pair off gloves 2 Necklassis
Marckt A.W. 1 Cours towell Marckt A., 43 Scheans off thrid
40 Scheanes off Silck and 1 remnant of old rubond.

     Whar Upon the Said Robbert Hudjeson since the 19th day
off this Instande has ben Kept Close Prissoner in Ower Fortt.
Wee Humbly desier Your Honors orders and directions in and
[abo]udt this Bissenis, Which shall bee stricktly Ob[eyed] by
Us
                    Your Honors Most Obedient Servants
                        [Signed:] Jn. Moll
                                   Pieter Alrichs
                                   J. D:Haes
                                   Will. Sempill

[Addressed:] To the Honorable Madjor Edmund Andross Knight
              Leftenantt and Govrnor Gennerall off all his
              Royall Heinessis Terratories in America att
              Fortt James In New Yorke
per Mons. Dela Grange
[   ]

---

1. See NCCR:322 for a transcription of the court's copy of
    this letter. Damaged portions have been recovered from
    this source. For Matthias Nicolls' reply dated May 19,
    1679 see NCCR:323. A transcription of Nicolls' copy
    of the latter appears in PA 5:712.

2. i.e., Robert Hutchinson.

3. NCCR has "neckcloaths." Final -sch was pronounced [s]
   at this period in Dutch. The spelling possibly reflects
   John Moll's Dutch accent.

4. i.e., filleting: a strip of material similar in use
   to ribbon.

5. i.e., sleeves.

6. NCCR has "broad holland Linnen."

21:55   [NO CALENDAR ENTRY AND NO DOCUMENT]

21:56   [THE PETITION OF ADAM WALLIS CONCERNING GOODS
         STOLEN FROM HIM BY ROBERT HUTCHINSON][1]

                         To the Right Honorable Sir Edmond
                         A[   ] Governor of New Yorke and
                         his Heig[   ] territories in
                         America.

         The humble petitione of Adam W[   ]

[   ] heaveing left one Chist at New Castle [   ]nt
to Maryland, and the Chist standing [   ] of
Robert Hutch[   ] Came for his Chist hee found
[   ] which were found in the [   ]
said Robert, And your honnors pet[   ] goods
againe from the worship[   ] of New Castle, they heave
[   ] to your honnor.

     May it therfor please your Honnor [   ]tione
that I am a poore labour[   ] heaveing nothing bot
what I [   ] dayllie labour to geive orde[   ]
your honnors heigh sheeriffe in New Cast[   ] to delyver what
goods properly belon[ ] to mee which are now in his Custody,
And your Honnors petitioner shall e[   ] pray etc.

_____

1. See 21:54 and PA 5:712 for related documents.

21:57 [LIST OF PATENTS SENT TO CAPT. CANTWELL][1]

[   ] 13th 1679 Patents sent to Capt. Edm. Cantwell by Mr.
John Shackerly which were refused to bee
signed when hee [   ] here.

[   ] Mr. Laurentius Carolus. Tacquirassy in
Delaware River. besides Marsh.............. 350 Acres

[   ] Henry Stevenson and John Richards
Batchelors Harbor in Del. Bay [   ]
besides marsh.............................. [600]

[   ] Henry Allison. Tillmouth Haven.
Del. Bay. besides marsh................... 400

4   Thomas Philips in Del: Bay. besides marsh.. 600

5   Cornelys Verhoofe. New Seven=hoven
in Del. Bay................................ 1218

6   Maurice Daniel in Del. River. no marsh
mencioned. granted before to John
Bradburne in 1671 who deserted it.......... 190

7   Cornelys Jansen in Del. Bay. no marsh
and certifyed by the Court................. 622

8   Richard Peaty. in Del. Bay no. marsh
and certifyed by the Court................. 421

[   ] James Loten. in Del Bay. and well
certifyed.................................. 400

[   ] Henry Harman. Harmans Choice in
Del. Bay.................................. 400

[   ] Erick Mallock, Olle Nielson and [Christiana]
Thomason in Del. River besides meadow, part
granted before to Mr. An[drew] Carr........ 950

12   Hendr. Molesteyn, John Kiphaven junr.
Cor. Verhoofe, and Harman Cornelys in
Del. Bay.................................. 800

13   Mr. John Moll Del. River 600 acres purchased of Goldsmith etc.................... 1000

14   Tho: Jacobsen, Olle Paulson, and Arent
Johnson in Del. River...................... 248

15   John Johnson, James Eustasen and [Peter]
Hendricksen in Del. River.................. 300

16   Laurence Cock, Erick Cock, Otto E[rnest]
Cock, Goner Rambo and Peter Nielsen a
tract of land called Shakhamux[unk] in
Del. River................................. 16[00]

17   Bryan Omella who had purchased [   ]
Claes Kersen and Bernard Brand [   ]
Delaware River and in possesin besides
Hayland etc............................... 400

18   Peter Petersen and Caspar Fish in Del.
      River. with meadow, it being part of
      a tract of land granted to Andris Carr....... 500

19   Peter Cock. Shackamunck, in Delaware
      River. his owne land. besides the meadow
      etc.. 650

[Endorsed:]   [   ] sent [   ] Cantwell by Mr.
               Shakerley May 13th 1679.

---

1. This document is written in the hand of Matthias Nicolls.
    Damaged portions have been recovered from DYR and WWS.
    Other transcription in NYCD 12:620.

21:58a   [WM. CLARK TO GOV. ANDROS CONCERNING SURVEYOR'S
           FEES AT WHOREKILL][1]

                    Whoorekill the 14th 3/mo.; Called May 1679

[Governor Andros]

      [Si]nce thee ware pleased when I was at york; To Aske me
[if] there was anything I Knew that related to this place for
thee [to] settel or order; doth Imbolden me to Lay one thing
before [thee]; which I obsarve to be A greavence; and that
which doth [prevent] the better seating of this County; And
that is thay that [have] land here are not at any Certainty
what thay must [doe fo]r the survaying it; The planters that
Comes out of Mary[land] are and have bene in an Expectacion;
that thay should pay [no] more then is paid for survaying
there; which is one hundred pounds of Tobacco for the first
hundred Acres; And fifty pounds for the second hundred Acres;
and Twenty five pounds for evrey hundred Acres after to A
thousand Acres; soe that the survaying of one Thousand Acres
of Land Comes to but three hundred and fiftye pounds; But
Instead thereof sume have paid here Two Thousand pounds of
Tobacco for survaying one Thousand Acres; And none that I hear
of have paid lesse then one Thousand pounds for survaying one
Thousand Acres of Land; which may be done in one days [work or]
Less which is Looked on as a greate Burthin [   ] [   ]ich
Complained on by the planters; And thay doe [say] it doth
hinder others from Coming to seat in this County; that had
thoughts of Coming; This I thought fitt to signifie unto thee,
Being allways willing to Appeare in that which may be for the
prospirity and well being of that place which I eat my bread
in; And Leave it to thy Consideracon to returne such Answer
and directions here unto; As in they greate wisdom shall
[   ]; An as this finds Acceptance with thee; I shall
take the more freedome hereafter as things presents; And
subscribe my selfe thyne to sarve
                         Thee In what I Can
                    [Signed:] Wm. Clark

[Addressed:]   To [   ] Andros [   ] In New
               York
                         Present

[Endorsed:]   [   ] May 14 16[   ]

---

1. Other transcription in NYCD 12:620.

21:58b   [COPY OF CORNELIS VERHOOFE'S PETITION TO BE
          CONTINUED AS CLERK AT THE WHOREKILL][1]

[The majority of this document has suffered water damage]

[Last two lines:] These petition Granted by the Court. True
Copie Examined per mee
                              [Signed:] John Avery

[Endorsed:]   [   ]on gran[   ] the Court at the
              Wh[   ]Kill and confirmed by the Go: to bee Clark.
              May 27: 1679. Also about Fees.[2]

---

1. Cornelis Verhoofe submitted his petition to the Whore-
    kill court where it was granted. John Avery then made
    a copy of the petition and sent it to New York for con-
    firmation. See PA 5:713 for Matthias Nicolls' reply
    to the magistrates confirming Verhoofe's petition. See
    also 28:109a for a letter from Gov. Andros to John
    Avery confirming the court's decision.

2. Endorsement is written in the hand of Matthias Nicolls.

21:59   [JOHN KIPSHAVEN'S PETITION FOR A PIECE OF
         LAND AT THE WHOREKILL][1]

                        To the Right Honorable Sir Edmund
                        Andros Knight Seignieur of Saus-
                        marez [   ] Governor Generall
                        Under his Royall [   ] of all
                        his Territories in America etc.

The Humble petition of John Kipshaven

Sheweth...
[The remainder of this document has suffered water damage]

[Marginal notations:]
The Apostajle or   This peticion is granted
answer from the Go;   if as alleadged, and to bee
was to this Effect   survey'd in Order to a patent.
                            M. N. Secr.

27th of May 1679 if as alleadged, to bee survey'd in order to
a pattent.

[Endorsed:] Jan Kippshaven for a piece of Land neare some
             other by him purchased at the Whorekill.[2]
Granted if as alleadged. May 27, 1679.

---

1. See PA 5:713 for Matthias Nicolls' reply to magistrates
   at the Whorekill in which an order on John Kipshaven's
   petition is issued. The notations and endorsement are
   in the hand of Matthias Nicolls.

2. See DYR:95 for a confirmation granted to John Kipshaven
   for a piece of land at the Whorekill.

21:60   [PETITION OF JOHN VINES TO BE SHERIFF AT THE
         WHOREKILL][1]

                        [   ] Right Honorable Edmund
                        Andros Kn[   ] of Saus-
                        marez Lieut and Govern[ ] Gen[   ]
                        of all his [   ]ritories in America
                        etc.

The Humble [ ]tition of John Vines of the Whorekill.

[The remainder of this document has suffered water damage]

[Marginal notations:] Upon the Courts Choice and recommendacion of Cornelys Verhhofe to bee Surveyor at the Whorekill -
Confirmed till further order.

[   ] Courts [   ] allowed and Confirm'd for
the yeare as the Court is.

[Endorsed:] John Vynes peticion to the Go: to bee sheriffe of
             the Whorekill.
Granted upon Courts Recommendacion. May 27, 1679.

[   ] of the Whore[   ] Go: about being [   ]
with answer, and answer likewise to Cor: Verhoofe to bee
Surveyor there. May 27, 1679.

1. See PA 5:713 for Matthias Nicolls' reply to the magistrates at the Whorekill concerning this petition. See
   also 28:109a for a letter from Gov. Andros to John
   Avery confirming the order on John Vines' petition.
   The marginal notations and endorsements are written in
   the hand of Matthias Nicolls.

21:61   [PETITION OF IMMIGRANTS FROM ENGLAND TO
         SETTLE NEAR THE FALLS]¹

Honorable Sir

       Wee whose names ar here under Subscribed Latly ar Com
From Old England with Intent to inhabitt in This Contry And if
your Honor Pleases to Grant us an order under your hand too
Setle between Mr Pitter Alderidges² Plantacion and The Falls of
Delloware River Wee Shall be willing to Imbrace it and to hold
it according to the Custom of The Contry being a Fitt Place for
Husbondmen: We may have Land in Jersie Side but we ar willing
to becom Tenants to his highness the Duke of Yourk if your
Honor please to give us the grant and to Cleer the Indians
that may [   ] to send for the Rest of our Famil[ ]
[   ] [ ]ttions which Looke for a Retorne from [
   ] your Answere by This barrer Wee shall waite for it before
we settle and Shall Rest

                           Your Humble Servants
[Bu]rlington   Although unknowne
June the 23rd 1679.   [Signed:] John Akarman Sen.
                                      John Akarman Jun.
                                      Robert Hoskins
                                      Daniel Brinson
                                      Thomas Scoly
                                      Robert Scoly
                                      William Cleark
                                      John Budd
                                      John Mifflin Sen.
                                      John Mifflin Jun.
                                      Robert Lucas
                                      John Lucas
                                      Samuel Cleft
                                      Tho. Revell
                                      Tho. Potts

1. Other transcription in NYCD 12:623.

2. i.e., Peter Alrichs.

21:62   [LUKE WATSON TO GOV. ANDROS CONCERNING MISCONDUCT
         OF JOHN AVERY]¹

Whoore Kill the 30th June 1679.

[Hon]ored Sir

    Your Honnor hath beene pleased to Joyne me in Commission
with others As A Magestrate for this County, which I have ever
sence bene both willing and radye to sarve you and my Countrey
to the best of my Judgment; And haveing that Trust reposed in
me, I Look upon my selfe oblidged to Informe your Honnor of
such miscarige and misdemeaners as happen or falls out that
Cannot be rectified [her]e; And that is the Gros[e] Abusses
that hath bene Commited by Capt. John Avrey presedent of this
Court; both relateing to t[he] Trust reposed in him, and other
ways;

    [1st] That when the rest of the Magestrats Could not Con-
sent to Do[e] and determaine things as he would have it; Contrary to our Judg[ment] He have in a Greate Rage and feurey
went out of Court Cursing and Swaring; Calling of the rest of
the Court Fooles Knaves and Rouges; wishing that if ever he
satt Amongest us again; that the devil might Com and fetch him
away; and also threeting [sic] and presently after did strik
one of the Magestrats with his Kane; and had he not bene prevented by the spectators; might a done m[uch] damiage that way,

    [2ly] He Tooke upon himselfe to Marry the widow Clament
to o[ne] Bryant Rowles; without publiquecation not with standing she w[as] out aske² at Least a Moneth to an other man;
namly Edward Cooke The which when the said Cooke hard that she
was marryed [to another man said that it would be his death
And presently went] home fell sick and in about forty Eighte
houres after [dyed;] [he] Left it on his death that hur Marrying was the Cause of [his dyeing]

    [3ly] He Took upon him to grant A Licence to Marry Daniel
Browne to Sussan Garland widdow; without any publiquecati[on,]
which Marrige was Effected; notwithstanding it is Generally
knowne; or at Least; the said Daniel Conffesses that he knows
no other but that he have a wife Liveing in England;

    [4]ly one Judith the wife of Thomas Davids being sub-
spected to have stoolen sume goods from severall persions, the
goods be[ing] found in hur Custidy; was had in Examinaction by
me; [And] at First she did Confidently Affirm that she brought
the said goo[ds] out of Mary Land; and that thay ware hur owne
Lawfull goo[ds,] but she well knowing that it would be proved
to be otherw[ise] did soone Conffess that she ded steele them,
and [fr]om whom; upon hur Conffession I made hur [   ]
and Commited hur to the Custidy of the Cunstable Till the next
Court then Following; but soon After Capt. Avrey sent a noate
by hur Husband to the Cunstab[le] requiring him to give hur
hur Libiurty; threetening both me that had Commited hur and the
Cunstable that did detaine hur soe that the Canstable being
subprized with fear ded discharge h[ur] out of his Custody; In
short he the said Capt. Avrey is an Incourig[er] and upholder
of Dronkingnes Theeft Causing Swaring and Fighti[ng] to the
Affrighting Amazing and Terifieinge of his Majesties quiet
peacable Subjects; whoes grose weeckednes and unhuman Con[ver]-
sation if a timely stop be not put to it; may Justly be Expected to bring downe gods Heavey Judgments upon this place;

[51y] I goeing into the house of Helmainas Wiltbanck on the fifteenth day of this Insint June being The Lords day; whare the said Capt. Av[ery] was Drounke; whoe soone after brooke out in a great Rage and feurey; (without any provecation Calling me beagerly Rouge) and theefe with maney more reflecting speaches; saying that he would prove me to be both Rouge and Theefe; and that I was not worth one grot[3]; I ded till him that if he would not give me Satisfacion; for the abusse he had Cast upan me; that I would sue him; To which he replyed; That he would faine see any Magestrate that would dare to signe a warrant or Sumeance Against him; And that what he had said he would not be Accountable to any Court but onely to the Govener; and that he is above any power here; see that the other Commisoners have Refeused to signe A Sumeance Against him; he Curses and Swares at such A rate that he Frights all others from doeinge anything in order to the bringing him to Justices;

All which I have hear Charged Against the said Capt. Avrey I shall be rady to prove by the Testamoney of Severall sufficent wittneses; when ever ther unto requiered by your Ho[nor] with much more stuffe of the Like nature, I Could doe no Less [   ] for the Clearing of my selfe from haveinge any unity [with] such his Abomenable wicked practies Life and Conversasion.

And My Humble Request unto your Honnor is that you will be pleased to give such order and directions that the said Capt. Avrey may be Compell[ed] to make good his Charge Against me; or Else to give me such satisfacion as shall Appeare to be Just and Equiel; which is the thing desiered and Humbled Crav[ed] for by your Honnors.

Obedeant and Faithfull Servant
[Signed:] Luke Wattson

[Endorsed:]   [   ] Luke Watson from the Whorekill
                Complain[   ] against Mr. Avery[4]

---

1. Other transcription in NYCD 12:624.

2. i.e., outask: to publish the bans of marriage in church for the third time.

3. i.e., groot: 1/40 of a guilder.

4. Endorsement is written in the hand of Matthias Nicolls.

21:63   [COPY OF THE COURT RECORD CONCERNING THE
         ADMINISTRATION OF WM. TOM'S AND WALTER
         WHARTON'S ESTATES][1]

                    Att a Court held In the Towne

of new Castle by his Mayesties
Authority this first of July
1679.

Present
Mr John Moll
Mr Peter Alrichs
Mr Fop Outhout   } Justices
Mr Joh. D Haes
Mr William Sempill

Johannes Dehaes and Ephraim Herman In Court Tendered
themselves to bee security for the Administration of Capt.
Cantwell upon the Estates of Mr. Tom and Mr. Wharton Decea[sed.]
a true Coppy out of the
Records Exam. per
[Signed:] Eph. Herman Cl.

[Notation:] for Capt. Cantwell. Mr. Johannes de Haes and
Mr. Ephraim Hermans were security before the Court at Newcastle
[   ] Capt. Cantwells [   ] Administracion [   ] Toms
and Mr. Whartons Estates. July [ ] 167[ ].[2]

1. See NCCR:345 for the original court record from which
    this copy was made.

2. This notation is written in the hand of Matthias Nicolls.

21:64a   [MATTHIAS NICOLLS TO CAPT. CANTWELL CONCERNING
          PHILIP POCOCK'S SURVEY NEAR THE FALLS][1]

Sir

        The Governor [   ] appointed Mr. Philip Pocock[2] to
[   ] lands of the purchase neare the [ ]lls for some
persons lately come [   ] with any obstrucions
or shall bee hindred by the Indyans, you are de[   ] upon
applicacion made by [   ] of them bee assisting to them with
your [   ] and to goe to the Indyans and admonish them of
their dutyes and the purchase sold by the [   ]
                    I am Sir
                       your humble [   ]
                    [Initialed:] M N
N. Y.
July 9, 1679.

[Endorsed:] [   ] 1679. Copies of a Letter to Capt.
             Cantwell about Mr. Pococks survey[ ]g of Land at
             Del. Falls.

1. This first draft of a letter to Capt. Cantwell is

written on the reverse leaf of a council minute.
Matthias Nicolls apparently used the blank side after
the minute was entered in the council book. See 20:79
and 20:80 for documents which relate to this tract of
land.

2. See NYCD 12:626 and PA 5:715 for Philip Pocock's
    warrant to survey this tract of land.

21:64b   [COUNCIL MINUTE CONCERNING THE CARGO FOR
          THE FRIGATE CASTLE][1]

                            At a Councell March the 30th 1675.

    The loading of the Castle Frigott being taken into Con-
sideracion [   ] to former Resolucion the[ ] upon.

    An Accout being de[   ] thereof, There was Report made
of [   ] planck to bee there on boar[ ] [   ].

    Standards and Knees 169 - as per the Boateswaines [Ac-
count] which by Computacion is 2077 foot.

    It was judged by Capt. Hyatt Master of the Castle that the
ship is capable of taking in about 1000 foot more, and that
to bee the Outride.

    Its farther judged by the Officer of the ship that 2600
foot of timber being taken in, the remaining 400 will bee best
to bee left for other drye goods, as Beaver hides Peltry etc.
which cannot bee taken in, if the whole Complement of 3000
[foot] of Timber should bee shipt.

    Capt. Burton [and] Capt. Hyatt suppose that 7 or 8000
Pipe Staves [may] bee taken in to fill up the voyde place,
which the Capt. and his Officer will undertake to provide.

    Whereupon [   ] ordered that present Care bee taken
[   ]nging on board, the remainder of the square [timb]er,
Leaving out 400 foot [ ] was propos[   ]

----

1. This document represents a first draft of a council
    minute written by Matthias Nicolls. He later entered
    this minute in the council book and cancelled the copy.
    Nicolls then used the reverse of this leaf to write a
    first draft of a letter to Capt. Cantwell (21:64a).
    Damaged portions have been recovered from Council
    Minutes 3:32.

21:65   [DUPLICATE COPY OF 21:68]

21:66   [COPY OF A COURT ORDER GRANTING A RESURVEY
          OF JOHN STEVENS' LAND]

                         [ ] A Speciall Court held f[   ]
                         Whorekill the 19th Day [   ]¹

                    Mr Helm. Wiltbanck
Com.   Mr. Edw. Southrin   Mr. Alex. Molestine [   ]
         Capt. Paull Marsh   Mr. John King [   ]

John Stevens petitioner.

     Granted unto John Stevens purchaser of the Land of Peter
Perry, William Willoughby and Robert Dicks that the persons
Lands soe purchased by the said John Stevens shall Bee Re-
surveyed according to pattents for the proper use of the said
John Stevens with an Addition of Six hundred acres thereunto
Adjoyning and the said Assignment by the Said Resurvey from the
Aforesaid persons unto the aforesaid John Stevens shall bee
Authentyque in Law.
                         Vera Copia
[Signed:] Test. Cornelis Verhoofe Cl. Cu. Whorekill

_____

     1. The date according to SCR:12 is March 19, 1676/7, not
         1679 as entered in O'Callaghan's Calendar. Only
         Alexander Molestine was still a justice in 1679.

21:67   [JOHN BRIGGS TO MATTHIAS NICOLLS CONCERNING JOHN
          RICHARDSON'S LAND AT THE WHOREKILL]¹

                         Whorekill July [ ] Anno 167[ ]

Honored Sir

        In the Relation of [   ] In the matters
of [   ] Att New Yorke [   ] one
John Richardson [   ] wherein many
Differances [   ] of Any Clayme pretended of any
[   ] John Stevens to the which Said [   ] Richardson
hath had the Courts [   ] In the Said [   ]
at the [   ] but [   ] which they [   ] where

[   ] John Richardsons [₂   ] as you may see
by the Inclosed order of [   ] Court² So the Said John Richardson being [   ] Very Responsible Estate and is Ready [   ]
Willingly to transport himselfe [   ] with his wife and
family and all his Esta[   ] Whereupon did promise to give
bond for Sum 100 lb. of money to the Court if was [   ]
for the true performance of Said transpo[   ] hee being
[   ] about the quantity [   ] 18 [   ] all will
[   ] here [   ] Esteem him very much [   ]
Incouragement by [   ] and [   ] Crave your
favor [   ] my matter [   ] Affaires will bee
thanck[   ] oblidged to Satisfie you for the Som [   ] and
allso [   ] John Shackerly In [   ] Should acquaint
you of the [   ] to Inlarge at present So I am
                          Your most Humble Servant
                        [Signed:] John Brigs

[Addressed:] To the [   ] Honorable Capt. Nicolls Secretary
              of New Yorke province.

              Capt. Crygier [   ]

[Endorsed:]   Mr. [   ] John Briggs from the Whorekill with
              two orders of Court there. July 13th 1679.
              patents.³

---

1. This letter is written in the hand of Cornelis Verhoofe.

2. See 21:68 for a copy of this court order.

3. Endorsement is written in the hand of Matthias Nicolls.

21:68   [PETITION OF JOHN RICHARDSON CONCERNING A LAND
         DISPUTE AND THE ORDER OF THE COURT THEREON]¹

                    At a Calld Court Held for the
                    Whorekill the 12th Day of July Anno
                    1679.

                   {Capt. John Avery}
         ⎧Mr. Francis Whitwell⎫   Mr. Luke Watson⎫
Com.   ⎨Mr. Alex. Molestine ⎬   Mr. John Roades ⎬   Present
         ⎩Mr. John Kipshaven ⎭   Mr. James Wells⎭

John Richardson petitioner.

     Whereas the petitioner hath made Appeale By the Evidence
of John Bridges thereunto Sworne and Mr Francis Whitwell Confirming the same that hee the said petitioner was by his
Tenant Thomas Crompton the first Setler In Building Clearing
and manuering the said land according by a Certificate [from
and in the hand of Thomas Philps Deceased the Deputy Surveyor

which Certificate][2] Bearing Date July the 18th 1676. The said
Tenant [   ] silently Departed by which one John Stevens or
his order haveing taken possession of the said house and Land
Which said Clayme and possession taken by the said John Stevens
Doth not as yet Appeare to the Court to be the said Stevens
his Just Right.

        Therefore the premises being Considered, [   ] the Court
to Grant the petitioner quiett and peaceable possession of said
House and Land notwithstanding the said petitioner to bee
Answerable to Any other Just Claymen title or Interest.
                        Vera Copia
[Signed:] Test. Cornelis Verhoofe Cl. Cu. Whorekill

[Verso:]
        These are In his majesties name to will and Requier you
upon Denyall of the premises of this within order to Levy by
Way of Execution the said premises within mentioned and Deliver
peaceable and quiett possession thereof unto John Richardson
the petitioner or his order according to Law and for so Doeing this shall bee [your] warrant for the same Given under my
hand the 14th Day of July Anno 1679.
To Mr John Vines Sherriffe
or the Deputy   (Was Signed)
Test. Cornelis Verhoofe Cler.   John Avery
                        Vera Copia
Test. Cornelis Verhoofe Cl. Cu. Whorekill

        These within and above mentioned premises being Executed
and Delivered according to the tenor thereof July 17th Anno
1679
                        (signed)
                per mee John Vines Sherriffe
                        Vera Copia
[Signed:] Test. Cornelis Verhoofe Cl. Cu. Whorekill.

----

1. This document is a duplicate copy of 21:65 which has
    been omitted. The order of the court appears only on
    the reverse leaf of 21:68. Other transcription in
    NYCD 12:626.

2. This phrase within brackets does not appear in 21:68
    and has been inserted here from 21:65.

21:69   [COURT ORDER CONCERNING THE LAND OF JOHN STEVENS
         AND A WARRANT FOR THE EXECUTION THEREOF][1]

July[2]   At a Calld Court Held for the
                                Whorekill the 25th Anno 1679

                Capt. John Avery

Com. {Mr. Alex Molestine }   Mr. John Roades } Present
      {Mr. Luke Watson   }   Mr. James Wells }

John Stevens petitioner

    Whereas at a Called Court Held for the Whorekill the 12th
Day of this Instant Last past[2] one John Richardson then Did
make Appeare that hee the said Richardson had Been the first
Setler by a tenant named Thomas Crompton upon a parsell of
Land now Appeares to Bee In Difference Between the said Richardson and John Stevens, The Court then Did order the said
Richarson Upon his Approvement peaceable and quiet possession
of the said howse and Land In Difference notwithstanding the
said Richardson to bee Answerable to any other Just Clayme
title or Interest which title the said petitioner now by patten
from the Honorable Governor producing this present Court Concerning the Land In Defference for the which the Court therefore hath Considereth the premises that the said John Stevens
Shall have the Enjoyment and peaceable possession of the said
Land and his howsing According to the tenor and premises the
said patten Doth mentioned notwithstanding Both or Either
party or parties may have further Redress Before the Honorable
Governor and Councell   Alias Execution
                        Vera Copia
[Signed:] Test. Cornelis Verhoofe Cler. Co. Whorekill

[Verso:] These are In his majesties name to will and Requier
you to Levey the premises within mentioned by writ of Execution
and Deliver Enjoyment and peaceable possession according to
Law unto John Stevens or his order and for Soe Doeing this
shall bee your warrant for the same Given under my hand the
Day and yeare within written.

To Mr. John Vines Sherriffe   (Was Signed By)
or his Deputy.   Luke Watson and
                                 Alex: Molestine
                        Vera Copia
[Signed:] Test. Cornelis Verhoofe Cl. Co. Whorekill

    The premises within and above mentioned have Demanded
from the hireling and on John Glover being there In the howse
upon the Land as Keeping possession for John Richardson Behalf which Answered and Replyed they had one order of Court
with which they were possest and by that said order they would
keep possession which Rapport Given unto Capt. John Avery and
Mr. Alex: Molestine Justices of the peace.   (Was Signed)
August 21st Ao. 1679   Per mee John Vines Sherrif[ ]
                        Vera Copia
[Signed:] Test. Cornelis Verhoofe Cl. Co. Whorekill

---

1. Other transcription of court order in NYCD 12:627.

2. The month was written in by a second hand.

3. See 21:68.

21:70   The Answer of John Richardson Defendant to the
         Bill of Complaint of John Stevens Appeallant.

The Said Deft. by Protestacion not Acknowledgeing or Con-
fessing the matters in the said bill of Complaint Contained to
be true in Such manner and forme as in the Same they are Sett
forth, and Alleadged, Sayth that the said bill of Complaint is
very untrue, uncertaine, and Insufficient in the Law to be
Answered and the matters therein surmised Enviousely Devised
and unconscionably Contrived Imagined and Sett forth only on
purpose to vex and molest this Defendant and to putt him to
greate Travill Expences and Charges of Suite without any Just
Cause or Good matter as this Deft. hopes to prove to this honnorable Court Nevertheless the Advantage of Exception to the
Insufficency and uncertainty of said Complaint and all other
Advantages to this Defendant at all times here after saved The
said Deft. for Answer sayth That True it is That on or about
the 18th of July 1676 this Deft. being then an Inhabitant in
Maryland and Desireous to Remove himselfe and family and to
setle on the West Side of Dellaware bay Applyed himselfe to
Mr. Thomas Phillips Deputy Surveyor (who as this Deft. was In-
formed had power to Survey and Lay out Tracts of Land for Im-
provement in those partes) for a Convenient Accommodacion and
Settlement suitable to his family and servants who Accordingly
Layed out and Surveyed to this Deft. a Certaine Tract of Land
Called Willingbrook on the West Syde of Delaware bay and on the
North Side of a branch of a Creeke of the said Bay Called Duck
Creeke Bounded as by the Certificate[1] under the hand of the
said Thomas Phillips may Appeare and Containeing about 2000
Acres by vertue of which Survey this Deft. became Possessed of
the said Tract of Land and Immediately proceeded to make Improvement thereon by building a good and Substantiall house and
on or aboute the 18th of August following Did make a Contract
and Agreement with one Thomas Crompton[2] for some time to Live
thereon and to Improve the same by Cleareing of Land Rayseing
of Stock Planting An orchard Fenceing and all other Improvements of husbandry untill this Deft. Could wholy remove himselfe and family which was accordingly followed and the said
Thomas Crumpton by Right of this Deft. putt in possession of
the premisses as this Defts. Tennant and his said Tennant there
Remained Quietly Peace[   ] and undisturbed for the space of
About 3 Yeares. And on or about the 20th of September following
the Deft. with Leave from the Authority made Purch[   ] Indian
Right from one Petocoqui[3] Commonly C[   ] (Christian) for
which he gave full Sattisfaccion [   ] as by the Deed of Sale
which was Likewise Acknowledged by the said Indian in Open
Court at the Whorekill in December 1679 and Proved by the
Wittnesses thereto may appeare and the Deft. being Soe possesed
as aforesaid in or aboute the month of June 1679 the Compll.
who Never before made any Clayme or pretence by violence and
force of Armes Came upon the said Land and the said Thomas
Crompton his wife and family turned out of Doores to the
greate hazard of their Lives and Kept Possession thereof

forceably whereupon this Defendant Peticioned the Court held
at the Whorekill the 12th of July 1679[4] for Recovery of his
Possession who ordered that the Deft. Appeareing to be the
first Settler to have Quiett and Peaceable Possession of the
said house and Land and the 14th following Execucion issued
out thereon[5] to putt the Deft. in Possession wa[ ] Executed
accordingly and he againe Repossed [   ] withstanding the which
the said Compll. procured a Sarv[   ] [   ] made to him of
1400 Acres of this Deft. [   ] and privately makeing Returne
thereof ha[ ] obteyned a Pattent from your honnor which Includes [   ] on Passing of which the Deft. Beeleives his Right
to [   ] as aforesaid was unknowne to your honor and by [   ]
meanes thinking to take advantage of the Deft. [   ] Labour and
Charge the 25th of July 1679 Peticioned the Cou[ ] at the
Hourekill where produceing said Pattent Possession was Ordered
to be Given to the said Stevens[6] accordingly bu[ ] The Deft.
haveing before that seated the said house and Land Againe to
one John Glovier hee Refused to give possession thereof to the
Compll. and kept the same untill by force or surprise the said
Appell. againe Gott the Possession whereupon the 12th of Febuary
1679/80 An Accion of Trespass and Ejectment[7] was brought in the
name of the said John Glovier (as Casuall Ejector) against the
said John Stevens for Recovery of the Possession of the said
house and Land but the said Accion was exsecuted in the Name
of the Deft. whereupon a full and faire Tryall before a Jury
the Deft. obteyned a Verdict that by Evidence the Deft. being
the first Settler hath Right to what he hath seated and the
Court passed Judgment accordingly and the Deft. became againe
Repossesed[8] and Soe Remaines but for the further trouble and
Vexacion of the Deft. the said Complaintant hath Appealed to
this honnourable Court from Said Judgment where this Deft. is
well pleased his Case shoudl be heard and Determined in a
Course of Equity before your honnor and this honnorable Court
where he doubts Not to Prove the truth of the above and his
Right to said Land etc. as aforesaid and hopes if he hath beene
any wayes Negligent in not obteyneing a Pattent for the same
(which his far distance of habitacion or Ignorance hath Occas-
sioned) In Equity his Laboure and Charge of Improvement which
some times alone gives a Right and propertey (there beeing
Roome and Vacancy Enough) will not be swallowed by the Co-
vetious Desires of the Appeall. who is Possesed of a Large
Tract of Land (In Quantity 1300 Acres) and hath onely hyred out
a Coople of Servants to another man to manure the said Tract of
Land which Keepeth other familys of that would settle in those
partes, which if hee hath The Defts. Land allsoe which hee
Layeth Clayme [   ] to and Calleth his by the Report of the
Neighbourehood, It is (in Circ[   ]teiance Neare 20 Miles in
those partes) And that your honnour will see Noe Cause to
allter but to Confirme the Verdict and Judgment of the Court
at the Whorekill and this Deft. in his Quiet Possession and
Allow him his Cost and Dammage by the Needless Occassion of the
Compll. soe unjustley Susteyned which Amounts to Aboute the
Sume of one hundred Pounds Sterling

        And This Deft. Shal Ever Pray etc.

[Entitled:] John Richardson Deft. Answere to the Complaint
        of John Stevens Complaintant.

---

1. See 21:88 for a copy of this certificate.

2. See 21:74 for this contract.

3. See 21:89 for this deed of sale.

4. See 21:68 for this petition.

5. See 21:68 for this court order.

6. See 21:69 for this court order.

7. See 21:88 for this order of ejectment.

8. See 21:88 for the verdict of the jury.

21:71   The Case of Tymen Stiddem declaring his right
         to 600 acres of Land lyeing on the Northside
         of the Fish Creeke alias Brandewyns Creeke,
         Just below the Falls of the said Creeke.

That about 18 yeares since Moens Andriessen and Walrawen
Jansen obtained a grant and permission from the then Commander
William Beeckman to take up the above said Land, in which Land
Moens Andriessen had two parts and Walrawen Jansen, one parte,
and they planted it foure yeares And then the said Moens
Andriessen sold his house and lott togather with his shares of
this Land to the said Tymen Stiddem, and Walrawn Jansen sold
his one share unto Jacob Vander Veer. per ut. Depos. of Walraeven Jansen, and Moens Andriessen No. 1.2.

That since the said Jacob Vander Veer sould his house and
lott att Cristina to said Tymen Stiddem, togather with this
same land soe that the said Land was baught by and belongs to
the said Tymen Stiddem, per ut. Walraevens Depos. No. 1 and a
note under Jacob Vander Veers hand No. 3.

That for the space of fourteen yeares last past the said
Land hath been accompted to belong to Tymen Stiddem and that
it is Called by his name and Walraevens, which is of Late taken
in by Jacob Vander Veere, in his resurveigh of his Island, and
that 15 yeares past there was Corne sowed on the said Land.
Vide Depos. No. 4.

To prove the title of Moens Andrissen and Walraeven Jansen Vide Depos. No. 5.

That the 18th Jannuary 1678/9 The said Tymen payed 4
yeares Quitt Rents for the said Land. per ut. receipt of
Eph. Harman.[1] No. 6.

That Jacob Vander Veer By his Resurvey of his Island In-
cluding the said Land, Caussed the said Tymen to make his
Addresse to the Court att New Castle[2], declareing his right att
Large as by his Complaint No. 7.

That the said Court the 5th of March 1677/8 did Order
that the Land which said Tymen has baught of Walraeven Jansen
and Moens Andriessen, he may Cause to be surveyed and Ot-
taine a Pattent for the Same. Vide Order of Court No. 8.[3]

The said Tymen Stiddem's right being as aforesaid he
humbly prayes the Same may be Confirmed to him by Pattent from
the Honorable Governor which may free him from further Trouble
or Molestacion.

[Entitled:] The Case of Tymen Stiddem.

---

1. i.e., Ephraim Herman who was receiver of quit-rents in
   Delaware.

2. See NCCR:291 for Stiddem's complaint.

3. See NCCR:182 for this court order.

21:72   [AN ABSTRACT OF THE PAPERS RELATING TO THE LAND
         DISPUTE BETWEEN TYMEN STIDDEM AND JACOB VAN DER
         VEER][1]

1. A dep.[2] of Walraven Jansen. That Mr. Beeckman as Commander at Del. granted to Mons Andriesen and him 300 margen
   of land at the Fish Creeke, neare Christina, of which Moens
   Andries had 2 parts which hee sold Timen Stidden, and
   Walraven - 1 part which hee sold Jacob Vander Veere Feb.
   25 1678/9.

2. A dep. of Moens Adriesen, relating to the sale of the
   whole to Mr. Timen Andries[3] Jan. 25 1677/8.

3. A bill of sale of Jacob Vander Veers right to Timen Stidden under both their hands. Its writte upon ill paper
   that sinks[4] so not well to bee read. 1667 on the backside.

4. Hans Peterson and Justa Poulsen dep. to prove the land to
   bee Mr. Timens. Feb. 24 1678/9.

5. Matthias Matthiassen de Vos. dep: that hee was at first
   joyned with Moens Andriesen and Walraven in this land it
   being granted to him with them by the dutch Commander Mr.
   Beeckman, but that afterward changing his mind hee left
   them and hath severall times heard that Dr. Timen Stedden
   was lawfully possest of the whole. July 23 1679.[5]

6. Mr. Ephr. Harmans receit of 4 bushells of wheat Quitt Rent
   of Mr. Timen Jan 18 1678/9.

7. The last declaracion put into Court by Tymen Stidden, relating the whole Case, This was depending when the order

came to stop proceedings The Consideracion said to bee
given by Mr. TYmen to Jacob Vander Veer, for his house and
Lott at Christina was 200f and for an Oxe hee sold his
right to the land hee bought of Mr. Walraven, which the
said Jacob Vander Veere since claymes by Vertue of a
Resurvey by Mr. Wharton by an Order from C. Cantwell.

8. The former order of Court in March 1677/8 wherein Jacob
   Van der Veer is cast.[6]

1. Jacob Vander Veers patent from Go. Lovelace for an Isl. and
   a piece of land neare it March 24 1668/9 by vertue whereof hee claymes this land, denyes ever to haye sold to
   Tymen Stidden what hee bought of Walraeven.[7]

2. A draught of the Isl. and land adjacent, by Mr. Wharton
   resurvey'd according to h[ ] patent Apr. 7th 1676

3. A paper signed by 5 persons of the pertenesse [   ] Jac.
   Van der Veeres land that if Mr. Timen have this hee will
   bee undone, a rough sort of draught Sept. 15 1679.

4. Walravens transport to Jacob Van der Veer. Timen Stiddem
   is a wittnesse.

[Entitled:]   The substance of Dr. Tymens and Jacob Van der
              Veeres papers which were delivered them back.

---

1. This document is written in the hand of Matthias Nicolls.
   See NCCR:324 for his letter to the New Castle court
   requesting all papers in this matter.

2. i.e., deposition.

3. A mistake by M. Nicolls for Tymen Stiddem. cf., 21:71
   for a reference to this sale of land.

4. i.e., "deteriorates."

5. See 21:93 or 21:94 for this deposition.

6. See NCCR:182 for this court order.

7. See DYR:156 for the confirmation of this patent.

21:73   [AGREEMENT BETWEEN JOHN STEVENS AND THOMAS
        CROMPTON WITH AFFIDAVITS RELATING THERETO]

      Artukells of Agrement Maid Betwext Johne Stevens of one
partje and Thomas Crumptone of the other partje

Wittnesth   That Wheras Johne Stevens doe Allenet[1] Lett and
              mak over [   ] Crumptone one percell of Land
              Laying one the West Sed of delo[   ] near Duck
              Craek for the Terme of Sevne yeirs and the said
              [   ] is to be at the Charges of Bulding only
              the said Thomas [   ] to gett Tember For what
              houssing is Bult upone the said [   ] Johne Stevens
              is to Bueld or Caus to be Bult one foftje foott
              hou[   ] yeir and the said Johne is to Lett the said
              Thamas have one Cows m[   ] [   ]eir and what
              servants the said Johne doe putt upone th[   ]
              [   ] that is planted upone the plan-
              t[   ] Cattell or hoggs is put in by Bothe part-
              ies is for the use [   ] and non to be dis-
              possed of without Bothe parties consent[   ]tjone
              of the tyme that the stock be equaly deveidid Be-
              tw[   ] Likweis the said Thomas dothe in-
              gag himselfe to doe his Best In[   ] Chorring
              and Bulding upone the plantatjone and all other
              Thengs [   ] for the use of the plantatjone
              as suffegent fencing and [   ] thenks usefull For
              the plantatjone and Likweis to make a suffeg[   ]
              Trinnell Fence[2] to secure what appeltreis is to be
              plantid and in cais [   ] mortalatje of the said
              Thomas then if the Weeff of the said Thoma[ ] a
              suffecjent man to Manneig the Crapt or Crapts[3]
              then shee [   ] Injoy her housband Labour accord-
              ing to the Agement [sic] abov[   ] mentjned
              and Likweis to the Leve Suffecjent fencing at thee
              experatjone of the tyme to this Agement Bothe
              p[   ] have Interchanble sett ther hands and
              sails this

Febb. 1676/7   [Signed:] John Steevens
Signed and Sailled in
the presant of Wts.[4]
[Signed:] James Veitch   Thomas TC Crumpton
           Christophe E Ellett   his mark
                   his mark

                        Entratt In Records
                        July 29th Anno 1679
              [Signed:] Test. Cornelis Verhoofe Cl.
                         Cu. Whorekill

[Verso:] [   ]tefar Ellet aged [   ] swears that he saw
the conditions signed, sealed and delivered by Tames Cromton
[   ] Steevens for his indenture. [   ] by mee the
[   ] September anno 1679[5]
                Cris E far   [Signed:] Geret Otto
                Ellet

[   ] Davids aged about 28 yeares [   ] Date
being about March List In the prese[   ] Stevens and
Thomas Crompton were the [   ] Thomas Crompton Did owne these
within [   ] unto the said John Stevens. [   ] the said
Evan Davids Declareth tha the [   ] Crompton had the use of
the said John Stevens [   ] Hoggs and one man servant untill hee [   ] Allsoe heard the said Crompton saye [   ]
[   ] Richardson never did Give him possession of [   ]
and your Deponant did upon th[ ] account of [   ] Stevens
helped the said Crompton to [   ] house upon the Land.
[Signed:] Evan Davids [   ]fore us Sept. 29th Anno 1679
[Signed:] John Avery
           Luke Watson

1. i.e., alienate.

2. i.e., a trunnel or trennel fence: a type of plank fence
    which is fastened together with treenails.

3. i.e., crop or crops.

4. An abbreviation for "witnesses."

5. This deposition was written in Dutch by Gerrit Otto.

21:74   [DUPLICATE COPY OF 21:88/89]

21:75   [WARRANT TO THE COURTS IN DELAWARE FOR THE
         ARREST AND EXTRADITION OF RICHARD TURNER]

                                    New Yorke the 9th of August 1679

Gentlemen

        Though I hope itt hath been your practice, this is upon
the Applicacion of the high Sheriffe of Accamack[1], Capt.
Jennefer, to desire you that upon his [o]r any authorized from
him demand you give present [or]der for the apprehending
Richard Turner a Sawyer [   ] being sentenced by the Court of
that County [   ]cution for debt brook prison and fleed
[   ] your parts, and that you assist any such person sent
after him, to Convay him safely back to Accamack with Care if
not so practised you are to observe in all the like cases for
the future being Certified thereof and persuit authorized by
the Cheife magistrates of the respective places, being in
haste occations onely this private intimation which I thinke is
According to Law and ought to be observed among the Kings subjects and will bee sufficient to you from
                            your affetionate friend
                              [   ] A[   ]

[Addressed:] [   ] magistrates of the [   ] Kill New-
              castle or [   ]land Courts in Delaware [ ]y
              and River.

---

1. Accomack, Virginia.

21:76   [MATTHIAS NICOLLS TO JOHN AVERY CONCERNING
         CAPT. NATHANIEL WALKER'S PATENT]¹

                                New Yorke August 23rd 1679
Capt. John Avery

        Sir Capt, Nathaniel Walker having the Last yeare, pro-
duced a Survey² under the hand of Cornelys Verhoofe of a parcell of Land Layd out for him at the Whorekill, called Cedar
neck, containing six hundred and Eighty acres, the which was
afterward certifyed by your Court, upon my writing to them
from the Governour about it³: And the said Capt. Walker having
the Governours Grant of a patent⁴ for the same, hath for the
present respited it, upon his desire that there may bee in-
certed in the said patent, besides the number of Acres aforemencioned, a certaine swamp Lyeing in the meddle of Cedar neck,
together with the sand Hills and pines by the sea side, with
the slashes, marshes, or broaken land, betweene the said neck
and the sea, and Rehobay bay, and the Indyan Inlett to the
southward all which the Governour is willing to comply with him
in, provided it will bee no prejudice to any towneship or persons seated thereby and before his voyage to the Eastward,
which hee began this day fortnight, had hee not beene very full
of business had writte to you about it [   ] bu[ ] being so prevented, ordered mee to doe it, so that my Request to
you is that you will propose it to the Court and if it will bee
no prejudice as before, that you will with the first opportun-
itie returne mee your Result, that Capt. Walker may no longer
bee delayed, about his patent, who when hee comes to settle
amongst you, will I doubt not, prove a good Neighbour and Inhabitant, I have not f[   ] on this occasion, so Subscribe
                          Sir
                          your friend and Servant
                       [Signed:] Matthias Nicolls

[Endorsed:]   [   ] Capt. Avery at the Whorekills on
               behalfe of C. Walker Aug 23rd 1679 with other
               papers [   ]cerning his bus[   ]

---

1. Other transcription in NYCD 12:631.

2. See 20:117 for this survey.

3. See 21:16 for this letter.

4. See 21:37 for this patent.

21:77   [CAPT. CANTWELL TO JOHN STEVENS CONCERNING THE
         LATTER'S LAND DISPUTE WITH JOHN RICHARDSON][1]

Sept. the 10 Day 1679:

Mr. Stevens Sir

      I Received yours of the 27 Last past wherein you Desiar to
Know wheather I gave power to Thomas Phillips to grant warrants
for Land I never gave any such power to him or any body else
nor Did I give John Richards a warrant for no more then three
hondered acres which I sent by you from the Whore Kill when
you Came there to me nor did I ever see the Said Richards to
the best of my Knowledge but once at John Edmondson house in
Chaptanke who then asked me if I would Confirme a Certificatt
he had of Thomas Phillips for twelve hondered or two thousand
acres of Land I asked him his name he answered John Richards or
Richardson I made answer that I gave Thomas Phillips no such
order he made answer that I need not fear my pay and prefered
me payment for the Survay in John Edmondson: hand which I would
not exept of and Tould him I Demanded no payment of him nor
would I Confirme the Certificatt where upon John Edmondson
Tould the Said Richards that he would not pay: him without I
would Confirm the Certificatt I Demanded what that was Edmondson tould him that he had bought the Said Land of the Richards
for thirteen thousand pounds of Tobbacco: or there abouts I
made answer that was none of his honor the governors orders for
he would not allow of any Sale of Land before a Settlement So
I parted with him without any further talke onely that the Said
Richards Sead if that I would not Confirme the Certificatt that
he would go to his honor the governor [up]on which I answered
he: might Do his pleasure Sume tyme after I mett with Thomas
Phillips and I asked him whey he had Laid out Such a Quantity
of Land for John Richards his answer was that he had forced him
to Do it and Treatned him if that he would not Do itt he would
beat him Thomas Phillips never made any Returne to me of the
Same or if he had I would not have Exepted of the Same Knowing
itt was Contrary to his honor the Governors order this was
when I was Last in Chaptanke and I never hard any thing of
sence untill Thomas Crompton Come to me the 7 Day of July 1677:
who tould me he Lived upon John Stevens Land and Exept I would
furn[ish] him with Sume Corne he Should be forced to Disart
your Land where upon I let him have three bushell of Rye which
he Sead w[as] anof untill now Corne would be Ryp[e] as for any
power Thomas Phillips [had] of me I have here with Sent you a
Copy this being all att present from
                            Sir your Loveing friend
                      [Signed:] Ed. Cantwell

[Addressed:] To Mr. John Stevens or in his absence to Mr. Peter

Bayard to Be: Delivered as above att new yorke
These

---

1. Other transcription in NYCD 12:631.

21:78   [CAPT. CANTWELL TO GOV. ANDROS ABOUT LAND
        NEAR THE FALLS][1]

Right honnorable

        Sir   In pursute of your honnors order[2] am Come up here
in Company of Mr. Alrichts and Mr. Israel Helm, and sumoned the
Indiens together and told them your honnors order Concerning the
laying out of the land In order of the setting out of land.
There answer was they did not hinder the Same So farre as the
Indiens had sold which they have marked and that is from the
begining of the falls downe to the lower end of Orechton Island
and noe further. Whereupon wee made answer and Showed them the
deed of sale which was made to your honnor. Neverthelesse
they denied the laying out of the land, or to Suffer to Setted
without purchassing of the Same for they are the right owners,
and never have had the Vallew of a pipe. Matapis standes with
them, and Ockenickan, who are the Chiefe owners of the Land.
The said Ockenickan saying that none wil nor shal Come Upon the
land without Satisfaction.

        Likewise wee have treated according to your honnors order
about the land not yet purchased. They would give Us noe
answer till they considered of it being a busines of Con-
sequance, being here taken Verie Ill, I Cannot expresse my
selfe as wont onley remaining
                        Right honnorable your honnors Most
                        humble and obeidiant Servant
                            [Signed:] Ed Cantwell
[Bu]rlinton the 18th Sept. 1679

[Addressed:] To the Right honnorable [   ] Andross Knight
              Governor [ ]neral of all his Royall [   ]
              in America
                    at New Y.

[Endorsed:] Capt. Cantwell from Burlington in Delaware to the
             Go. Sept. 18th 1679.[3]

---

1. Other transcription in NYCD 12:632.

2. See 21:64a for this order.

3. Endorsement is written in the hand of Matthias Nicolls.

21:79   [CAPT. JOHN AVERY TO MATTHIAS NICOLLS CONCERNING
          CAPT. NATHANIEL WALKER'S LAND AT CEDAR NECK]

                         Whorekill the 28th of September 1679.

Sir

        Yours from the 23rd of August[1] have Received concerning
Capt. Nath: Walker his Land Called Cedar Neck the which have
Accordingly pased to the Court Concerning the premises therein
mentioned which the Court hath Examined and Conclude that...

[The remainder of the text has suffered water damage   ]

                              Your most Humble Servant
                         [Signed:] John Avery

[Addressed:]   To the [   ] Honorable Capt. Matthias Nicolls
               Secr. of New Yorke province. These.

_____

    1. See 21:76 for this letter.

21:80   [NO CALENDAR ENTRY AND NO DOCUMENT]

21:81   [AFFIDAVIT OF THOMAS GARVASS CONCERNING THOMAS
          CROMPTON'S TRANSFER OF LAND TO JOHN STEVENS]

        Thomas Garvass Aged 29 yeares Declareth that sum time in
the summer last past at Thomas Cromptons Departure out of this
place hee the said Crompton Delivered possession of the Land
hee had Dwelt and now Left unto John Stevens man named Theo-
philes for the Use of the said John Stevens And further Sayeth
not.

Sworne Before Us   Thamas ⊤ Garvass
Sept. 29th Anno 1679   his / marke
[Signed:] John Avery
           Luke Wattson

21:82   [MATTHIAS NICOLLS TO CAPT. CANTWELL ABOUT LAND
        NEAR THE FALLS]1

New Yorke Oct. 10th 1679

Capt. Cantwell

        Sir   Yours of the 18th Sept.[2] from Burlington the Gover-
nor received wherein you acquaint him with your comming thither
in company of Mr. Alricks and Mr. Izrael Helme and summoning
the Indyans when you told them to his honnors order for [
    ] and settling the land there about the [   ] Falls they
pretend not to hinder the land [   ] was sold, which they
[   ] further the Orichtons Island [   ]
deed of sale made to the Go: and denyed and laying out and
suffering any other land to bee layd out till purchased from
the right Owners who you name to bee Matapis, and Ockenickan
as cheifes.

        You also mention your treating according to order about
the land not yet purchased to the which you say they will give
no answer till they have consider'd of it as being a buisnesse
of Consequence, so breake off being indisposed as to your
health.

        The Go. having beene but litle time he[re since h]is re-
turne from Pemmaquid, where hee had be[ene] or was absent from
here seven weeks; (The Intervall being the Assizes, and the
day after goeing early for Albany,) Hee ordered mee to returne you this answer to your letter that hee is much unsat-
isfy'd as to the Indyans bogling about that purchase and yours
and others Informacions of all the right Owners of the land on
which hee depended, Hee doth therefore positively order you,
(if not prevented by sicknesse) if possible to attend him [   ]
his returne from Albany, which [   ] doubt will bee sometime [   ] also that you give notice [   ]
Sachems that stand in opposicion together with one of them
that sold the land to bee here at that time likewise, that
there may bee a right understanding of the matter, and a prevention of future Contests thereupon. So much I had in charge
to signify to you, being

                        Your friend and servant

[Endorsed:] Copie of what [   ] C. Cantwell, [   ] sent
             by M[   ] Oct. 13 167[9].

----

1. Other transcription in NYCD 12:633.

2. See 21:78 for this letter.

21:83   The Names of the Magistrates in the severall
        Courts at Delaware on the west side.[1]

At Newcastle

Last Commission
Oct. 1678

- Mr. John Moll
- Mr. Peter Alricks
- Mr. Foppe Outhout
- Mr. Gerritt Otto
- Mr. Johannes de Haes
- Mr. William Semple
- Mr. Abraham Man

At Upland

Last Commission
Sept. 1676

- Mr. Peter Cock
- Mr. Peter Rambo
- Mr. Izrael Helme
- Mr. Otto Ernest Cock
- Mr. Lasse Andries
- Mr. Olle Swansen

At the Whorekill

Last Commission
Oct. 1678

Capt. John Avery
- Mr. Francis Whittwell
- Mr. Alexander Molestein
- Mr. John Kippshaven
- Mr. Luke Wattson
- Mr. John Roades
- Mr. James Wells

At the upper Plantacions on the
Westside of New Jersey

Commission being
the first dated
August 1677

- Mr. Tho: Olave
- Mr. Daniel Willes
- Mr. John Kensey
- Mr. John Pinford
- Mr. Jos: Helmesly
- Mr. Robt. Stacy
- Mr. Ben: Scott
- Mr. Richard Guy

At the lower plantacion on the
westside of New Jersey: Salem

Commission being
the 2nd dated
Oct. 26 1679.

- Mr. James Nevill
- Mr. William Penton
- Mr. Richard Guy
- Mr. Edward Broadway
- Mr. Edward Ward
- Mr. Richard Hancock

[Entitled:]   Magistrates at Delaware

---

1. This document is written in the hand of Matthias Nicolls.
   cf., 21:109. Other transcription in NYCD 12:634.

21:84   [COURT ORDER CONFIRMING A PATENT GRANTED TO
         WALTER DICKINSON][1]

                          At a Calld Court Held for the
                          Whore Kill the 30th Day of October
                          Anno 1679.

                         {Capt. John Avery}
Com.   {Mr. Alex. Molestine}   Mr. John Roades}   Present
        {Mr. John Kipshaven }   Mr. James Wells}

Walter Dickenson petitioner.

        Whereas the petitioner producing a patten[2] From the Honor-
able Governor of a Certaine tr[act] of Land scituated at St.
Jones Therefore the [Courtt] Grant and Confirme the previledges
Apportin[ances] premises bounds and Limitts the said patten
Do[th] Express to Injoy peaceable for and unto the petit[ioner]
Alias Execution
                            Vera Copia
[Signed:]   Test. Cornelis Verhoofe Cl. Cu. Whore Kill

[Endorsed:]   An Order of Court at the Whorekill. Walter
              Dickinson concernd. Oct. 30th 1679[3]

_____

1. Other transcription in NYCD 12:635.

2. See DYR:184 for this patent.

3. Endorsement is written in the hand of Matthias Nicolls.

21:85   [MEMORANDUM BY MATTHIAS NICOLLS ON EPHRAIM
         HERMAN'S REQUEST FOR LAND][1]

                      November 4th 1679.

        Mr. Ephraim Hermans this day upon his departure, desired
mee to give to the Governor the following Memo. vizt.

        That Mr. Izrael Helme had a Grant under the Governors hand
for 200 acres of Land, just below Chiepiessing which is neare
the Falls, but its now layd out to some of the Quakers, by Mr.
Pocock.

        Mr. Ephraim Hermans desires a piece of Land towards the
Falls of about 200, or 300 acres, which if granted, hee'd take
Care for its present settlement.

        Olle Swansen, (one of the Magistrates up the River) being
an old Inhabitant, having divers Children and but little Land,
desires the Quantity of about 200 acres, there about also.

Lausa Cock the like.

[Entitled:]   Mr. Ephraim Hermans Memo. for land att Delaworr.

[Notation:]   Lasse Cock to come up about indions refusing to
goe of land purchased.

---

1. Other transcription in NYCD 12:636.

21:86   [COPY OF 21:85]

21:87   [MEMORANDUM OF ITEMS SENT TO DELAWARE][1]

[Th]o. Jacobsen, Olle Paulsen and Arent Johnson
a patent[2] 248 acres in the River by Christina....... 2 beavers

Paulus[3] and Amilius de Ring a patent for a
double Lott in Newcastle........................... 2 beavers

Maurice Daniel a patent for 190 acres............. 2 beavers

Bryan Omalle a patent for 400 acres.............. 2 beavers

Mr. John Moll a patent for 3 Lotts in towne........ 2 beavers

Do. Petrus Teschenmaecker [   ] a new Lott
in the Towne...................................... 1 beaver

[Hendrick][4] Vanderburgh a patent for a Lott [   ]. 1 beaver
                                                          12 beavers
                                                           6:12:0

Do. Teschenmaecker more for
the Commission under the [   ]   1: 8:0
for his ordinacion and [   ]
                                                           8: 0:0
Mr. Moll more 2 beavers   1: 5:0
                                                           9: 5:0

C. Cantwells Lettres of Administrations
2:13:4   2:13:4
                                                          11:18:4
The Law book   3: 0:0
                                                          14:18:4

[Endorsed:]   Things [   ] Delaware [   ] Hutchenson
              [   ] Dec. the [   ] 167[ ]

---

1. This account is written in the hand of Matthias Nicolls.
   Partly transcribed in NYCD 12:636.

2. All of the patents in this account appear in DYR:185-
   187.

3. The patent in DYR:186 records Matthias instead of
   Paulus.

4. Recovered from DYR:186.

21:88/89   [COPIES OF COURT PROCEEDINGS RELATING TO THE SUIT
            BETWEEN JOHN STEVENS AND JOHN RICHARDSON][1]

Whorekill

     Copie: John Stevesn was Atteached to Answer John Glovear
In a plea of trespass and Ejectment wherefore the Said John
Stevens the Six and twentieth Day of January Anno 1679 Last
past the plantation of the Said John Glovear Scituate and be-
ing on the West side of Delaware bay Called Willing brooke on
the northside of a Branch of a creeke of the Said bay Called
Duck Creeke Beginning at a Bounded poplar by the Branch Running
Up the Branch Southwest three hundred perches to the Land of
William Stevens to a bounded white oake neare the head of the
Branch then SouthEast paralell with the Land of the Said
William Stevens one hundred and fifty perches to a Bounded
white oake by a Swampe and by a Line Southwest one hundred and
Sixty perches to a Bounded poplar on a Knowle in the Woods and
by a Line South East three hundred and Eighty perches and by
a Line Drawne Southwest one hundred and Sixty perches to a
bounded oake and by a Line Drawne northEast Six hundred and
twenty perches to a Bounded Oake and by a Line South East
three hundred and seaventy perches to the first bounded poplar
Conteining two thousand acres of Land with force and Armes Did
Entre and him the Said John Glovear from his farme and terme
there of Doth Eject Expell and amove and other Injuries to him
Did against the peace of our Soveraigne Lord the Kinge and to
the Damage of the Said John Glovear one hundred pounds Sterling.
                    pledges ad. prosequend.[2] ⎱ John Doe
                                              ⎰ Rich: Roe

     And the Said John Glovear by Griffith Jones his Attorney
Comes and Complaines that whereas the Said Griffeth Jones as
Attorney to John Richardson of Dorchestor County in the pro-
vice of Maryland planter by his Certaine Lease in Writting
Sealed with his Seale as his act and Deed Delivered in behalfe

of his Said Attorney and here in Court produced bearing Date
the Six and twentieth day of January Last past Did Demise Grant
Sett and to farme Lett unto the said John Glovear all that
plantation on the West Side of Delaware bay Called welling
brooke on the north Side of a Branch of a Creeke of the Said
bay Called Duck Creeke Beginning at a Bounded poplar by the
Branch Running Up the Branch Southwest three hundred perches
to the Lands of William Stevens to a bounded white oake neare
the head of the branch then South East paralell with the Land
of The Said William Stevens one hundred and fifty perches to a
Bounded white oake by a Swampe and by a Line Southwest one
hundred and Sixty perches to a Bounded poplar on a Knowle in
the Woods and by a Line SouthEast three hundred and Eighty
perches and by a Line Drawne Southwest one hundred and Sixty
perches to a bounded oake and by a Line Drawne northwest nine
hundred perches then by a Line Drawne northEast Six hundred
and twenty perches to a bounded oake and by a Line SouthEast
three hundred and Seaventy perches to the first bounded poplar
Conteining two thousand acres of Land, the Said Demised premises with the Apportunances Unto the Said John Glovear ·and
his Assignes from the twentieth Day of January then Last past
before The Date thereof Untill the End and terme and Duering
the full End and terme of five Yeares from thence next In-
sueing fully to bee Complait and Ended by Vertue of Which
Said Demise the Said John Glovear the Day and yeare first above
mencioned Into the premisses aforesaid with the apportunances
Entred and was thereof possessed untill the Said Defendant
Samuell Styles afterwards to witt the Said Day and year first
mencioned into the premisses afore said in the peaceable and
quiet possession of the Said John Glovear being with force and
Armes etc. Did Enter and him the Said John Glovear from his
farme aforesaid and terme aforesaid thereof not yett Ended did
Eject Expell and amove and Still Doth with hold and other
harmes to the Said John Glovear then and there Did against the
peace of our Soveraigne Lord the King and to the Damage of the
Said John Glovear one hundred pounds Sterling And there Upon
hee bring this Suite etc.   Jones proquer.[3]
                    [Signed:] Test: Cornelis Verhoofe: Cler.

At a Court Held for the Whorekill the 10 · 11 · and 12 · Dayes
of february Anno 1679/80

                    (Capt. John Avery)
         (Mr. Fran: Whitwell)   Mr. Luke Wattson)
Com.   {Mr. Alex. Molestine}   Mr. John Roades } present
         (Mr. John Kipshaven)   Mr. James Wells)

John Richardson plt.}
John Stevens Deft. }   In a plea of trespass and Ejectment.

     By Conseht of both parties Griffeth Jones Attorney for
John Richardson and John Stevens Doe Joyne Iss[ue in] the action now Depending the Deft. plead not [Guilty] troyes him Selfe
Upon the Court the Court Condisent [the plt.] Shall have a Jury
Capt. John Avery Entred [his decent] the Jury is agreed and
find by Evidence John Richardson being hee is the first Setler
to have Right to the Same hee hath Seated the Court pass Judgment according to the Verdict of the Jury. The Deft. appeales
from Judgment to the next Court of Assizes to beheld at New

Yorke Before the Honorable Governor and Councell: The Court
order both plt. and Deft. to put in Sufficient Security to
prossecute and Answer the Said Appeale.

The pannell of the Jury

Mr. Edward Southrin	George Young	Richard Levick
Samuell Gray	Daniell Browne	Charles Johnson
Otto Wolgast	William Futcher	Richard Peaty
Helm. Wiltbanck	John Hackister	Thomas Howard

[Signed:]   Test. Cornelis Verhoofe Cler.

Copie: July 18: Anno 1676.
Laid out for Mr. John Richardson and James Shackleday and John
Richardson Senor a tract of Land Called Willing brooke on the
West Side of Delaware Bay and on the northside of a Branch of
Creeke of the Said bay Called Duck Creeke beginning at a
bounded poplar by the branch Running Up the branch South west
three hundred perches to the Land of William Stevens to a
Boundeth white oake neare the head of the branch - then South
East paralell with the Land of William Stevens one hundred and
fifty perches to a bounded whitt by a Swampe and by a Line
Southwest one hundred and Sixty perches to a bounded poplar on
a Knowle in the woods and by a Line [
                     ]^4 hundred perches to a bounded [
] a Line Southwest one hundred [   ]
to a bounded Red oake and bys [   ] hundred perches [   ] Bounded oake then by a Line northEast
Six hundred and twenty perches to a bounded oake then and by
a Line South East three hundred and twenty perches to the
first bounded poplar Laid out for two thousand acres.
[By or]der of Capt Edmund
[   ]ll Survor generall   By mee
The blanck Left was torne in the   Thomas Philps Deputy
originall Befor it Came to my hand.   Surveyor
       [Signed:]   Test. Cornelis Verhoofe Cler.

Knowall men by these presents that I Thomas Crumpton of
Dorchester Countey in the Province of Maryland doe Stand firmly
bound and obleidged me my heires Executors Administrators or
Assignes unto John Richardson of the Same Countey and Province
Planter in the full and Just Quantity of Ten Thousand Pounds
of good Sound Merchantable Tobacco and good Sufficient Caske
to Conteyne the Same to be paid in Some Convenient Place in
the Province of Maryland or on the West Side of Delaware bay
to him the Said John Richardson his heires Executors Administrators or Assignes or Certeyne Attorney, as wittness my hand
and Seale this the 2nd Day of Sept. 1676.

The Condition of this obligation is Such that if the
above bounden Thomas Crumpton me my heires Executors Administrators or Assignes shall well and Truly keepe Covenant full-
fill and Satisfy Every Claws in a Conditionall Covenant of
Articles beareing Date the 18th of August 1676 and Likewise
according to the Last Article in the said Condition Quietly and
peaceable Deliver or Cause to be Delivered up at the Expiracion
of Nine Yeares to the said John Richardson for his heires

Executors Administrators Assignes or Certaine Attorney and to
Noe other person or persons or in any time Dureing the said
Terme of Nine Yeares then this obligation to be void and of
None Effect or Else to Remaine in full force and vertue
Seigned Sealed and Delivered   Thomas Crumpton
In presents of us.   his $\mathcal{TC}$ marke (seale)
Thomas $T W$ Williams
    signat
Charles $C G$ Grindey   Entred in open Court December the
    signat   9th 1679 by Wm. Wattson and Thomas
Wm. Wattson   Williams
[Signed:] Testis True Copie Exam. per Cornelis Verhoofe Cler.

     Articles of Agrement made Concluded and Agreed upon Bee-
tweene Thomas Crumpton of the one party of Dorchester County
Planter and John Richardson of the other party of the Same
Countey and Province Afore Said Planter This 18th Day of
August 1676.

Maryland Witnesseth.

     Whereas the Sayd John Richardson doth Demise and grant to
the Said Thomas Crumpton one parte of a tract or parcell of
Land Called wellin brooke Lieing and being on the west Side of
Deleware bay Neare a Creeke Called Duck Creek for and Dureing
the time and terme of Nine Yeares together with all benifits
and priviledges thereunto belonging for the use of him the
Said Thomas Crumpton for the said Terme of Yeares (That is to
Say about the quantitey of Twoo hundred Acres of the said
Tract before mentioned
2dly. The Said Jno. Richardson Doth Covenant and agree to and
with the said Thomas Crumpton for to find and allow him Six
Sow Shoates and one Young bore to deliver them at the Now
Dwelling plantation of him the said John Richardson, the said
Tho: Crumpton Doth Engage to Transport to the said Land before
mentioned and to use the best of his Endevour Carefully to
Looke after and Raise as he Cann of the stock upon the Land
the one half of the Increese and principall to the use behalfe
behoofe of the said Thomas and the other halfe to the onley
behalfe behoofe and use of him the said John Richardson his
heires Executors Administrators or assignes Likewise the said
John Richardson is and doth Covenant to furnish him the said
Thomas Crumpton Two Cowes the one the said Thomas is to pay
him for the other upon his own accompt the said hoggs Equally
Divided Every Two Yeares and kill all that is killable only a
shoate Left to breede on and the Increse of the Cattle for the
female at the Expiracion of the Said terme Equally to be Devided and the male as the parteys hereafter Shall agree.
3dly. The Said John Richardson doth Covenant to find and allow
him the Said Thomas Three hundreed Aple Trees at his Now
dwelling plantation and the said Thomas Crumpton doth Engage
to Transport them to the Sayd Land and to plant them thereon
and Sufficiently Fence and Tend them and 3 Yeeres after the
Transporting them to plant them out at an Equall Distance as
men Doe Generally plant beareing trees in orchard and the
profitt that shall arise from the Said Trees in Every Respect
the one halfe to the one party the other halfe to the other
party only Dureing the said ter[me] of Yeares the said Trees
to be Transported this present Yeare or as the said partys

they shall agree:
4thly. At the Expiracion of the Said terme of yeares the said
Thomas Crompton doth Cov[enant] and Engage to and with the
Said John Quietley to Deliver the possession of the said Land
howseing Orchard or orchards Gardon or Gardons fence or
Fence[s all] Tenantable and Good in Repaire unto him the said
Jno. Richardson his Heires [Executors] Administrators and
Assignes or Certeyne Attorney, and Discharging the said terme
of Yeares to pay to the said John Richardson or his order One
fatt Capon [yearly] Upon the feast of St. Michall, if Demanded
as a Due Rent to the Said John R[ichardson] as witnes my hand
and Seale the Day and Yeare above writen.

                         Thomas _TC_ Crompton (seale)
Testis.   Signatt
Wm. Wattson   John Richardson
Tho. Barker   Signatt _IR_ (seale)
Edmond _O_ Riall
  signatt

William Wattson Declared upon Oath that hee Did Draw the within
wrighting and Saw John Richardson and Thomas Crompton Assigne
and Seale the within wrighting and made Delivery there of as
their act and Deed before the wittnesses within mentioned who
Did attest the same In open Court the 10th December 1679
[Signed:] Testis True Copie Exam. per Cornelis Verhoofe Cler.

       Know all men whom these presents may in any manner of waye
Concerne that I Petocoque Indian Comonly Called amongst the
English Christian haveing for the value and Consideration of
three Matchcoates haveing Received 4 yd. feese⁵ and 1/2 yd.
buttons and thred to the value of two of them and one Match-
coate more to be paid to me the said Petocoque or Mehoxey my
brother have by these presents sould and Doe acknowledge to
have Received full Sattisfaction for the Sale and worth to our
Contentes and Likeing and Doe demise and graunt and wholly sell
and possess and deliver up our possession from us our heires
Executors Administrators Assignes or any other person or persons Either English or Indians unto John Richardson of Dorchester Countey in the province of Maryland Planter a tract
or parcell of Land Lyeing and being on the West Side of Del-
leware Bay on the South Side of a Creeck Called Duck Creek
Conteyning and Now Layd out for 2000 Acres by English with all
benifits and Priviledges thereunto belonging as hawkeing hunting
fishing fowleing or any other use the said John Richardson shall
think fitt or any one here shall order or appoint Eyther
heires Executors Administrators or Assignes Likewise I Doe by
these presents Ingage to defend the said John Richardson his
heires and Assignes etc. from all Indians or others in the
Quiett possession of the said Land that my selfe Nor Noe other
Indyans shall hunt or Kill Eyther deere fish foule or any other
Game Eyther wild or Tame upon the said Land for Ever without
the Especiall Leave or Licence from the said John Richardson
his heyres Executors and Administrators or Assignes further I
Doe Engage to Assist and help the said John Richardson or any
one that Doth belong to him that Live or Shall hereafter Live
upon the said Land if eyther his or their hogs or Cattle shall
Runn astray in the woods to use the best of my Endevoure to
drive them to the plantation or plantations they Doe belong
to upon his or their Request to the true and honest Intent and

and performance and Keepeing Covenant with this present obligation I have hereunto sett my hand Sealed with my Seale the
20th of September 1676

Signed Sealed and
Delivered in the presents of us
Thomas Crumpton
    TC
    signat
Charles C G Grandy
    signat
Thomas I W Williams
    signat

forgot I doe Acknowledge to
have Received Eight bottles of
Rum as part of Sattisfacion as
witnes my hand (all at one
time though forgott by the
wrighter
    The marke of
    ᒍᐯᑌᐯᔕᒍᒪᔑ   (seale)
Petacoque or Christiany

Acknowledged In open Court by the said Christian Indian
December the 10th 1679.

William Wattson declared upon oath that hee did draw this
writeing and saw the Indian deliver the same as his act and
deed etc. to the Receiveing of the whole Consideration thereof
and Thomas Williams Sworne that hee saw the Assigneing sealeing
and Delivery thereof
[Signed:] Testis. True Copie Exam. per Cornelis Verhoofe Cler.

      To the Worshipfull Commissioners of
      Dorchester Countey

    The Humble Peticon of John Richardson humbly sheweth that
whereas your peticoner Transported from Maryland to the West
side of Dellaware River and to a place in the said River Called
Duck Creek and on the South Side of the said Creeke A Certaine
Man Called by the Name of Thomas Crompton there to keepe possession in my Name and for my use one Certaine house that I
Built there together with 2000 Acres of Land belonging to the
same and are out of purse in seating of the said Crampton for
the prevention very Considerable in seating the same Notwithstanding John Stevens of Dorchester Countey in the province of
Maryland Gent. hath by violence and force of Armes turned him
the said Crumpton out of Doores together with his wife and
family whereby their lives and health were hasarded And what
the said Crompton Did there in matter of Cleareing fenceing or
building w[as] only for the proper use of the said John Richardson or for the heires or Assignes of the said John Richardson
or whomseoever the said Richardson shall order [all] that is
herein Conteyned I the said Thomas Crompton doe sweare to bee
[nothing] but truth therefore the above said Richardson your
peticioner humbly Cra[veth the] Countey Seale for Testimoney
that this is the oath of the above said Thomas [Crompton] and
your peticioner shall ever pray etc. as witness my hand and
seale the 5th of Au[gust] 1679

Phins. Blackwood
John Rawllings
John Saulsburrey

the Mark of
   TC
Thomas Crompton   (seale)

          August the 6th 1679
Sworne before us
      Raymond Stapelfort
      Wm. Stephines
      Wm. Smithson Cler. Com. Dorr.   (Seale Countey)
Affirmed by oath by the said Clerk December 10th 1679 before us.

Testes
Luke Wattson
Sander /M Mallson
[Signed:] These a true Copie Exam. per Cornelis Verhoofe Cler.

The Deputicion of William Watson aged 34 Yeares or thereabouts Sayeth that in the yeare 1676 Sometime in that month of
August or There aboute he Came in Company of Jno. Richardson
to Thomas Phillips his howse with some others and the said
Thomas Phillips Jno. Richardson and others did goe to the
branch of Duck Creeke and there hee Did see a house upon a
branch side and the said Thomas Phillips and John Richardson
did say that he the said John Richardson Did build the Same
and Thomas Phillips Did Carry your Deponant and the Rest of the
Companey to a Marked Tree by Another branch and Says he had
Surveyed that Land for the said John Richardson being 2000
Acres and your Deponant Did Ask him whethor he had Power to
grant warrants and Survey he Sayd hee had Soe your Deponant
the Same time Did obteyne Another Certificate for 500 Acres of
Land for himselfe of the Sayd Thomas Phillips and when wee
Came boath to the said Thomas Phillips his house he Did Shew us
a Letter which your Deponant Read which Came from Capt. Cant-
well which Did Certify his Power to Come from him further your
Deponant Sayth to his Certaine knowledge the said John Richardsons horse Did Carry by his order and a man that he hired with
them Some Goods of one Thomas Crampton his wife and Children
from the Deponeants house in hunting Creek in Choptancke in
Maryland with Intention as they had made a Contract betwene the
said Thomas Crampton and John Richardson to goe to the said
Land in Duck Creek branches and there to Remaine for Nine
Yeares his time that he went from your Deponants house was
Sometime in the begining of October 1676 and further the Deponant Saith Not as witnes my hand this 9th Day of September
1679. Sworne in Open Court December the 10th 1679.
                                    Wm. Wattson
[Signed:] Test. True Copie Exam. per Cornelis Verhoofe Cler.

Edmond Ryan aged 36 Yeares of thereabouts Deposeth and
saith That John Richardson of the Freshes of Choptanke River
in the Province of Maryland was the first Cleerer and Im-
pruver of the Land Called Wallinbroo Lying on the west side
of Dellaway Bay adjoyneing to the branches of a Creek Called
Duck Creeck which Cleareing was Began by him this Deponant
for the said John Richardson the 18th Day of July 1676:

Maryland Dorchester County coram me[6] 7th die August 1679.

        Wm. Stiphens Wm Smithson Clr   (Seale of
        Raymond Stapelfort   the Countey)
Affirmed by Oath by the said Clerke before us December the
10th 1679
Test. Luke Wattson   [Signed:] True Copie Exam. per
Sander /M Mallston.   Cornelis Verhoofe Cler.

Peter Bawcombe aged about 49 Yeares being Deposed and
Saith That aboute Juley in the Yeare 1676 The Deponant Being in
the house of Thomas Phillips and hard the said Thomas Phillips
and one John Richardson Say then that they had Surveyed the
Land upon Duck Creeck branches for the Said John Richardson and
the Said John Richardson built a house there upon the Said Land
presently after before hee went Downe to Chaptanck and about
Sept. or Oct. followeing the Said Richardson Sended up the
Said Land Thomas Crompton as Tenant with his wife and family
to Seate the said Land and furnished him with Corne and Meale
and Your Deponant heard Thomas Crompton Say often times hee
Seated the said Land for John Richardson as his Tennant further
your Deponant heard Robert Dick and William Willoughby Says
that They Never would Come up to Seate their Land if They
Could have Given all the Lands in thes Parts for the Plague
and Trouble of the Muscitesh and would Sell thier Land to your
Deponant for a pair of Shoes apeere and your Deponant told
them if they would Not Seated they had Noe Right of Land here
and [your] Deponant tould them he would Not by it and further
Saith Not
Sworne before us   Peter Bowcombe
November 14th Anno 1679
Fra. Whitwall
Luke Wattson

The above Said Deponant further Declares that he heard
the above named Thomas Philips Saye that he had Power to grant
warrants for Land to any person and to Survey the Same and
Did grant a warrant for the same Land to John Richardson.
Declared in Truth before us.   Peter Bowcombe
The Day and Yeare above writen
Fran. Whittwell   [Signed:] True Copie Exam.
Luke Wattson   per
                                     Cornelis Verhoofe
                                       Cler.

Christopher Jackson Aged 30 Yeares or There abouts Being
Examined and Sworne in Open Court upon his Oath Saith that
John Richardson in the Yeare 1676 Did agre and Pay your De-
ponant for to help Gett timeber and to bring it in Place for
the building of one Certaine Dwelling house on a Certayne
Peice of Land which hee the Said John Richardson had Surveyed
for him on the West Side of Dellaware Bay on The branches of
Duck Creeke and that time here was Noe manner of worke Done on
any parte of that Land where hee the Said John Richardson had
Surveyed for him at That Time to my Certeine knowledge and
further Saith Nott.   Christipher Jackson
Sworne in Open   his marke ⋎
Court December 10th 1679
[Signed:] Testis: True Copie Exam. per Cornelis Verhoofe Cler.

[Entitled:]   1679 Copy of proceedings of the Court at
              Whorekill.

---

1.   The pages of these copies of court proceedings are
     numbered consecutively 1-11 with page 4 left blank. A
     duplicate copy of these proceedings is represented by

documents 21:74, 21:90 and 21:91.

2. i.e., pledges ad prosequendam or "pledges to prosecute."
    They were originally those persons who became sureties
    for the prosecution of the suit. It later became a
    formal matter to append their names to the declaration
    since the plaintiff was no longer liable to be punished
    for a false claim, and the fictitious persons John Doe
    and Richard Roe became the universal pledges.

3. i.e., Jones pro querente or "Jones for the plaintiff."
    This is a reference to Griffeth Jones who was an
    attorney.

4. These brackets and those following in this return of
    survey represent a missing portion of the original
    document which Cornelis Verhoofe notes at the end of the
    copy.

5. i.e., frieze.

6. i.e., "before me."

21:90/91   [DUPLICATE COPY OF 21:88/89]

21:92   [COPY OF THE COURT PROCEEDINGS RELATING TO A
          SUIT BETWEEN GRIFFETH JONES AND THOMAS SHAW]

Whorekill County

    Copie: Thomas Shaw was Atteached to Answer Griffeth Jones
In a plea of trespass to his Dammage twenty pounds Sterling.

                pledges to prossecute[1] $\Big\}$ John Doe
                                                      Rich: Roe

    And the Said Griffeth Jones In his owne proper person
Comes and Complaines That whereas the Said Thomas Shaw the
nynth Day of february in the two and thirtieth year of the
Raigne of our Soveraigne Lord King Charles the Second over Eng-
land etc. at a Certaine plantation Called willing brooke In
the Jurisdiction of this Court In the present and against the
Command of Richard Leverett Constable for the precincts of St.
Jones in the Jurisdicion aforesaid upon the body of the Said
Griffith Jones then and there being in the peace of God and

our Soveraigne Lord the King with force and armes (viz) with
Clubs Staves and other weapons did make an Assault and him the
Said Griffeth Jones did beate wound and Evill Entreate Soe
that of his Life hee was In Dispaire and other harmes to him
Did against the peace of our Said Soveraigne Lord the King and
to the Said Griffeth Jones his Dammage twenty pounds Sterling
and upon this hee brings his Suite.

                                        Jones:
[Signed:] Test: Cornelis Verhoofe Cler.

     Copie: At a Court Held for the Whorekill the 13 and 14th
Dayes of Aprill Anno 1680.

Com: {Capt. John Avery   }   Mr. John Kipshaven}
       {Mr. Fran: Whitwell }   Mr. Luke Wattson }
       {Mr. Alex: Molestine }   Mr. James Wells   }

Griffeth Jones plt.} In a plea of Trespass
Thomas Shaw Deft. }

     Upon the Debeat of the matter the plt. Craveth a Jury the
Deft. Plead hee haveing made Satisfaction for that offence the
Court Before the Jury find for the Deft. the Court Entred
Judgment no Caus[ ] of action and therefore Grant a nunsuite
for the Deft. against the plt. with Costs the plt. Entred
Appeall from the Said Judgment before the Honorable Governor
and Councell at the next Court of Assizes to beheld at New
Yorke The Court ordered the plt. and Deft. to putt in Sufficient
Security to prossecute and Answer the Said Appeale according
to Law Alias Execution.

                    pannell of the Jury:
Mr. Helmanus Wiltbanck} John Hackister } John Dupree
William Clark   } William Hamilton} George Young
Joswah Backstead   } Johannis Kip   } Edward Pack
Robert Hart   } Otto Wolgast   } Bryand Rowles
[Signed:] Test. Cornelis Verhoofe Cler.

     Copie: Richard Levick Aged 31 yeares or there abouts
Sayth that there was a warrant Directed to him for Atteach the
bbody of Samuell Styles and allsoe to Serve a Lease of Ejectment and In Company there went Griffeth Jones and wee were
pursued by one man named Thomas Shaw and when wee were peaceable Entred Into the Said house on the branch of Duck Creeke
Came in Thomas Shaw after us and Said the house was his.
Griffeth Jones Sayd that when hee had Done the buseness hee
Came to Doe hee would begone and I Sayth that I had warrant
from the magistrates Said Shaw Replyed hee Cared not a turd
for the magistrates nor their warrants neither and then with a
Stick hee Struck the Said Griffeth Jones and Closed with him
and Layd hold of him by the throate and then John Glovear
asked the Said Shaw why hee was Soe Rash and tooke hold of his
hand which was then holling of Griffeth Jones his throate the
Said Shaw Cryed out give mee my Stick I often Cryed out peace
In his majesties name John Glovear Came from him and hee with
his Stick Struck John Glovear one blow on his head and an

other blow on his arme and further Sayth you Glovear would I
had you in the woods and Still Disobeyed and further Sayeth not
this was Sum time about the Second day of february 1679/80
                                              Richard Levick
Sworne In open Court february the 12th 1679/80
[Signed:] Test: Cornelis Verhoofe Cler.

     Copie: John Glovear Aged 40 yeares or thereabouts Sayeth
that hee Did See the man named Thomas Shaw about the Second
Day of february Last Strucke Griffeth Jones and with one of
his hands Did Lay hold of his throate the Constable then Commanded peace Severall times In his majesties name and Said hee
had a warrant hee the Said Shaw tooke the Said papers and
threw them on the Ground and Said hee Cared not a turd for the
magistrates nor theyr warrants neither and Still Disobeyed Soe
then I asked of him why hee was Soe Rash hee Still Cryed give
mee my Stick and presently hee Came to mee and Struck one
blow with his Stick on my head and an other blow on my arme
and Sayth you Glovear would I had you in the woods and further
Sayeth not.
                                              John Glovear
Sworne In open Court february the 12th 1679/80
[Signed:] Test: Cornelis Verhoofe Cler.

[Entitled:] Appeale from the Whorekill Court to the Court of
             Assizes

             Griffeth Jones plt.
             Thomas Shaw Deft.
                                    1680

_____

1. See 21:88/89 F. N. 2.

21:93 [COPIES OF DEPOSITIONS RELATING TO THE LAND
        DISPUTE BETWEEN TYMEN STIDDEM AND JACOB VAN
        DER VEER][1]

Copia   I underwritten William Sempill doe hereby declare that
on the 23 day of July Last past one Mathias Mathiasz de Vos
came to mee at my house in New Castle with one deposition
written as I: suppose by Mr. Ephraim Herman or his Clerck,
Conserning Some Land then in Controversy betweene Mr. Tymen
Stiddem and Jacob V: Veer, and the said Mathias, desiering mee
to give him his oath to the same deposition I made answer that
hee Should Come att one other tyme because I supposed him then
to bee In drinke but the said Mathias replyed that hee was not
in drinke, and desiered mee to dispatch him alledgeing if hee
was not sworne att that tyme hee should bee forced to come

againe and sweare att Court, for Mr. Tymen would Subpene him
and then hee Should Loose more tyme and the Lyke upon which
I Looking over the deposition demanded of the said Mathias
what hee could Sweare hee thereupon did to mee declare the ful
substance in Every perticular, which was in the foresaid deposition written; by which I finding that the said Mathias was
in his ful sences tought good to Read the deposition over to
him and haveing done the Same, I demanded of him, whether hee
understood what was therein written and whether itt was the
truth and if hee could Swear the same, The said Mathias Replyed Yes upon which I gave him his oath to the afore said deposition and did then also subscrybe the same; during all
[   ] said Tyme Mr. Samuel Land Stood by and heard all
above [   ] that Mr. Ephraim Herman was not
to [ ] knowledge Conserned neither did I heare the said
Mathias make any the Least mention of him all which I declare
to bee the Truth, and in Confirmacion whereof I have here unto
and to the true Coppy of the aforementioned deposition here
annex Set my hand att New Castle the 6th day of Jannuary
1679/80

                              (was signed)
                              Will: Sempill

        Samuell Land Sub Sherrife of the precincts of New Castle
delcares that all what is mentioned in the within written declaration is the whole Truth and nothing but the Truth and
that hee was personally present when Mr. William Sempill Examined and administred the oath unto Mathias Mathiassen de Vos;
In Testimony whereof hee has hereunto Set his hand In New
Castle this 9th day of Jannuary 1679/80

                              (Signed)   Samuel Land

Examined by and Sworne
before us the day and yeare
abovewritten
  (Signed)
  Jno. Moll
  Pieter Alrichs
  J: D'Haes

        The deposition of Mathias Mathiasz De Vos aged forty Seven
yeares or there abou[tes] Delcares that the dutch Commander
Will[ ] Beekman whilst he was Governor of Crist[ena] did give
and grant unto this Deponant togeather with Moens Andriessen
and Wallraven Johnson De Vos a certayn [Peice] of Land Lyeing
and being [on] the north syd[e of] Brandawyne or Fish [Kill In
Cristena Aforesaid upon which said Land this deponant] togeather with the other twoo a[foresaid] Participants did make a
begining [and] worke but this deponant Chang[ing his] mynd
resolved other wayes and [thereupon] Left his said Land to the
aforesaid M[oens] Andriesen and Wallraven Johnson [de] Vos and
as the Deponant has sever[all] tymes heard sence doctor Tymen
S[tiddam] have bought the said Land and was Lawfully Possesed
of the same and further sayeth not.

In wittnesse whereof the Deponant have hereunto set his

hand att New Castle In Dellowar River this 23rd of July Anno Domini 1679. This is the true Copie of the Deposition of Mathias Mathiasen Devos Examined and Sworne before me the day and date above written. In wittnesse whereof I have hereunto set my hand att New Castle the 6th day of Jannuary 1679/80
(was signed)   Will: Sempill

These aforestanding three Testimonys are True Coppyes of their originalls Examined and Compared by mee
[Signed:]   J.d:Haes

[Endorsed:]   Some delcaracions and deposicions made at New-castle in Delaware about the difference betweene Mr Tymen Stiddem and Jacob Vanderveere. 1679/80.3

---

1. The damaged portions of Matthias Matthiassen de Vos' deposition were recovered from 21:94.

2. See 21:94 for a copy of this oath.

3. Endorsement is written in the hand of Matthias Nicolls.

21:94   [COPY OF A DEPOSITION MADE BY MATTHIAS MATTHIASSEN DE VOS RELATING TO A LAND DISPUTE BETWEEN TYMEN STIDDEM AND JACOB VAN DER VEER WITH CONFIRMATION OF HIS OATH]1

Copia: The Deposition of Mathias Mathiasen de Vos aged forty seven yeares or thereaboutes Declares that the Dutch Commander William Beekman whilst hee was Governor of Cristena did give and grant unto this deponant togeather with Moens Andrisen and Walraven Johnson Devos a Certayne Peice of Land Lyeing and be-ing on the north syde of Brandawyne or Fish Kill In Cristena Aforesaid upon which said Land this deponant togeather with the other twoo aforesaid Participants did make a begining and work but this deponant Changing his mind resolved other wayes and thereupon left this said Land to the aforesaid Moens Andriesen and Wallraven Johnson de vos and as the Deponant has severall tymes heard sence docter Tymen Stiddam have bought the said Land And was Lawfully Posesed of the same and further sayeth not.   In witness whereof the Deponant have hereunto sett his hand att New Castle In Delowar River this 23rd of July anno Domini 1679.   (was signed)   Mathias Mathiasz
Examined and Sworne   De Vos
before mee in New Castle
the date above written
(was signed)   Will Sempill

[Verso:]   This 9th day of January anno 1679/80 apeared before us Matthias Mathiasen de Vos and has taken his Possetive Oath that all what is mentioned In the within written Deposition is

the whole truth and nothing but the Truth and that there is nor
was no other deposition written by Mr. Epharim Herman or any
Clerck of his for him; Concerning the primsses or any Part
there of as allso that he Came upon his own accord and was
verry Earnest wi[ ] the said Herman to write by himselve or
his Clerck the Said Deposition for him much Less that he Should
have In the Least Degree Intyced him perswaded or forced him
unto the Swearing of any word or words Mentioned In the said
Deposition and that all what hee has Declared In and aboute
the Same whas upon the request of Timen Stiddem.

In testimoney whereof the Deponant has put here unto his
hand In new Castle the day and yeare above written
                              (was signed)
                              Mathias Matheasz d'Vos
Examined by, and Sworne
before us at the Same
tyme and wryting of the
above written deposition;
  (was signed)
  John Moll
  Pieter Alricks
  Joh: D'haes
  Will: Sempill

This above standing together with the within written
depos[   ] are both True Coppies of [   ] originals Examined
and Comp[   ] by mee.
                    [Signed:] J. d'Haes

[Endorsed:]   Other deposicions relating to Mr. Tymen Steddam
              and Jacob Vanderveere.[2]

---

1. See 21:93 for a copy of the deposition.

2. Endorsement is written in the hand of Matthias Nicolls.

21:95a   [EPHRAIM HERMAN TO MATTHIAS NICOLLS ABOUT
          AFFAIRS IN DELAWARE][1]

                              New Castle Jan. 17: 1679/80

Honorable and Worthy Sir

     Your Kind Letters of the 24th and 28th of Nov. Laest[2] by
Mr. Ralph Hutchinson, together with the Inclosed Pattents I
Received, and humbly Returne you thenkes for your Soe Carefully delivering my Letter to his Excell. itt Cheefly Consisted
in proposals and ther's noe doubt but his Excellency in his
wisdome will doe for the best; Your youngest Letter Counter-
mand[ing] the Elder, the bill Drawn (which other wayes Should
have ben by mee accepted:) is not come to my hands; The

quackers wil sometymes bafle; according to your orders I have
delivered to Capt. Cantwel (who's well Recoverd) the 2 Letters
of Administration and to Mr. Moll his Pattent and doubt not but
they will make you Sattisfaction; which I in your honors behalfe will put them in minde of when occasion presents; Do.
Tesschemaker hath promissed to make Sattisfaction in the spring
for the pattent and the other wrytings 40 Shillings in wheat
as by your Selfe demanded, which I thinke is Soe reasonable as
can bee Considering the trouble which to my Knowledge yourselfe had in that buisnesse, Hendrik Vanden Burgh his Pattent
I have delivered whoe promissed not to fayle of makeing Sattisfaction as Soon as opportunity of Sloopes, present; also
Matheus and Emilius deRing, the Rest are to have their Pattents
when payment made; as for The Lawe booke Its Yett in Capt.
Cantwells hands, and I hope the Court wil find out Some way for
your Sattisfaction of which I Shal Not fayle to put them in
Minde againe att their next meeting; - I have heard nothing
further of the buisnesse of Jacob V.Veer and Tymen Stiddem, I
am not neither was I in the Least Conserned with the one or
the other; I question not but hee whoe has the most Justice of
his Syde will prevayle; but am mutch troubled to heare that Mr.
Beeckman in Jacob Vander Veers behalfe (as I am Informed) hath
gon about to make his Excell. beleeve that one of the wittnesses by name Mathias Mathiasz deVos, Should have ben by mee
as itt was forced or perswaeded to give in Testimony in Tymens
behalfe; which is utterly false; and therefore to Cleare my
Selfe of that Scandall I have Summoned the Said Mathias before
a Court of magestrates, and there the old depositio[ ] was
Exam: and a New Certifyed, and also the Testimony of Justice
Will: Sempill before whome the Said Mathias first Swore, of all
which I have Imbouldned to trouble yourSelfe with the Coppies
here Inclosed;[3] and humbly request your Selfe to Shew them to
his Excellency and if need bee the originalls written and
attested by the magestrates themselves, Shall bee Sent Newes
wee have Little here, there's of late a fleet of shipps arrived
in Maryland, but the newes not Come heither Yett; all things
are at present here well, the quackers Still multiply there
being Some come out [of] [England] by the way of Maryland 2
months pa[st;] my father[4] is and has ben all this winter Extreame weakly, yet presents his humb[le] Servis to your good
Selfe; Sir if you please to dignify mee with your Correspondency
itt Shall bee [mo]st acceptable; myne and wyves humble Servis
to your good selfe and Lady, with thenkes for your Kind
Rememberance to us, and harthy wishes of your Prosperity and
welfare and a merry good New Yeare I therewith Rest:

                          Sir Your most humble Servant
                          to his power whylst
                          [Signed:] Eph: Herman.

[Addressed:]   For the Honored Capt. Mathias Nicolls t'Cheefe
                Secretary of the Province of New Yorke;
                Present In New Yorke

[Endorsed:]   Mr. Ephraim Hermans New Castle in Delaware Jan:
               17th: 1679/80[5]

_____

1. Other transcription in NYCD 12:641.

2. cf., 21:87 for M. Nicolls' memorandum of items dealt
    with in these letters.

3. See 21:93 and 94 for these papers.

4. Augustine Herrman.

5. Endorsement is written in the hand of Matthias Nicolls.

21:95b   [JOHN OGLE TO JOHN BRIGGS CONCERNING THE
          PAYMENT OF A DEBT]

John Brigs   at Newcasel Jenwer 20, 1679

    I do declear that I hawe not resewd nothen pert nor persel
of that nin honder pond of tobakoe that yowe ar to pay to me
for the hors yowe boght of me therfor I do expeact you wil mak
good payment to Wm. Hamilton acording to yowr promis for I
hawe not reseawed any setisfaction of Mr. Shakerly nor any
other person so I do expeact wil mak good pay and yowe wil
oblig yowr frind
                              [Signed:] John Ogle

21:96a   [JOHN MOLL TO MATTHIAS NICOLLS ABOUT
          AFFAIRS IN DELAWARE][1]

Captyn Matthias Nicolls   New Castle January the 20th 16[ ]

Honorable Sir   Both yours of the 26th November and the 4th
De[c.] I recived per Ralph Hudjeson[2] att my returne From Maryland the 24th [past] With a small pakett Returninge You Menni
thaeks for your Care and Tr[ouble] tharin, as also about the
Land att Chiepiessinge, I Supose itt will bee best to L[et]
that dorment thel[3] the Purtches is made Sertaine from the
[Headens] and Without dis Yett itt is moost Secur I thnck to
Keepe ower old Schoos thill [wee have] New [ones] Capt. Cantwell is g[on] for Maryland and Expected Back aga[ine] everi
Ouer, he[e told] Mee You had Writt [hi]m, which Caused mee to
refaine off Communicatinge [to him] Whatt you write [mee] Con-
serninge the same.

    [I am sorri] Ralph Hudjeson has priudised him selve so
much [in] [   ] [off his tyme which] Wee I supose are
not able now to [re]call [after] [   ] ower Verditt, hee
beeinge dissattisfied and Unwilling [to] Hande unto [   ]
Robbert prest upon us for Judgement upon the bonde of awarde,
which wa[s held in su]spence after that as I remember, and than
Wee givinge him Leaffe, and perswedit [   ] was, to stande

to the awarde reather than unto the farfiture off the bonde,
h[ee] Contesende unto itt; whar upon Wee past one order against
him for the said [awarde] with a proviso that what soever Ralph
Hudjeson should bringe in betw[een] that and the next Courtt
and prouff to have payd for his Brother Robberts accoun[t]
since the awarde, itt should bee alowed unto him as partt off
paymentt, [but] hearinge Nothinge of him Execution was Issued
outt against the Estate off Ralph For the account off Robbertt
Hudjeson about [two] month a[go] Wee past ower said order, and
som Month after that the said Effectes we[re] Executed by the
Creditors of Robbert Hudjeson as beeinge his Estate, Nevertheless I advysed him Upon your Recommandation to draw op a
[peti]cion unto the Courtt which hee did and receved his
answer almoost unto [the] same effecte as above.

I hope when his Excellencys Leagir[4] will admidt him hee
will bee plea[sed to] give such orders as hee in his Wisdom
shall thinck meed about ow[   ] [wee] doe waent a Survayer Verri Much, Reperation off [the] [5] and Fortt, to
Know how to pay the pore man which leaves[5] thare by his Ex-
cellenc[ys] Cullers[6] for the Fort, a Seale for ower Office and
Sundry other things as Wee [have] often mensionett, I discourst his Excellency also about the Quitrents that pla[ce]
havinge no Weate, nether are they able to portich itt for Tobacco meight [   ] Tobacco as in Virginia and Maryland which
his Excellency promised Mee to take into [con]sideration, You
knowe who[7] Letell Aportuniti ther whas to finnis [the] thinge
unto the porpis When I was thare, I hope Wee shall see his
Excellency here next summer to Rectefy all whatt is Waentinge
and a'mis.

Wee have Receved No Letters from his Excellency about the
difference betw[een] Timen[8] and Jacob Vander Veer nor ani other
Matters, I supose Mr. Beakm[an has] too good one opinion off
the said Vander Veer Iff all or moost the Inhabit[ants] off
ower presincx whare off thad man his temper I whould nott
[bee on] the Bench upon ani terms Ye[9] rether forsake and Leaff
all wha[tever] I have Received the Pattin for the ground whare
my dewellin[g house stands] and the gaerden behind itt, Which
in [G]erritt Van [Sweeringen] as also in Capt. John Carr there
tyme wa[s K]eept intyerly [unused] When I had bought itt ther
were sum old apple trees Gr[own upon] the plase which is now
Called the Lands Street, Capt. Cantw[ell was] schewinge Mee by
the Old Duch map that thare whas to bee a Fo[ ] sixty fott
wide I whas Willinge to Condesend unto itt and Caused m[ee] to
Cutt down the Apple trees which gruw thare as Iett apeers by
the Str[eet] whare by I not onely Last[10] 60 Fott off ground
butt Cost mee a bor[   ] more to fence itt in, and in the
patten itt seams is Enterd 3 bushel[s of wea]te per acre for
Quit rents, My Predesessers have payd butt one b[ussel and I]
paid one bussels since I have had itt, I hope not dat my
Sevile[   ] Neibours, my Lass[11] off ground, and Exter-
ordinari Char[   ] shall Cause mee to pay 2 bussels of
Weate Yearly pray Sir bee pleased [to ac]quantt his Excellency
with itt, I bought itt together and nott in p[arts I sha]ll
make you Honest satisfaction att the Springe the same I blief[e
Mr.] Tesschenmaker Mr. De Ringe etc. they have More than 3
Lotts a pers[ ]

Wee have promised next Court [to grand Ralph Hud]jeson
one order upon Capt. Cantwell for the funerall Charges off Mr.
Wharton Which is above 1200 g[   ] others have bin buried
as Hansom for 1/3 off the monni and less, to my thinkinge Wee

have bin as Civill and favourable [to] that man as hee in
reason Can Expecte [as] ower Records upon all Ocasions shall
make itt apeere [   ] the Chanseler of Maryland I know allows
all Administrators alyck for funerall Charges Iff they will
bee Astravigand they must doe itt upon ther own bu[rthen] not
u[pon] the Crediturs accoumpt.

Itt [is v]arri nessessary Wee should Know how his Excellency aproufft off Ca[pt. Cantwell his] accounts, for sum
small Metters must bee paid which Iff the [fynes will] Nott
defray itt, Wee must request his Excellency to admitt off a
[small] Levy to doe itt.

The Land grant[ed] unto Robert Tallent [and] Thomas
Snellinge You Know can not bee La[yd] oud thill itt shall
plea[se his Ex]cellency to nominate and apoint us a Sur[veyor]
which wee doe [Expect, niews wee] have none by way off Mary-
[land onely that some schips lat]ely are [arrived.]

Whissing your selfe and your good Leady [a pros]perus
Marry and blessed New Yeare with abondence more [to come] I
and My Wyffe Salute you both Verri Keindely, and shall [re-
maine]
                    Honorable Sir Your moost
                    Hum[ble]
                        [Signed:]   John Moll
P.S. Pray presentt my
Humble Servis with a
Merri New yaer to [   ]
Capt. Napte[   ] the Master
[   ] is in haest Vale.

[Addressed:] For the Honorable Capt. Matthias Nicolls, Sec.
              Att New Yorke [   ]

[Endorsed:] [   ] 1679. [   ]
             [   ]

---

1. Other transcription in NYCD 12:642. The damaged portions
   have been recovered from this source.

2. Ralph Hutchinson.

3. i.e., "till."

4. i.e., "leisure."

5. i.e., "lives."

6. i.e., "colors."

7. i.e., "how."

8. Tymen Stiddem.

9. i.e., "yea."

10. i.e., "lost."

11. i.e., "loss."

21:96b   [THOMAS WOLLASTON TO JOHN BRIGGS ABOUT A DEBT]

Mr. Brigges

     Sir   having this apeartunaty to wright to you by Mr.
Hamelton, this is to acuainte you that Mr. Shakerly Returned
your bill to me againe and said you could not pay it Last yeare
which I wrott to you by Mr. Ralfe Hutheson[1] and sence by Petor
Baccombe[2] and he brought me answer that you denied the bill and
you oued me aney thing at all thearfore I would desire you to
Looke after Mr. Shakerlyes Estate if you have payd aney thing
upon the bill for he gave noe further accounte but that you
could not pay it the Last yeare, thearfor I would desir you to
make use of that prinesible I tooke to be in you of an honest
man for you Know that I paid the bill by your ordar and to doe
you a cindness and have binn ought of my tobacco soe Longe soe
havinge noe more att present but rest yours to Command
                                   [Signed:] Tho. Wollaston
N. Castle Januer the 25th anno 79/80

[Addressed:] These
              for Mr. John Brigges
              att his plantion in St. Joneses

---

1. Ralph Hutchinson.

2. Peter Bawcom.

21:97a   [PHILIP POCOCK TO GOV. ANDROS CONCERNING THE
          DEATH OF ROBERT HOSKINS AND THE SURVEY OF LAND
          NEAR THE FALLS]

May it please your Honor

     After my comeing from Yorke being taken sick in my Journey
to New Castle first at Wood bridge then at Puskataway and last
of all at the Falls of Delaware River where I was forced to
Continue five Weekes before I could recover my strength to be
able to travall in which time haveing many occasions to discourse concerning Robert Hoskins one of the persons that
petitioned your Honor for Land at the falls of Delaware which
as I informed your Honor had a Plantacion Survey for him by
vertue of your Honors warrant Authorizeing me soe to doe as
alsoe the said person was since unfortunately drowned and
thinking it my duty to give your Honor an account as well of
the manner of his being found as alsoe of the proceedings of
these persons whoe pretend to Administer upon what Estate he
had there being as yet noe officer or publick person in that
New Settlement whereof he was a membor, to give your Honor any
informacion I hope it [ ] plead my Apology with your Honors
Clemency for my presumption in giveing your Honor this trouble
without any Command soe to doe the manner of his being drowned

was as Followeth goeing from William Biles his Landing (one of
his Neighbours with whome he did then work) in a Canoe to
fetch Clay there being noe person with him in the Canoe after
Long expectation of his returne some days afterwards, some
servants of Thomas Lamb as I take it of the other side of the
River goeing in a Boate or Canoe by the place where Robert
Hoskins went to dig the Clay found a paddle of which [   ]
Notice to the Neighbours, whereupon William Biles desireing
them to [   ] and the body being found did hire or promise
pay to three persons [   ] and strip him Robert Scoely one
of your Honors Tenants being of the [   ] afterwards the
Corps by order from William Biles was conveyed to [   ]lington[1]
and there buryed there being noe Crowner[2] to apply themselves
to notwithstanding they did call together 8 or 9 men to view
the Corps [   ] Daniell Wills Robert Stacy and Thomas Gar-
diner pretending to [   ] Estate and as I understand have
appraised it at 45 lb. Wm. Biles [   ] intending to Move
your Honor for Letters of Administation as being [   ] to
the Deceased Pretending a right to the Land that was Surveyed
[   ] Notwithstanding he never seated it and that your Honor
by Commanding [   ] lines Paralol to the other Lines have
Clear[   ] The Indian Sackamaker comeing to Mr. Wheeler,
wher[   ] [   ] in my Sicknes gave me opportunity to inquire
why they [   ] their Covenants with your Honor in Sale of the
Land Sackaquewom and the fall Indians still affirming that
they sold noe more than from the falls to the Lower End of
Aurictans Island Okonickon Nokewson and the Chiepiessing Indians
pretending a great Antipathy to Seckaquewom and his Company for
selling their Land without theire Knowled [sic] and say that
they received noe part of the pay Notwithstanding to my Knowledge they hold good Corespondence among themselves for 4 or
five of the Chiepiessing Indians being drunck forced from Mr.
Wheelers Wife and Servants in his absence halfe an Ankor of
Rum and afterward sent Nomnekos Knoweing him to be acquainted
with Mr. Wheeler to make their peace and agree with him to pay
for the Rum which pay [   ] brought according to Namnekos his
word and the Cask returned Namnekos [   ]ing one of the fall
Indians, I hope your Honor shall not find much trouble or
Cleare them from those parts if as they told me soe soone as
theire indians come from Hunting the Chiefest of theire Sachems
intend to come to your Honor and make finall Conclusion for
that which is unpurchased alsoe which I doubt not but they wilbe
ready to doe if they be nor preiudic[   ] by some of our owne
Inhabitants I should have acquainted your Honor sooner with the
Contents of this Letter had I had an opportunity I must now
[   ] your Hononrs patience a little farther to acquaint your
Honor that presenting [   ]y Commission for Survey to the Court
of New Castle they seemed to scruple [   ] which were by your
Honor allowed to Mr. Wharton, the trouble wilbe [   ] to
me then to him and the care wilbe more because most of this
bus[   ] Resurveyes and devisions of Land taken up in
partnership [   ] in Maryland double fees are
allowed but I desire noe more [   ] Honor thought fit to
allow my predecessor and will alsoe I hop Judge [   ] to
allowe me noe Lese but Submitting to your Wisedome I have
[   ] Surveyes more within the Compass of the Land acknowledged [   ] sold by the Indians) to make and then I shall
give Honor [sic] an account of the [   ] returnes, thus
praying for the prosperity of your Honor and begging pardon
[   ] my prolixity and presumption I subscribe

                        Sir your Honors [   ]
                        and obedient Ser[   ]
Swan Wick by
New Castle   [Signed:] Ph. Pocock
[   ] February 1679/80

[Addressed:]   To The Noble Sir Edmund Andros Knight Cheife
               Governor of New Yorke
                              etc. present

---

1. Burlington.

2. i.e., coroner.

21:97b   [CERTIFICATION THAT WILLIAM IS THOMAS YOUNG'S
          OLDEST SON]1

                              Att a Court held in the
                              J[   ] of New Castle
                              february the [4th] Anno
                              1679/80;

        Upon the Request of Mr. Ralph [Hutchinson] the Court
(haveing Informed [themselves)] Doe Certify; That one William
Y[oung] was Reputed and owned to bee the Eldes[t son] of Thomas
Young of St. Jones's' [Creeke] deceased;
                              This is a True Coppy
                              of the Records Exam. [   ]
                              [Signed:] Eph. Herman [   ]

[Endorsed:]   [   ] of Ralph Hutchinson
          about Wm. Youngs being the eldest son of Tho.
          Young who had sold him his patent. Dated Feb.
          3 and 4.2

---

1. See NCCR:381 for the original record from which this
   copy was made. Damaged portions have been recovered
   from this source.

2. Endorsement is written in the hand of Matthias Nicolls.

21:98a   Articles of agreemente made betwene John Steevens
          of the one party and Sammuell Stiles of the other
          party1

     [Wit]nesseth That where as John Steevens doe alinate
[le]te and make over unto Samuell Stiles one Plantation neere

Ducke Creeke for the terme [o]f two yeares and for to doe his
beste indeaver in [S]eatin and cleareing and for the helpe for
to git timber [for] to bild what houses theire shall be
occacion of [for th]e good of the plantation and for to Looke
after [what] nussere² the Said Steevens shall send up, and
trim [and] fense them in from the Cattell and hogs, and if the
[said] Steevens shall put one hand theire this yeare [for] to
have equall Sheare with the said Stiles: and what [hogs] shall
be put one the Land by both parties shall [Be ea]qually devided betwene them both, and none shall [be ki]lled with oute
both parties consente; and at the [end]e of the two yeares for
to devide the hogs be[twe]ne them both and for to Let the said
Stiles have [two] coues for to give him milcke this yeare and
what [Cat]ell and mares the said Steevens shall put one the
[Land] the said Stiles is for to doe his beste indever [for]
to Looke after them, and for to Leave sofitient [fe]nsin at
the end of the time and if the said Stiles [sha]ll neglecte or
refuse for to keepe Covenant with the said Steevens; it shall
be Lawfull for the said Stevens for to turne the said Stiles a
way when [he] shall thincke fit, and to this agreement both
par[ties] have set to their hands and fixed theire seales
[this] forth day of February Anno Domini 1679
[Sealed] and delivered   [Signed:] John Steevens
[in the p]resence of us   his
[   ]   Samm ⌒ Stiles
          his   marke
[   ] Daves
       marke

[Entitled:] [   ] Condicion in Delow. bay

---

1. Other transcription in NYCD 12:644.

2. i.e., nursery.

21:98b   [THOMAS SPRY TO MRS. JOHN SHACKERLY ABOUT
           OUTSTANDING DEBTS]

Mrs. Shakerly   After my Love and service to yourselfe and
children with my wifes also, being both very sory for the Loss
of your husband These are to aquaint you, thatt I have occacion
for thatt money which your husband owed me when he went from
my house which was for yours and your famelyes accomidations
while you were in my house, the summ as you will se by the
account was five pound ten or twelve shillings in good Lining¹
and Duffels att first Cost which he was to send me forth with
besides 3 pints of rumm and two pound of sugar, as alsoe a
botle of spiritt of scurvy gras² with a quarter of mutton you
had when went away which was nott putt to account, which I hope
you will aquaint him who is the administrator, that itt is my
dew, as for your mony which is in Mr. Darbys hand I se them
here attach itt so forget it. I did like wise attach som,

which is never the further of from you, itt Lying still in his
hands, withoutt the administrator order he shall satisfie my
Just Due which I hope you will do the best you Can there in
pray Mrs. Shakerly send me my fower Razors, your husband had of
mine, that Mr. Mors gave him, and he told me he had them in
his Chest att New Yorke, for I want them, schaving no more butt
desire to here from you by the first opertunity, I rest your
freind to his power

                              [Signed:]   Tho. Spry
Newcastle Feb. 11th 1679/80

[Addressed:]   To Mrs. Sarah Shakerly att her house in New Yorke
     per am   These present   QDC

---

1. i.e., linen.

2. "scurvy-grass" or "scurvy-cress" is a cruciferous plant
    used as a cure for the scurvy.

21:99   [EPHRAIM HERMAN TO JOHN MOLL ABOUT RUMORS
          CIRCULATING AGAINST HIM AMONG THE SWEDES]

Mr. Moll   Feb. 15th 1679/80

Sir   Upon your desire, I declare, that some tyme in November
Laest, I being att the house of Peter Cock in the Schuylkill;
There hapned some discours to passe, and amogh the rest the
wyfe of Jonas Nielsen in a Spytful and rayling manner did say
that some of us whoe had ben att New Yorke Laest Summer had
sayed that all the sweads in the river were rebellers etc. and
that itt was done as they supposed to make the Sweads odious in
the Governors Sight and the Lyke; I replyed to Know nothing
of itt and desiered hur to tell Me whoe itt was, Shee thereupon togeather with Justice Peter Cock and all the Company
there present did tell mee, viz That Jacob vander Veers wyfe
togeather with Evert Fin at their Comming bake from New Yorke
had Informed and for a Certaine truth related to them at
Taokanink in a full Company of a great many people that Mr.
Moll had informed the Governor that all the Sweads were rebellers against the Government and great deal More, My Answer
was that I verrily beleeved that Jacobs wyfe and Evert Fin
had belyed Mr. Moll and qave them severall reasons whereby
I supposed itt to bee but a faalshood Invented by Jacobs wyfe
and Evert Fin to Incense the people in the River against you,
Soe att Laest they seemed to bee better sattisfyed; and afterwards I have heard itt againe of other Sweads related the same
has Mr. Alrichs also heard; and if you make any further Inquiery
in itt you'l find wittnesses anof of itt; which is all with
[   ] humble servis and My wishes of a good morrow [   ]
and Lady from Sir

                         Your humble Servant
                    [Signed:]   E. Herman

[Addressed:] For Mr. Mol

21:100   [PHILIP POCOCK TO GOV. ANDROS ABOUT THE
         SURVEY OF CRANE HOOK][1]

May it please your Honor

        haveing now a fit opportunity of Conveyance by Robert Wade
hath caused me once more to presume to give your Honor the
trouble of the perusall of a line or two onely to informe your
Honor that the inhabitants of Crane hoock Lyeing within the
Jurisdiction of this Court of New Castle being 6 persons and
haveing held theire Land Some yeares by vertue of a dutch pattent and desireing to have theire Land Surveyed and to have
confirmacion of theire Said Land by your Honor and haveing Imployed Mr. Wharton accordingly to Survey and devided the same
equally amongst them which by theire patent was granted in an
intire parcell accordingly Mr. Wharton Surveyed the whole but
dyed before it was devided Now haveing Still the Same resolution of Surveying in order to your Honors confirmation:
They tell me that Capt. Kantwell had said that what Mr. Wharton
had begun he had order from your Honor to finish: in which not
being Satisfied I went with two of the men to Speak with Capt.
Kantwell who affirmed the Same to me and told me hee would
Shew your Honors order Soe to doe: but hee could not then find
it upon which I told him he might pick out here and there what
hee pleased under pretence of doeing what Mr. Wharton hath not
finished but whe[reas] the pay is already received and the work
not done, I suppose he will hardly intermeddle I had forgotten
in my other[2] which I hope your honor hath received and vouch-
safed to peruse to informe your Honor that I have performed
your Honors Command in runing the Back line and altereing the
2 lower most in the Survey at the falls: thus Craveing Your
Honors pardon for this and my former presumption Submitting
this matter to your Honors Consideracion and assureing your
Honor that I Shall not further trespasse in disturbing your
Honors more weighty consideracions with any more Letters of
this Kind onely once more beseeching your Honors pardon I subscribe

[Swanwic]k by New Castle   Sir
[20th Feb.] 1679/80   Your Honors Humble
                               and most obedient servant
                      [Signed:] Ph. Pocock

[Addressed:] To the Honorable Sir Edmund Andros Chiefe
              Governor of New York etc.

---

1. Other transcription in NYCD 12:645.

2. See 21:97a for this letter.

21:101   [JOHANNIS KIP TO CORNELIS STEENWYCK ABOUT
         JOHN SHACKERLY'S ESTATE][1]

Mr. Corneles Stenwyck

    Since my arrival at the Hoerekill on the 5th of March I
find nothing special to write about other than the estate of
John Shakerly, deceased. Everything is in such disarray that
I don't know where to begin and how best to put things in
order, for the book and bonds are but a guess. Since so many
receipts and various expenses have been entered in the book
incorrectly and erroneously, some people will deny having incurred them under oath. For this reason I am afraid to bring
the book into court. In order to prevent all the trouble which
certain people are ready to cause, I suggest that it be placed
before one or two commissioners and settled in this manner.
Then if any refuse to pay debts, to summon and compel those who
are able to make payment; and those who are unable to pay, to
give security to pay the following year. In any case I request your advice on the same which I shall follow.

    For the present I can offer no account about the situation
in St. Jones; but, God willing, I intend to go there the first
of next week and see what the situation is. I shall at the
first opportunity write more extensively about it.

    The plantation at Mispelen[2] should not be sold before the
second Tuesday in April, the day the court sits, because the
largest amount of people congregate then and we shall thus
have the highest number of bidders at the sale.

    I must close due to lack of time and paper, cordial
greetings from me

your faithful servant
[Signed:]   Johannis Kip

[Addressed:]   Mr. Corneles Stenwyck
              Merchant at New Yorcke
              This

[Endorsed:]   Johannis Kipps Letter to C. Steenwyck 18 March
              1679/80

---

1. This letter has been translated from the original
    Dutch.

2. i.e., Mispillion Creek.

21:102a   [JOHANNIS KIP TO CORNELIS STEENWYCK ABOUT
           JOHN SHACKERLY'S ESTATE][1]

Sir

        Since my last letter dated 20 March[2] I have been at St.
Jones to put everything in order, but I am encountering considerable obstacles. Partly because the people cannot make
payments, saying that I've come unexpectedly. Since their
tobacco has all been sent off, I doubt that anything can be
done about it this year; and partly because there are so many
errors in the accounts. I have summoned them all before the
court in order to settle accounts with everyone and to be on
firm ground next year. John Brickx, who is the greatest debtor
in Mr. Shackerly's book, acknowledges his debts for the most
part, but he holds a note from Mr. Shackerly for some rum
which is due him. With this he is trying to balance his
account. Or he requests having the rum itself before he pays
for the tobacco. The rum comes out of the sale of the yacht
so that he presumes to have nothing else for his plantation
than that. If possible please inform me about it as soon as
possible and what I am to do in the matter so that I can act
accordingly in court, which sits the second Tuesday in April;
because [   ] the court I have everything settled to the
best of my ability and knowledge, I plan to go to the South
River to see what the situation is there.

        The plantation-account cannot be settled either; so little
has been done there that can impede the expenses, and I cannot write up its account because all the tobacco has not yet
been stripped. I have taken an inventory of animals and servants: there are 3 male servants, 1 female servant, 41 head
of cattle, large and small, and 4 horses, large and small.
According to them there are 60 hogs in addition to the cows
which I chose not to have shown to me. I shall receive about
4 to 5 hogsheads of tobacco on Mr. John Shackerly's account.
I cannot report the [   ] quantity because it hasn't been
packed yet.

        No more for the present. Please excuse anything that I
may have misstated. If you point out the error I shall grate-
fully attempt to correct it. Cordial greetings from me and I
remain
                              Your obedient servant
                        [Signed:] Johannis Kip
In the Whorekill
Anno 1680 the 3rd of April

[Endorsed:] Johannis Kipps Letter 3 April 1680

---

1. This letter has been translated from the original
    Dutch.

2. See 21:101 which is undated but carries March 18 on the
    endorsement. This may be either an earlier letter or
    an error by the clerk who endorsed it.

21:102b [DEPOSITION OF JOHANNES DE HAES CONCERNING
JOHN SHACKERLY'S PROMISE TO PAY A DEBT DUE
JOHN BRIGGS][1]

Johannes D'Haes, declares upon oath that Some tyme Laest
Spring, John Shackerly deceased Comming up from St.
Jones's' to this Towne of New Castle this deponant, asked said Shackerly
whether John Briggs had not sent some tobacco for him, John
Shackerly answered againe, well John Briggs had soe faithfully
promissed mee payment and nowe hee deceives mee, and therefore
I will send the Sherrife upon his bake upon which John Shackerly
answered againe well out of kindnesse I will pay you one thousand lb. tobbacco for John Briggs if you will stay with the
rest till next yeare, to which the deponant answered noe I will
not stay for a pound of itt and some small tyme after John
Shackerly Came to Your deponant and sayed if I should pay you
twoo thousand pound of tobbacco for John Briggs would You bee
Contented to stay with the rest til next Yeare, to which this
deponant Replyed if you doe pay 2000 lb. of itt there will bee
but Litt [sic] Left behind and with that I will bee Contented
to stay with John Briggs till next Yeare and thereuppon John
Shackerly asked the deponant whether hee would take him for
his paymaster to which the deponant made answer, Itt is all
one whoe payes mee, when I Receive my payment I deliver up the
bill and not before; and a Little whyle after, this deponant,
came to John Shackerly and asked him whether hee would pay him
for John Briggs but Shackerly answered noe I can not pay this
Yeare, to which this deponant answered, well then I find out
John Briggs, and I will make him pay mee; And this deponant
declares further that hee never tooke John Shackerly for paymaster and discharged John Briggs and did not Knowe in the
Least that John Shackerly had Received the Tobbacco from John
Briggs, And further sayeth nott In Testimony whereof the Deponant hath hereunto Set his hand In New Castle this 3rd day
of April 1680.

[Signed:] J.D.Haes

Sworne Before mee
[Signed:] John Moll

---

1. This document is written in the hand of Ephraim Herman.

21:102c [FRANCIS WHITWELL'S PETITION FOR A COMMISSION
TO KEEP AN ACCOUNT OF STRAY HORSES]

St. Jones Aprel 12th

Honrabl Governer

Thees Few lines are to aquaintt your honor that ther is
several stray horses and mares in thees persinkes and many of
them wild and not marked and sevrel hath bene taken up but no
account hath been given of them but Convarted them to ther own

uses but if your honor would grant me A Comesion to take them
up I Shall be redy to give your honor An Acount of the same
this is all from him that rests in obeadeance to your honors
pleaser

[Signed:] Fra. Whitwell

[Addressed:] These to the hands of his honor the Governor
present

[Endorsed:]   [   ] Mr. Fra. Whitw[   ] att
            St. Jones delawo[   ] of stray horses.[1]

---

1. Endorsement is written in the hand of Matthias Nicolls.

21:103   [1680 CENSUS OF THE HOUSEHOLDERS FROM
          CEDAR CREEK TO DUCK CREEK][1]

These are to Certify the Honnourable Sir Edm[   ] Andros
Knight Governor Generall of New York and all his Royall Highness Territorys in Am[   ] of the Inhabitants that are Re-
sponceble housekeper[   ] their familys Inhabiting in Ceader
Crick Muther K[   ][2] St. Jones and Duck Crick

In Ceader Creek[3]

Robt. Hart.............. 3 in family		
upon Joseph Cowdree plantation 3 in family		dead
Mr. Bowman.......... 2 or 3 in family		of Groves
George Collens on Shakerlys plantation		disputab[ ]
Jno. Curtis............. 4 in family		quaker
Jno. Richardson......... 6 in family		
Thomas Groves........... 2 in family		Muder[4]
Thomas Heiffer.......... 2 in family		
Alexander Ray........... 2 in family		
Thomas William and Jno. Deshaw. 2 in family		

In St. Jones and Duck Crick

Mr. Fraunnces Whittwell.. 5 in family		
Mr. Jones............... 1 in family	[	]
Mr. Joshua Barksteede.... 3 in family		
Mr. Rob. Bedwell........ 3 in family	[	]
Allex: Humphry.......... 3 in family		
Mr. Isaack.............. 2 in family		
Jno. Brinckloo.......... 2 in family		
Gabrill Jones........... 3 in family		
Richard Levey........... 2 in family		
Mr. Wallter Dickason..... 5 in family		
Mr. Wm. Berry........... 2 in family	[	]
Jno. Briggs............. 6 in family		
Jno. Burton............. 2 in family	[	]
Henry Stevens........... 3 in family		
Daniel Jones............ 2 in family	qua[ ]	
Wm. Winsmore........... 1 in family		

```
Jno. Stevens.............. 3 in family
Thomas Bostick............ 2 in family
Robt. Beates.............. 3 in family
Jno. Hillyard............. 3 in family
Symon Irons............... 4 in family
Thomas Willson............ 4 in family
Peter Boyard.............. 2 in family
Wm. Greene................ 2 in family
Ch: Ellett................ 2 in family
Wm. Sherwood.............. 1 in family
```

These are the familys from the uper part of Ceader Crick to the
uper part of Duck Crick being 99 persons, to the best of the
Knowledge of him who Remaines

                              Your Honnors most humble Servant
                              [Signed:] John Brigs

[Endorsed:] N. Y. 23 apr[il 1680][5] inhabitants names in St.
Jones in delawar.

---

1. Other transcription in NYCD 12:646.

2. This is "Murder Kill" which appears often in variant
   forms such as "Murther" or "Mother Kill."

3. This heading and the notations in the margin are written
   in the hand of Matthias Nicolls.

4. This marginal notation and brace by Nicolls was added
   to distinguish those inhabitants living in Murder Kill
   from those in Cedar Creek.

5. The year has been recovered from O'Callaghan's Calendar.
   The endorsement is written in the hand of Matthias
   Nicolls.

21:104/105   [A 1671 LIST OF THE INHABITANTS FROM
               MATINICONK ISLAND TO NEW CASTLE][1]

Matincum [   ]nd[2]
Peter Aldricx
Lass Cock

Wicka Coe[3]
Swan Swansa
Olla Swansa
Andrew Swansa

Moy Mansy[4]
[   ]s Bancks
[   ]llen
[   ]derson

[   ] Molickka

Passaymunt[5]
[   ]bert Ashman   10
Thomas Jacobson
Caleb Carmen
William Duncke
John Ashman
Thomas Flayle
Francis Waker[6]
Frederick Andrews
Peter Ramboe
Hance Mansa
Andrews Inkhorn   20
John Boulsa
John Eustace
Mathias Holsten

Kincesse[7]
Jonas Neildson
Peter Andrews
[   ] Sneeer
[   ]abeth Dalbo
[   ] Cock
[   ] Otto
[   ] Bone   30

[   ]ons Hook[8]
[   ]rews Trumpeter
[   ] Collman
[   ]la Francis
[   ] Salloon
[   ]ews Salloon
[   ]ias Matson
[   ]rick Collman

Callcons Hook
Isreall Helme
Henrick Jacobson
Olla Kooko   40
John Minsterman
Hance Peterson

Ammersland
Henrick Johnson
Bartill Eschillson
Olla Slouboe
John Grilsaw
Mathias Mattison
Martin Martinson
Jacob Clementson
Hendrick Tauta   50

Tinnacum
Mr. Andrew Carr
Hance Walter

Upland
Niels Lausa
Nields Mathiasson
Eusta Benes
Hance Urian
Urian Keen

James Sanderline
Mr. Lausa the Minster[9]

Princes Dorp
Ufroe Popagay[10]   60
Peter Nieldson

Marquesse Kill
Hendricke Massan
Umus Eustason
John Hendrickson

Marquess Hook
Olla Nieldson
Olla Rausa
Hance Hopman
Chareles Janson
Po[ ]ell Corhold

Tredredene Hoock[11]
Michall Rongell 70
Olla Toersen
[   ]thas Nelidon[12]
Hendricke Neildson
Neilds Neilson

Skill Pott Kill
Andrews Mattson
Hans Petersen

Christeene
Andrews Urinson
James Mett
John Stalcopp
Jacob Vander Veere 80
Mr. Teeman[13]

Deer Point
Andrews the Fine
Seneca Brewer
Vald Raven

Bread and Cheese Island
Tho. Jackobson
Thomas Snelling
Clocker Olla

Swartnuten Island
Tho. Wolleston
Bone Backer 90
Garet Otta
Harman Otta

Feren Hook
John Ericks
Paules Lawson
Paules Poulson
Mathias Johnson
Henrick Lawsa
Peter Wooley

Long Hooke
Olla Shoemaker

Urin Boathman[14] 100
John Kett
Laurance or his sonn

Mill D[ ]pe
Peter Clauson
John Tison
John Clauson
William his [   ]

Cran[   ][15]
Mons Pou[   ]
Hendricke [   ]
Bartle the [   ]
Pella Park[   ]
[   ] Mats[   ]
[   ]
Askell Fin[ ]
Lass Eskellson
Smaul Peterson
John Skrick
Olla Toersin
Simon the Finn
Mathias the Finn
Evert the Finn 120

[   ]rden Hook
[   ]e Bran[ ]e
[   ]ke Johnson
[   ]r Dewhit
Widdow Bowmer[16]
Widdow Sericks
Rouloph
Hance Hanceson
Arntt Johnson
Hance Miller
John Hulke
[   ]ian Johnson 130
[   ]thias Esclesen
[   ]cas Peterson
[ ]lla Toersin
[   ]ret Sanderson
[   ]nce Blocke
[   ]lis Douxen
[   ]n Barneson

[   ]w Castle
[   ]n Carr
[   ]bart Dericke
[   ]cham the Coopper 140
[   ]ll Berrown[17]
[   ] Cantwell
[   ] Crab
[   ]
[   ] Rosamond
[   ]ias Linburgge
[   ]ricke Johnson
[   ]cke Time
[   ]ent Eegbourson
[   ]ias De Ringe 150
[   ] Snerling
[   ] Oudhout
[   ] Erskin

[ ]n Garetsin
James [ ]afford
William Thom
William [ ]ckler
Cornelius Winehard
John Martinson
Garett Smieth 160
Barnet Egbertson
Anna Peeterson marryed to Andrees[18]
Hance Bones
Evert Garets
Peter Alricks[19]

[Entitled:] A List of the Inhabitants of Delaware River.

[Endorsed:] [ ] List [ ] Inhabitants [ ]
Delaware
1671[20]

---

1. This 1671 census appears so late in the documents because it was apparently filed with the preceding census (21:103) which is dated 1680. See 20:81a for a 1671 list of inhabitants at the Whorekill. For 1677 lists of "tithable" inhabitants in New Castle and Upland see NCCR:159 and UCR:77. Other transcription in NYCD 12:646.

2. Matiniconk Island.

3. Wicacoa.

4. Moyamensing.

5. Passayunck.

6. i.e., Walker.

7. Kinsessing.

8. Probably "Carkoens Hook." cf., UCR:79.

9. Domine Laurentius Carolus Lokenius.

10 Armegart Printz. Ufroe is an English attempt at Dutch juffrouw: "madam." She was the wife of Johan Papegoja who died in 1667.

11. Possibly a confusion of the Swedish name "Tridie Hoeck" with the Dutch name "Verdrietige Hoeck" for this neck of land above Christina.

12. Possibly a misspelling of "Neildson" or "Neilson."

13. Tymen Stiddem.

14. Jurian Boatsman.

15. Crane Hook.

16. This name is crossed out.

17. Probably "Michael Baron."

18. This notation is written in the hand of Matthias
    Nicolls.

19. This name was added by M. Nicolls.

20. Endorsement is written in the hand of Matthias Nicolls.

21:106   [PETITION OF CORNELIS JANSEN FOR A REHEARING
           OF A DIFFERENCE WITH H. WILTBANK][1]

To his Excellency Sir Edmond Andros Knight etc. [ ] Governor
Generall under his Royall Highness of all his Territories in
America

       The humble Petition of Cornelis Janse.

Whereas there is past a Judgement of the Court at the
Whorekill of the diffrence between this petitioner and Harmanus
Wiltbank about a parcell of Land.

This Petitioners humble request is to have a grant of a
rehearing and a tryall by a Jury at the Whorekill, to determine
the Cause and this petitioner shall ever pray.

[Endorsed:]   A Peticion Cornelius Jansz Whorekill. April 1st
              1680.[2]

---

1. See PA 5:711 for the governor's order on this petition.

2. Endorsement is written in the hand of Matthias Nicolls.

21:107   [DANIEL WILLS TO MATTHIAS NICOLLS ABOUT
           A LETTER DELIVERED BY JACOB LEISLER]

    Loveing freind Captayne Nicolls   heare this day came to
burlington on[1] Jacob Leysler with A writeing from thy self,
which I read over in the absence of Thomas Olive whom thou
derected thy writeing unto and I being att the toune but
axadentally and could not meet with Any of the other Commissioners, att the presant time, soe conveniantly could not
answer thy desire by this barer, noe more at presant from thy
freind
                             [Signed:] Daniell Wills

Burlington the 6th
day of the 2nd month
comonly caled
April 1680

---

1. i.e., one.

21:108   [PETITION OF THE INHABITANTS OF CREWCORNE
          AGAINST THE SALE OF LIQUOR TO THE INDIANS][1]

Aprill the 12 1680

To the Worthy Governor of new York

  Whereas wee the Inhabitants of the new seated Towne nere
the falls of Delloware (called Crewcorne) findeing our selves
agreived by the Indians when drunck, Insomuch that we be and
have been in great danger of our Lives, of houses burning of
our goods Stealeing and of our Wives and children a Frighting,
Insomuch that wee are affeared to go about our Lawfull occasions,
least when wee come home we[ ] finde them and our concernes
damnifyed. These things considered we doe humbly and Jointly
desire that the selling [   ] and other strong liquors
to the Indians may be wholly s[ ]ppressed which if done we
shall live peaceable

        [Signed:] Willi Biles
            Rich Regway[2]
            Samuell Feild
            John Akarman
            Robt: [   ][3]
            Robt: Scholey
            Tho: Scholey
            Danial Brinson
            William Cooper
            George Browne
Mr. Gilbert Wheelers house broake open by Indians and Peter
Aldrix Mans house on The Island and another hou[ ][4]

           Gilbert Wheeler[5]

[   ] Hoskins drowned[6]
[   ] Estate att Burlington

---

1. Other transcription in NYCD 12:645.

2. Richard Ridgeway. cf., 21:131.

3. Probably Robert Lucas. cf., 21:131.

4. This note is written in a second hand.

5. This name and the following notes are written in the
    hand of Matthias Nicolls.

6. See 21:97a for Philip Pocock's report on the drowning
    of Robert Hoskins.

21:109   [A LIST OF JUSTICES COMMISSIONED IN DELAWARE][1]

Apr. 5. 1680
When Mr. de la   Commission to the Justices at the
Grange was agoe-   Whorekill dated Oct. 8th 1678 vizt.
ing, the Go: thought
to renew the   John Avery
commissions but   Francis Whittwell
resolved to stay   Alexander Molestein
till Mr. Ephr.   John Kippshaven
Herm:[2] came.   Luke Wattson
                               John Roades and
                               James Wells.

Commission to James Nevill Wm. Penton etc. on the West side of
New Jersey[3] at Salem or Swamp Towne Oct. 26. 1679.

The like Commission for the Upper plantacion on the west side
of New Jersey Aug. 7. 1677.

Tho. Olive   ⎫
Dan. Willes   ⎪   A new Comission to the
John K[   ][4] ⎪   7 remaining. any 4 to be
John Pinford   ⎬   a Court etc. as the Common
Jos. Hel[   ][5] ⎪   Court.
Robt. Stacey   ⎪   I doe further [   ]
Benjam. Scott and   ⎪   Mar. 25. 1680
Richard Guy.   ⎭

[Endorsed:] Court [   ] for Delaware to be renewed 1680.

[On a separate leaf:]
     Newcastle Court
In the place of Mr. Abraham Man,[6]
The same - any 4 in court
                         Mar. 25, 1680

     Upland Court
The same - onely in the place of Peter
Rambo to put Robert Wade.

[On a separate leaf:][7]

          Peter Cock
          P. Rambo
          Isr. Helme
          Otto Ernest Cock
          Lasse Andris

Olle Swansa

John Moll
P. Alrich
Fop Outhout
Gerrit Otto
Joh.d.Haes
Wm. Sempill
Abr. Man

[On a separate leaf:][8]
[   ]
Mr. Withwel
Mr. Jones
Mr. Briges
Mr. Glover
Mr. Hart
Mr. Barkstead
Mr. Peck
Mr. Winsmor
Mr. Hiliard
Mr. Richissen
Mr. Bawcum
Mr. Berroy Bishop

---

1. cf., 21:83 which is related to this document and is also written in the hand of Matthias Nicolls.

2. Ephraim Herman.

3. West side of New Jersey replaces: East side of Delaware River, which has been crossed out.

4. John Kensey. cf., 21:83.

5. Jos. Helmesly. cf., 21:83.

6. This line is crossed out.

7. The following represent nominations for justices at Upland and New Castle.

8. This list, which is not in Matthias Nicolls' hand, represents nominations for magistrates at St. Jones. See 21:110a and 21:145b for petitions to establish a court at St. Jones.

21:110a   [PETITIONS OF FRANCIS WHITWELL ON BEHALF OF THE PEOPLE AT ST. JONES FOR THE ESTABLISHMENT OF A COURT][1]

Most worthy and honorable Sir after my dew respets to

your honor I thought good to aquaint your honor with some of
the greeven[   ] of the Inhabetans in and About St. Jones and
Duck Creek understanding that they shall be exposed to goe
eather to Dellawar[2] or the Horkel to Corte being so fare distant and the [   ] and exposed to great hardnes which hath
[   ]ed some of ther health locally they cannot [
]nences for mony wich being fifty or sixty miles some of
them from ther homes wich we hoped ever sence we Came heare
that we should be eased of thes grevences hoping that we might
as the people Increas have obtained better Convenences for the
ease of the power[3] Inhabetance to have another Court and the
Court bee Keep[   ] about St. Jones whear ther is great resort
out of Mer[   ] and would be Bettr Incureged for the
s[   ]ing of [   ] place hear it being as popeles[4] as any
place betwene the horkill and Delawar and I Dout not but persons may be found as sufesant to Determn a Case or Difrancess[5]
thar may be Among them as is in some other places in this Bay
if your honor ware pleased to make Choice of them from the
north side of Seadr Creek to the south side of Duck Creek is
About sixty miles or more which if your honor would take it
into your Considracion to Compose the same into A County it
would be very exept[   ]ll to the powr Inhabetance who othr
wayes will be [   ] great Charge both in speding ther substance and predages[6] in the necklect o[   ]ther busenes [   ]
for we doe undrstand that the delawar men hath sued to your
[   ] that ther County might Com as fare as St. Jones but we
hope that your honor will be Bettr [   ] so if not it would
great discureg[   ] both that are hear and thar is to Com so
[   ] your honor will take it into [   ] Considracion
as a [   ] I rest in [   ] your honors pleasur whil
I am   [Signed:] Fr. Whitwell

[Verso:][7]
    Humbly shew to your honor the greiveances and great
hazards and perils both by water and land that wee are putt to
in goeinge [   ] to the Whorekill downe to the Court held
there that nott onely the distans of some and more of us
beinge 50 and 60 miles butt [   ] many places the unpassablenes
of the way for man and beast by reason of high tides and upon
suden freshes that there is not possivility of goeing over
for eyther over the Creeks and marshes thereto adjoyneing butt
in jeopardy of life to both which hath given disincourgement
to sev[   ] persons comeinge to seat in these parts from
Maryland beinge nere there to that they have desisted from
proceedinge any further in there designes of setlement rather
then to goe to hazard theire lives downe to the whorekill
which Inconveniency continues nott onely in summer time butt in
the winter season is far more greiveous by reason of severall
dangerous branches which are to be past through with great
difficultie and hazard And foras much as these upward parts
have exceedingly encreased and severall considerable families
lately removed from Maryland to these parts and others dayly
addinge to the setlement [   ] then
any other parte of this County And for that nott onely the
[   ] of the County and towns of Delaware [   ] that if the Inhabitants [   ]
should be ordered [   ] eyther places [   ]
Inhabitants [   ] cause some or most to withdraw back and
withhold other [   ]

    [   ] humble reverence leave the discuss of
the whole [   ] your honors [   ] and consideracion and
doubt nott butt for the encouragement of us the Inhabitants and

others who may and are expected to come amongst us [
] adjecent to Maryland your honor of tender Care and Clemency of setlinge the place preserveinge us under the shun-
shine [sic] of your honors happy Government from all future
greveances perills and dangers and for the ease and Incouragement of all such persons as may settle in these parts your
[sic] will be pleased to order and give and authority for a
Court to be held in some convenient place in St Jones Creeke
and that all persons from the Northside of Cedar Creeke to the
South side of Blackbird Creeke may by your honors order be required to doe suite and service to [   ]
thereof Not doubtinge butt your Honor [   ]
men in the precincts thereof when your honor may [
]

[Endorsed:] N.Y. 15 May 1680 from St. Jones Delawar for
             N. Court there.[8]

---

1. See 21:145b for another version of this petition which
   is in the same hand as the one on the reverse leaf of
   this document.

2. i.e., the court at New Castle.

3. i.e., poor.

4. i.e., populous.

5. i.e., differences.

6. i.e., prejudices.

7. This version of the petition is written in a second
   hand.

8. Endorsement is written in the hand of Matthias Nicolls.

21:110b   [DEPOSITION OF PETER GROENENDYCK CONCERNING
            AN ACCOUNT AGAINST JOHN SHACKERLY]

        The deposition of Peter Groenendyk aged 35 year or ther
abouds,

        Saied that Mr. John Shackerly deceased became Indebted
unto Mrs. Mary Phillips the quantity of twoo hundered twinty
six gallon of Rume as by a note from under his hand may appeare
the 30th day of July 1679, within my hearing the said John
Shackerly would a [   ] the said Rum on the Account of Mr.
[   ] your deponant saied not
                        [Signed:] Peter Groenendyk

Horkil this
[   ] 1680   Sworn before me
                        [Signed:] Luke Wattson

21:111   [WILLIAM BILES TO GOV. ANDROS ABOUT AFFAIRS
          AT CREWCORNE NEAR THE FALLS]

Crewcorne the 17th of the 3rd month Caled may 1680

Govenor   According to thy warrent to me directed Bareing date
the 20th of aprill 1680 I did summon Gilbert Whelar and Barnet
Keerce to appeare Beefore thee and thy Councill in New Yorke
and hath also according thy warrent Bearein the same date
warned the people of oure towne to meete to gether for to
Chuse Comissioners or magastrates and they hath chosen those
foure whose names are under written since my Returne home wee
hath Been very quiet with the Indians and the people heare are
very well satisfied with what thee hath done in order to Keepe
them quiet which is all at present from him whoe is Ready to
serve the in what I may
                                [Signed:] Willi Biles
George Browne
Robert Scooly
Robert Lucas
Samuell Feild

[Addressed:]   to Edmund Andros Govenor   this deliver In
               New Yorke

[Endorsed:]   The returne of William Biles Constable of Crooke-
               horne at the Falls in answer to a speciall, May
               12, 1680[1]

---

1. Endorsement is written in the hand of Matthias Nicolls.

21:112   [DANIEL WILLS TO GOV. ANDROS WITH A NOMINATION
          LIST FOR COMMISSIONERS AT BURLINGTON][1]

     According to thy warrant wee have herein sent the names
of Five persons in order to the renewing of our Commission:
And this is deisred by us all, That the Clause in the next
Commission (vizt.) (concerning the laying out sufficient
Quantities of Land for the People) may be left out, wee being
satisfyed that the Land was bought by us and paid for; And
therefore according to every ones Quantity wee are willing   ·
that every one should have his just right and share thereof.

                                [Signed:] Daniell Wills
Burlington the 15th of the 3rd moneth 1680.

                    x Thomas Olive ⎫ old Commisioners
                    x Daniell Wills ⎬
                    x Robert Stacy ⎭
                    x Mahlon Stacy
                    x William Emley   Commissioners
                      Thomas Lambert

                      Thomas Budde
                      Thomas Gardner   Commissioners

                      William Peachy   Sheriffe
                      Thomas Revell   Clerke

                      Thomas Olive[2]

[Endorsed:] N.Y. 20th May - 80 returne from Burlington.

        The returne from the Falls.[3]

---

1. The check marks before the names were apparently made
    by Matthias Nicolls in selecting five commissioners
    from the list.

2. This name is written in a second hand and may signify
    Olive's endorsement of the list.

3. Endorsement is written in the hand of Matthias Nicolls.

21:113   [DECLARATION OF THOMAS BUDD CONCERNING A
          MISLAID PAPER][1]

                      New Yorcke May 22nd 1680

      I doe heare ingeniously relate that concerning [   ]
paper which was subscribed two, I doe not Kn[ ] what is become of it but heare I truly decl[   ] that I have not Intent
to keepe that paper [   ] subscription but am realy sorry
that I ever was concerned therin and If it shall come to my
hand againe I doe heare promise to deliver it to one of the
Comishoners to bee torne in peeces
                          [Signed:] Thomas Budd

[Verso:] Upon his submission he is discharged May 22 1680
                          M.N.[2]

[Endorsed:] Thomas Budds acknowledgment about the sub-
             scriptions. Delaware the East side. Burlington
             May 22 1680.

---

1. See 29:99 (printed in NYCD 12:650) for a council
    minute on this matter.

2. This order and the following endorsement are written
    in the hand of Matthias Nicolls.

21:114   [JAMES NEVILL TO GOV. ANDROS ABOUT THE
         APPREHENSION OF SOME RUNAWAYS FROM VIRGINIA][1]

Governor

     About the 12 instant 2 person in the habit of a Seaman
came to this place pretending himselfe to be mate of a Ship
called the Marygold bound for Gynny[2] and was to touch at New
york to leave Some passengers there with whom the Master had
condicioned and to have 100 lb. for their passage which money
was on board the Ship with much goods for the Gynny Trade and
comming to Cape-May the Ship Struck ground and Stuck fast the
Seamen escaped in a Greenland Shallop that belonged to the
Ship, the Master his sone and 5 passengers were drowned, and
that he had left 4 Seamen at Cohanzy[3] and the Shallop in
Morriss-River[4], he desired assistance with men and Boates
pretending he could Save much goods and rigging if he could
get help, I sent him to the Magistrates at New-Castle who made
provission for his aide, but before they were ready, this pretended Mate escaped away, they then Suspected him, and Sent
huy and cry after him; but hither have not taken him; with in
24 houres after his escape a person came to New Castle from
Virginia, who came in pursuite after these Seamen; I haveing
notice thereof Sent four men to Cohanzy apprehended the four
men that were there, and Sent them to the high Sherriffe at
Newcastle, where it appeared that the pretended Mate with
these four men were Servants in Virginia and had Stolne a
Shallop from thence and left her towards the mouth of Delaware
river; At the first report here, of the Ship being fast in the
Sands as aforemencioned, William Maltster, Edw. Lumley, Tho.
Watson, John Salter and John Wooldridge went from hence Secretly
in a great Cannooe to finde out the afore named Shallop at
Maurice River intending to take her to the Ship and to bring
what they could from thence with out being accountable to any,
but coming where the Shallop lay, they found her fore part
burn't, they took her Cable, Grapling and Rudder-Irons and a
Smale Cock-boate about 8 foote by the Keile and returned to
William Maltsters plantacion where they left them untill they
Could make Sale thereof; which I haveing Notice of, have Secured till thy pleasure be known concerning them; the Cable
I Suppose to be between 20 and 30 fathom, a large Grapling,
the boat is Supposed to belong to the Shallop; I desire thee
Send an answere hereof to thy true
Salem the 26th   Friend
[ ] the 3 mo. 1680.   [Signed:] James Nevill

[Addressed:]   For The Govenor of New-yorke etc. These with
               Care.

[Endorsed:]   N.Y. 8 June 1680 from Mr. Nevill of Deloworr of
              runawayes Boat that found at Maurice River[5]

---

1. Other transcription in NYCD 12:650.

2. Guinea.

3. Cohansey. Probably the area where the Cohansey River
   empties into Delaware Bay south of Salem, N.J.

4. Maurice River. Also called "Riddare Kill" by the Dutch
   and Swedes. It empties into Delaware Bay between

Cohansey River and Cape May.

5. Endorsement is written in the hand of Matthias Nicolls.

21:115   [EPHRAIM HERMAN TO GOV. ANDROS ABOUT LAND IN   1
          DELAWARE WITH ORDERS BY MATTHIAS NICOLLS THEREON]

                        300 acres a p.[2]

      Twoo Pattents for 600 acres of Land Granted by his Ex-
cellency Sir Edm. Andros unto John Morgen and John Denny both
deceased the said Land Lying on the west syde of Delowar River
towards the mouth thereof, betweene The Land of Morris Liston
and Duck Creeke

      The Pattens to bee called In. The Land is heitherto not
seated noe quit rent paid and the persons that first tooke
itt up boath deceased without heirs.

      To bee made over by Patent to Mr. Ephraim Hermans,
granted him by the Go.[3]

      His Excell. has granted to Laurens Cock the Land formerly
granted unto John Ashman and Sam: Jeckson by Pattent from
Governor Andros, Lying on the west syde of Delowar River and
on the north Syde of Duke Creeke Cont. 600 acres of Land The
Pattents to bee delivered him by Capt. Cantwell hee paying
all the Charges and [the] Arrier of the quit rent due.

      Lasse Cock and Eph: Herman Grant [for] Each 200 acres of
Land up the River Just [below] Chiepaessing at a place Called
Taorackan

[Endorsed:] Mr. Ephraim H[ ]mans paper to the Governor about
             Land for him and Lausa Cock. June 1, 1680 orders
             thereupon.[4]

_____

      1. Other transcription in NYCD 12:651.

      2. This notation is written in the hand of Matthias
          Nicolls.

      3. This order is written in the hand of Matthias Nicolls.

      4. Endorsement is written in the hand of Matthias Nicolls.

21:116a   [DEPOSITION OF SAMUEL STILES CONCERNING HIS
           EJECTMENT BY JOHN RICHARDSON][1]

                         June the 7th 1680.

     This day Samwell Stiles Aged Forty foure years or there
Abouts Came before us and deposed on his oath that on or about
the Third day of April Last past; That John Richardson Came
with severall other persons to the house that John Stevens
seated him upon near Lettel Creeke in the Whoore Kill precents:
and demanded him to give him the said Richardson possession of
the house and Land and threetened this deponant that if he
would not give him possession that he would send him to prisson;
and that he had brought up Servants to put on the plantacon;
and said that if he this deponant did not give him possession
that he should pay for the Lorse[2] of his Servants time; soe
Through fear of being Ruened in prison; I this deponant went
away and Left him the said Richardson in possession of the said
house and Land; and Further sayeth not;   Samuell ⟨∩⟩ Styles
                                                 his mark
Sworne In open Court
[June] the 8th 1680
[Signed:]   Test: Cornelis Verhoofe Cl. Cu. Whorekill

[Entitled:]   Samuell Stiles evidens

---

     1. Other transcription in NYCD 12:652.

     2. i.e., loss.

21:116b   [COPY OF A COURT ORDER IN A LAND DISPUTE   1
           BETWEEN WALTER DICKINSON AND BARNARD HODGES][1]

Copia   Att a Court held for the whore
                            kill the 8th day of June 1680

               ⎡Capt. John Avery   ⎤ Mr. John Kipshaven ⎤
Comissioners ⎨Mr. Francis Whitwell ⎬ Mr. Luke Watson   ⎬present
               ⎣Mr. Alex: Molestine ⎦ Mr. James Wells   ⎦

Walter Dickinson plt.⎤ in a plea of Trespas
Barnard Hodges   deft.⎦

     The matter in difference betweene the said plt. and deft.
beinge concerneinge the right and Title of a Tract of Land
called Mulberry Swampe scituate in St. Jones Creeke after a
full heareinge of the matter on both sides and the Said Cause
beinge upon the defts. mocion putt upon Tryall of a Jury and
after a full debate on both sides the Jury haveinge duly considered of the difference in Question doe agree in theire
verdict and finde for the plt. with one penny damage and Coste
of suite als. Execucion

Test. Corn. Vrhoofe Cler.
Vera Cop: ex. per me

	£ s d	[Signed:] Griff Jones
The Sheiriffs Fees	00-09-00	
Cler. Fees [2]	01-02-06	
Americament[2]	00-05-00	
Jury Fees	01-01-00	
Evidences	01-04-00	
	04-01-06	

[Endorsed:] Copie of Court order, Walt. Dickinson Plt.
             Barnard Hodges deft.[3]

---

1. See 21:123 for a contemporary copy of this court
   decision with additional material concerning the case.
   Other transcription in NYCD 12:652.

2. Same as "amercement": an arbitrary fine imposed by the
   court.

3. Endorsement is written in the hand of Matthias Nicolls.

21:117   [PETITION OF WALTER DICKINSON CONCERNING A
          LAND DISPUTE WITH BARNARD HODGES]

To the right honorable Sir Edmond Andros Knight Seigneur of
Sansmarez Lt. and Governor Generall under his Royall highnes
James duke of yorke etc, of all his Territories in America

     In all humble manner showeth unto your honor your dayly
Orator Walter Dickinson of Talbott County in the province of
Maryland beinge ambitious and desireous for the benefitt of
himself Children (beinge a person well knowne in the said province of good estate and for severall yeares ever since his
comeinge and Seateinge therein as a planter to live in good
fame and reputacion and honest behavior and nott willinge
ever to wronge or trepas abridge or Covett any mans estate
but what he legally purchased of others or tooke upp upon
Condicions of plantacions) to take up or purchase an estate
for himself and Children within the Sunshine of this honorable
Government In order where unto your orator heveinge contracted
to himselfe a certen Tract of Land lyeinge in or nere St.
Jones Creeke in this Government called by your orator by the
name of Mulberry Swampe containeinge foure hundred acres or
thereabts which said Land was thentofore surveyed for one
Thomas Merritt who never Seated the Same butt dyed as is reported in his voyage for England which said premisses your honor
by your patent under seale [   ] this honorable Government
ready to be produced to your honor confirmed to your orator
his heres and Assignes under Such lymittacions and services as
therein is expressed and which your orator ever hath byn and
Still is ready to yeild obeidience to do the Seatinge and Im-

proveinge where of your orator hath nott onely byn att great
Costs chardges disbursements and expenses in contracting for
the Same both in his money paid for the purchase thereof and
his severall Journeyes and disbursements of duties for Confirmacion thereof which if the same were duly calculated your
orator could plainely make appeare that the Same would double
amount to the vallue thereof Butt your Honor for the Incouragement Said Government hath byn att great Costs and Chardges in
Transportinge servants goods and Chattells [   ]
llue to the Said plantacion which never yett could returne to
my proffitt [   ] For that one Barnett Hodges of St.
Jones Creeke pretendinge aright [   ] beinge a man
of meane Capacity and onely himselfe and wief and as it [
       ] hath Severall tymes [ ]ott onely given out Scurrilous
and [   ] as old Rogue old Quakinge dog and that he
would [   ] hundred pounds bag [   ] and he would
finde [   ] meaneinge in Law here and a[   ]yf he could
nott doe here his [   ] his owne minde then he would goe
with the Cause for England as yf your [   ]ncell were
nott of Capacity to determine the Same Butt alsoe hath and
[   ] threateinge speeches against your orators servants there that yf they or any other on behalfe of your
orator putt a foote upon the said land he will either kill
maime or wound them though your orator when desperately sick
and little hopes of life willinge to depart in Charity to the
[   ] and to declare and manifest to the world his ambition
to die and depart this transitory life [   ] good will
to all persons did send to the said Barnett Hodges to come to
your orator in his Sick Cond[   ] and your honor for Quiett
enjoyment of the premisses out of meere good will after lardge
Tenders of [   ] by way of Guift to him for a finall end of
all future Clamors which he refused and though your orator was
in such weake Condicion would nott vouschafe¹ to come nere
your orator butt presisted in his base dirty scurrylous language both to your orator and Threates to his servants where-
uppon your orator after Recovery of his said sicknes brought
his accion of Trespas against the said Hodges (he makeinge use
with one John Newell his mate of the plantacion to make Corne
on) onely for Tryall of your orators Titles so which accion
the Said Hodges appeareinge and giveinge in his speciall matter
in evidence and a Jury Impanelled of able and indifferent men
for Tryall of the same the Jury found for your orator as by
the Judgment² dated the eighth of June Anno 1680 may att lardge
appeare Nevertheles the said Hodges still molesteth your orator
and continues his said menaces careinge nott what he doth or
can doe soe that your orator may be dispossed or kept out with
stronge hands from the premisses and hath endeavoured all
sinister wayes and meanes to deale under hand with others to
defraud your orator of his Just right sayinge he cared nott
who had ytt Soe your orator had itt nott and did by one John
Burton of St. Jones Tender to your orators Attorney to give
him halfe the said Land and two hoggs to speake little and
desist in the said Cause and after verdict against him said he
would give his right to [   ] to sue for the same soe that
the Old Rogue (your orator meaneinge) might be disseised of
[   ] And since your Honor hath byn pleased to erect a Court
att St. Jones is with confederacy with the said John Burton and
John Glover more violent then ever in his wordes against your
orator and his Attorney for puttinge him under execucion for
this Costs recovered against him where he yett remaines your
orator haveinge made faire offers by his Attorney to the said
Hodges which nothinge availes Butt now is by some dissemblinge
Confederates persuaded to continue his molestinge your orator

and now the Court beinge come to St. Jones they Question nott
butt recover the Land for him to have a Jury for theire owne
Butt your orator is ready to make appeare to your Honor That
he by law is nott bound to answeare the Said Hodges upon the
same matter neither ought any venisne[3] to arise from a place
where the Inhabitants doe beare noe good will to your orator
butt have given out theire Judgments in Chimney Corner Law and
discourse against your orator The premisses Considered (And for
that your Honor May further understand that your orators
Attorney did tender him an appeale after verdict and charged
itt to him and Since hath offered the Said Hodges to determine
the Same by consent without further Chardge to him before your
honor which he utterly refused) your orator humbly praies your
Honor to take the same into your Honors most serious Consideracion that your Honor would be graciously pleased to grant to
your orator a decretall order for Quiett enjoyment of the
premisses without further Trouble or molestacion or otherwise
yf the Said Hodges findes himself greived the Same may be discussed before your Honor whose grave Judgment and deliberacion
upon the matter will doubtlese putt a full period to the
buisnes your orator yf knoweinge he should have had such
trouble and vexacion for the quietinge enjoyinge of the just
right he hath to the premisses had byn att first better to have
desisted to seate then have byn troubled by such an invetirate
malicious [   ] the said Hodges who still prosists to
vex and molest your orator and still [   ] your orator
be releived by your Honor To whom your orator [   ]
premisses to doe as your Honor in your grave wisdom.

---

1. i.e., vouchsafe.

2. See 21:116b for a copy of this judgment.

3. A misspelling of "visne" which is a former spelling of
    the legal term "venue."

21:118   [WILLIAM CLARK TO GOV. ANDROS REFUSING TO TAKE
          THE OATH OF OFFICE WITH A STATEMENT WHICH HE
          REQUESTS BE ACCEPTED INSTEAD]

              Whoore Kill the 21st 4th month Called June 1680

Governor Andros;

      Sence the Arrivell of John Roades here by Peter Groundik
Sloop; I was sumanced to A Court by vertue of A warrant from
the; to take the oath of A Justices of the peace for this precents; According to thy Commission to others with myselfe
directed; I am and shall be with Gods Asistance to the best of
my knowlidge; for ever redy to sarve thee and my Countrey in
that or the meanest Capasety that I may be Thought Capable of;
But as to the Ceremony of an oath; It is not unknowen unto

thee; That it is A Generall princab[ ] Receved and Releaved
Amonest the people of the Lord Called Quakers; of whome I owne
myselfe to be A member That wee ought not to sware; According
to the Command of our savour Christ; 5th Mat. 34 Whoe said
sware not at all; And the Exhorttacion of the Appostel James;
5th James:12 who said Above all things my Brethren sware not;
neither by Heaven nor by Earth; nor by any other oath; soe that
for fear of offending the Lord, and for no other end; I Cannot
take the oath; But Insteede thereof I doe give A paper in
writing signed by me; which is recorded in the Court; And
give satisfacion to the rest of the Commissioners; A Coppie
thereof I have under written sent thee; And if thee will be
pleased to Accept of it Insteede of an oath; I hope I shall
discharge the Trust reposed in me Faithfully to the best of my
understanding; But if this will not be Accepted; my Request is
that thee will be pleased to Excuse me and Appoint sume other
person in my place; be pleased to favour me with thy result
therin; for I shall not be soe forward to Act in that stacion
as when I have thy Conformaition; I shall not at present enlarg
but Approve myselfe true and faithfull in thy services

[Signed:] Wm. Clark]

Whereas the Governer of New York hath beene pleased by
his [ ]cion; To Appoint And Authorize me William Clark to
be one [ ]tices of the peace for the Whoore Kill percents;
Insteede thereof I doe hereby [ ] and Ingage to discharge
that offices faithfully to the best of [ ] understanding; And
to doe or shall (wittingly or willingly) doe any thing; [ ]
to Law and Justices; I doe hereby oblidge my selfe to suffer
[ ] under goe such fine or ponishment; as if I had Actively
taken [ ]; As wittnes my hand this seaventeenth day of
the moneth [ ] June one Thousand six hundred and Eightye;

[Signed:] Wm. Clark

[Addressed:] This
To Governor Andros at Fort James in New York
Present

21:119   [CORNELIS VERHOOFE TO GOV. ANDROS CONCERNING
          HIS DUTIES AS SURVEYOR AND OTHER MATTERS]

Right Honorable Sir   Whorekill the 23th of
                                    June Anno 1680.

Not to obstrude your Excellencys more Waighty Affair[ ]
thought Good to Acquaint your Honor with Sume of the particulars
of Land Concernes here in these partes, Since it hath Been
your Honors Good Will and pleasure, to Constitute mee Surveyor
here, which Doth as yet Remaine Sume What ill favored, and is
as not Come to Good perfections as yet, being your Honors orders
from time to time have been but Little observed heitherto,
have made Severall Surveys both of Seated and Unseated Lands,
of which Should have made Sum Returnes Before now, but haveing
been a Long Time In Grea[ ] want of paper, and In the Spring

of the Year is here allway[ ] most Employments for Either
Clerks or Surveyors, Am fully Resolved to Bee with your Exc.
my Selfe and bring all my Returnes my Selfe, which Will be in
Sume time of August next if god Will permitt, on purpose to
Give your Honor my Acknowledment In Every particular, as need
may Require, and for Sum Certaine Errecting particulars for the
future, In my Small opinium, by your Honors Good Will and
pleasure, if your Honors prudent Wisedome See Good Cause for
it, of Which In part have mentioned more at Large to Capt.
Matthias Nicolls Secr.; hope your Honor please to pardon In
What I may bee amiss, I am Willing to act Dispence my Uytmust
Endeavors for the Well, Speedy and quiet Inhabiting of this
partes, which Doth much Lay in the good mannagement and fayth-
full Care of a Surveyor, have Cleared Severall Defective Surveys, formerly made In theire Due Right, to the best of my
Understanding and Know no otherwise yet, but Doe Remaine with
quietness among the Inhabitants, have not further to Inlarge
onely Did Lately Understand that the Lord Baltemore Governor
of Maryland had Sumned all his Justices of the peace, to take
oath to What purpose I have not yet heard of Shall for the
present Soe Remaine
                    Your Honors most obedient Subject and Servant
                    [Signed:] Cornelis Verhoofe

[Addressed:]   To the Right Honorable Sir Edmund Andross
                Knight Governor Generall and Vice Admirall
                Under his Royall Highness James Duke of Yorke
                and Albany etc. of All his Territories in America
                These

21:120   [WHOREKILL COURT TO GOV. ANDROS CONCERNING
          THE PARCELLING OUT OF LAND][1]

Honorable Governor   Whoore Kill the 26th, 4 mo. Called Jun.
                         1680

        Thy Commicion wee have recieved; And in obedeance there-
unto have proceeded etc; whareas there have heather to bene A
nedglect in geting A prisson here; for want of which there
have bene not long Sence A prissoner for debt whoe was a
Stranger made his Escape; which may prove Damage either to the
County or Shreeife[2]; for the preventing of the like for the
futter[3]; wee have ordered A prisson Stocks and wheeping post;
forth with to be built; which will Cost betwene three or foure
Thousand pounds of Tobacco; here is also greate want of A Court
house; the which will Cost about five Thousand pounds of Tobacco; our request is that Thee will be pleased to Impower us
to make a Tax to Leavey the Same on the Inhabitants; there was
Sume Certain Land formerly Laid out by Capt. Cantwell for a
Towne; which was to be devided i[nto] Lots of 60 foot in
breath and 200 foot in Leinght; and the land and [woods] that
Lye back ward to be Common for feed of Cattell and firwood;
it being in all about 130 Acres of Land; Some which time
Armainas Wiltbanck[4] have got the Said land Survayed; but wee

doe not understand that he have any patton for it; he demands
A bushell of winter wheate A yeare of any person that Shall
build upon the Said Towne Lands; which is Soe high A rent that
it gives no Incurigment for any to build; wee Shou[ld] think
one halfe of that rent would be an nouffe; but that wee leave
to thy ordering and to whom the rent Shall be paid; wheather
to the due of york or to Armainas Wiltbanck; here is a greate
Marsh that lyes at the north west Side of the Towne; which if
it Should be at anytime here after taken up by any peticoler
person it would be a greate In Convenencey to those that doe
or Shall here after live here; As alsoe the Cap⁵ whar there is
good pin Trees for building; the land Lettel worth; both which
wee desier may Lye in Common for the use of the Towne; It hath
bene Spoake here as if thee ded Intent; as an Ease to the
Court to Impower the Survayer to grant warrants to Lay out land
to Such persons as Shall Com to take it up; But wee being
Senceable of the Ill Consequence that will attend that; doe
desier that thee would be pleased to for bear giveing him any
such power; for our precents is now but Small; And he for the
Lucher⁶ of geting the more money; will Lay out Such Large tracts
of Land for a peticoler person; that migh Sarve many fameileys
to live Comfortably upon; there have bene Expearance of the
Like; As when Capt. Cantwell had the Same power he Survayed
Three Thousand Acres of princabl Land at Prime Hook for Henry
Smith; And others of the like nature migh be mentioned; And
wee have good Cause to resolve for the time to Com to grant
Less Tracts of Land to perticoler persons then have bene formerly granted for this County as it is now devided is not above
halfe soe big or large as St. Jones; nor will not hold halfe
soe many people; neither [is] the land soe generally good as
that is; And this being the Anciante[st]⁷ [place] wee thinke
with Submisson; might a bene Continowed at least [Equi]l with
the other; which if thee please may be redrassed in [the] next
Commicon or Sooner; which may be by devideing by [M]urther
Creeke and Soe downe wards; when Capt. Avrey was in Commicon
he ded peticon the Court for three Thousand Acres of land; for
three persons Liveing in Acamack⁸; which the Court ded grant
to be taken up in any part of this precents that was not all-
rady survayed and taken up; sence which Cornelous Verhoofe
have at the request and procurement of the Said Capt. Avrey
and one of the three persons of Acamack Survayed and Laid out
the Said three Thousand Acres of land at prime hook; most of
it being [the] land that was taken up and Seated by Henry Smith;
now [whea]ther or no thee will Allow the Said Henry Smith the
three [thousan]d Acres of land by him taken up and Seated; wee
doe [not in] the least despute; But however wee Humbly Conceave that no part of it ought to a bene Survayed for any person whatsoever; without A Speacell warrant obtained from thy
Honore; It hath bene to much in use here for Sume persons to
Sall Land befor thay make any plantacon or Settelment there
on; And Espeacally by Capt. Avrey; whoe have Sold Severall parcells of Land; by which he have gotten greate quantieys of
Tobacco; wee would be willing to have thy posetive order as to
that Concerne; wheather thee Allow of Such things or not; thee
ware pleased to Send A Caske of powder heather for the Sarvices
of this place; which Said power hath bene all Sold and Im-
barseled⁹ away by Capt. John Avrey to the Indians and others;
And if there should be any occation for powder here; there is
not any to be got here for money; wee haveing as in duty bound
Laid these things befor thee; doe desier that thee will be
please to give such order and directions therein; as in thy
greate wisdome Shall Seeme most meete; the which wee Shall be
rady to observe and follow; this is the what needfull at

present From thy

                                True Serants
                    [Signed:]   Luke Wattson
                                John Rodes
                                John K Kiphaven
                                  his marke
                                Otto Wolgast
                                Wm. Clark

[Addressed:] This To Governor Andros at fort James in new york
              present

[Endorsed:]   N.Y. 30th June 1680 from whorekill in Delawarr.
              from new court of Clarck[10]

---

1. Other transcription in NYCD 12:654.

2. i.e., sheriff.

3. i.e., future.

4. Helmanus or Hermanus Wiltbanck.

5. Cape Henlopen.

6. i.e., lecher.

7. i.e., ancientest or oldest.

8. Accomack, Virginia.

9. i.e., embezzled.

10. Possibly "new clerk of court" was intended here; Wm.
    Clark had recently replaced Cornelis Verhoofe as clerk
    at the Whorekill court. This endorsement is written in
    the hand of Matthias Nicolls.

21:121   [THE COURT AT ST. JONES RECOMMENDING CORNELIS
          VERHOOFE FOR SURVEYOR AND CLERK]

To the Right Honorable Governor

       Wheareas it hath Been your Honors Good will and pleasure
to Appoint and Constitute us your Imferior Justices for This
new St. Jones County which for the Good mannagement to our
Said County Concerning the Land Affaires and the Increasing of
Inhabitants In quiet possessions of Land to the Same will
thinck fitt and Requisite to Recomend Cornelis Verhoofe to your
Honor that hee may bee the fittest and best Surveyor to Remaine here hee being acquainted with Every Survey and with the
woods all Soe that is yet to bee Surveyed by his former

Discoveries made and with the most part of the people that may
bee Expected here wee Know no otherwise but Said Verhoofe hath
Rectified all or most Defective Surveys formerly made and Doe
not heare nor Know of Any unjust actions by him Like wise hee
the Said Verhoofe is best fitting persons for our Clarke all
Soe Knoweing of our former buseness will Cause more Ease and
benifet for your Inhabitants in both Effects and undoubtedly
more for the good of the Contrey In Every Respect for the
Confirming There of wee Leave to your Honors good will and
pleasure Soe Remaine In all Humbliness your Honors most
Dutefull

                                    Francis Whitwell
                                    John Hillyard
                                    Edward pack
                                    Robert ℞ Hart
                                       his marke

primo July Anno 1680

True Copia Examined[1]
[Signed:] per Luke Wattson

[Endorsed:] [   ] Verhoofe [   ]
             by the Magistrates [   ] County to be Sur-
             veyor and [   ] there.

_____

1. This copy is written in the hand of Cornelis Verhoofe.

21:122   [COPIES OF COURT PROCEEDINGS FROM THE
          WHOREKILL RELATING TO A DIFFERENCE BETWEEN
          PETER GROENENDYCK AND CAPT. JOHN AVERY]

                        Att A Calld Court Held for the
                        whoore Kill the first day of May
                        Anno don. 1680;

Commiconers {Mr. Alexander Moulston {Mr. Luke Wattson} present
            {Mr. John Kipehaven   {Mr. James Wells }

Peter Groundik plt.   }
Capt. John Avery deft. }

     Wharas the deft. the last Court Appealed from the verdict
of the Jurey; the deft. Inpersuance for the Judgment to the
said verdict of the Jurey given in the last Court upon A
defferance then depending betwene this plt. and this deft., of
which verdict the deft. then Appealed, the Court there for hath
Examined the Matter of the proceedings from the Last Court and
pass Judgment to be entered Against the deft. to pay forth
with According to the verdict of the Jurey being The summe of
Two Thousand one hundred and sixteene pounds of Tobacco and
23 lb.;00^s:07 1/2^d of money, one shilling of damages with

Cost of suite Alias Execution And the bonds past for the pro-
ssecution and Answering the Said Appeal from the order of the
last Court to be void and surrendered to each party; and if
the deft. be A Greeved of this Judgment may if please entry
[sic] Appeale to the Honnorable Governor and Councell According
to Law;

                    Test Cornelous Verhoofe Cler.

A True Coppie taken and excamined
[Signed:] per Wm. Clark

                              lb: S: d
The Shreeiffes fees   0:19:00:
Clerks fees   3:04:00
Jurey fees   1:16:00
Courts fees - 500 lb.   5:19:00
          of Tobacco

      These are in his Matjesties name to will and require you
to Levy the Contents of this within mentioned order and Charges
by way of Execution upon the Estate of Capt. John Avrey and
pay the Same unto the plt. within named and this Shall be your
warrant for the same dated this 17th day of June Anno; 1680;
                              Luke Wattson

To Mr. John Vines Sherriffe
or his depity

                    Test Cornelous Verhoofe Clerk

A True Coppie taken and excamin[d]
[Signed:] per Wm. [   ]1

                    whoore Kill the 22nd, 5 mo. 1680
Loveing Friende

      Peter Groundik thyne of the Thurteenth Insint I have re-
ceved as also the 40 yds. of osinbrig 4 Ells of blew Linnen
and 1/2 lb. of thrad; and According to thy request I doe here
with send thee A Coppie of the order of Court and Execution
the obtained Against Capt. Avrey; the Coppie of what was
Apprised I sent thee per Thomas Carr; I have also sent thee per
Capt. Othow2 five pounds of white Lead and five pounds of Redd
Lead the Redd Lead is to be use[ ] first in priming as thy
work man will Informe thee; I have delivered the enclosed
Letters as directed; and if in any thing elce I may sarve thee
spare not to Command; which with my kinde Love and respects to
thy selfe and deare wife is all at present from him that is
                    Thy Asured Lo. Friende
                    [Signed:] Wm; Clark

[   ]am to pay unto Thomas Hearse that went in my boate
[   ]:7s:6d in goods at new york; and least he Should be there
[   ] for I com my selfe I have given him a bill upon thee for
the [   ] which I desier thee to pay if he Coms to thee
befor me [   ] goods that tobacco will Answer; I am thyne to
sarve
                    [Signed:] Wm. Clark

[Addressed:]   This To Peter Groundik Merchant in new york
               deliver

---

1. William Clark.

2. Gerrit Otto.

21:123   [PAPERS FROM THE WHOREKILL AND ST. JONES
          COURTS RELATING TO A DIFFERENCE BETWEEN
          WALTER DICKINSON AND BARNARD HODGES][1]

Copie   At a Court Held for the Whorekill
                            the 8th Day of June Ao 1680.

Com: ⎰Capt. John Avery   ⎱   Mr. John Kipshaven⎱
      ⎱Mr. Francis Whitwell⎰   Mr. Luke Wattson   ⎰ present
       Mr. Alex. Molestine   Mr. James Wells

Walter Dickison   plt. ⎱ In a plea of trespas
Bernard Hodges   Deft. ⎰

        The matter In Defference Between the plt. and Deft. Con-
cerning the Right and title of a tract of Land Called Mull-
berry Swamp Situated In St. Jones his Creeke After a full
hearing of the matter on Both Sides and the Said Cause being
Upon the Defts. mocion put Upon tryall of a Jury the Said
Jury after a full Debeate on Both Sydes the Jury haveing Considered of the Defference In question Doe agree In theire Verdict and Doe find for the plt. with one penny Dammage and Cost
of Suite.
                    [Signed:] Test: Cornelis Verhoofe Cler.
                         Certified that no Judgment of
                    Court is Entred Upon the above Jury Ver-
                    dict Unto this Day being the 23th Day
                    of August Anno 1680: [Signed:] Test.
                    Corn: Verhoofe Cler.

[Verso:] Copia
These are In his Majesties Name to ateach the Body of Barnard
Hoddges and him in safe Custidy keep without Bayl or Mainpris
untill he say and satiefie the within named Wallter Dickourson
as weel the some of four pounds one shilling and six pence
starling Cost of suite as allsoe one penny Dammige according
to the within mentioned order wittnes Mr. Francis Whittweell
Chefe Justis of our Court att St. Jones the [ ] Day of July
1680.
[Signed:] Teste John Brinckloe Clerke

---

1. See 21:116b for a copy of the judgment in this suit.

21:124   [WILLIAM CLARK TO PETER GROENENDYCK ABOUT THE
          APPRAISAL OF JOHN AVERY'S ESTATE, WITH OTHER
          RELATED PAPERS]

                                    Whoor Kill the 9th 5/mo. 1680;

Loveing Friende

        Peter Groundik; at thy request I here send thee a Coppie
of the Apprizment of the goods and Cattel taken upon executcion
at thy suit of Catp. Avrey; the Cows the Shreefe[1] brought the
day that thee went from home and Left them in my yard; I gave
no recept for them; sevriall of them have no Calves nor big
with Calfe they all save Two Cows and Calves gott out of my
ground and went back a gaine within a day or two; I Shall not
need to tell thee how grosely thee are abused in the Apprizing
of the Cattel; but how thee Can help thy selfe I Cannot see;
I Shall not enlarge but with my respects to thy selfe and
wife I remaine thy true Friende

                                    [Signed:]   Wm; Clark

Wee the Apprizers hereunto subscribed; Chosen to Apprize the
goods of Capt. John Avrey that was by the Shreefe taken upon
Execution at the suit of Peter Groundik as followeth;

Two houses the one Called the Ketch; and the other Calld the Court house both Standing upon the Towne Lotts on the Whoore Kill at......................	Tobacco	1500 lb
one seane neatt[2] at....................		0300
two sows big with piggs at.............		0316
		2116

As wittnes our hands this 24th day of June

          Luke Wattson   ⌠ Edward Southrin
          John Roades   ⌡ Wm. Clark

A True Coppie

[   ] I was Chosen by the praysers Luke wattson Wm. [   ]
John Roades and Edward Southrin; in the prease [   ]
Cattel in the [   ] Jurey; and I have [   ] a Cow
with Calfe [   ] a Cow this [   ] of June 1680;
Helm. Wiltbanck

A true Coppie taken and Excamined
[Signed:]   per Wm. Clark

[Addressed:]   This To Peter Groundik Merchant in new york
                deliver

---

1. i.e., sheriff.

2. i.e., seine net.

21:125   [JOHN WRIGHT TO GOV. ANDROS ABOUT LAND IN
          DELAWARE][1]

Ano 1680 July 10th

Sur   The nesesety of this publick case pots me upon a Resolve
to communicate my moste in impershall thoughts to you what ever
hazard I expose my selfe unto; my deuty I owe unto god and my
Cuntries good the trust Reposed in mee by them; the Care I have
of your honers Reapetation and to Free my selfe of any Charge
in doeing my mesidg to halfes whereby any anamosityes may arise
through misundarstanding; all which commands me to tell you
that it will be both safe and honireabell to grant the pleases
for a towne arthough[2] my Charity obblidge me to beleve, that
being the yndines[3] not bought of in the Case of hinderance but
with all I have not enuf to make them beleve, but it will in-
dainger the loseing of all there to you. then the next thing
will be not only the Removeall of seaverall persines out of
this Coliny but apeales hom may be made. Surr the Reseleutions
of seaverall men of good Istats is not eseley turned whoes
intrust is so Nerely Concarnied in the satlin of a towne there
both For there owne seafety and seaverall other Respects, and
Considering the eminance of the persin or persines which may
be there advocate askeing nothing but what may Corispond with
the Deukes intrest it is esey to gess at the efeackt but as
harde for me to here of any thing that may Iclips your honers
fame amongst us to whome under god I am behoulding to fore my
all there being a sentance of death given upon my Concarnes
by the Courte of Martines Vinyarde[4] had not your Cleminessey
given me a Resericktion I had bin Now but the prodikt of a
sifer and for this veari Reasin pardin me if I be twoe curis[5]
in informeing you what may harme your honner Hombly Concaiveing
that my pore abilityes doe not comprehend publick afayrs which
I am Nowe pot upon not of Choise but of Nesesety but with all
desier to make treuth and the ginarall good the sole Reule of
what I here prosicute; Surr take it and measar it [by] your
owne stan[dard] which will descover that his or ofesars per-
feckshon to be nothing but h[is] intrust and will pass over
treuth obeadance and the Care of the [go]od of ot[hers] which
are the maine upholders of the Common welth; Sewarly he hath
forgot that we are Com out of an exspensive war with the duch
whoe ware mastars of all our fortines here had not his Riall
Hiness pot his [Life] in hazard whoes valar and fortine hath
pot us into poseshon of this Contry whoes ende Doughtles was
for the good of the [h]olle in desposeing of Lands in a dewe
proporshon that he maye finde [   ] the acomideashon of
the genirall good and must the Comonwelth blede the treserey
exspendid to invest one pertickerler in Large trackts of Land
indeed [it is] the Nerest way to bring the Kings subiects to
be under a worse slavarey then to be undar a foriner and by
the waye we may observe the greate prise and worth of a Comman-
welth and how Nere [ace]nn[6] it is to the Crowne and [he] that
is an enemy to the one is noe frind to the [other;] Surr I
have observed [you] to seapress the eveles thereof in your
time [paste] hopeing you will doe the same for the time to Com.

[Then goe] on moste Nobill Sur in your wontid pracktis
that not we maye have [Case to pr]aise you alone but the sur-
viveing ginireation may have Case to singe [praises] with
aclimeashons of Sur Edmand Andris.

[So Conclea]de our eyes are towards you that we may take
just measers of ouer [good fortines by yo]ur doeing this not

to detaine your Honnar from your more [beater inp]lyment I
take Leave and subscribe my selfe to be your most Loyell
[Hombell Obe]adant Sarvant

[Signed:] John Wright

[Addressed:] For Surr Edmand Andris Governer of Newyorke.

[Endorsed:] Mr. John Wright July 10th 1680 For land at
Chiepiessing neare the Falls.[7]

---

1. Other transcription in NYCD 12:655.

2. i.e., although.

3. i.e., Indians.

4. He was convicted "for speaking contumelius werds"
against the Duke of York. See Charles E. Banks, The
History of Martha's Vineyard, I:269.

5. i.e., curious.

6. i.e., akin.

7. Endorsement is written in the hand of Matthias Nicolls.

21:126   [CORNELIS VERHOOFE TO GOV. ANDROS RECOMMENDING
HIMSELF TO BE CLERK AND SURVEYOR AT ST. JONES]

Whorekill the 10th of July: 1680.

Right Honorable Sir.

My Last from the 23rd of June[1] hope is by your Honor
Received, the 26th of Dito moneth followeing, my occasion Commanding mee abroud up this bay, were as I Did heare the Alterations for the Ellecting of the Court there, by your Honors
orders, And did allso understand that your Honor hath Constituted Mr. Eph: Harmon Surveyor for St. Jones County[2], which
Caused much Admirations to my and Likewise understand the same
by the Inhabitants, the Inhabitants same thes to bee Doubtfull,
may Cause new Differenc[ ] to have Deputy Surveyors there Imployed againe, as Before, which hath been heitherto the ill
Conditions Concerning the Land, untill I now have Cleared all
Errours and Defectives, Concerning all those Lands there, in
that part, So that may boldly Saye there is nothing a wanting
but your Honors further Instructions, for the which purposes
and the Returnes of mee Surveys to give your Honor a full
Account In Every particular I am Dissigned to your Honor I
find the new St. Jones Court and the Inhabitants there, very
much Inclining for to have theire former Clerke, Sherriffe,
and Surveyor againe, for which said Court have Intreated mee to

send this Inclosed[3] to your Honors Veiw and Approbations (which
Comman Reason Cannot otherwise adjudg but that no fitter Surveyor Cann bee heere) may it please your Honor I Imploy no
Deputies but Doe all Surveys my selfe, Surveyors that stay at
home and know no otherwise but that theire Deputies bring upon
paper to them I Dare not trust to that but what I Doe my selfe
since I have Knowne In my time here that many Errours Did Derive
from them whereas yet being Defferences, of these 3 and 4 yeare
standing Came by the Default of Deputy Surveyors, if I had not
lyeing under the Yoke of Mr. Henry Smith so long by his
malicious Constant Imforming against mee and had Continued Surveyor I Durst have Laid a good wedfee to have had more as many
Inhabitants by this time as wee have now, and now have Indured
much hardness, made many Discoveries and have brought all the
Incouragement to the Inhabitants and Strangers that now within
this year or two it is a Likelyhood to have this part much
populated with people therefore I Humbly Crave your Honor to
Continue mee Surveyor for the bay of Delaware as I was Before
not onely for the good of my selfe but for the Contrey Allso:
Mr. Ephr: Herman Affirmed to the Court at St. Jones hee had
more to Doe as hee Could mannage and Did not Desier to bee
Surveyor there but his Honor was pleased to force it upon him
Shall bee very well pleased with your Honors Resolutions hope
these few lines may not obstrude your Honors more Waighty
Affayres Shall Referr the further Enlargeing of the premises
untill I Come to See your Honor my selfe Shall bee sum Certaine Day In Aug[   ] next if god willing have not heard Any
newes Either out of Maryland or any place Ells Con[   ] In
the Intrim to Remaine Allwayes Read[   ]

               Your Honors most Dutifull [   ]
            [Signed:] Cornelis Verhoofe

[P.S.] The Ellection by your Honors Comission for the magistrates here was Confirmed Accordingly by the 17th of June Last
the Court was pleased then to Sweare mee againe to Continue
Clerke and Mr. John Vines to Continue Sherriffe who Doth not
Reconing to bee a possitive Sherriffe untill your Honors Approbation I my selfe pleaded to save the oath being twice sworne
before but the Courts opiniun was not so: The Expresse send
by your H[   ] to the magistrates here is Dispatched according [   ] Subscriptions.

[Addressed:] To the Right Honorable Sir Edm: Andross Knight
              Governor Generall And Vice Admirall Under his
              Royall Highness James Duke of Yorke and Albany
              etc. of all his Territories In America. These

[Endorsed:] July 10th 1680. from Cornelis Verhoofe to be
             Clerke and Surveyor att St. Jones Delaware.

---

1. See 21:119 for this letter.

2. See PA 5:720 for Ephraim Herman's warrant to be sur-
    veyor at New Castle and St. Jones.

3. See 21:121 for this petition.

21:127   [THE PETITION OF PETER GROENENDYCK FOR THE
         SETTLEMENT OF A DEBT]

                          To the Right Honnorable Edmont
                          Andros Governor Generall over the
                          nord. parts in Ameryca.

The humble Peticion of ⎫
Peter Groenendyck   ⎭

Sheweth

     That whereas Your peticioner att the Whorkill hes ob-
tained on order against Capt. John Avery[1] for the Sume of
23-01-07 1/2 in mony and 2116 pounds of tobacco for the wich
said sume of mony and tobacco Execution was Granted and served
upon sume of said Capt. Avery his astate and preased[2], but so
it is that said goods is preased so extrordinary onresonable;
as your honnor if please by the Proceedings there of may see
so that your peticioner should bee a greate looser there by.

     There for Your Peticioner humble Requests your honnor will
be plased to take this in his Cerius Consideration and to Grant
your peticioner on order that the said goods may be sould att
a pubblike outcry or other ways that the preasers may bee
Compelled to Keepe the said goods at the prise as it is
pra[   ] them and that your peticioner may have his Just due
According to order and so your peticioner Shall pray for Ever.

[Entitled:] Peticion to the Governor.

[Endorsed:] Peter Groenendyke Aug. 6 1680.[3]

───────────────────────

    1. See 21:122 for a copy of this court order. See also
        21:128.

    2. i.e., "appraised."

    3. Endorsement is written in the hand of Matthias Nicolls.

21:128   [COUNCIL MINUTE CONCERNING A JUDGMENT OBTAINED
         BY PETER GROENENDYCK AGAINST JOHN AVERY][1]

                          At a Councell held in New Yorke
                          the 6th day of August 1680.

     Upon a peticion from Mr. Peter Groenendike[2] about a
Judgment[3] obtained by him at the Court of the Whorekill against
Capt. John Avery for the summe of twenty three pounds one
shilling seven pence halfe penny, and two thousand one hundred
sixteene pounds of Tobacco for which said summe and quantity
of Tobacco the sheriffe layd an Execucion upon divers Effects

and Goods of the said Capt. Averyes which were referred to
apprizement but the Rates the same were apprized at were so
high that they were not sufficient to satisfy the peticioners
debt, whereupon hee prayes reliefe; The same being taken into
Consideracion.

[   ] That the Sheriffe doe make payment [   ] the
peticioner according to the [species][4] in the Judgment sett
forth, for the which if sufficient Goods are not already taken
in Execucion by the Sheriffe hee is to seiz much more as being
publickely sold in vendue as will satisfy the debt according
to Law. [   ] of the Governor in Councell.
                                [Signed:] Matthias Nicolls Secr.

---

1. See 29:185 for the council minute from which this
   revised minute was made.

2. See 21:127 for this petition.

3. See 21:122 for this court order.

4. Recovered from 29:185.

21:129a   [TESTIMONY OF FRANCIS WHITWELL CONCERNING
           SOME BLANK SURVEY WARRANTS GIVEN TO THOMAS
           PHILIPS][1]

Francis Whitwell Aged Forty years or ther Abouts declareth that Capt. Edmand Cantabel[2] as was understud had
poure[3] to grant warants whear upon the yeare seventy Four or
seventy Five did grand your deponent severall Blank warrants
For the taking up of Land whear upon your deponant did put
some of the Land warrants in to Thomas Philaps hands then Survar[4] deputed by Capt. Cantabel to survay Land for the use of
seyrel[5] persons as your deponant ordred him but of what was
Left of the Said Blanks the said Thomas Philaps Came to your
deponant and said he had ordr From Capt. Cantabel to aske your
deponant for the remainar of the said Blank Warants Whear upon
your deponant Did to the Best of his knowledg dliver the said
Blanks to the said Thomas Phileps then debety Survar[6] Furdr
sath note.

Sorne before me this twenty fift day of August 1680.
                                [Signed:] per Ed: Pack

[Entitled:] Whittwells Testimoney

---

1. Other transcription in NYCD 12:656.

2. Edmund Cantwell.

3. i.e., power.

4. i.e., surveyor.

5. i.e., several.

6. i.e., deputy surveyor.

21:129b   [TESTIMONY OF JOHN BRINKLOE CONCERNING
            JOHN STEVENS' LAND AT ST. JONES][1]

[John Brinloe aiged about] 36 years [or there] about Doth
take it [upon his testim]ony that John Stevens doth hould a
track of Land which is by Estemation five miles from Ducke
Creeke with in a mile or there abouts of St. Jones Creeke which
Containes to Severall Thousand ackes of Land more then hee
thinks Ther is within his Lyne which hath beene a great hind-
rence to severall families that would made better Improvement
upon itt then hee doth.

Tested by me [Signed:]   John Brinckloe

Sworne before me this twenty fift day of August 1680.
                                    [Signed:]   Ed. Pack

[Entitled:]   John Brinkloos Testimoney.

---

1. Other transcription in NYCD 12:657, from which damaged
   portions have been recovered.

21:130a   [PETITION OF BARNARD HODGES FOR A REHEARING
            OF A LAND DISPUTE WITH WALTER DICKINSON][1]

                        To the Right Honorable Sir Edm.
                        Andross Knight Governor General and
                        Admiral under his Royall Highnes
                        James Duke of Yorke and Albany and
                        all his Territories In America.

The Humble Petition of Barnard Hodges Sheweth in all Humbly
maner.

    That whereas the Petitioner had formerly a warrant for

400 ackrs of Land Granted by the worshipfull Corte of the
Whorekille the which I Imployead Wolter Worton to Seurvay and
he apointead his Debutey William Talleur[2] houe[3] did seurvay the
Lande and Gave me a seurtificat Datead 5th of May 1678. The
which Wolter Worton Deying I adresead my seulefe a Gane to
[the Corte of the] Horekille houe Gave me an Order for the Re-
survay of the sad Land by Corneliya[s Verhoofe Ho]ume I agane
Imployead to seurvay and did seurvay the 15 day of Jeuley 1679
the [time of the above] sad seurtificates ware Returnead Into
the Yeouffeis[4] one by Cournelleus Ve[rhoofe and the out]her
Deleveread to Captan Mathieus Nickles by the handes of [
       ] [and aullsoue] purcheisead the sad land of the Indyane
by a Considrable valleue to the [content as] maapeyer[5] yeunder
theare handes and Sealle barig Dattead[6] the 20th of [   ]
[1678 and] Seatead and Improvead the sad Land by my seullefe
and fammally [this month of nove]mber 1677 by werteu[7] of a
proclamasion from your Younneur and [yeuere seance bin] an
improver apon the sad Land; and stille willig and Readeay to
yealde all [tribute to the Laues of this Government, Seans your
Pettisoner hath Improved and Bestouead the [Care and Charg of
to Seurv]ayes and seteling the Land Going throu maney hard-
shipes by leying [in the Wendes maney] neightis and Maney Dayes
travell and Loues of all my childeren and In[dangering my on[8]
and my] wives Livefe onley for the saicke of this Land. And
nou on Waulter Dickisson leaving] In Maryland Clameth the sad
Land by werteu of a Bille of Salle [from Captane] Edmon Cantwell have neare[9] seatellead nor seurvayed the sad Land nor
aney [on for him seans the] Last redusing of the Govermeant,
But your pettisioner wous Latley in[formed the one Thomas
Mearr]it formerley Did Lay a Clame to the sad Land[10] In
Governor [Lovelace Is tine, the which] sad Merit Did Departe
for Ingland and thare Resides] haveing Desertead thare by his
Clame and tiytelle to the sad Land; but houevere y[our pet-
tisio]ner hath bin Molleustead by the sad Dickison houe Imployed a Cunning aturney [ ]ne namead Grifin Jones, which said
Jones fore sume Extrordinarey fee Did yeundert[ake to r]emove
your Petisonr from the sad Land allthou the Sad Jones had
formerly agreed [wit]h your Petisonor and barganead with him
to tack your petisonors Caus In hand. [It] Can be mad appere
appon Youth[11] If nead requiread and wous ofered at the Cort
of the hore [Kill.] The sad Jones aristing your Petisoner By
an accion of trespas and Connig and seutel[lg][12] bro[ug]ht It
to a tryeall sumtime Delaying and Oufering to Grant a non seut
and sum [time of]ring to Com to treyall tille such time your
Petisonr Nabours and the Moust yundersta[nding me]an of the
Contey ware Departead the Cort, So that the Court Could not
Get above 7 Men for a J[ury an]d feue or none of them that ware
summened and swornt to attend the Courte and Moust of [them]
[ ]ttireat[13] men and absolute strangers to the Caus In hand,
houe Gave a Verdit [Against the] Petisoner thou the titille
of the Land wous nevor brout In quiston at the tryall on
Eather side [whi]ch wous So Suprising to the Corte and Standers
by that the Court woull not Give Gug[ment[14] in a]ney maneur
of way. Never the Leas seans the abovesad Vardit, and the
Devission of the Co[ntry[15] the sa]d Jones hath obtanead an
Execysion without Paill or mane Pris[16] under the Hand [of Mr.
Francis] Witwell which is to the Intent to Ruyen your Petisioner
your Petisonor Rem[ang In Danger] Bye werteu there of and
Moreover threattining to throue Doun your Po[ur Petisoners
hou]ses and to Drive In the Cattell to Destroy his Corne. So
that your Petisoner s[hall be leuft ho]lley Remmeddeles yunles
your Youner will be Pleased to Grant a [Rehering In the Surva]y
whare the sad Land Leyes and your Petisonor shall ever Pray.

The Truth of wout Is Related to your Youner In this
[Petision I Dout] not but If it Pleas youre oner to In quire of
Cour[nelius Verhouf or] aney of the Justis of the Hore Killes.
Thay will sertif[ye youe at Large,] If so be thay Be at
Yourcke.

[Addressed:]   To the Right Honorable Sir Edmand Andross Knight
               Governor Generall and Vice Admirall under his
               Royall Highness Jeames Duke of Yorck and Albany
               and all his Therritorie In America

[Endorsed:]   N.Y. 11th Sept. 80 Barnard Hodges from Whorekill
              for diference of Land.[17]

---

1. Other transcription in NYCD 12:657, from which damaged
   portions have been recovered. Note that it is a
   peculiarity of the spelling in this document to prefix
   y- or ye- to words beginning with a vowel.

2. William Taylor. See 21:130b for this return of survey.

3. i.e., who.

4. i.e., office.

5. i.e., may appear.

6. i.e., bearing date.

7. i.e., virtue.

8. i.e., own.

9. i.e., ne'er.

10. See DYR:150 for the confirmation of his patent in 1671.

11. i.e., oath.

12. Possibly "cunningly and subtly" was intended.

13. Possibly "illiterate."

14. i.e., judgment.

15. Reference to the establishment of a court at St. Jones
    which previously was under the jurisdiction of the
    Whorekill court.

16. i.e., bail or mainprise.

17. Endorsement is written in the hand of Matthias Nicolls.

21:130b   [RETURN OF SURVEY FOR BARNARD HODGES' LAND
           AT ST. JONES]

May the 5th Anno 1678

        Laid out for Barnatt Hodges a track of [   ] Called
Hodges Deserts lying and being on The [   ] side of Delaware
bay and on the north s[   ] of a creik Called St. Joanses Creik
being a pers[   ] of Land formerly Laid out for on Merredy[1]
beg[   ]ing att a bounded Red oake being the first bound[   ]
Tree of Richard Levick[2] and Gaberle Joanses[3] Thence by there
line north east 320 per.[4] to a bound[   ] hickerry being ther
upermoste bounded [   ] Thence South east 200 per. by a
line [   ] to the upermoste bounded tree of Walter W[   ]
Land then Doun the said Line South west 320 [   ] To the Creik
side then by the said Creik to the Bounded Tree Containing
400 acers by m[   ]

                              [Signed:] Wm. Taylor

[Entitled:] Wm. Taylors Survey for Barnard Hodges.

────────────────

    1. Thomas Merritt. See DYR:150 for the confirmation of
        his patent.

    2. cf., 21:103 where this name appears as Levey.

    3. Gabriel Jones. See the census (21:103) where he is
        listed directly above Richard Levey at St. Jones.

    4. Abbreviation of "perches."

21:131   [COMPLAINT OF THE INHABITANTS OF CREWCORNE
           AGAINST GILBERT WHEELER FOR SELLING LIQUOR
           TO THE INDIANS][1]

To our Honorable Governor of N. York

Sir

        The nessessity of our greivance drives us to trouble you
once more with a complaint (though unwillingly) against our
neighbor, who will not be restrained from selling of strong
liquor to the Indians, whom he entertaines at his house by
great numbers, and sells it to them by both great and small
measures, which sometimes they carry a litle distance from his
house and makes them selves drunck with it, Then they revill
and fight together, and then they com furiously and break our
fences and steales our corne, and breaks our windows and dores
and carryes away our goods, and worryed 3 of our chatle in one
day with their dogs, which oppression if it continue will force
som of us from our Plantations, we being very weake at the
present for resistance and ignorant in their Lingo whereby we

can not appease them when they are mad with drinck which considered we humbly desire that selling them strong Liquors may
be wholely suppressed amongst us by vertue of a Warrant from
your Honor to make distress upon proof given to the Elected
Commissioner for the time to come for breach of that Abreviate
of the Law which Will: Biles brought us, which when we made our
Complaint to him he told us his order was nothing worth, which
we accounted was sufficient, but by his words we perceave that
he intends to sell Rum himself. So hopeing your Honor in
Charity will help us we remaine Your Honors humble

<table>
<tr><td></td><td>Servants and Tennants</td></tr>
</table>

Crewcorne Sept. the 13 1680   [Signed:] Robt. Lucas
Memmorandum the Person   Richard Ridgway
complained of is Gilbert   George Browne
Wheeler   Danell Britten
                                 Samuell Feild
                                 Mary Acerman

[Entitled:]   Complaint Inhabitants of Crewcorne about Gilbert
            Wheelers Selling Drinke to the Indians.

---

1. See 29:230 for a council minute on this petition.
   Other transcription in NYCD 12:658.

21:132   [THE WHOREKILL COURT TO GOV. ANDROS REQUESTING
            ORDERS ON SOME PUBLIC AFFAIRS][1]

1st.   order to Make a Leavey to build a prison and Court house;
      stocks and wheeping post;

2   the Towne Lotts, whoe the rent shall be paid to wheather
      to the duke of york or Armainas Wiltbanck;

3   the Marsh at the northwest end of the Towne and the Cap[2]
      to be Common to the use of the Inhabitents;

4   The In Convenency that will Attend the survayors haveing
      power to grant warrant to persons to tak up land without
      the Court;

5   that the County as it is now devided is not above halfe
      soe big as St. Jones and not soe good land; that it
      would a bene more Equilly devided if our County had ex-
      tended to bocking bridg Creek;

6   As to the 3 thousand Acres of Land that hath bene Lately
      survayed on the nect of prime hook for three persons
      Liveing at Acamack; greete part of the Land formerly and
      now seated by Henry Smith;

7   wheather any person shall be Allowed to see the dukes
      Land before thay make Improvement thereon;

8   As to the Caske of powder that the Govenor sent how it
      hath bene Imbasseled and made a way by Capt. Avrey; and
      how that if there should be any occation there is not
      any now in the precents for the defence of the Countrey;

[9]   To give the Whoore Kill sume other name;

These are the princable things that the Court of the Whoore
Kill wrot to the Govenor about; And Humbly Craveth Answer
therunto;

[Endorsed:]   N.Y. [14 Sept. 80 Mr.] Clark [of Whorekill]
              Memorand[um for] said parts concerning publick.[3]

---

1. Other transcription in NYCD 12:659, from which damaged
    portions have been recovered.

2. i.e., cape.

3. Endorsement is written in the hand of Matthias Nicolls.

21:133   [PETITION OF AMBROSE BACKER ABOUT SPARING THE
         HORSE THAT KILLED HIS DAUGHTER-IN-LAW][1]

                           To the Right Honorable Sir Edmond
                           Andross, Knight, Captine Generall
                           of all his Royall Highness his
                           Territoryes in Americka and Govor-
                           nor of new yorke

The petition of Ambrose Backer

Humble Shewith
                                                         2
      Thatt whereas on the 10th of this instant month Sept.
your petitioners Dafter in law[3] went to take your petitioners
Cartt horse, with intention to bring the said horse home, to
fech som wood home outt of the woods which your petitioner
then had occation for, Now your petitioners Dafter law going
to take the said horse as formerly she had Donn, nott thinking
to be resisted, and the said horse having a mare in his Company which he always accompanyed with, she beeing yonge and
nott fearing the horse went Close up to him, and toke hold of
him, Now he perceiving the mare to go from him, would nott be
stopt by your petittioners Daftere law, and thereupon Kickt
her with his foott so violently, that in the space of an hower
or two shee dyed, wher upon Capt. Edmond Cantwell Coranor of
the river of Dellaware Imediatly in the said place Summonsed
a Jury of Inquest, which Jury upon Sarch and Inquiry found the
Said hors to be the Cheife Cause of the Girles Death. Insomuch
that by the Juries verdict the horse Belongs to the King, Now
thus itt is may itt pleas your honor your petitioner having

Lostt his Daughter and by her losse and the verdictt of the
Jury lostt his horss, although nott yett apraized, with outt
your honor be mercyfull unto him and his pore famely. his
livelyhood being in Carting wood outt of the woods for the
towne, he having no other hors, and thinking in his conchiens[4]
he hath losse enough of his Daughter besids funerall Charges,
etc. Humble prays your honor that as he is a pore Laboring
man and no other horse nor Creature to fech him wood home, to
relive his wife and Children, butt the said Condemned horse,
which your petittioners neighbors will attest[5] never before
this time, was ever Knowne seen or heard, to have acted any such
thing, or ever proffered the same abuse, to any Your Petittioner' Therefore humble prays,

    Your honor thatt your honor would Be so Clementiall and
    mercyfull To give him the horse againe (which is now in
    [   ] Coronors posession) to fech wood for the releife of
    him his wife and children he having alreddy had loss
    enough he leavs his Condittion to your Honors Compation
    hoping your honor will be so mercifull as to Consider the
    Condittion and State of your pore suplyant
                        And he for your Honor shall
                        Always pray as in Duty Bound -

[Entitled:] Peticion of Ambrose Backer about a horse Condemned
             for Killing his Daughter.

---

1. See NCCR:437 for the order of the Council in New York
    concerning this petition; and 29:230 for a council
    minute on this petition.

2. The year, although not stated, is 1680.

3. i.e., daughter-in-law.

4. i.e., conscience.

5. See 21:134 for the deposition of Backer's neighbors.

21:134   [DEPOSITION OF AMBROSE BACKER'S NEIGHBORS
          ATTESTING TO THE BEHAVIOR OF HIS HORSE][1]

Newcastle Sept. 16th 1680

     We underwritten being all Neighbors of Ambrose Backer,
Do, Declare that to Oure Knowledg either by hearing or Sight
we never heard nor have Seen nor understood that ever the
Cartt horg that belongd to him and did Lately strike his
Dafterlaw[2] Did ever be fore this time ever strike att any man
woman nor child butt wass always a quiett good Condittioned
hors this was attest under our hands the Day and yeare above
written

[Signed:]   John Moll
Will. Sempill
G. Dyerckse[3]
Reynier vander Coelen
James Walliam
Thomas Spry

---

1. See 21:133 for Ambrose Backer's petition.

2. i.e., daughter-in-law.

3. Gysbert Dircksen.

21:135   [FRANCIS WHITWELL TO GOV. ANDROS CONCERNING HIS
LAND ON DUCK CREEK AND HIS DESIRE TO BE MADE
SHERIFF]

Most worthey and honered Sir

Whereas your exelency haveing granted me A Carton tract
of Land situat[   ] Laying in Duck Creek and being seated thereon with my Famely Ind[   ] the Inprovement thereof which I
have not beene A want[   ] place whear I Com and more in
this place then any one pertic[   ] to the Expence of A great
deal of mony and Lose that I have [   ] by Fire which
burnt me upwards of one hundred Foott of [   ] and the
greatest part of it Full of tobaco upon the said Land be[   ]
thousand Acors which was to my dameg one hundred pound st[
] the Acasion of Laing thes thingss before your Exelency is
dout[   ] Exelency should be wrong informed by some persons
that h[   ] in thes parts From Long Iland who had som
pretences [   ] Land for A town which none would Like them
but all [   ] that I have belonging to my Land for the Coming
att the Wa[   ] being all sunken and more only that part
which they Cou[   ] att present I am seated upon the outer-
most part A pretty Di[   ] that Convenence affore mencioned
but am now A bulding wit[   ] to remove to the said Convenence it being your Exelencys plea[   ] it me doubts not
the Confirmation therof ther being other [   ] yett anofe
that may be Judged bettr Convences both for wa[   ] all so
for medow but opasett over the Creek ther for hoping tha[   ]
exelency will be pleased that wee who have been the First
I[   ] in this parts of the Cuntry may be In Cureged
In the Injoymen[   ] Convenences and preveliges that your
Exelency hath given us [   ] is all that doth Induse into
this place so Leaveing it to your Exelency [   ] have one
thing more to Aquaint your Exelency that as yet your exe[   ]
not Comisionated any person in this County to be Shrefe[1] but
[   ] hath deputed att the present to serve in that offess
untill your [   ] pleased to depute whom your Exelency
think Fitt the person [   ] now serve name Pettr Bacom is
a person that hath Formrly a[   ] good Fasion but is Falen

to decay and groweth ansent[2] an[   ] to Labor iff your
Exelency will be pleased to be slow itt [   ] he would kindly
exept of it From your Exelency and [   ] thought by the
Cort to be the Fittest person that that your ex[   ] make
Choyce of withall I Conclud in obeadence to your exe[   ]
[pl]easur Whil I am
St. Jones the 20th   [Signed:] Fra. Whitwell
Novembr

[Addressed:] This For The Right honnor. Govern. over the
              nord. part of ameryka Present att New York

---

   1. i.e., sheriff.

   2. i.e., ancient.

21:136   [EPHRAIM HERMAN TO JOHN WEST CONCERNING
           WARRANTS FOR HIM AND EDMUND CANTWELL TO
           APPEAR IN NEW YORK]

Mr. John West[1]

     Sir Comming home 3 dayes agoe from St. Jone[ ] County
where I had ben Surveiging of Lands I found your Letter dated
the 10th of Nov. togeather with his Excellency the Governors
warrantt Inclosed for my and Capt. Cantwells attendance att
New Yorke, the said Letter was sent to my house but the day
before my [   ] home which was the 29th of Nov. I suppose itt
[   ] ben detayned otherwayes itt might have foun[ ] mee att
home before I went downe, and also Capt. Cantwell whoe went
12 dayes sence for St. Maries In Maryland;

     Sir Imediatly upon the receipt as above I sent Expressly
for Capt. Cantwell and think to stay for him till monday next
itt being fryday today, in which tyme if [   ] doth not come I
shall sett on my Journey alone and hope to bee att New Yorke
to wayt on his Excellency within this 8 dayes of which I
humb[ ] desire you to Informe the Governor which with [   ]
my humble servis to your good selfe is a[ ] att present from
Sir

                         Your very humble Serv[   ]
N Castle   [Signed:] Eph. Herman
Dec. 3rd 1680

[Addressed:] To Mr. John West att New York These with Mr
              Corn: V: Borsum Q.D.G.

[Endorsed:] [   ] from Eph[   ]
             a New Castle [   ] to N Yorke.

---

   1. John West was clerk of the court of assizes.

21:137   [COMPLAINT OF JOHN ROADES AGAINST HELMANUS
          WILTBANCK]

                              To the Worshipfull Commissioners of
                              the Whorekill the Humble Declaration
                              of

[   ] Roades Plt. against }
[   ] Wiltbanck Deft.   }

     The Plt. Declareth that the 16th Day of August [   ]
Last past the Deft. Caused the Plt. to bee unjustly Imprisoned
without bayle or maineprise Contrary to Law by or upon a pretended Complaint made by Mr. Edward Southrin against the Plt.
is Damnified the quantity of twenty thousand pounds of tobacco
Besides the Impearing of the Plt. his Credit and health the
Plt. being Kept In prison the quantity of four times four and
twenty howers and at the next Court then Recovered nun suit
against the Complainant for being unjustly molested.

                    Now soe it is that the plt. Craveth your worships to
                    Consider the plt. his Cause according to Law and
                    grant unto the plt. your worships order for the above
                    said quantity of 20000 lb. of tobacco for the suf-
                    fring of unjust Imprisonment with cost of suite.
                              And the plt. shall pray
     Vera Copia   [Signed:] Cornelis Verhoofe Cl. Cu. Whorekill

21:138   [COURT PROCEEDINGS CONCERNING THE REMOVAL
          FROM OFFICE OF CORNELIS VERHOOFE]

Deale Alias Whoorekill;

Coppie

     The Courts Complaint And Accusation Against Cornelous
Verhoofe the Clark of this Court; That he have bene nedglegent
Carles willfull and parshall in his offices And that he hath
nedglected to enter into the booke of Records; the Bussines of
the Court and Countrey And have threatened to Cutt out of the
book of Records Severall orders of the Court; which the Court
Caused to be entered theirein; And Also that he the Said
Cornelous Verhoofe was the Last Court Soe dronk in the time of
the Court Sitting; That he the Said Cornelous Verhoofe was not
Capable to doe the bussnes of the Court that belonged to his
offices as Clark of the Court. As also Severall other mis-
demenors and unfaithfullnes in his offices as Clark;

     The Court doe therefor order and determin that the Said
Cornelous Verhoofe Shall not at any time After the date hereof;
Act as Clark of this Court and Countrey; And that the Said
Cornelous Verhoofe doe forth with render and deliver up unto
the Judge of the Court the books and all papers whatsoever
that doe Concerne the Clarks place; And all writings that doe

any ways Concerne the Court and Countrey that are in his Custidy as Clark upon payne of Imprissonment; Given under our
hand this 11th day of the Moneth Called Febuary Anno; Domini;
1680;

John Roades was Absent ⎧ Luke Wattson   Otto Woollgast
from that Court upon   ⎨ John Kiphaven
[   ] Exterordney occation ⎩   [Signed:] Wm: Clark

The Court make Coyce of William Clark to be Clark of the
Court for the time Coming; who Accepting of the books and papers
that ware in the Court was [   ]livered by the Court to remaine
in his Custidy; At [   ]ch time the Said William Clark gave in
steede [   ] oath A paper or writing under his hand [   ]
followeth;[1]

Whareas the Court did see good Cause to Turne out
Cornelous Verhoofe from being Clark of this Court; And have
made Coyce of me William Clark to be Clark of the Court; I doe
there for hereby promise and Ingage to doe the bussnes of the
Court and Countrey; to the best of my knowlidge; And to keepe
A True Record of the Courts proceedings; And if I doe nedglect
or enter any thing Contrary to Law And Justices; That then I
doe hereby obligge my Selfe to Suffer and under goe Such fine
or poinshment as if I had Acttifely taken the oath; As wittnes
my hand this 11th day of the Moneth Called Febuary Anno;
Domini; 1680;

entered upon Record by   ⎧ Coppee [Signed:] Wm: Clark
(the) order of the Court; ⎨

To the worishfull Justices of deale Court the Humble peticon
of Cornelous Verhoofe

Shaweth

That your peticoner desiers A Referance or Rehearing upon
the Complaint prefered by the Court this day Against your
peticoner;

The Court being willing to hear what the said Cornelous
Verhoofe had to Say; Left him to his Libiarty to make his
defence; And Aske him if there wore any thing in the Complaint
that was not True; or that the Court had Laid any thing to his
Charge that he was not Guilty of; which he did not deney but
that what the Court had Charge him with was True; But Alleadged that the Court had not power to Turne him out of his place;
but that he ought rather to have bene find for his offences;
To which the Court Answered that he had bene offten [   ]
find formerly; and still no Amendment [   ] that he growe more
nedglegent and willfull; [   ] which the said Cornelous Verhoofe Craved A Jurey [   ] Court Granted him A Jurey which was
rady to [   ] upon the bussines; But the said Cornelous
Verhoofe Refused to put his Cause to the Jurey After desiered;
and by the Court Granted;

The Court ordered his peticon And Answer to be
[   ]corded; soe that he might be Left without
[   ]use; A True Coppie [Signed:] Test Wm: Clark Cl.

---

1. See 21:118 for William Clark's letter to the governor
   in which he refuses to take the oath of office and
   submits a statement in lieu of the oath.

21:139   [JUSTICES OF DEALE TO GOV. ANDROS CONCERNING
          THE DISMISSAL OF CORNELIS VERHOOFE AND THE
          APPOINTMENT OF WM. CLARK AS CLERK]

                            Deale formerly Called the Whoorkill;
                            21st March 1680/81

Honorabl Governor

     Wee the Justices for this County Appointed and Com-
miconate[ ] by your Honor are oblidged to give you an Account
of the nessesety wee wore in to Turne out Cornelous Verhoofe
from Being Clark of this Court and County; For that he was
soe nedglegent and unfaithfull in the discharging of his duty
belonging unto his offices; and the Trust reposed in him; As
may more at Large Appeare by the Charge the Court drew up
Against him And his Apswer there unto; A Coppie thereof wee
here Enclose send you[1]; he was by A Complaint made to thy
Honor; for keeping of Falce Records and other Abusses; About
Two years and a halfe Sence; Turne out of the Said Clarks
offices; with this order from the Governor; That he Should not
be ever Imployed in the Said offices of Clark; unless he Should
Clear himselfe from being Guilty of the Said Charge; which he
never yet did; nor never Can; But at that time here being no
person fitt to Act or officoate in that offices; Capt. John
Avery being the First in Commicon here; did take him in Again;
ever sence which time he have bene in the offices of Clark;
Till the 11th day of the Last Moneth; Att which time the Court
discharged him From being any Longer Clark as Aforesaid; And
for as much as wee are oblidged by an order signed under the
hand and seale of the Governor; bearing date the 14th day of
September Anno; Domini; 1676;

     That when the Clarks offices is vacant; To Recommend A
fitt person for Clark to the Governor for his Approbacion;
The Court haveing Thought Good to make Coyce of William Clark
to be Clark of the Court and County; whoe wee [   ] is A
very fitt and Capoable person for that offices; [   ] that
wee Can repose Trust and Confiedence [   ] wee haveing pre-
vailed with him to Accept [   ] that Charge upon him;

     [   ] therefore hereby Recommend him unto your
[   ] your Approbacion and Confirmacion in the [   ] of
Clark; And allthough he is one in Commicion [   ]

Justices for this County; wee doe not Judge [   ];
But that as he is very [   ] he may be very servicesable
in both stations [   ] Like have bene by the Governors
Commicon [   ] on Long Island and New Jersey; for A
[   ]er to be Clark of the Court; wee have no [   ]
present; save onely to Crave your Answer [   ]probacion of
the same; And subscribe our [   ] yours to be Commanded
[Signed:] Luke Wattson   Otto Wolgast
John K Kiphaven
his marke

---

1. See 21:138 for these court proceedings.

21:140   [THE ST. JONES COURT TO CAPT. BROCKHOLLS
          REQUESTING PROTECION AGAINST LORD BALTIMORE]¹

Capt. Brookuls²   St. Jones 10th of Agust

honered sir haveing att this time Acasion to writ to you
worthenes Craveing your pardon for many mistaks that sha[   ]
not be giveing your honer or titl Acording to deserts but
giving A short and Brefe Acount of some publek and maters that
doth both Consern us and his royall hinesses not douting your
honers Care and Dilegance to Instruct us in thes things which
may be for the softy and preservation both of us and his royall
hyneses in trest which many of us A cording to ower abelety
will not be Bacward to mentain allso hoping that his royal
hyness and your honer will mentaine owr rights and preveleges
granted us in assisting against me Lord Baltymour which we do
expet evry Day to Come and Subdew us with Force and Arms to
Bring us undr him and all soe hath mad proclemation who will
Come into thes persinkt to take Land he will mentaine ther Intrest and take from us thos preveledges granted us under this
govenment which Is Intended as we undrstand About the Later
part of this Instant month to make ther progress both in surveying of Land and allso settl A Corte under his Athorety we
do not know how he may Deall with us for we have sene A very
bad asspet³ befor us for som Few years past which was the rune
of many your pepol which had ther houses and provisons Burnt⁴
which may be our Cass if we do Apose them so we hombly Crave
your Instructions how We shall act for our Safty expeting it
if it be your honers pleasur by this Bearar for if it be so
as it is reported that his royal hines hath serendrd it to me
lord Baltemore we must submett so being satisfied til we Can
have report from your honer [rest] In obeadance to your honers
pleasur⁵
[Signed:] Fra. Whitwell
John Hillyard

[Addressed:] Thes For his honer Capt. Antony Brookas
Governor of new york.

1. Other transcription in NYCD 12:662.

2. Capt. Anthony Brockholls. Gov. Andros departed for
    England Jan. 7, 1681, leaving Brockholls in charge of the
    government.

3. i.e., aspect.

4. A reference to Lord Baltimore's destruction of the
    Whorekill settlement in 1673.

5. See Hazard's Register of Pennsylvania, 3:33-34, for
    Brockholls' reply to this letter. Also printed in
    NYCD 12:668.

21:141   [COPIES OF ALL PROCEEDINGS AND RELATED PAPERS
          IN THE DIFFERENCE BETWEEN ABRAHAM MAN AND JOHN
          MOLL][1]

Copia[2]

        This is to Sattisfy all whom this may Concerne that John
Moll of the Towne of New Castle was by a Jury att New Yorke att
the Court of Assizess[3] found guilty of the Indictment pro-
ssecuted by Abram Man In the behalfe of our Soveraigne Lord
King Charles which may be proved by the hands of the Jury yett
after the verdict past against the said Moll, part of the
Justices of the Court did say they would Cleare the said Moll;
and that I Should take care to pay the Charge therefore for
that unlawfull Prosedings and Actings I did Appeale from their
Lawless Judgement to King and Councell then after there was An
Appeale granted thy Tould me that I Should putt In a thousand
pound Sterling Security to Prosecute which Security I did Tender Provided they Could Shew me Law I was bound to doe itt;
they Could Show me no Law butt the baire order of part of the
Justices of the Court so that the said Moll is nott Cleared
by Law as yett; Therefore I am Now bound for England with gods
Leave to prossecute the Said Indittmenent against Moll I shall
be goeing by the first Shipping; Therefore this is to desi[re]
all people that hath any Accounts to make up that they would
send them as Sone as they can; and the Latter End of this next
month they shall have their Just due; Requiring all that oweth
to him they may doe the same as Wittness my hand this 31 of
October 1681
                            (was signed)
                            Abraham Man
This is a true Coppy of the originall

Mr. Arnoldus De Lagrange and Samuell Land being sworne
Declareth that being at the house of Abraham Man; aboutt the
28th day of october Last past heard Mr. Abram Man, Say thatt
all Causes that had bin tryed in the Court of New Castle were
Ilegall that were tryed withoutt a Jury and that any man which
was Cost in Such actions where there was no Jury, the party
might take his goods where he found them though taken upon
Execution and seize them as stolen goods and that the power of
the Court was of no Validety and their Lawes Likewise becaues
they were nott made by an act of Assembly In Wittness whereof
we have hereunto Sett our hands this 4th day of november 1681.

(was signed)
Arnoldus De Lagrange
Samuell Land

[   ] Before us the day and [   ] above Written
                       [   ] Moll
                       [   ] Alrichs
                       [   ] Haes
                       [   ]mpill

November the 4th 1681.

[   ] and sub Sherrife of New Castle doe declare that
hav[   ] and Directed to my selfe and Samuell Barker for
to [   ] Boddy of Abram Man of Christena before the Magestrats of [   ] to be Examined and proseded against as
his Merritt should Requi[   ] his abusive words which he
had Writt against the Court of [   ] thereupon We Repaired this day in pursuance of the Warrantt [   ] of Abram
Man, I Entred the house and the Constable [   ], Man seing
the Constable Comming Locked him outt [   ] and me In;
forbidding the Constable upon his perill to come [   ];
Whereupon I Required him and Commanded him [   ] name to
goe along with me having served the Warrant Upon him att which
he desired to see the Warrant I Lett him have itt in his hand
and he Read the Warrant over twise and then sayd what he had
Writt in the paper that he sent to be publisht; he would proofe
to be true saying he wrote nott against the Governor butt the
Court of Assizyes and that he would prove all that he had writt
against them, And for the Warrant which I served upon him he
would nott obey itt; for he Denyed any Power that the Magestrats
of New Castle had and that he would nott obey any Warrant nor
Warrants from any of the Magestrats of New Castle and he was
Vexed that Ever he obeyed them or their Warrants butt he would
never doe itt againe for the future though he dyed for; I
againe Required him to obey the Warrant and goe along with me;
saying he must and should goe; he tould me he would goe with
me, butt he must putt his cloaths on first; whereupon he went
into another Roome to dress himselfe and when he had putt on
his Cloathes I Know nott whether he went into the Roome againe
for a hatt or a cap butt he went his way unknowne to me which
way he gott out I know nott; Leaving me Locked up in the house
so that I was forced to come out through a Winder to be att
Liberty, The which I doe aver to be true and further att present sayeth nott.

(was signed) Samuell Land

Sworne before us this 8th day of November Anno Domini 1681

(was signed) John Moll
Joh. De Haes
Will. Sempill

I Samuell Barker Constable of Cristena doe Declare that
having [   ] speciall Warrant directed to Samuell Land and my
selfe for to bring [   ] the Boddy of Abram Man of Cristena before the Magestrats of [   ] Castle to be Examined and proseded against as his merritt shou[   ] Require; itt being for
his abuse to the Governor and Court of Assi[   ] in pursuance
of which sayd Warrant we Repaired this day to [   ] house of
Mr Abram Man wherupon Samuell Land Entred [   ] Man seeing
me coming with my stafe loked him the said [   ] in his house
and me outt of Doors for the space of one ho[   ] Longer
During which Time the Said Man made his Escap[   ] the said
Land and his wife Loked in the house so that [   ] was
forced to come outt of a Winder to be att Liberty [   ] I
doe aver and am Ready to Atteste The same upon [   ] under
my hand this 4th day of November Anno 1681. [   ]

Whereas Abram Man of Christena Creeke did [on the 1st day
of this] Instant month of November send into Court a Cert[aine
paper under] his owne hand there to be publisht and ther fixt
[up att the Court dore] In which paper he doth in a high nature
Abuse the Gove[rnor and Generall] Court of Assizes and doth by
his speeches to severall [publicqly Seeme to] Endeavor the Dis-
quiet and Disturbance of his Mayesties peacea[ble subjects
Contrary] to the Knowne Lawes of England,

These are therefore in his Mayesties name to will and
Requiere you that you bring before us the Boddy of the said
Abram Man within this Tow[ne] of New Castle to be there Examined
and proceded against as the Merritt of the Cause shall Require
according to Law; for the doeing of which this shall be your
Warrant Given under our hands att New Castle this 3 day of
November 1681.[4]

To Mr Samuell Land
Sub Sherrife and Mr
Samuell Berquer
Constable of Christena
and Assistance if occasion

(was signed)
John Moll
Peter Alrichs
Gerrett Otto
Joh. De Haes
Will. Sempill

All the aforestanding are true Coppies Exam. and Compared per
mee
[Signed:] Eph. Herman Cl.

---

1. See 21:142 for the covering letter to these papers.

2. See NCCR:497 for a transcription from the original
   record.

3. See NCCR:496 for a copy of the Court of Assizes'
   verdict.

4. See NCCR:514 for a transcription of this warrant from
   the original record. Damaged portions have been recovered from this source.

21:142   [THE NEW CASTLE COURT TO CAPT. BROCKHOLLS
         CONCERNING ABRAHAM MAN][1]

Right Honorable Sirs

     The 1st of this Instant month of November being our
ordinary Court day, one Francis Jackson Late Servant to Mr.
Abram Man Appeared in Court and there did Deliver a Paper
Written and signed by his said master Abram Man[2] whoes order
was that itt should be there publisht and then fixed up: Upon
which wee Resolved to send for the said Man and after Exam:
further to proceed against him to which porpose wee Issued
forth a Warrant But the said Man made his Escape from the under
Sherrife and keeps now att Present In Pensilvania and Burlinton;
Wee send your honor herein Inclosed the Coppies of all the
papers and other proceedings[3]; and Desire your honor further
order and Instructions for our further Rule in this and the
like occasions; The Proclamation[4] which Mr. Moll brought along
with him is published; wee having nothing att present further
all things Continuing well as before; we Remaine:
                    Right Honorable Sir
               Your Honors Most humble Servants
New Castle   [Signed:] John Moll
[11] Nov. 1681   Pieter Alrichs
                                   J.D. Haes

[Addressed:] To the Right Honorable Capt. Anthony Brockhols
         Esq Dep. Gov. and the Rest of [   ] Councill
         in New Yorke
                    These per Capt. Blagge

[Endorsed:] November [   ] from the Magistrates
         att New Castle Concerning Abram Man

---

1. See NCCR:514 for a contemporary copy of this letter.

2. See 21:141 for a copy of this paper.

3. See 21:141.

4. See NCCR:496 for a copy of the Court of Assizes' verdict.

21:143   [EPHRAIM HERMAN TO CAPT. BROCKHOLLS ABOUT
         AFFAIRS IN DELAWARE][1]

Right Hono[rable]
Sir

     His honor Sir Edmund Andros, was pleased to Imploy mee to
receive the Quit Rents due for Land to his Royall highnesse of
which my Receipt I have ben accomptable to his said honor and
the accounts Stated allow[ ] and ballanced till 25th of March

1680. this Laest Year I sent to Mr. Wells his honors Stuard,
in the sloope of Capt. Cregier 150 sch. wheat and in the sloope
of Mr. Leysler 50 sch. more besydes some wheat paid here to
Capt. Cantwells order by his honor Governor Andros speciall
order; Now this is to acquaint Your honor that within that part
of this River now Called Pensilvania are severall persons whoe
are in Errier and still debtors for quit Rents and other rents
due to his Mayestie or his Royall highnesse; Therefore doe
humbly referr itt to Your honors Consideracion, whether itt is
not necessary that som[ ] person whome your honor thinkes fitt
bee Impowred by your honor to demand and Receive the same
Arrier[ ] there and also the quit Rents here belowe, and that
Your honor Lykewyse Intimate the same to Esq: [M]arkham the
Governor of said province; [Ye]sterday arryved here a ship
from Bristol haveing [had 9] weekes passadge, but brings Little
Newes only [that se]verall Ships more are bound for this River
and [that Esq. Pen wil] follow next Spring all things [else
Continuing well] in England as before; Mr. Man [was appr]ehended
and hath Given bond and security for his [appeara]nce att the
Cort of azzyses and his good behavior in [the meane]whyle,
all things Continue well here as [before which] is all att
present from Right Honorable Sir

                                   your honors most humble Servant
[Newcastle 16th   [Signed:] Eph: Herman.
Dec. 1681][2]

[Addressed:]   To the honorable Capt: Anthony Brockholls Deputy
               Governor of the Province of New Yorke Present
               Att New Yorke These per Capt. Cregier

---

1. Other transcription in NYCD 12:662, from which damaged
    portions have been recovered.

2. O'Callaghan's Calendar records the date as Nov. 19,
    1681. See PA 5:729 for Capt. Brockholls' reply to this
    letter in which he acknowledges receipt of the Dec.
    16th letter.

21:144   [EPHRAIM HERMAN TO CAPT. BROCKHOLLS ABOUT
          AFFAIRS IN DELAWARE][1]

Right Honorable;
Sir

     In my Laest[2] per the Sloope of Capt. Cregier I wrott your
honor about the receipt of the arrier of the quit rents: That
itt was necessary some person should be Impowred thereto; and
also of Mr. Ab: Mans haveing Given bond for his answering Att
the next Generall Court of azzyses; Sence which there is
arryved here; a shipp from Bristoll with Passengers for Pensilvania; and more are Expected dayly and Cheefly att the Spring
when itt is said that Esq. Pen will come over in owne Person;

Esq. Marckham the Governor of the said Province has desiered
our Magistrates to Joyne, and Lay out the 12 myles above this
Towne mentioned in his mayesties Pattent to said Esq.
Pen; and
they not Knowing whether sufficiently thereunto Impowred doe
humbly desire your honors order therein and alsoe doe desire
to Know whether; to begin att the verry Towne it Selfe or att
the End of the Liberty of the Towne; The news goeth here that
Esq. Pen is about or has gott these Lower Parts alsoe from his
Mayestie and that itt wanted only his Royall highnesse Con-
firmaci[on] whoe was in Scotland and Dayly Expected att Whyte-
hall; I doe now Send to Mr. John West 15 Certiciates of Sur-
veys³ which are all viewed and allowed by the Cort, the severall [pe]rsons Conserned doe most humbly desire [to] have Pattents of Confirmation on the same [all] things further doe
Continue here well [a]s before; The Laest assembly in Maryland
[h]ave Prohibited Corne and all sorts of other provisions [to]
bee Exported, Itt is said and feared that a warr [w]ill Ensue
betweene them and the Sinneco Indians Which God Prevent; for
in my Judgement the Constitution of that Country Is such that
a warr with Such a Strong Ennemy will proove verry distructive
to them; which with my humble Servis presented to your honor
and Lady wieshing you a Merry Christmas and New Yeare, is all
Att present; from

                          Right Honorable Sir
                          Your Most humble Servant
                          [Signed:] Eph: Herman.
New Castle 27th of
decemb. 1681

[Addressed:] To the Honorable Captain Anthony Brockholls
              Deputy Governor Present In New Yorke. These

---

1. Other transcription in NYCD 12:663. See PA 5:729 for
    Brockholls' reply to this letter.

2. See 21:143 for this letter.

3. See NCCR:503ff. for these certificates of survey.

21:145a Jan. 30. Summons in the case of John Glover
         against Samuel Stiles; plea trespass and
         ejectment.¹

---

1. There is a notation in the Ms. folder that this
    document is missing. The heading has been taken from
    O'Callaghan's Calendar.

21:145b   [PETITION OF THE INHABITANTS OF ST. JONES
           FOR A COURT]

To the right honorable Sir Edmund Andros Knight Seigneur of
Sausmarez Lt. and Governor Generall under his Royall Highnes
Duke of Yorke and Albany etc. of all his Territories in America

    Wee whose names are hereunto subscribed liveinge and am-
bitious to abide under the Sunshine of your Honorable Goverment
Inhabiteinge in the upward part of the Whorekill County

    In all humble manner shew unto your honor the great
greiveances Hazards and perills both by land and water that wee
undergoe to the Whorekill Court nott onely the distance beinge
to some of us 50 some 60 miles want of Comodacions of man or
beast there butt the unpassable dangerous waies by reason of
perillous Creekes which many tymes cannott be past over by man
or beast the hazardous large marshes and myreous and difficult
branches which are past through to the said Court which doth
nott onely putt us to greate straits and jeopardy of our Lives
butt hath and doth great disincouragment to others intendinge
to seate in these upward parts from Maryland that some have
desisted in theire designes rather then in hazard of theire
lives to goe downe to the said Whorekill Court And forasmuch
as the greivances aforesaid are Insupportable to us and these
parts dayly encreaseinge with diverse considerable families
with considerable Estates and more intendinge to remove from
Maryland that wee are these altogether yf not more populated
then the other part of the County And nott onely the Incon-
veniences aforesaid yf nott by honor remedied butt alsoe the
Towne of Delaware beinge in like manner Inconvenient to these
upward parts That should the Inhabitants hereof appeare att
either Court ytt would nott onely cause the present seaters to
withdraw back hence and disincouragement of others designed to
seate here

    The Premisses considered with all humble reverence wee
leave the discuss of the whole matter to your Honors grave and
wise consideracion And hope your Honor for the Encouragement
of us the present Inhabitants and others that are comeinge to
seate in these parts Out of your wonted Clemency Tender Care
and willingnes att all tymes for encouragement of seaters and
preserveing us under the sunshine of your happy Goverment from
all dangers and removeinge Inconveniencies and perills that
might ensue and for the Ease and propserous setlement of these
parts will be graciously pleased to order authorize constitute
and appoint a Court to be held in some Convenient place in St.
Jones Creeke att such tymes and upon such daies as your Honor
in your wisedome shall thinke fitt and that all persons Inhabiteinge from the Northside of Cedar Creeke to Southside of
Blackbird Creeke be ordered and required to appeare doe suite
and service obey proces in Law and bee deemed and taken to be
within the Jurisdicion of the said Court and yeild obeideyance
to the authority thereof Nott doubtinge butt your Honor may
make and finde persons capable in the precincts thereof for
administracion of Justice and others as ministeriall officers
to attend the same Court and execute all proces and orders and
Keepeinge and makeinge Recrods of proceedings and acts done by
Authority thereof

                    And wee as in duty bound shall ever
                    pray for your Honors health and
                    happines That Age [may Cr]owne your

Snowy haires with Cesars Honors and with Nestors yeares.

[Signed:]

[Fran. Whitwell]
[Petter Bawcom]
[John Baswell   his marke]
[Daniell Arnestead]
[E. Pack]
John Richardson Junr.
Rich. ℛ Griffin
    his ⋊ marke
Henery H Stevenson
John Dawson
Henery Plomen[2]
John Walker
Walter 𝗪 Powell
George Martens
Jafeth 𝓗 Gresen
    his marke
Isaac Balstek
Thomas Bolsticke
Simon Ironnse
[Alexander Humphrey]
[John Brinklo]
[Gabriel J]onses
[Christophe]r Jecson
[Dav]id Margin
[Abr]om Brate
Isack Webe
John Webster
Thomas Heffer
Allesxander Raey
Williom Sparces
Thomas Cliford
John Getes
Rabert Bedowel
Richerd Levike
John Cortes
Thomas Williom
Thomas Groves
Tho. Hill
John Hase
Robert Johnson

Griff Jones
John Glovaer
Robert Porter
Arthur Alstone
Robert Willen[3]
Thomas Willon
William Willon
John ℛ Richeson
John Hilard
Robrt ℛ Parnatry
    mark
Artre 𝐴 Allston
    mark
John Brics
William Berry Junr.
John Lloyd
John ℓ Barratt
    his makre
John Burton
Daniell Jones
Wm. Winsmore
Eavan Davis
John Cavely
Ed. Pynar
John Disshaa
Benony Barnes
Feby Oreme[4]
Christopher Ellitt
Wm. Greene
Robert Franssen

The shipe goeing away wee had nott time to gitt the rest of there names but wee thinke there may bee above 100 tithabels.

---

1. See 21:110a for a rough draft of this petition. Other transcription in <u>NYCD</u> 12:664, from which damaged portions have been recovered.

2. Possibly intended for <u>Bowman</u>. cf., 21:103.

3. This name and the two following are possibly misspellings or variant forms of <u>Willson</u>, cf., 21:103.

4. i.e., Fabian Orme. cf., <u>NCCR</u>:334.

21:146   [PETITION OF CORNELIS VERHOOFE TO SURVEY
          SOME OF HIS OWN LAND]

To the Honorable Capt. Antony Brockholls Deputy Governor over
new yorke province.

The Humble petition of Cornelis Verhoofe In all Humble manner

Sheweth

    That Whereas Sir Edmund Andross Knight Governor Generall
of this province haveing Deputed and Imployed your petitor as
Surveyor for Deale alis Whorekill precincts In Delaware Bay
not withstanding it being understood by the magistrates and
Sum of the Inhabitants there that your petitior Cannot Lawfully Survey any Lands for him Selfs and your petitior haveing occasion to have Land Surveyed which hee allready Doth
possess Inhabite Improve and manure and the Great Distan[ ]
and ill Conveniency to gitt other Surveyors for the Same
neithe[ ] theire Commissions take any Effect there for Surveying In the Said precincts where your petitor being Impowred to Survey Therefore your petitior Humble Creave your
Honor Will bee pleased to Grant your petitior an order for the
Surveying of Such Lands as your petitior is allready with Concerned In Deale and St. Jones County and Such warrants for
Lands as the Courts of Said Countyes hath or Shall bee pleased
to Grant your petitior and of Said Surveys to make a Due Returne to the office of Records.

                    And your petitior as In Duty bound
                    Shall Ever pray for your Honors
                    prosperity

                    [Signed:] Cornelis Verhoofe

21:147   [JOHANNIS KIP'S FEES AS ATTORNEY FOR CORNELIS
          STEENWYCK THE ADMINISTRATOR OF JOHN SHACKERLY'S
          ESTATE]

    Mr. Johannes Kip the attorney of Mr. Cornelis Steenwyk
the administrator of the Estate of John Shackerly deceased
De[   ] to Cls.[1] fees in the following actions against the
afternamed persons att a speciall Court[2] Caled by the said
Kipp in New Castle the 19 of May 1680.

Recording the Governors Letter of
administration.. £0:2:6
Recording Letter of Attorney from
Mr Steenwyk... £0:2:6
1 Summons against John Cocx   £0:1:=
   Ent. the Courts order and   0:2:6
   agreement Coppies..................... 0:1:=
                                         £0:4:6

1 Summons against Edmund Cantwell   -1:=
   Ent. the Courts order and agreement   -2:6
   Coppies.................................   1
                                                     £0:4:6

1 Summons against Edmund Cantwell as
   attorney of Gab. Minviell................   1
   The order of court and agreement   2:6
   Coppies.................................   1:
                                                     £0:4:6

1 Summons against Tho. Spry................   1
   The order of court and agreement   2:6
   Coppies.................................   1
                                                     £0:4:6

1 Summons against John Ogle   1
   The order of court etc................... 2:6
   Coppies.................................   1
                                                     £0:4:6

[   ] Eph: Herman   1
   [   ] of Court etc.   2:6
   [   ]pies................................   1
                                                     £ 0:4:6
                                                     £1:12:-
                           Brought over   £1:12:-
1 Summons against Edmund Cantwell
   as a debtor to Shackerlys Estate..........   1
   Ent. act. for tryall..................... 2:6
   Ent. and record defts. oath.............. 1:
   The Courts order......................... 1:6
   Coppies.................................   1:
                                                     £ 7:-

1 Summons against John Kan.................   1
   Ent. declaration etc..................... 1:0
   Ent. act. for tryall..................... 2:6
   Judgement................................   3
   Coppies.................................   2
                                                     £ 9:[ ]

1 ditto against John Darby.................   1:-
   Ent. declaration......................... 1:
   Ent act. for tryall...................... 2:6
   Judgement................................   3
   Coppies.................................   2
   Ent. and record the defts affidavid....... 1
                                                     [   ]

Itt being a speciall Court the fees are
allowed double............................. [   ]

Errors Excepted per Eph: H[   ] 3
      from above [   ]
1681   More for drawing a [   ]
May 9   for Hend. v. Burgh [   ]
           desire 4:8

----

1. i.e., <u>clerk's</u>.

2. See <u>NCCR</u>:415 for these court proceedings.

3. Ephraim Herman, in whose hand this document is written.

21:148   [EPHRAIM HERMAN'S ACCOUNT WITH JOHN SHACKERLY]

John Shackerly Deceased his account whilst hee was in
Partnership with Reynier the baker:

Dr.
1676
Dec. 6   To 1 Packet Inckhoren.................   f 3:[ ]
17 ditto   To 4 hhds. tobacco upon the account
            of the osnab.[1] w. d'haes[2]   542:1[ ]
            To Clr. fees for wryting a deposition
            about a Lost anker   3:-
1677
June   To 4 hhds. tobacco by Shackerly
            rec. in N. Castle....................   505:-
            To 1 Knyf fetched by Reynier   2:
            To 1 hhd. tobacco the 3 april 1677
            of Hend. Williams....................   140:-
            1 Emty new anker Kept and
            then sould for 8 gl.................   8:-
1677
            To 20 sch. wheat from Lasse Cock   100:-
            3 plankes had of Mr Bayard on
            my account.........................   9:-
            To wryting a Letter of attorney........   8:-
                                             f 1320:1[ ]

            John Shackerly sence hee was
            Reyniers Partner...........Dr.
[   ]   To Clr. fees against Jannetie Viddette and
            against Salter as per account deb.
            att Upland   2:2:8..................   f 85:[ ]
[   ]   To fees against ditto Viddette........   3:[ ]
[   ] house fees paid.......................   12:[ ]
[   ] Cooren by you accepted........   24:1[ ]
[   ]ut Jeacox Land.................   10:[ ]
[   ] 2 Sundry tymes...............   12:[ ]
[   ] fees paid....................   8:[ ]
[   ] Oldfield and Henry Salter.....   20:-
[   ] against Vidette etc...........   10:-
[   ] Oldfield and Salter and actions.   6:[ ]
[   ] non suits against Oldfield and
                            Salter etc.....   16:-
[   ] against Jo. Claessen..........   3:
[   ]ver to the other syde   f 1530:19
Dr. Brought over from the other syde   f 1530:19
1678/79
March   To drawing a Large deed of the
            Land of Briggs etc..................   20:-
            5 Depositions recording about Briggs
            Land................................   6:-
            drawing an ample declaration etc.
            against Briggs etc..................   7:-

```
            1/2 a deed of sale with John Williams      8:-
            Clr. fees in 4 severall Court dayes..     23:10
            paid the Sherrife                         16:-
                                                    1611:[  ]
Creditor:
1676
June        By osnab. Linnen which Johannes
            d'Haes bought of Shackerly            f 569:4
            By 1 firking of soape of Shackerly       35:-
            By severall goods bougt and rec. of
            Reynier.........................         376:10
                                                  f 980:14
            By freigt of some goods from N.
            Yorke which I cannot Exactly
            remember how mutch the summe
            was but suppose to the ulmost it
            to bee noe more then about 150 gilders   18[    ]
                       See on the other syde      f 11[      ]
            Ditto Creditor
            Brought over from the other syde       1130:14
            By Henry Salter                           21:-
            By 4 Sch. Salt at 10 g.                   40:-
                                                  f 1191:14
            By ballance due on this account          419:15
                                                    1611:9
```

N. Castle 1682   [Signed:] Eph. Herman

[Entitled:] Ephraim Hermans Account.

---

1. i.e., osnaburgs.

2. Johannes De Haes.

21:149a   [THOMAS WOLLASTON TO JOHN BRIGGS ABOUT A DEBT][1]

[   ] Briges

        Sir I have sente by the bearer hearof John Ogle your bill
wich you ordered me to take up from the taylor William Jonson
which you may be soe cinde as to take it to Consideration that
I have binn oute of my moneyeys neare thre years you say you
payd Mr. Shakerly one hh. of tobacco you Cannot mak it apere
for Mr. Shakerly sould me at his Comin up from your houes to
New Castell befor sevorell sufficent wittnes that he had not
receved one pound and Like wis you sent by Mr. Hambleton that
I should send from undar my hand that Mr. Shakerly had not
given me Credite for the hh. of tobacco which I did hoping
that you would have binn soe sivell as to have pay it to Mr.
Hamleton whoe I ordered to receve it thearfor I would desire
you to pay it to the bearer or give him a new bill in my name

to pay next fall in tobacco or porke acordin to your promess
or Eles send me your answer for I will take some othear Corese
for I will not be Keepe oute of my moneys mutch Longer Soe
havin noe mor att present [   ] rest youres
                              [Signed:] Tho. Wollas[   ]
Whitte Clay Creeke
Agte. the 25th anno 1680.

[Addressed:]   These for: Mr. John Brigges att his houes in
               St. Joneses Creek

---

1. See 21:95b and 21:96b for letters related to this
    matter.

21:149b   [AFFIDAVIT OF JOHN OGLE CONCERNING JOHN
           BRIGGS' DEBT]

        John Ogl aged thirty tow or ther Abouts Declareth upon
othe that he did never recieve of John Shakele any part or
pearsel upon the acount of John Brigs and Fordr sath not
                              [Signed:] John Ogle

Sworne the 27th of Agust
1680 before me   [Signed:] Fra. Whitwell

21:149c   [ASSESSMENT OF JOHN SHACKERLY'S ESTATE AT
           ST. JONES CREEK][1]

[   ]sement[2] of the Plantagie at St. Johns Creecke the
[   ] to John Sackerly deceased done by John Brigs
[   ] ackers of land at 3000 lb the 200 ackers is lb.   2625
[   ] tobacy huyse nieu 'tsamd[3] 5000 lb. tobacy is lb. 2500
[   ] 60 voet toebacys hous out[4].....................lb. 600
[   ] houge booth 1600 lb Is voor d'half [   ]
al waerd[5]...lb. 800
[   ] 2900 lb. toebacy...........................lb. 450
[   ]s part 5 at 600 lb a pies...................lb. 3000
[   ]or Sackerly and third 9 1/3 at 300 lb per
pies...lb. 2800
[   ] voor 2 Jaer[6] servings 1000 lb. Is   lb. 500
[   ] amoust 2 Jaer tother[7] 6 meneths [   ]....lb. 750
[   ] 1600 lb...................................lb. 800
[   ] years and of 1 jaer lb 800   lb. 400

[   ] at 50 lb. per hog Is lb 3000   lb.   1500
                                                                        lb. 16725

---

1. cf., 21:102a for Johannis Kip's inventory of the
    chattels at St. Jones. The handwriting style, the use
    of Dutch words and the spelling of English words indi-
    cate considerable Dutch interference in the writer's
    English.

2. Probably "assessment."

3. 17th c. Dutch Samd or tzamen meaning "with" or
    "together with."

4. Dutch oud meaning "old."

5. al waerd, ie. "all worth."

6. Dutch jaar meaning "year."

7. i.e., the other.

APPENDIX

The following items are related to documents
20:98, 20:103, and 21:30. For their significance consult the footnotes of each
document.

20:98   [THE ORIGINAL PREAMBLE TO THE RULES OF GOVERNMENT
         FOR DELAWARE]

Whereas upon a peticion of the Magistrates and [   ]
Newcastle and Delaware River, Governor Lovelace did resolve and
orde[ ] and in par[ ] settle the Establisht Lawes of this
Government, and appoint some Magistrates under an English De-
nominacion accordingly, In the which there haveing been an
Obstruction by reason of the late warres and Change of Goverment: And findeing now an absoulute Necessity for the well
being of the Inhabitants, to make a speedy settlement, to bee
a generall knowne rule unto them for the future, Upon mature
deliberation and advice of my Counsell, I have resolved and by
vertue of the Authority derived unto mee, doe hereby in his
Majesties Name Order as followeth.

20:103   [FIRST DRAFT OF A REPLY TO PROPOSALS FROM
         DELAWARE]

Gentlemen

I have received your Letters (by the Expresse sent hither)
with severall other papers and writings relating unto Major
John Fenwycks actings on the Eastside of Delaware River by his
granting Patents for Land, and refusing to obey my speciall
warrant etc. As also touching your more peculiar affayres;
Whereupon having taken advice of my Councell,

It is Resolved, It importing his Majesties service, and
the good and quiet of those parts and Inhabitants, That Major
John Fenwyck bee sent for with the first Convenience hither,

and if there bee occasion, That the Commander, and Magistrates at Delaware doe use force for seizing and sending him.

That there being no Lawfull Authority for Major Fenwycks giving forth Patents for Land, Its not thought fitt to returne back those Sent hither, But the persons who have paid their moneys for them, may have their remedy at Law for the same, against the person that gave them.

Upon the Complaint of Jean Paul Jaquet, That hee hath beene dispossest by Major Fenwyck for some Land on the Eastside of Delaware River, Ordered That the said Jean Paul Jaquet bee repossest of what Land hee was in possession of, on the Eastside of Delaware River at the Last comming in of the English Government, the which the Court at Newcastle is to take order about, and if occasion the Commander at Delaware is to assist then.

In answer to the Proposalls sent by the Magistrates of Newcastle for my Approbacion, It is as followeth.

1. To the first Proposall, Ordered That one of his Royal Highnesse Law Bookes shall bee sent them.

2. To the second, That the Inhabitants of the Towne of Newcastle, and within a mile thereof, doe keepe watch but that none bee obliged to come to the watch farther. The other part of the Proposall about souldyers to bee sent hither, to bee taken into farther Consediracion.

3. To the third about a publick seale, Care will be taken against the next yeare, In the meane time to make use of their owne seales, as is usuall for Justices of the peace every where.

4. Allowed That a prison bee built in the Fort, and the Sheriffe to bee responsable for prisoners; For the allowance or Fees, to bee airected by the Law booke, with regard to former Custome and Practice.

5. The Order made about killing of Wolves, to bee confirmed for the present yeare, and till further Order.

6. Fines to bee granted to the Court, for the present yeare and for the two yeares last past, to bee applyde for publick uses; for the which the Sheriffe and Receiver or Receivers to bee called to account, and pay in the same to the Courts order, who are to make a Returne to the Governor, how disposed of. The Sheriffe for his paine[ ] in collecting of Levying the same, to have five shillings in the pound, and for extraordinary Charge, to bee farther allowed by the Courts as there shall bee cause.

7. That towards the farther defraying of publick Charges in the Towne of Newcastle, as also up the River, and in the Bay, there bee a Levy made of one penny in the pound upon every mans Estate, to bee tax't by indifferent persons thereunto appointed by the respective Courts, and by the said Courts to bee disposed of accordingly, whereof an Account to bee given hither.

8. That former Orders Prohibiting Sloopes and Vessells goeing up the River above Newcastle to trade, bee duely observed

as heretofore.

9. That a weigh-House bee allowed in the Towne of Newcastle,
for The which a sworne Officer to bee appointed.

Nov. 23rd 1676   To the Magistrates of Delaware

[Endorsed:]   In answer to the proposals sent from Delaware.
Nov. 23rd 1676.

21:30   [FIRST DRAFT OF A LETTER TO THE NEWCASTLE
COURT CONCERNING JANE ERSKIN]

Upon the Addresse and Complaint of Jane the wid. of
Serjeant John Erskin late of Delaware to the Go., setting forth
that suddenly after her said husbands death before any account
was taken of tne Estate Left by him (hee dyeing Intestate) or
any Administrator appointed, Mr. John Moll one of the Justices
there seized by attachment on a parcell of Tobacco as it lay
in bulke but not stript, in a Tobacco house, and so continued
neglected by the said Mr. Moll and Agents or the Undersheriffe
who attacht it Untill the greatest part was damnifyed and the
rest apprized under Value that very low and received by the
said Mr. Moll who also with divers house hold Goods taken in
Execucion, to the great prejudice of the said wid. and her
children and upon another Execucion obtayned by Wm. Semple her
Cowes Likewise seized on, very much to the prejudice of the
said widdow and her Children: By the Governors order and
direction I am to acquiant you, that the proceedings herein
have beene very irregular, and that the Administracion (belonging to the wid. if refused by her) the Court ought to have
appointed one or more to have administred and taken that trust
upon them, and having appointed a time for the Creditors to
make their Claymes, have taken Care for the payment of the
Creditors equally with due regard to the wid. and children but
to take notice that all Estates of houses or lands in this
Country, are as lyable to pay debts as moveables, So that the
[   ] have received any proporcion of the said
Estate [   ] to bee accomptable for the same to the administrators and if any damage hath happen'd to the Tobacco by
occasion of the Attachment, through the want of Care of the
Undersheriffe or those that employed him the same is by them
to bee made good.

As to the difference betweene the said widdow and Mr.
Ephraim Hermans as one of the Overseers of Martin Rosamonds
children deceased, concerning a small Lott of land in the
Towne for which her husband had a patent and possest the same
for neare fourteene yeares shee cannot bee ejected out of the
same by any pretence of former title, or later patent, but by
due Course of Law.

[Endorsed:]   To the Justices of the Court at Newcastle about
the wid. Erskin. No. 6 1678.

INDEX

MANSA, Hance, see MOENSEN,
Hans
Manslaughter, penalty for 36
Maques Indians, see Mohawk
Indians
MARGIN, David, signs petition
357
MARKHAM, William, governor of
Pennsylvania 355
MARLETT, Gideon, patent 109
Marreties/Marities/Marquess
Hook 125,142; census 307
Marretiens/Marikes/Marquess/
Marcus Kill 9,142; census 307
MARRIOTT, William, patent.107
MARSH/MASH, Paul, officer at
Whorekill 169,170,180
MARSHALL, John, patent and
quit-rent 28; see also
MARTIALL, John
MARTENS, George, signs petition
357
MARTENSE/MARTENSZ, Jacob,
witness in suit 142,143
Martha's Vineyard, 332
MARTIALL, John, receiver of
tobacco 54; received tobacco
due Andrew Carr 56; see also
MARSHALL, John
Martin's Vineyard, see
Martha's Vineyard
MARTINSEN, Martin, census 306
MARTINSON, John, census 309
Mary of Leverpoole, ship 176
Marygold, ship, 318
Maryland, 11,12,13,21,23,26,
112,124,140,155,161,164,165,
182,189,191,192,193,280,294,
296,315,338; eastern shore
14; unable to give help 30;
on her guard 31; squatters
from on Whorekill 39; run-
away servants 39; plans to
take over Delaware 47; sur-
veyors fees in 137,138;
persons from surveying
illegally 153-154; Quakers
in 291; planters from 250,
279,314,356
MASSAN, Hendrick, census 307
MASTEN, Will, 197
MATAPIS, sachem, 271,273
MATHEWS, James, witnesses
land transfer 169
Mathias the Finn, census 308
MATHIASSON, Niels, census 306
MATHISONE/MATTISON, Mathis/
Mathias, see de VOS, Matthias
Matthiassen
Matiniconck Island, 3,4,5;
defense post for 50; lease
of 229; census 305

MATSEN/MATESEN/MATTSON, Andres/
Andries/Andrews, fined 10;
patent and quit-rent 28;
census 307
MATSEN/MATSON, Erick/Erike,
fined 7,8
MATSON/MATSE, Jan, fined 8;
signs protest as deacon 95
MATSON, Margerett, widow,
fined 8
MATSON/MATSEN, Matijs/---ias,
fined 8; census 306
MATSON/MATSA, Neals, 9; patent
and quit-rent 29; land of
129
MATTHIASON, Peter, declaration
about right-of-way 114
MATTLOCK, William, signs
petition as Quaker 231
MAULSTENE see MOLESTINE
Maurice River, 318
May, Cape, 318,319
MAZINELLO, [Tommaso Aniello,]
93,94f
MEGERAS, sachem, 18
MEGGES, Francis, witness 213
MEHOXEY, an Indian, 281
MELINTON, Oliver, patent 110
MENNINCKTA, sachem, 17
Merchandise, prices of 139,196,
197,198,199,360; lists of
329,360
MERRITT, ---, Mr., 20
MERRITT, Thomas, 340; patent
and quit-rent 29; land of 233;
deceased 321
MERTEN, George, petition about
land at Whorekill 190
METT, James, census 307
MEULESTEYN see MOLESTINE
MICHAELS/MICHIELS, Jan, 45;
juryman 16; census 100
MIFFLIN, John, Sr., petitions
for land 253
MIFFLIN, John, Jr., petitions
for land 253
Militia, commissions to
officers 43,44,70; form of
commission for officers 63;
asks to be excused from
watch at fort 123
Mill D---pe, census 308
MILLER, Hans, census 308
Mills, see Sawmills and grist-
mills
Mills Island, 14
Minister, 8,10,28,225,276;
conduct of 68; at Wiccakoe
76; unbecoming language of
87; to be questioned 91;
lead mutiny 92; sent to New
York 93; church protests